Reading Instruction That Works

Reading Instruction That Works

The Case for Balanced Teaching

◄o►

Michael Pressley

The Guilford Press
New York London

A few years ago while I was conducting research in a classroom that included publishing of student-written books, I overheard a little boy, DJ, reflect, "Why doesn't anyone ever dedicate their book to me?" I told him, "I'll see what I can do." I'll never forget DJ. This one's for you . . . and for other unforgettable DJs, too.

© 1998 Michael Pressley
Published by The Guilford Press
A Division of Guilford Publications, Inc.
72 Spring Street, New York, NY 10012
http://www.guilford.com

Printed in the United States of America

This book is printed on acid-free paper.

Last digit is print number: 9 8 7 6 5 4 3 2 1

Library of Congress Cataloging-in-Publication Data
Pressley, Michael.
    Reading instruction that works : the case for balanced teaching / Michael Pressley.
      p. cm.
    Includes bibliographical references and index.
    ISBN 1-57230-308-5 (hard). — ISBN 1-57230-319-0 (paper)
    1. Reading (Elementary) I. Title.
LB1573.P72 1998
372.41—dc21
                                           97-44072
                                               CIP

CONTENTS

INTRODUCTION

This is a book about effective elementary literacy instruction, intended for the many constituencies who have a need to know about what works to develop readers in elementary school. It is intended especially for those who want to form research-based opinions about effective elementary literacy instruction, including reading educators and specialists, staff developers and in-service professionals who focus on reading, teacher educators, graduate students, policymakers concerned with reading and elementary education, and parents who feel a need to know more about the reading instruction that is occurring and could occur in schools. In short, this is aimed at a broad audience who want an accessible and reader-friendly review of the research evidence pertaining to beginning reading, and that doesn't require them to have technical background knowledge in reading research.

I make the case in this book for a balanced perspective on reading instruction, rather than stressing either a whole-language or skills-first instructional orientation. Balanced-literacy teachers combine the strengths of whole language and skills instruction, and in doing so, create instruction that is more than the sum of its parts. The case for balanced instruction is most forcefully and completely made in the latter two-thirds of the book, because it is much more convincing following coverage of the predominant approach in elementary language arts (i.e., whole language, reviewed in Chapter 1), the nature of skilled reading (which involves a balancing of activities, reviewed in Chapter 2), and the nature of difficulties in beginning reading (Chapter 3).

Perhaps the most common advice to writers is to "write what you know about." Not surprisingly, what people know and believe comes through in their writing. This book is about what I know and believe, based on my interpretation of research on reading and reading instruction, but my belief structure about that topic is also informed by my lived experience as a reader and a student as well as by my scholarly study of reading and reading instruction. I overview that life in this Introduction, because I think it will help you to understand better the ideas favored in this book.

MY LIFE AS A DEVELOPING READER

Many of the conclusions offered in this book align with the facts of my own life as a student learning to read. I grew up in a home filled with what are now referred to as "emergent literacy experiences," with the early years at my house consistent with the best preschool literacy development practices, covered in Chapter 4 of this volume.

I met Dick, Jane, and Sally as a grade-1 student in the fall of 1957. From the earliest days of grade 1, I was learning whole words, consistent with the approach used in the reading series featuring the three children who have become cultural icons representing all that was good and bad about America in the mid-20th century (Kismaric & Heiferman, 1996). In a 1995 letter, my former first-grade teacher, Miss Lindley McKinney, confided to me that she did follow the whole-word approach with a lot of phonics added to the instruction. Her memory is very credible given my own recall of lessons, in which there was much sounding out of words and much reflection on the sounds in words. I have learned from personal experience that effective instruction need not be entirely consistent with any one perspective but rather can be a blending of perspectives, a major conclusion of this book.

Although learning to read in the sense of decoding went well for me in grade 1 and after that, I made less certain progress in becoming a good comprehender. For example, in junior high school, my strategy with high school textbook assignments was to read them again and again, which I now know to be a strategy of choice for many students, including college students at elite colleges (Cordón & Day, 1996). That strategy works poorly and demands a great deal of time. As a result, I became exceptionally anxious about school, grades, and exams as a junior high school and senior high school student. For example, during junior year, I was required to read a book a week in the college preparatory English section in which I was enrolled. I always read my book, but I must admit I always had a great deal of fear that I would be quizzed on books read, for I was having difficulties understanding and remembering much of what was in them.

I was exposed to some comprehension-strategies instruction during junior and senior high school through the SQ3R (Survey, Question, Read, Recite, Review) approach (Robinson, 1961), which involves skimming a text first; asking questions about it based on the title, headers, and pictures; and then reading, reciting, and reviewing. It seemed difficult to execute and certainly did not improve my comprehension and memory noticeably. I knew even then that there had to be better strategies. There are, and they will be covered in Chapter 7 of this book.

In college, I learned the value of prior knowledge. My first year at Northwestern University was exceptionally demanding. There was no hope of keeping up with many classmates in some of the subjects I was taking, for they had better background knowledge than I did in those subjects. I was not entirely left out of the prior-knowledge-advantage club, however, for through some enrichment opportunities in high school, I knew a great deal about chemistry, and thus, freshman college chemistry was much easier for me than for other students. By the end of freshman year, I understood very well that background knowledge was critical to understanding and learning, both from when I was disadvantaged in prior knowledge relative to others and when I was advantaged. There will be much about the importance of background knowledge to reading comprehension in the pages of this book.

I started to use reading and study strategies very extensively during college, generally picking them up from classmates. By the late undergraduate years, I was on my way to becoming a strategic reader. It took a while to get to the level of strategy use now evident in my reading, however. At middle age, I can read books very quickly in subject areas in which I possess a great deal of prior knowledge. I have learned to overview books and to skim in order to avoid detailed reading of parts of texts covering material I already know. I attempt to relate what I am reading to my prior knowledge and beliefs, explicitly looking for points of similarity and dissimilarity with other conceptions I have encountered. I pay special attention to and read very carefully those sections of texts that are likely to be useful to me later, sections I want to understand well and remember. At midlife and midcareer, I am a skilled reader, who can communicate with confidence the ideas encountered in books. As a scholar studying reading, I also have come to understand that exceptionally strategic reading is rare in college students, requiring years of reading experience to develop. That work is taken up in Chapter 2 of what follows.

DEVELOPMENT AS A SCHOLAR OF READING AND READING INSTRUCTION

My scholarly experiences had profound effects on the ideas in this book. Specifically, my thinking was influenced by my background in psychology, especially developmental and educational psychologies. This disciplinary preparation in psychology prepared me for conducting experimental analyses of reading and reading instruction, but also to adapt my skills and outlooks as new issues in reading have come to the fore. Work from a number of disciplines is reviewed in this book, as is research carried out with a variety of methodologies, consistent with the diversity in my own research.

Education as a Research Psychologist

I majored in psychology at Northwestern between 1969 and 1973. While at Northwestern, I conducted a senior honor's thesis that placed me in a number of schools in Evanston, Illinois, for much of my senior year. There was much innovation going on in the Evanston schools at the time, informed by research and a variety of scholarly perspectives on education. My time spent in the Evanston schools did much to stimulate my career-long interest in how research can inform the education of children.

In August 1973, I drove to Minneapolis to begin a PhD in child psychology at the University of Minnesota. Thanks to a cooperative agreement within the Big Ten, I was able to take some of my doctoral work in the Department of Educational Psychology at the University of Wisconsin–Madison and carried out research there for the concluding 2 years of my graduate program. I emerged in 1977 with a PhD. Since then, I have been involved in a series of interrelated scholarly efforts that prepared me for the task of writing this book.

Research on Human Development and Instruction

I conducted much research on natural strategy development and strategy instruction during graduate school and the years immediately following completion of my PhD. A major conclusion that followed from this work was that sophisticated intellectual strategies develop over many years. However, I also became aware of much other work supporting the conclusion that even children in the early elementary grades can be taught strategies they would naturally acquire only many years later, if at all. That is, I discovered early in my research career that natural development is often slow and uncertain relative to development via instruction.

Research on Skilled Reading

Excellent developmental researchers understand that to know development, it is essential to know about what is developing. Studies of highly skilled performances can be very informative about factors that should be encouraged during development. In the early 1990s, I carried out a study of exceptionally skilled reading, having university professors think aloud as they read articles in their areas of expertise (Wyatt et al., 1993). The outcomes in that study were consistent with the outcomes in other think-aloud studies that Peter Afflerbach and I reviewed in *Verbal Protocols of Reading: The Nature of Constructively Responsive Reading* (Pressley & Afflerbach, 1995). The case made in that book, and reviewed in Chapter 2 of this volume, is that exceptionally skilled reading is very active reading, from before reading begins to after it is concluded. Much of the activity can be described as strategic responses articulated with prior knowledge related to the topic of the reading. Pressley and Afflerbach (1995) refer to excellent reading as constructively responsive reading because good readers are continuously attempting to construct meaning. Their meaning-construction activities are consistently in response to ideas encountered in text, with the responses very much influenced by the reader's prior knowledge that can be related to the text.

This book takes the position that the development of constructively responsive reading is an appropriate goal for reading educators, and one that can begin in the elementary years, in particular, through comprehension strategies instruction (Chapter 7). I came to this position—that comprehension strategies can and should be taught to children—largely through my research on reading instruction. That work has also informed my thinking about beginning reading instruction, including teaching about decoding.

Research on Elementary Reading Instruction

My best-known work in reading focused on the development of comprehension skills through strategies instruction. The main research tactic was to study schools where such instruction was making a big impact and to understand the nature of such effective instruction. Many of the insights about comprehension instruction covered in Chapter 7 of this book were developed in this program of research.

This work on comprehension strategies instruction was followed by studies of instruction in primary-level classrooms known to produce high literacy achievement. The work at the primary level continues as this book is being written, with the research to date going far in informing Chapter 6 of this book, which is concerned with the nature of effective primary-level teaching of reading.

When I began my studies of excellent teaching, I went in with an open mind. What I have emerged with as a function of those interactions is a well-informed mind about what instruction can look like when it is done well. I am much in admiration of excellent elementary teachers, and I am very grateful that some of them have admitted me to their classroom communities to observe what they do. When I think of my work in excellent classrooms, I am reminded of the motto of Northwestern University, my undergraduate alma mater: "Whatsoever is true, whatsoever is honorable, whatsoever is just, whatsoever is pure, whatsoever is pleasing, whatsoever is commendable, if there is any excellence or anything worthy of praise, think about these things" (Philippians 4, Vs. 8). It is good advice, especially with respect to the study of teaching. Much more can be learned about teaching by studying good teaching than by lamenting bad teaching. I have done the former and that goes far in explaining my perspectives on instruction that are detailed in this book.

When reading the descriptions of excellent teaching covered here, give the teachers the credit rather than me. I was privileged to showcase their work with my efforts in collaboration with many graduate students. In particular, Pamela El-Dinary, Rachel Brown, and Ruth Wharton-McDonald were important colleagues in these research efforts. Together, the outstanding teachers who were studied and the graduate students who worked with me helped me to shape more complete perspective on the nature of balanced elementary literacy instruction than existed previously. As effortful as it was to do it, my students and I always found this work interesting and fun, and we were honored that some of the outstanding teachers we observed became our coauthors and friends. I have been privileged to have great people working with me throughout my career.

Integrative Scholarship on Reading Instruction

I have never been a researcher who has carried out his work unaware of related research (Kiewra, Cresswell, & Wadkins, 1997). Throughout my involvement in reading research, I have studied carefully the major conceptual and empirical works related to reading and reading instruction (e.g., Pressley with McCormick, 1995; Pressley, Woloshyn, &

Associates, 1995). Those efforts went far in defining the conclusions advanced in Chapters 4 and 5 of this book, respectively about literacy development and instruction before school begins and the nature of decoding instruction.

Participation in Development of a Reading Instruction Series

In addition to my research and scholarly writing, in 1991 I became part of the author team of an elementary reading program. My interactions with my coauthors, including Marilyn Adams and Carl Bereiter, did much to increase my understanding of the nature of reading instruction that makes sense. In particular, this experience sensitized me to many of the issues surrounding decoding instruction, including the tensions that constitute the whole language versus phonics debate.

HISTORY AND PURPOSE OF THIS BOOK

Much of this book is an expansion of a series of lectures that I gave between 1994 and 1997, in my role as a principal investigator at the National Reading Research Center (NRRC) and the National Center for English Language Arts Achievement (CELA), to many audiences across North America. Both of these centers were funded by the U.S. Department of Education, Office of Educational Research and Improvement (OERI), and I am grateful to OERI for its financial support of my research during the 1990s. I am also grateful to the University of Maryland at College Park (1989–1993) and University at Albany, State University of New York (1993–1997), the universities at which I was appointed when this book was conceived and written. The NRRC and CELA both provided support for this book during 1996–1997, when the bulk of the work on it was completed.

Because this book started out as a series of talks, the ideas have been tried on many audiences. I think of this book as being like a Marx Brothers movie. Their films were funny because they were first tried on the road as plays. The brothers benefited from audience reactions, only keeping the good stuff in the final film version. Similarly, I have tried many ideas about reading and reading instruction on my audiences, who have made very clear which arguments have been more credible to them. Those are the arguments that made it into this book. My goal was to write a book as informative and compelling about reading and reading instruction as Marx Brothers' films were entertaining. I leave it to you, the reader, to decide whether I succeeded.

This book can be read alone but will be more useful as a gateway to the literature on reading and reading instruction. There will be some who complain that the parenthetical references in the body of the text interrupt reading and hence distract the reader. I have opted for this approach, however, for I find that alternative referencing systems—for example, footnoting—do not make as clear who did and claimed what. I have erred on the side of providing more references rather than fewer because my experience is that those interested in elementary reading want a great deal of information, and specifically, they want to know where they can go to get more information about points that they consider critical. Thus, I have provided references for each chapter because I am aware that some readers are much more interested in some topics than others. Each chapter is intended to contribute to the overall book as well as to serve as a stand-alone reference for readers who want information on any of the topics covered in the individual chapters.

In closing this Introduction, I want to point out that in the chapters that follow, much will be said about reading achievement as defined by objective measures, because that is the benchmark of effective instruction for many 1990s policymakers and educational administrators. For me, however, there is another way to think about such instruction, a way that brings it to life much better than does a focus only on the test scores. My colleagues and I have been impressed that effective literacy education environments, in which children are learning how to do difficult things and, in fact, do them well, are also happy environments. One has far fewer disciplinary encounters with children who are much less in dispute with one another than one has in other classrooms. Thus, one of the reasons to love effective literacy instruction is that the engagement it produces (see Chapter 8 of this volume) leads to more harmonious classroom relations. My associates and I frequently have found ourselves wishing that many more children could experience the kinds of classrooms that we have been privileged to study, not simply because the classrooms are good for children's academic development but also because such classrooms are warm, wonderful places. When teachers become excellent literacy teachers, they also seem to become agents of peace in children's lives.

If you find what follows to be compelling, I am pleased. Never forget, however, as you read, that much work remains before the ideas detailed in this book are translated as completely as they might be into literacy instruction in elementary schools. There is much more research that can be done, and much implementation that needs to occur; more commitment to refine implementation through continuing inquiry is needed. I expect to revise this book, perhaps in a decade or so, and I pray that when I do, much revision will be in order because progress will have been made in the scholarly analysis and dissemination of effective reading instruction, as well as continuing reflective evaluation of literacy development through state-of-the-art teaching.

REFERENCES

Cordón, L. A., & Day, J. D. (1996). Strategy use on standardized reading comprehension tests. *Journal of Educational Psychology, 88,* 288–295.

Kiewra, K. A., Cresswell, J., & Wadkins, T. (1997, March). *Biographical sketches of prolific researchers: R. Anderson, R. Mayer, and M. Pressley.* Paper presented at the annual meeting of the American Educational Research Association, Chicago.

Kismaric, C., & Heiferman, M. (1996). *Growing up with Dick and Jane: Learning and living the American dream.* New York: Scott Foresman.

Pressley, M., & Afflerbach, P. (1995). *Verbal protocols of reading: The nature of constructively responsive reading.* Hillsdale, NJ: Erlbaum.

Pressley, M., with McCormick, C. B. (1995). *Advanced educational psychology for educators, researchers, and policymakers.* New York: HarperCollins.

Pressley, M., Woloshyn, V. E., & Associates. (1995). *Cognitive strategy instruction that really works with children* (2nd ed.). Cambridge, MA: Brookline Books.

Robinson, F. P. (1961). *Effective study* (rev. ed.). New York: Harper & Row.

Wyatt, D., Pressley, M., El-Dinary, P. B., Stein, S., Evans, P., & Brown, R. (1993). Comprehension strategies, worth and credibility monitoring, and evaluations: Cold and hot cognition when experts read professional articles that are important to them. *Learning and Individual Differences, 5,* 49–72.

1

—◄〇►—

WHOLE LANGUAGE

Effective reading instruction is a topic that has commanded a great deal of attention in recent years. One motivation for this attention is that learning to read is painfully difficult for some children. There are students in every school in the nation who are experiencing difficulties becoming readers.

A second motivation for attention to reading instruction is that, in the eyes of many parents, there is an obvious culprit when their child does not learn to read in school. They believe that their son or daughter is the victim of the reading instructional approach currently most in favor. In the 1990s that approach has been whole language.

Whole language is an approach to literacy education in which natural development of literacy competence, with students immersed in real literature and daily writing, is favored over literacy development through explicit teaching of basic reading skills. Instruction of skills occurs in whole-language classrooms on an as-needed basis only, and then only in the context of reading and writing rather than as a focal point of instruction. Many suspect that the reading problems of the current generation of students are more pronounced than those of previous generations because of whole language, and that students who might be at risk for reading failure are at even greater risk in whole language classrooms than in environments in which instruction is more explicit (Pressley & Rankin, 1994).

I emphasize that this is not a book about the whole-language versus skills-instruction debate. My view is that the whole-language philosophy has had some profound and very positive effects on elementary literacy instruction and that many whole-language practices should be in elementary literacy programs. However, from my perspective, other practices should be there as well, and much of the chapters that follow are devoted to making a case for balancing decoding and comprehension skills instruction with elements of whole language to create an effective and attractive elementary literacy curriculum.

Getting to that balance requires understanding of whole language, which can be challenging. Those most strongly identified with whole language have often resisted attempting to define it precisely in terms of curricular practices, arguing that an approach that is whole cannot be easily reduced to parts. Even so, for many others, it is helpful to think in terms of particular instructional practices associated with an educational philosophy. One scholar, in particular, did much to clarify the nature of whole language in terms of practice. Bette S. Bergeron's (1990) article on the subject captured a great deal of attention when it first appeared in the *Journal of Reading Behavior* and continues to be referred to by scholars and practitioners interested in the nature of whole language.

BERGERON'S DEFINITION OF WHOLE LANGUAGE

Bergeron (1990) lamented in the introduction to her article that the term "whole language" was being used too loosely. She believed that this had the potential to undermine the credibility of whole language as an instructional approach as well as lead to misuses of it.

Methodology

Bergeron's approach to defining whole language has a lot of credibility. First of all, she analyzed journal articles, which tend to contain the most up-to-date information as well as the most carefully thought out ideas. Bergeron exhaustively searched for and reviewed all journal articles on whole language published between 1979 and 1989, the period of time during which whole language as it is currently known was conceived and shaped. The articles reviewed included ones by important figures in whole language, such as Kenneth Goodman, Jerome Harste, Sharon Rich, and Bill Harp.

Bergeron's (1990) analysis began with an initial list of characteristics and practices that she expected might be reported as part of whole language. As the study proceeded, however, the list of practices expanded, informed by what was in the articles, with the final list of practices then used to score all of the studies.

Findings

Bergeron's (1990) analysis produced a great deal of information about various issues pertaining to the definition and practice of whole language.

Definition

Bergeron (1990) found that two-thirds of the manuscripts she reviewed contained definitions of whole language—all different. Although the majority of articles provided information about the roles of constructing meaning and functional language in whole language, there was less agreement that whole language was pupil centered (44% of articles), involved empowerment (42%), was communication oriented (38%), integrated language arts (36%), encouraged risk taking (30%), included both reading and writing (17%), involved both oral and written language (16%), or was based on a cuing system for reading (i.e., use of semantic, syntactic, and letter-level cues to recognize words rather than relying primarily on letter-level cues; 14% of articles). In short, there was little agreement among the contributors to the whole language literature about the basic definition of the approach.

Whole-Language Instructional Techniques and Strategies

Just as there was little agreement with respect to definition, there was little agreement about the instructional techniques and strategies used in whole language. Yes, 81% of the articles specified literature as important in whole language, and 64% identified process writing as part of whole language. About 65% of the articles discussed the cooperative nature of students in whole language classrooms. A little more than half (56%) talked about the affective dimension as part of whole language teaching. There was less agreement about other practices, however, with a little more than 40% of articles endorsing sharing, invented spelling, independent reading as part of whole language, thematic units, child-centered teaching, learning of skills in the context of real reading and writing, and student choice with respect to literacy activities. More than 40% of articles also specified that whole-language teachers were interactive with their students, with the teachers viewed as learners as well. A little more than 30% of the articles specified student writing of journals, reading aloud, and reading independently as part of whole language. Dramatics, choral reading, predictable books, reading corner, student dictation of stories, learning centers, teacher modeling, teacher analysis of reading miscues (i.e., teacher analysis of student reading errors to discern student reading strategies), daily reading, daily writing, kidwatching (i.e., for assessment), and teacher–student conferences all garnered fewer mentions in the articles. Bergeron's (1990) interpretation of her outcomes was that the diversity in instructional recommendations probably reflected the diversity of practices in whole-language classrooms.

Bergeron (1990) also notes some instructional elements and practices that are inconsistent with whole language: the whole-word approach, which was the approach used in the Dick-and-Jane era with students introduced to words to learn by sight, and phonics, with few of those writing the articles analyzed by Bergeron expressing any concern about phonics whatsoever. Nor does whole language involve the teaching of skills out of the natural context of reading and writing. Worksheets are not part of whole language, nor is teacher concern with accuracy during decoding. Ability grouping is viewed as conflicting with whole language.

A few years after Bergeron (1990), an analysis using a similar approach was published—that is, involving the careful analysis of articles published in carefully reviewed journals relating to whole language. Moorman, Blanton, and McLaughlin (1994) came to conclusions generally consistent with the ones drawn by Bergeron. However, they also came up with a telling way of organizing their findings in terms of oppositional metaphors capturing what whole language is and what it is not. They argued that the authors of the various articles they reviewed emphasized naturalness and personal ownership of teaching and learning as characteristic of whole language environments, but found that whole language classrooms do not include artificial instruction (i.e., experiences that are not real reading and writing, such as isolated skills instruction) which is controlled by authorities outside of the classroom (e.g., basal publishers).

What may be surprising to readers is that despite the murkiness in definition and in the descriptions of whole language practices in the journal articles, there have in fact been many volumes written about the nature of whole language, albeit with the more detailed ones coming after Bergeron (1990) did her work. It is worthwhile to spend some time reflecting on those volumes, because they are very revealing about the nature of whole language.

VOLUMES ABOUT WHOLE LANGUAGE

In the late 1990s, there is much that can be read by anyone interested in learning about whole language. I could not possibly cover the many books on the topic, but will instead highlight some of the especially important authors in this section.

Frank Smith and Kenneth Goodman

There are a few volumes, continually cited whenever whole language is discussed, in which the case was originally made for making meaning construction the primary goal in learning to read from the very start. In these classics, there is deemphasis of the letter- and word-level processes that are involved in decoding of text in favor of higher-order meaning construction as the driving force in reading. Moreover, meaning construction during good reading is depicted as much more affected by the prior knowledge of the reader rather than determined by the information in the text.

An edited quote from the second chapter of Canadian Frank Smith's (1979) *Reading without Nonsense* provides the flavor of this line of thinking, including clear antagonism for any conception of reading that focuses on letter- and word-level skills:

> One essential skill of reading that no reader is ever taught is to depend upon the eyes as little as possible . . . undue concern with marks on the printed page can only make reading more difficult . . . visual information is not enough for reading . . . the more you know in advance about a book, the easier it is to read. . . . Readers have nonvisual information about the choices available to an author, and make full use of their knowledge to reduce their own uncertainty about what successive words might be. . . . In other words, the reader knows so much that for every letter the author supplies, the reader can provide the next himself, without even looking. (pp. 12–30)

Among his many complaints about reading instruction, Smith (1979) objected to phonics, making the case that good readers routinely recognize words without sounding them out, and that often, a word cannot be recognized until its meaning has been comprehended. For those beginning readers who encounter words they do not know, Smith offered the following advice:

> The first alternative and preference is—to skip over the puzzling word. The second alternative is to guess what the unknown word might be. And the final and least preferred alternative is to sound the word out. Phonics, in other words, comes last. (p. 66)

In the concluding chapter of his 1979 book, a chapter concerned with the teaching of reading, Smith continued his attack on the teaching of letter- and word-level skills. Indeed, his list of ways to interfere with learning to read includes the following: "Ensure that phonics skills are learned and used" and "Identify and treat problem readers as early as possible" (p. 138). As will become clear as this book proceeds, it would be hard to imagine advice less consistent with the scientific data on reading and reading instruction produced in the last 15 to 20 years. What is so striking in reading Smith's writing, however, is the certainty of his claims. If you reread the quotes I provided, you see no hesitancy, no tentativeness about the thinking. Smith is not advancing hypotheses but rather conclusions, implying as he does that any other conclusions simply are not supportable.

Although the emphases and specifics vary, Frank Smith (1971, 1975, 1979) as well as Kenneth Goodman (1986, 1996) produced many reiterations of the theme that learning to read is more about learning to guess words well, based on the meaning cues in the text and the prior knowledge brought to the text, with letter- and word-level cues definitely less important in word recognition. Goodman is no less assertive than Smith in his writing. Thus, despite quite a bit of evidence to the contrary at the time of his writing, Goodman (1996) concludes his Chapter 4, "How Proficient Reading Works," with the following:

> In these experiments [i.e., thought experiments that Goodman led readers through in the chapter] you studied your own reading process. You discovered how you achieve *effectiveness* (by successfully constructing meaning) while also being *efficient* (getting to meaning with the least amount of time, energy and visual input). You saw that reading was a far more efficient process than successively recognizing letters in words could ever be. And you discovered how active your mind could be in making sense of print. (p. 52, emphasis in original)

If there be any doubt from that summary that Goodman holds no respect for the bottom-up processes involved in decoding text (i.e., translation of visual letter cues into sounds), the summary at the end of his next chapter, "How Developing Reading Works," leaves little doubt: "In the pre-Copernican world of understanding reading we thought accurate, rapid letter and/or word recognition was the center of the process and somehow comprehension followed. But now we know that reading is making sense of print" (p. 61). By the end of Chapter 7, "The Reading Process: Cycles and Strategies," there is no doubt, with this conclusion offered:

> By calling reading a psycholinguistic guessing game, I wanted to emphasize the active role of the reader in making sense of written

language as a new key element in our understanding of the reading process. I wanted people to take distance from the view that reading is the accurate, sequential recognition of letters and words. I wanted them to understand that, in order to make sense (construct meaning), readers:

- make continuous use of minimal information selected from a complex but incomplete and ambiguous text;
- draw on their knowledge of language and the world;
- use strategies for predicting and inferring where the text is going.

In short, I wanted them to understand that readers engage in informed guessing as they read. (pp. 115–116)

As it turns out, Smith and Goodman are correct that prior knowledge plays important roles in reading; that will be considered in detail in the chapters that follow. Where they are wrong, which will also be considered in detail, is in their belief that semantic cues and meaning cues in text should have priority in word recognition. The scientific evidence is simply overwhelming that letter–sound cues are more important in recognizing words than either semantic or syntactic cues, despite the constant assertions to the contrary by Smith and Goodman (see especially Chapter 5 of this book).

Although Smith's and Goodman's writings did much to inspire the whole language movement, their writing was not very helpful with respect to implementation of whole language. To the extent that they deal with implementation, Smith and Goodman both are more anti-instruction than pro-instruction, believing that learning to read depends much more on whole reading and writing experiences than on teaching about the parts of words and how those parts can be combined (i.e., phonics instruction). Goodman (e.g., 1993), in particular, argued that learning to read is analogous to first-language acquisition, that it is a natural by-product of immersion in print experiences:

What we've learned from the study of language development, both oral and written, is that language is easy to learn when we deal with the whole of it as we use it functionally to make sense. Little children are understanding and making themeselves understood in oral language long before they fully control the sound system. That's because they learn language in the context of its use. Children learn written language in the same way. They may learn the names of letters as they're learning to read, and even have some sense of how they relate to sounds. But they can learn the abstract phonics system only in the context of trying to make sense of meaningful print. They're good at learning language when it is in authentic, meaningful context. They're not very good at learning abstractions out of context. (Goodman, 1993, p. 109)

Goodman (1993) concluded his book *Phonics Phacts* with a list of reasons not to teach letter-sound relationships out of the context of actual reading and writing, including (among others) the following:

- Such instruction turns reading from a process of making sense into one of saying sounds for letters.
- It ignores the meaning and structure of language. Phonic instruction distorts children's processing of language by taking instruction out of the language context.
- It begins with abstractions instead of functional, meaningful language that's easy to learn.

In summary, the most important fact about phonics, according to Goodman (1993), is that it should not be taught because it does not need to be taught. Children can discover letter–sound regularities from experiencing actual print and doing real writing. As will become clear as this book continues, however, that is too sanguine a view about children's abilities to discover phonics regularities.

Constance Weaver

In my mind, the gold standard with respect to presenting whole language theory to teachers in a coherent way is Constance Weaver's (1994) book. Weaver does a very credible job of presenting the case that Smith, Goodman, and others began—that meaning making should take priority in reading at all times, including as children are learning to read. Better than Smith and Goodman, however, Weaver presents more contemporary theory and research pertaining to meaning-construction processes.

For example, she emphasizes schema theory, which was the driving force in much of reading research in the 1980s. She leads her readers through the restaurant schema. Most Western adults understand what happens at a restaurant, from prior to arrival at the restaurant until departure (i.e., making reservations, arriving, being seated, getting the food, eating, paying). But the restaurant schema is more complicated than that. Adults recognize how each of the events in going to a restaurant plays out differently in specific restaurants, such as truck stops, fast food restaurants, cafeterias, ethnic restaurants, family restaurants, cocktail restaurants, and expensive restaurants. Even within these categories, adults have very well differentiated knowledge; thus, many adults know what differences to expect at a variety of ethnic restaurants, such as Greek, Italian, Mexican, Chinese, and Thai establishments. This schematic knowledge is very important in getting through the restaurant event, with our expectations about what will happen leading us through a visit to a restaurant. Thus, while no one who knows about fancy Hungarian restaurants is surprised when a violinist shows up at the table, imagine the surprise if that were to occur at McDonald's or a Pizza Hut.

More pertinent here, when a child enters a McDonald's and encounters a menu, the child's reading of the menu is going to be colored by expectations based on prior knowledge of the restaurant. Thus, in McDonald's, a 6-year-old, when asked to read the top line on the menu over the counter, might say, "Big Mac," immediately. In contrast, if the words *Big Mac* were presented to the child at home on a piece of paper, the child might not be able to read them. The context cues that trigger schematic knowledge are very important in reading according to the whole-language perspective. Indeed, in the tradition of Smith and Goodman, Weaver (1994) makes a strong case that context cues and the schemata they trigger are prime players in reading. Because whole-language educators believe that schemata play a large role in comprehension, their approach is often thought of as a top-down approach. That is, the reader first gets the top level, big ideas, which inform his or her understanding of parts of the text. In contrast is the bottom-up approach, which involves analyzing individual letters to produce individual words which are combined to construct the meaning of the text.

There is little of the bottom-up approach in Weaver's view of reading and much of the top-down. She sums it up early in her book (Weaver, 1994) in the following way:

1. In isolation, most words do not have a single meaning but rather a range of possible meanings.
2. Words take on specific meanings as they transact with one another in sentence, text, social, and situational contexts.
3. Meaning is not in the text, nor will the meaning intended by the writer ever be perceived (or rather, constructed) exactly the same by a reader.
4. Readers make sense of texts by bringing to bear their schemata— their entire life-time of knowledge, experiences, and feelings.
5. Meaning emerges as readers transact with text in a specific situational context.
6. Thus, the process of reading is to a considerable degree whole to part, top to bottom, deep to surface, inside out. (p. 43)

As part of learning to read this way, Weaver goes on in her volume to specify how every component cited by Bergeron (1990) can play a role in whole-language classrooms. There is much in Weaver's book about immersing children in literature and encouraging them to write. According to Weaver, both play a critical role in learning to read, including learning to recognize words.

Weaver portrays written word recognition as involving analyses of multiple cues: semantic cues, syntactic cues, and graphophonemic cues. Consider the following sentence, which has one word missing: *Mike is writing a* _____. Could _____ be goat? No, it just would make no sense in this context. How about *lied*? Well, no, because *lied* is a verb, and knowledge of syntactic constraints rules a verb out in favor of a noun. How about *book*? That's more like it, for it is a noun that makes sense in context. With a little more processing of the graphophonemic (e.g., visual) cues—that is, looking at the other letters—it might become obvious that the word was *book*. But what if the first letter was *p* (i.e., p___)? In that case, *book* would not be thought of because you would process the first-letter cue of *p*, and thus not think of a word starting with a *b*.

For their conclusion that word recognition involves the use of these semantic, syntactic, and graphophonemic cues, whole-language-oriented scholars cite as evidence the fact that when a reader misreads a word, the misreading typically can be explained as semantically related to the actual word (e.g., for the sample sentence in the last paragraph, if the reader read *play*), syntactically sensible (e.g., for the sample sentence, if the reader said a noun rather than a verb), or graphophonemically related to the target word (e.g., for the sample sentence, if the reader read *boom* instead of *book*; Goodman, 1993). Of course, the problem with such miscue data is that they represent reading when it is flawed rather than reading when it is done competently. Although it is completely illogical to argue that processing during errorful reading is like processing during competent reading, whole language theorists consistently make this argument.

Moreover, the patterns of miscues observed during flawed reading are such that the whole-language enthusiasts have concluded that semantic and syntactic cues take priority over graphophonemic cues in reading, with processing of semantic and syntactic cues permitting more efficient use of visual cues. As Weaver (1994) put it:

1. Highly effective readers use preceding syntactic and semantic context to predict what is coming next (that is, to reduce the number of reasonable alternatives). On the one hand, their

reliance on prior knowledge and context makes their use of visual cues more efficient. On the other hand, it also generates predictions resulting in miscues, but ones that typically fit with the grammar and meaning of the preceding context.

2. Highly effective readers use the following syntactic and semantic context to confirm their prediction, or as an impetus to reread and try to correct.

3. Moderately effective readers use preceding syntactic and semantic context to predict, but they are less successful in noticing where grammar or meaning has gone awry, and thus, less successful in using following context to correct what doesn't fit.

4. Somewhat effective readers use preceding syntactic context to predict, but they are not as successful at using preceding semantic context to predict. (p. 142)

Given Weaver's belief that good readers use semantic and syntactic cues to a much greater extent than letter-level cues to recognize words—especially words they know from hearing them but have not seen before—it is sensible to play down the teaching of phonics and the analyses of letter-level cues to recognize words.

To say that Weaver (1994) plays down the teaching of phonics is to put it very mildly. Indeed, Weaver (1994) leaves absolutely no doubt where she stands with respect to the systematic teaching of phonics:

> *It's not necessary.* Just as they learn the patterns of oral language, so most children will unconsciously learn common phonics patterns, given ample opportunity to read environmental print and predictable and enjoyable materials, and ample opportunity to write with invented (constructive) spelling. (p. 197, emphasis in original)

There it is in a nutshell, the classic whole-language philosophy with respect to the development of word recognition skills: Do not teach decoding directly. Rather, immerse children in print experiences and opportunities to write with invented spelling, and they will learn to read.

Weaver (1994, pp. 197–199) goes on to list many reasons for not teaching decoding systematically, among them her view that visual processing is just one of the cuing systems that should be used, with semantic and syntactic cues reducing the need to process the visual characteristics of words. Weaver worries that phonics instruction will lead children to "sound out" words too much, with not enough attention paid to meaning. That phonics is very difficult for young children because it involves analytical and abstract learning is a consistent claim of whole language theorists, as expressed, for example, by Kenneth Goodman (1993):

> The phonic relationships in English . . . are . . . abstract: when we deal with phonics, we're dealing not with the relationship of language to meaning or to things, we're dealing with relationships between two abstract systems, oral and written language. (p. 106)

When all is said and done, Weaver comes to the conclusion that there are many reasons to develop children's knowledge of letter–sound relations and patterns through authentic reading and writing rather than through isolated skills instruction. Much of the book you are now reading is about making the case that Weaver (1994)–and other whole language theorists, such as Goodman (1993)–had it about half right with respect to the development of reading skills. Yes, authentic reading and writing are important in the development of literacy, but systematic instruction in skills is also very important.

Regie Routman

Regie Routman is a teacher who works in a school district that moved from conventional literacy instruction to whole language. As part of that, Routman became exceptionally well informed about the theoretical background supporting the whole language approach as well as specific practices that can be used in whole language classrooms. She has recorded her accumulated wisdom in two volumes, *Transitions: From Literature to Literacy* (1988) and, *Invitations: Changing as Teachers and Learners K–12* (1991). Both are bestsellers in the educator marketplace.

Whole-language practice in North America has been very much influenced by literacy instructional approaches in Australia, as defined, for example, by Brian Cambourne (1988, 1995), and in New Zealand, as described, for example, by Don Holdaway (e.g., 1979). Routman's writing reflects thorough familiarity with the work of these authors but also reflects her complete understanding of how whole language is being accomplished in North America. I am genuinely impressed with the set of beliefs she has come to as a function of her reflection on whole language theory and living whole language practice. As will become obvious as this book proceeds, I concur with most of them. The various tenets of her beliefs include the following:

- The developmental level of the learner must be respected.
- All students and teachers can learn.

- Focusing on the strengths must come first when looking at learners.
- We teachers need to demonstrate ourselves as "joyfully literate."
- Learners need many opportunities for "languaging."
- The learning process is highly valued.
- Evaluation is ongoing.
- The goal of education is independence.
- Learning is lifelong and requires thoughtfulness.
- The teacher is facilitator and colearner.
- Curriculum is negotiated, and learners have choices.
- "Demonstrations" are necessary for learning.
- Sharing is an important part of learning.
- Sufficient time is needed for optimal learning.
- Collaboration and social interaction foster literacy development. (Routman, 1991, p. 14)

Routman believes that literacy instruction should involve these key components: children reading and writing aloud, student sharing of reading and writing, teacher-guided reading and writing, and independent reading and writing (Routman, 1991, p. 31). Both *Transitions* and *Invitations* are filled with specific practices that teachers can incorporate into their classrooms. The books also include many insights about how literature can be incorporated into classrooms, students can be taught to respond to literature, spelling instruction can be accomplished so that it is consistent with whole language, content instruction can be integrated with language arts, and classroom management can foster whole language. Both books include "blue pages," which provide annotated bibliographies of references that might be helpful to teachers attempting to understand and implement whole language. The blue pages also provide lists of pieces of literature that are appropriate in whole language classrooms (e.g., books that invite readers into print, books that are particularly good for readers just learning how to make sense of text, ones that fit well into instruction in grades 1 through 6, books that invite writing, etc.) as well as appendices that can support various aspects of life in whole language classrooms. Routman's books are invaluable resources for elementary teachers.

There are disturbing aspects of her perspectives, however, with the most saliently troubling being her stance on instruction in word recognition for beginning readers. Routman advocates a problem-solving approach when beginning readers encounter words in print that they do not recognize visually, with the reader making choices between a number of strategies for identifying a word:

- Skip the difficult word.
    Read on to the end of sentence or paragraph.
    Go back to the beginning of the sentence and try again.
- Read on. Reread inserting the beginning sound of the unknown word.
- Substitute a word that makes sense.
- Look for a known chunk or small word.
    Use finger to cover part of the word.
- Read the word using only beginning and ending sounds.
    Read the word without vowels.
- Look for picture cues.
- Link to prior knowledge.
- Predict and anticipate what could come next.
- Cross check.
    "Does it sound right?"
    "Does it make sense?"
    "Does it look right?"
- Self-correct and self-monitor.
- Write words you can't figure out and need to know on Post-Its.
- Read passage several times for fluency and meaning. (1994, p. 226b)

What is wrong with this list of choices? For one, as will become apparent in the chapters that follow, sounding out a word is the preferred strategy of good readers and one associated with strong reading, in general, and yet, it does not appear on this list. Second, although there is growing evidence that recognizing words through known parts of words (e.g., recognizing the *-ail* in *pail* from knowing *sail*) is an effective decoding strategy, it is buried in a long list of strategies based on orientation to semantic context cues. What this egalitarian list of word recognition strategies represents is Routman's complete commitment to use of multiple cues for word recognition—semantic, syntactic, and graphophonemic, the approach favored in whole language.

In summary, I am certain that Routman is a very good whole-language teacher. Consistent with my belief that the practices and perspectives of excellent literacy teachers can be very informative about how literacy instruction should be carried out everywhere, I greatly admire much of what she has to say. I find myself most troubled, however, by her stance on the teaching of word identification, which is not in synchrony with a great deal of research data.

Even so, Routman is more balanced than some other whole-language advocates. For example, Routman makes clear, in her 1996 book,

Literacy at the Crossroads: Critical Talk about Reading, Writing, and Other Teaching Dilemmas, that at least some students, ones who have a great deal of difficulty in learning to read, really need intensive phonics instruction (pp. 99–100), that their problem is that they have not received systematic teaching of letter-sound relationships. This contrasts with other whole-language enthusiasts who actually contend that the source of difficulties for students who are very slow to read is that they have been taught phonics (e.g., Goodman, 1993, pp. 110–112; Weaver, 1994, p. 198)! In addition, Routman (1996) very soundly recommends that the aspiring whole-language teacher not throw out the spelling workbooks and basals until she or he is confident in teaching spelling using the contextual approach, a recommendation flying in the face of many whole-language opinions. Similarly, she dismisses the frequent recommendation by proponents of whole language not to teach handwriting. In general, there is a lot of reality in Routman (1996) that I have not found in other texts pertaining to whole language. She realizes limits of whole-language thinking that others identified with the movement do not.

IS WHOLE LANGUAGE SUPPORTED BY RESEARCH?

In this section I summarize evidence of the value of whole language in contemporary elementary instruction. Even so, whole language does not effectively promote all of the competencies that are required of skilled readers.

Stahl's Reviews

Steven Stahl has done more than almost anyone else to summarize the effects of whole language on standardized measures of reading achievement. Perhaps the most visible article ever published pertaining to research and whole language was Stahl and Miller's (1989) paper in the prestigious *Review of Educational Research.* The authors reviewed all of the comparisons they could find of conventional reading instruction using a published reading series (i.e., basal instruction) and whole language or a precursor approach to whole language, the language experience approach.

Based on their review of the evidence, Stahl and Miller (1989) contended that whole language and language experience approaches are more effective in kindergarten than in grade 1. They also concluded that whole language is effective in conveying some very general under-standings about reading and writing but that it is not particularly effective in developing word recognition skills (i.e., decoding), which is essential if students are to learn to read with good comprehension. The basis for this conclusion is that in 33 comparisons at the kindergarten level involving measures of reading readiness, whole language proved superior to basal approaches, with basal approaches faring better than whole language in only 2 of the 33 comparisons. In contrast, at the grade-1 level, 65 comparisons of whole-language/language experience and basal instruction were available, with 13 clearly favoring the basal, 9 favoring whole-language/language experience, and 43 indeterminate.

A particularly important finding in the Stahl and Miller (1989) study, and one that has gotten a great deal of attention (Pressley & Rankin, 1994), is that positive whole-language effects are much less likely with weaker students and students at risk because of low socio-economic status than with more advantaged students. Especially strik-ing were the outcomes pertaining to beginning reading (rather than reading readiness): For those 24 comparisons, the basal approach was favored in nine of them and whole-language/language experience was favored in none.

An intriguing finding was that despite the orientation in whole-lan-guage/language experience approaches toward comprehension, if any-thing, these approaches have had more of an effect on word recognition measures than comprehension. In neither case is the effect dramatic, however, with a modest effect in favor of whole-language/language experience on word recognition and a slightly larger negative effect of whole-language/language experience approaches on comprehension.

Stahl, McKenna, and Pagnucco (1994) revisited and updated the Stahl and Miller (1989) conclusions, based on a number of new comparisons of whole language with other forms of instruction. Again, whole language seemed to produce better outcomes with respect to some measures of reading readiness, although Stahl et al. (1994) alluded to some evidence that important readiness competencies, such as awareness that words are composed of sounds (i.e., phonemic awareness, see Chapter 5, of this volume), are not developed well by conventional whole language (e.g., Byrne & Fielding-Barnsley, 1993). What Stahl et al. (1994) found at grades 1 and 2 was a very modest positive effect of whole language on comprehension and a modest negative effect on students' decoding abilities. In general, Stahl and his associates found some support for whole language as a kindergarten approach. They found nothing to favor whole language after kinder-garten.

An Overview of Documented Positive Associations between Whole-Language Experiences and Literacy Outcomes

Although the effects of whole language on standardized tests have not been as positive as might have been hoped for by whole language proponents, there is nonetheless quite a bit of evidence that children benefit from experiencing whole-language education. Some of the most important findings are the following:

• One of the most striking and consistent findings in the research literature pertaining to whole language is that immersion in literature and writing increases children's understanding about the nature of reading and writing and stimulates children to do things that are literate (e.g., Graham & Harris, 1994; Morrow, 1990, 1991; Neuman & Roskos, 1990, 1992; Rowe, 1989). For example, there is a growing data base supporting the conclusion that when literature drives instruction, there are positive effects on students' autonomous use of literature and attitudes toward reading (e.g., Morrow, 1992; Morrow, O'Connor, & Smith, 1990; Rosenhouse, Feitelson, Kita, & Goldstein, 1997).

• Consistent experiences with high-quality literature foster growth in understanding of the structure of stories, which improves both comprehension and writing, as well as the sophistication of children's language (e.g., Feitelson, Kita, & Goldstein, 1986; Morrow, 1992; Rosenhouse et al., 1997). For example, when teachers and children share books, which is a frequent type of interaction in whole language environments, the children learn how to interpret stories and go beyond the literal information in the text to draw appropriate inferences (e.g., Cochran-Smith, 1984; Reutzel, Hollingsworth, & Eldredge, 1994).

• Just as broad reading expands the knowledge of adults (Stanovich & Cunningham, 1993), extensive experiences with stories expand children's knowledge of the world, as reflected, for example, by breadth of vocabulary (e.g., Elley, 1989; Robbins & Ehri, 1994; Rosenhouse et al., 1997). Having students read a great deal of literature that deals with science themes increases the elementary students' understanding of science concepts (e.g., Morrow, Pressley, Smith, & Smith, 1997).

• Despite concerns that practices such as invented spelling might interfere with development of conventional spelling and reading skills, the effects seem to be just the opposite: Good invented spelling is associated with skill in learning to read (e.g., Richgels, 1995).

It should be apparent from this brief survey of outcomes that whole language practices are associated with positive achievements in literacy. Anyone who wishes to argue based on standardized test scores alone that whole language does not have positive effects must confront this data and explain them away. I, for one, do not believe that these data can be explained away, but rather; that they provide the impetus for thinking very hard about how the advantages produced by whole language can be replicated in many more classrooms. If more convincing is needed, however, the work of one Ohio-based research team is especially worthy of attention.

Dahl and Freppon's (1995) Study

Although many researchers have offered evidence of whole language's effects on children's literacy development, two researchers are mentioned particularly often as fostering in-depth understanding about the impact of whole language versus more conventional, skills-oriented instruction: Karin L. Dahl of Ohio State University and Penny A. Freppon of the University of Cincinnati. Some discussion of their best-known study will make clear that there is much substance to their work.

Dahl and Freppon (1995) focused on how kindergarten and grade-1 students in whole-language and skills-based classrooms interpret reading and writing and the instruction they are receiving. One aspect of the study that is impressive is its duration, with students studied for two years, and each classroom in the study (four classrooms total each year of the study) visited twice weekly. Within each classroom, twelve students in particular were selected for intensive study. All of these focal students were from socioeconomically disadvantaged homes, approximately equally divided between African American students and Appalachian whites.

What were the skills-oriented classrooms like? There was a traditional reading readiness focus with a great deal of attention to letter-sound relations. Grade 1 involved a basal and associated workbooks and skill sheets. Phonics instruction occurred out of the context of actual reading, through skills and drills, with little discussion of how to apply phonics skills during actual reading. Although there was occasional journal writing, there was also copying from the board and writing workbooks. Round-robin reading was a daily occurrence in grade 1, although students also read trade books from the classroom library when their other work was completed. There was some choral reading. When there was storybook reading, the discussion of stories was usually limited to asking students to recall information in the stories. In short, Dahl and Freppon (1995) succeeded in finding prototypical skills-based primary classrooms, which are a far from extinct species in North America despite the widespread dissemination of whole language.

What were the whole language classrooms like? There were long periods of independent reading and writing. The teachers sometimes worked with small groups of readers and writers, and sometimes worked with individuals. The students read fine children's literature, much of it from well-stocked classroom libraries. Teachers often demonstrated reading strategies and skills, for example, in the context of storybook reading. There was a lot of shared reading in these classrooms, with teachers and students engaging in real dialogue about a story as it was being read. Writing was often in response to stories read by the children, with children being taught writing strategies and conferring with teachers about how they might revise their rough drafts. The writing cycle culminated in publication of student writing, consistent with the Writer's Workshop approach so often encountered in whole-language classrooms. Writing was an everyday thing, including journals and opportunities to share writing with others. One means of sharing was that students read each other's published books. Also, an important part of writing involved reflection on phonics, with students encouraged to use letter–sound relations to figure out how to write the words they wanted to use. In summary, Dahl and Freppon (1995) succeeded in identifying prototypical whole-language classrooms.

One strength of the study is that the extensive observation permitted the researchers to ensure that the classrooms they were studying were in fact consistently either skills based or whole language. Beyond the extensive observations of instruction, however, there was also extensive measurement of students in order to understand how they understood reading and writing and reacted to the instruction they were receiving. All focal students were assessed with respect to the following:

- Students were presented a printed sentence and were asked if there was anything on the paper. The responses to this probe were revealing about whether students understood written language as a system with accessible meaning.
- Major concepts of books and print were measured (e.g., reading is left to right, front to back).
- Knowledge of letter–sound relations was tapped by, for example, asking students to write 10 spelling words or asking them to write anything they could, then telling about the writing.
- Children were asked to recall a story read to them and to tell

a story with a puppet. This was intended to reveal students' knowledge of story structure.

- Children were asked to read a picture book to a doll, and encouraged to make it sound like a real story. How they performed this task was compared with how they told about a family event, such as a birthday party. By comparing these tellings, the authors were able to gain understanding about what the students knew about the syntactic and word-level features in books.
- By asking the child to talk about her or his own writing, it was possible for the author to make inferences about children's concepts of writing.

These measures, which were administered early in the kindergarten year and then late in the grade-1 year, along with the two years of actual classroom observations, permitted the authors to come to a number of conclusions about how progress in literacy development differed in the two types of classrooms. I review their results in some detail here.

Concern with Accuracy

An important tenet of whole language theorists is that mistakes are a natural part of learning. Thus, the message in whole-language classrooms should be that it is okay to take risks; accuracy is not a paramount concern, according to the philosophy. Interestingly, however, students in both the skills-oriented and whole-language classrooms were concerned with accuracy.

Phonics

There was more evidence of skill in application of phonics knowledge in the students in the whole language classrooms. For example, students' writing in whole-language classrooms often included approximations to words that included salient letters in the words, but this pattern was not observed in the students from skill classrooms. When they did not know words, the whole language students were more likely to use credible invented spellings (i.e., ones reflecting knowledge of letter–sound relations) than were the skills-based students. Another disturbing finding with respect to the skills classroom students was that when they sounded out a word incorrectly when reading, they were less likely to notice that the word did not make sense and more likely to accept the misreading.

Response to Literature

The whole-language students made many more sophisticated responses to literature than did the students in the skills classrooms. When whole-language students told stories and talked about them, there was evidence of greater knowledge about characters, story events, and plot structuring. In telling and talking about stories, whole-language students were more likely to relate accurate information from well-known children's literature. It was clear that the whole-language students had learned more about literature as literature from their two years of immersion in whole language. The whole-language students were appropriately critical as well, expressing ideas about how authors might have varied stories.

Coping Strategies

The authors observed much more coping in whole language classrooms when students experienced difficulties. In contrast, they observed more avoidance of challenging tasks in the skills-based classrooms. One reason for this difference in coping was that the whole language classrooms were more social-collaborative settings, so that it was acceptable and appropriate to work with friends when the going got tough. That is not to say that everything was wonderful in the whole-language classrooms with respect to coping. For example, the least capable writers in the whole language classrooms often socialized to avoid writing, and they often elected the nonwriting role in collaborations with other students (e.g., illustrating the story).

Sense of Self as Reader/Writer

The whole-language students more frequently viewed themselves as readers and writers. Only the best readers and writers in the skills-based classrooms seemed to be comparably aware of themselves as developing literates.

Engagement

Persistent engagement in reading and writing was striking in the whole-language classrooms compared to the skills-based classrooms. The students in the skills-based classrooms certainly did not seem to be interested in reading as an elective activity compared to the students in the whole-language classrooms.

Knowledge of Written Language Characteristics

In general, students had more similarities than differences in their understanding of concepts of print, knowledge of story structure, and concepts of writing, as well as other indicators of knowledge about written language. The one exception was that, by the end of grade 1, the whole language students knew more about how the syntax and wording of stories differ from natural speech than did the students in the skills classes.

Word Recognition Strategies

The whole-language emphasis on use of context cues came through when students' reading was analyzed in this study. When encountering an unfamiliar word, whole language students were more likely to use picture cues, skip unknown words, reread and self-correct, and comment about the story than were students from skills classrooms. The skills-based students relied more exclusively on letter-sound relationships to recognize unknown words.

Summary

There were plenty of positives favoring the whole-language classrooms over the skills classrooms in Dahl and Freppon (1995), and the outcomes in their study are broadly consistent with the list of advantages compiled across a number of studies summarized earlier in this section. Dahl and Freppon have published some other analyses of the classrooms analyzed in the 1995 report, which also favor the whole-language classrooms. For example, Freppon (1991) reported that students in whole language classrooms understood much better than skills students that reading is about getting the meaning rather than simply reading the words. Dahl (1993) analyzed the comments that the whole-language students made while they wrote. The students engaged in a great deal of self-regulated reflection on letter–sound relations as they wrote, with a great deal of attention to patterns in letters and words.

For all that was positive, there was an important difference between the classrooms that is telling from the perspective of many researchers studying reading. Although the whole-language students seem to have been learning much about letter–sound relations and how to use them, they seem not to have used them with as much certainty as students in skills-based classrooms. The whole-language students were much more likely than the skills students to rely on picture and semantic context cues. In the chapters that follow, the case will be made that this is a disastrous strategy—and that it points to a great weakness in whole-language instruction that does not include extensive, systematic coverage of word recognition in terms of consistent letter–sound and orthographic analysis of unfamiliar words.

Commentary

Some who are reading this book are probably wondering how whole language, which has enjoyed widespread dissemination, could have been studied so little. One side of the answer is that those most strongly identified with whole language are very little interested in studying it, comfortable in their philosophically and theoretically based convictions about whole language's effectiveness. The other side is that those same whole language proponents have been aggressive in challenging reading researchers who want to study whole language. Indeed, a few years ago, when three researchers (McKenna, Robinson, & Miller, 1990) proposed in an even-handed, statesmanlike way that more research on whole language might be desirable, they were blasted in print in one of the most widely circulated educational research journals by whole-language advocate Carol Edelsky (1990). Here is a sample of Edelsky's comments to McKenna et al.'s (1990) mere suggestion that whole language might be studied, which she viewed as inconsistent with her worldview and that of whole-language educators in general:

> They [McKenna et al.] don't know from *gornischt* (from nuthin') but they sure have *chutzpah* (unmitigated gall)!! . . . It is not necessary and often not in their interests for whites, Christians, and men [McKenna and his coauthors were all three] to appreciate that there might be a coherent perspective that drastically contradicts their own. . . . Between their paradigm blindness and their conceptual errors, it is no wonder that McKenna et al.'s proposed research agenda is off base. . . . Whole language objects to relative effectiveness studies because, with their typical reliance on test score data, they promote test-driven curricula. Such curricula and such studies weaken teachers and students and subvert whole language goals; that is, they feed into mechanisms for stratifying society. . . . After acting as self-appointed statesmen who can broker two conflicting points of view because they themselves supposedly are eclectic, after distorting or outright obliterating whole language assumptions, arguments, definitions, and research agendas with an imposed agenda that doesn't acknowledge its own paradigmatic bias, McKenna et al. then deliver the crowning

blow—they call on whole language proponents to collaborate in all this. Gei gezundt (lotsa luck to 'em). (Edelsky, 1990, pp. 7–10)

Fortunately, some very good scientists ignored such advisement (and other blistering attacks). Hence, there is a growing body of data addressing what whole language can do and what it does not do, with that research summarized earlier in this section.

To review, we now know that there are many general points of understanding about reading and writing that are promoted by whole language. Moreover, literature and writing immersion promote the development of important content knowledge and ability in writing. Despite these benefits, there are some important negatives. Decoding skills are not effectively developed in whole-language environments. Moreover, at-risk students may be especially disadvantaged when in whole-language environments. Comprehension is not necessarily improved by whole language. Thus, the mixed record of effects is one reason that whole-language philosophy has not been embraced wholeheartedly by many concerned with early reading. Another reason is that, like Edelsky (1990), whole language proponents often have packaged their ideas about curriculum as political perspectives, ones unlikely to persuade many reading educators.

POLITICS OF BEGINNING READING INSTRUCTION (AT LEAST ACCORDING TO SOME WHOLE-LANGUAGE LEADERS)

No one who has had any contact with recent discussions regarding elementary reading instruction could have missed the political tone of the whole-language leadership. I offer here a sampler of their political thinking.

Kenneth Goodman

One of the most important early documents in the great debates surrounding reading was *Becoming a Nation of Readers,* which was prepared largely by a group at the Center for the Study of Reading, University of Illinois, headed by Richard Anderson (Anderson, Hiebert, Scott, & Wilkinson, 1985). The Center and the writing of the document itself were supported by grants from the U.S. Department of Education. Consistent with substantial research that phonics instruction should be part of beginning reading programs, the report includes recommendations for systematic teaching of decoding. The Center would also oversee the writing of Marilyn Adams's (1990) *Beginning to Read,* which summarized the evidence supportive of decoding-skills instruction.

Kenneth Goodman (1993), in a chapter entitled, "The politics of phonics," characterized *Becoming a Nation of Readers* as a tool of the "phonics-first lobby" (p. 103) and the conclusions in *Beginning to Read* as "determined in advance by a federal government agency acting on the instructions of the Congress" (pp. 103–104). He concluded, "Some people further their own [conservative] political purposes by using phonics to frighten and politicize rural and working-class parents" (p. 98). Similar sentiments were also expressed by Goodman in his most recent book (Goodman, 1996).

Constance Weaver

Weaver's (1994) textbook includes an entire chapter (Chap. 7), "Phonics and Whole Language: From Politics to Research," largely dedicated to the proposition that skills instruction is part of the arch-conservative political agenda. Here are Weaver's words on the topic:

> There is substantial evidence that advocacy for heavy phonics instruction is coming particularly from certain individuals and organizations within the Far Right. For instance, the ultraright National Association of Christian Educators (NACE) and its action group Citizens for Excellence in Education (CEE) urge their Christian followers to insist upon the teaching of phonics in the school. . . . A publication of the Heritage Foundation, a conservative think tank in Washington, extols phonics as "the very first tenet of the back-to-basics approach," which is advocated as the best approach to the illiteracy problem. . . . A great deal of the force behind such advocacy seems to be the desire to promote a religious agenda and/or to maintain the socioeconomic status quo. (p. 295)

> Members of the Far Right who emphasize getting the words "right" and value so-called literal recall rather than construction of meaning also tend to insist upon the extensive and intensive teaching of phonics. Having children do extensive and intensive work with phonics suits their worldview . . . Intensive phonics instruction is necessary because only the ability to sound out unfamiliar words will guarantee word-perfect reading. . . . [Quoting James A. Chapman, whom Weaver presents as a member of the Christian Right], "whenever initial emphasis is placed upon meaning instead of identifying the exact words that are on the page, a student is implicitly learning that individual words are not important . . . the emphasis upon individual words has always been of paramount importance to Christian educators, who believe in the verbal inspiration of the Scriptures and in quality education. Orthodox

Christians believe that God gave every word of the Scripture, not just the thoughts." (p. 296)

Teaching intensive phonics is . . . a way of keeping children's attention on doing what they're told and keeping them from reading or thinking for themselves. (p. 296)

Weaver continues elaborating the case that phonics instruction is part of a plan to maintain a stratified society, one in which those who are now lower class spawn future generations of the lower class. According to Weaver (1994, p. 299), who was very much influenced in her thinking on this subject by postmodernist critics of education (e.g., Giroux, 1983; Shannon, 1992), this occurs because lower-class children arrive at school already far behind other children, because of, for example, restricted language experiences during the preschool years (see Chapter 4 of this volume). Such children are assigned to lower reading groups and are subjected to more skills instruction (e.g., phonics) than other children, because they are deemed to need it. As the first step in a long downward spiral, among other negatives, such boring instruction kills such students' motivation, perhaps eventuating in students dropping out of school. This dooms them to continue in the lower class, where they spawn children who begin the cycle again.

According to Weaver, the blame for membership in the lower class falls in part on the shoulders of scholars who document the efficacy of including skills instruction as part of early reading instruction. As she summed it up:

Unfortunately, this vicious cycle is all too likely to be encouraged by . . . Marilyn Adams's book *Beginning to Read: Thinking and Learning About Print* . . . cited approvingly by Far Right advocates even before it was published. . . . It seems likely that such heavy phonics instruction will serve to perpetuate the nonmainstream status of many of these students through the overt curriculum, which keeps them busy with skills work instead of real reading. . . . (pp. 301–302)

Regie Routman

Much of Routman's 1996 book, *Literacy at the Crossroads: Crucial Talk about Reading, Writing, and Other Teaching Dilemmas,* is concerned with politics. She makes the case that to some extent, political leaders and policymakers have scapegoated educators, and the literacy crisis is not nearly as pronounced as many policymakers make it out to be. This point is reasonably credible, consistent with the conclusions of a thorough analysis published by Berliner and Biddle (1995), which influenced much of Routman's theory. Routman is also aware that educational change will be resisted by many (her Chap. 4) and offers many suggestions as to how educators can work in their settings to overcome political resistance. Indeed, the entire 1996 book is a political document, specifically about how to make whole language more palatable to many stakeholders and thus, more likely to be the language arts approach of choice. For example, Routman revises the whole language story, stating early in the book, "*The reality is and has always been that phonics is part of whole language*" (p. 9, emphasis in original). That is, according to Routman (1996), whole-language teachers have always been in favor of teaching phonics to students on an as-needed basis and have always believed that phonics knowledge develops during authentic reading and writing.

In part, Routman's point is to defend whole language against its political critics, but it is also aimed at teachers who misinterpreted whole language to mean no skills instruction. Routman is blatantly honest about the existence of such teachers, as in, for example, a section of her Chapter 3 entitled, "I'm Whole Language—I Don't Teach Phonics." My only point of difference with Routman is that I do not believe that such teachers seriously misunderstood whole language as it was portrayed to them, for I have read the books they would have read, and it is easy to leave those books feeling that to teach skills is inconsistent with whole language.

Are These Political Perspectives Realistic?

To many, the political outlooks of these folks do not seem realistic; they seem, rather, to be far, far from the concerns of the many teachers who work very hard to develop literacy competencies in children. To the extent that such political assumptions have been addressed in formal studies, they have not held up. Consider, for example, the research in reaction to the perspectives of curriculum theorist Michael Apple (1982, 1986), who is sympathetic to whole language.

Apple argues that reading basal programs limit teachers' freedom, but more than that, actually deskill them. Rather than choosing among their various teaching skills to plan a reading curriculum, the teacher who relies on a basal surrenders control to an outside authority. According to Apple, this leads to an atrophying of teaching planning skills—and hence, the term "deskilling" (Apple, 1986, p. 209). The problem with this argument is that it just does not square with the data. In fact, according to several different investigations involving very different methodologies (Barr & Sadow, 1989; Baumann & Heubach,

1994; Hoffman, McCarthey, et al., 1995), teachers do not just follow the basal manuals but rather are extremely planful, picking and choosing parts of the basal program that make sense in their reading instruction. Of course, that basals do not deskill teachers is just one of a number of data-based conclusions that clash with the convictions of the whole language and like-thinking curriculum theorists.

In closing this section, I want to point out that my main intent in covering the political side of whole language is to make clear to readers why some whole-language proponents are so adamantly opposed to skills instruction: they believe that skills instruction serves political agendas not consistent with the best interests of many children.

I can understand their passions given their perceptions and convictions about the world. I simply do not agree with their perceptions and convictions and cannot make a conscionable case based on political considerations for not teaching children literacy skills. Indeed, my own view is that one part of any strategy to prevent disadvantaged children from being upwardly mobile would be to deny them effective literacy instruction, employing the most convincing scientific analyses available to determine effectiveness. I sincerely believe that those who would deny such instruction to children for whatever reason are, in fact, working on behalf of those who might prefer to prevent the disadvantaged from becoming more advantaged.

SUMMARY

1. Whole language has been a dominating force in contemporary elementary-level literacy instruction for more than a decade now. Dick, Jane, and Sally have been replaced by immersion in real literature, and there is a great deal more student writing today than there was in the mid-20th century. These practices have improved students' knowledge and their composing skills, as well as positively affected their attitudes toward reading.

2. Frank Smith and like-minded psycholinguistically oriented scholars formulated a top-down view of reading: According to their perspective, readers have hypotheses based on prior knowledge and ideas already encountered in a text, about which words might be coming up in the text that they are reading. Their hypotheses are also affected by knowledge of English syntax and the lexical constraints imposed by syntax, so that the good reader does not expect a noun in a part of a sentence that takes a verb. Finally, the letters and letter chunks in words (i.e., graphophonemic cues) are noted and processed. The proof that word recognition involves use of multiple cues in this

fashion is in the reading errors that are sometimes made. Particularly important, misreadings often are related semantically to words misread, which whole language enthusiasts take as evidence of the primacy of semantic cues over graphophonemic cues.

3. Educators committed to whole language have been assisted in implementing their efforts by the writings of Constance Weaver, Regie Routman, and others. Weaver's conception of language-arts education seems entirely consistent with the thinking of Frank Smith, Kenneth Goodman, and whole-language educational theorists from New Zealand and Britain. It is filled with recommendations to immerse students in print and writing. Teachers are to expect much of young learners as they give them the time and opportunities they need to practice real literacy; they also must permit them the mistakes that are part of learning to read and write. The teacher's role is largely to provide timely and appropriate feedback when mistakes occur, according to Weaver: to prompt students to reflect on their errors and in doing so construct new understandings about reading and writing.

Regie Routman's thinking seems to be less bound to whole-language principles than is Weaver's, reflecting her grounding in actual schooling. Even so, with respect to word recognition, Routman's prescriptions are much more consistent with Smith, Goodman, and other whole language-advocates than with the research-based perspective on word recognition that is outlined in the chapters that follow.

4. Although whole language is comprehensive with respect to language arts education, and many specific whole-language practices have been identified for encouraging development of reading and writing competencies, one issue seems to be more important than all others in differentiating the whole language perspective from others: Whole-language theorists and educators have a perspective on word recognition that contrasts with the positions of many others who are concerned with reading, especially beginning reading.

In addition, the whole-language approach to development of comprehension skills is read, read, and read. This is an old model of comprehension development. As will become evident in Chapter 7, there is much more that can be done to stimulate mature comprehension. Thus, my view is that whole language is an incomplete model of literacy development. By the end of this book, the case will be made that what is good in whole language should be combined with more explicit instruction of decoding and comprehension.

5. Whole language is a politically charged philosophy of curriculum. Whole-language advocates have claimed repeatedly that skills instruction is a tool of conservatives; used to maintain current socio-

economic and political stratifications. Those perspectives provide important insights into why opposition to skills instruction is so intense within the whole-language-education community.

REFERENCES

Adams, M. (1990). *Beginning to read.* Cambridge, MA: MIT Press.

Anderson, R. C., Hiebert, E. H., Scott, J. A., & Wilkinson, I. A. G. (1985). *Becoming a nation of readers.* Washington, DC: National Institute of Education.

Apple, M. W. (1982). *Education and power.* New York: Ark Paperbacks.

Apple, M. W. (1986). *Teachers and texts: A political economy of class and gender relations in education.* New York: Routledge.

Barr, R., & Sadow, M. W. (1989). Influence of basal programs on fourth-grade reading instruction. *Reading Research Quarterly, 24,* 44–71.

Baumann, J. F., & Heubach, K. M. (1994). *Do basal readers deskill teachers?* (Reading Research Report No. 26). Athens, GA, and College Park, MD: National Reading Research Center.

Bergeron, B. S. (1990). What does the term whole language mean? Constructing a definition from the literature. *Journal of Reading Behavior, 22,* 301–330.

Berliner, D. C., & Biddle, B. J. (1995). *The manufactured crisis: Myths, fraud, and the attack on America's public schools.* Reading, MA: Addison–Wesley.

Byrne, B., & Fielding-Barnsley, R. (1993). Evaluation of a program to teach phonemic awareness to young children: A 1-year follow-up. *Journal of Educational Psychology, 85,* 104–111.

Cambourne, B. (1988). *The whole story: Natural learning and the acquisition of literacy in the classroom.* Auckland, New Zealand: Scholastic.

Cambourne, B. (1995). Toward an educationally relevant theory of literacy learning: Twenty years of inquiry. *Reading Teacher, 49*(3), 182–190.

Cochran-Smith, M. (1984). *The making of a reader.* Norwood, NJ: Ablex.

Dahl, K. L. (1993). Children's spontaneous utterances during early reading and writing instruction in whole-language classrooms. *Journal of Reading Behavior, 25,* 279–294.

Dahl, K. L., & Freppon, P. A. (1995). A comparison of innercity children's interpretations of reading and writing instruction in the early grades in skills-based and whole language classrooms. *Reading Research Quarterly, 30,* 50–74.

Edelsky, C. (1990). Whose agenda is this anyway? A response to McKenna, Robinson, and Miller. *Educational Researcher, 19*(8), 7–11.

Elley, W. B. (1989). Vocabulary acquisition from listening to stories. *Reading Research Quarterly, 24,* 174–187.

Feitelson, D., Kita, B., & Goldstein, Z. (1986). Effects of listening to series stories on first graders' comprehension and use of language. *Research in the Teaching of English, 20,* 339–356.

Freppon, P. A. (1991). Children's concepts of the nature and purpose of reading in different instructional settings. *Journal of Reading Behavior, 23,* 139–163.

Giroux, H. A. (1983). *Theory and resistance in education: A pedagogy for the opposition.* Granby, MA: Bergin & Garvey.

Goodman, K. S. (1986). *What's whole in whole language?* Richmond Hill, Ontario: Scholastic. (Distributed in the United States by Heinemann)

Goodman, K. S. (1993). *Phonics phacts.* Portsmouth, NH: Heinemann.

Goodman, K. S. (1996). *On reading.* Portsmouth, NH: Heinemann.

Graham, S., & Harris, K. R. (1994). The effects of whole language on children's writing: A review of literature. *Educational Psychologist, 29,* 187–192.

Hoffman, J. V., McCarthey, S. J., Bayles, D., Price, D., Elliott, B., Dressman, M., & Abbott, J. (1995). *Reading instruction in first-grade classrooms: Do basals control teachers?* (Reading Research Report No. 43). Athens, GA, and College Park, MD: National Reading Research Center.

Holdaway, D. (1979). *The foundation of literacy.* Sydney, Australia: Ashton Scholastic. (Distributed in the United States by Heinemann)

McKenna, M. C., Robinson, R. D., & Miller, J. W. (1990). Whole language: A research agenda for the nineties. *Educational Researcher, 19*(8), 3–6.

Moorman, G. B., Blanton, W. E., & McLaughlin, T. (1994). The rhetoric of whole language. *Reading Research Quarterly, 29,* 309–329.

Morrow, L. M. (1990). Preparing the classroom environment to promote literacy during play. *Early Childhood Research Quarterly, 5,* 537–554.

Morrow, L. M. (1991). Relationships among physical designs of play centers, teachers' emphasis on literacy in play, and children's literacy behaviors during play. In J. Zutell & S. McCormick (Eds.), *Learner factors/teacher factors: Issues in literacy research and instruction: Fortieth yearbook of the National Reading Conference* (pp. 127–140). Chicago: National Reading Conference.

Morrow, L. M. (1992). The impact of a literature-based program on literacy achievement, use of literature, and attitudes of children from minority backgrounds. *Reading Research Quarterly, 27,* 251–275.

Morrow, L. M., O'Connor, E. M., & Smith, J. K. (1990). Effects of a story reading program on the literacy development of at-risk kindergarten children. *Journal of Reading Behavior, 22,* 255–275.

Morrow, L. M., Pressley, M., Smith, J. K., & Smith, M. (1997). The effect of a literature-based program integrated into literacy and science instruction. *Reading Research Quarterly, 32,* 54–76.

Neuman, S. B., & Roskos, K. (1990). The influence of literacy-enriched play settings on preschoolers' engagement with written language. In J. Zutell & S. McCormick (Eds.), *Literacy theory and research: Analyses from multiple paradigms* (pp. 179–188). Chicago: National Reading Conference.

Neuman, S. B., & Roskos, K. (1992). Literacy objects as cultural tools: Effects on children's literacy behaviors in play. *Reading Research Quarterly, 27,* 203–225.

Pressley, M., & Rankin, J. (1994). More about whole language methods of reading instruction for students at risk for early reading failure. *Learning Disabilities Research and Practice, 9,* 156–167.

Reutzel, D. R., Hollingsworth, P. M., & Eldredge, J. L. (1994). Oral reading instruction: The impact on student reading development. *Reading Research Quarterly, 29,* 40–59.

Richgels, D. J. (1995). Invented spelling ability and printed word learning in kindergarten. *Reading Research Quarterly, 30,* 96–109.

Robbins, C., & Ehri, L. C. (1994). Reading storybooks to kindergartners helps them learn new vocabulary words. *Journal of Educational Psychology, 86,* 54–64.

Rosenhouse, J., Feitelson, D., Kita, B., & Goldstein, Z. (1997). Interactive reading aloud to Israeli first graders: Its contribution to literacy development. *Reading Research Quarterly, 32,* 168–183.

Routman, R. (1988). *Transitions: From literature to literacy.* Portsmouth, NH: Heinemann.

Routman, R. (1991). *Invitations: Changing as teachers and learners K–12.* Portsmouth, NH: Heinemann.

Routman, R. (1996). *Literacy at the crossroads: Critical talk about reading, writing, and other teaching dilemmas.* Portsmouth, NH: Heinemann.

Rowe, D. W. (1989). Author/audience interaction in the preschool: The role of social interaction in literacy lessons. *Journal of Reading Behavior: A Journal of Literacy, 21,* 311–349.

Shannon, P. (Ed.). (1992). *Becoming political: Readings and writings in the politics of literacy education.* Portsmouth, NH: Heinemann.

Smith, F. (1971). *Understanding reading.* Hillsdale, NJ: Erlbaum.

Smith, F. (1975). *Comprehension and learning: A conceptual framework for teachers.* Katonah, NY: Owen.

Smith, F. (1979). *Reading without nonsense.* New York: Teachers College Press.

Stahl, S. A., McKenna, M. C., & Pagnucco, J. R. (1994). The effects of whole language instruction: An update and reappraisal. *Educational Psychologist, 29,* 175–186.

Stahl, S. A., & Miller, P. D. (1989). Whole language and language experience approaches for beginning reading: A quantitative research synthesis. *Review of Educational Research, 59,* 87–116.

Stanovich, K. E., & Cunningham, A. E. (1993). Where does knowledge come from? Specific associations between print exposure and information acquisition. *Journal of Educational Psychology, 85,* 211–229.

Weaver, C. (1994). *Understanding whole language: From principles to practice* (2nd ed.). Portsmouth, NH: Heinemann.

2

◄O►

SKILLED READING

Understanding the nature of skilled reading permits insights about what should be the goal of reading instruction. The analyses summarized in this chapter are among the most important influences on current efforts to develop powerful elementary reading instruction. The information in this chapter is essential for those who wish to understand why many researchers and reading educators are determined to increase the amount of decoding and comprehension-strategies instruction in the elementary curriculum.

LETTER- AND WORD-LEVEL PROCESSES

Researchers have used a variety of methods to understand how good readers process letters and words.

Eye Movements

During the past half-century, a number of researchers have studied reading at the letter and word levels by studying the eye movements of readers as they process text (Carver, 1990; Just & Carpenter, 1980; Rayner, 1992; Ygge & Lennerstrand, 1994). Much is now known about how eyes move during reading: Eye movements can be thought of as involving *fixations* when the eye is stopped briefly, looking at something, and *saccades* when the eye is jumping to the next fixation. Sometimes the eye will jump back to examine an earlier word in a sentence or paragraph: this is referred to as a *regression*. How does the eye know where to jump next? When reading in languages printed left to right, such as English, a reader processes the material a little to the right of the current point of fixation. More often than not, there is not enough processing of the material in the right periphery for the reader to know what the word is before it is fixated, but there is enough processing to permit the eye to make a jump to something informative—that is, to permit the eye to land on a word rather than a space between words.

When reading at a rate of 200 to 300 words per minute, good readers seem to process every single letter of text. One piece of evidence consistent with this point is that the longer a word is, the longer it takes a reader who is reading aloud to begin to pronounce it from the onset of perception of the word. In fact, every additional letter results in about a 10- to 20-millisecond delay in the onset of reading of the word (Stewart, James, & Gough, 1969, cited in Samuels, 1994). Another telling piece of evidence about how readers process individual letters is that if text is altered so that individual letters from words are deleted, reading is much slower (Rayner, Inhoff, Morrison, Slowiaczel, & Bertera, 1981). If you do not believe that single letters can make a difference, try reading an uncorrected letter typed by a pretty good typist in contrast to an uncorrected letter typed by an excellent typist. Mistyped and missing leters are vary distracting and slow reeding quite a bit, dn't they?

It is important to process every single letter during reading because letter-level cues are the primary means of recognizing words. This conclusion, based on eye movement and related analyses, clashes with the whole-language theory of word recognition. Whole-language theorists contend that reading a previously unseen word often involves making a guess based on the meaning of the text that has been encountered prior to the new word. From this perspective reading is very much a psycholinguistic guessing game (Goodman, 1967; Smith, 1971). However, this perspective simply is not supported by outcomes from eye-movement research. For example, if it were true, then good readers should have a pretty good idea of what the next word in text is going to be—that is, the word to the right of the word just read. They don't. When adult readers are reading a text on a computer screen that suddenly disappears, they can report the last fixated word reliably (McConkie & Hogaboam, 1985), but have a great deal of difficulty guessing the next word in the text, being correct about a quarter of the time. A skilled adult reader reading a text with content words missing has a very tough time guessing the missing words, doing so correctly with 10% accuracy (Gough, 1983). Need convincing? Try guessing the correct word that is missing from this sentence: The lanky ballplayer reached down to pick up a _____ that had jumped onto the field. Do you now think that skilled readers guess words on the basis of context cues? If you do, reflect for a moment how much easier it is to read this: The lanky ballplayer reached down to pick up a frog that had jumped onto the field.

Thus, one problem with relying heavily on semantic context cues is that many words will be read incorrectly. That is, the psycholinguistic guesses will be wrong because any of a number of words could fit into the context. Relying heavily on semantic context cues is a weak strategy, the preferred strategy of weak readers only, as a number of studies (Share & Stanovich, 1995) have concluded. This point is taken up in greater detail in Chapter 5.

With skilled readers, reading speed varies with the type of reading. Thus, during skimming, reading is faster because many words are skipped by the reader. In contrast, when a reader is attempting to learn what is in text, reading is a word-by-word affair, with fixations on most of the individual words. For a skilled adult reader who is reading material carefully, each word is typically fixated for about a quarter of a second. That translates to about 200 words per minute when readers are reading to learn material (McConkie, Zola, Blanchard, & Wolverton, 1982). The less the reader is concentrating on learning the ideas in the text, the faster the reading rate. Reading at a relaxed pace typically occurs at a rate of between 250 and 300 words per minute, and thus, more relaxed reading also is more word-by-word reading than anything else. Despite claims by speed reading programs, the fastest that humans can read and comprehend is about 600 words per minute (Carver, 1990, Chap. 21).

Decontextualized Word Recognition

The ability to read words even when there are no semantic context cues is almost a defining characteristic of the good reader (Share & Stanovich, 1995). A great deal of research effort has been devoted to determining how good readers recognize words as well as they do. Of course, for good readers, many words are sight words: well known from many past encounters. Recognition of sight words is said to be automatized, for reading these words requires little or no effort and is highly reliable (LaBerge & Samuels, 1974).

Much more telling about the skill of good readers, however, is that they typically can read words they have never seen before, even words that are really nonsense words or pseudowords, such as *swackle, preflob,* and *plithing.* They can do that because they can readily associate letters with their sounds and blend the sounds to pronounce a word. Sounding out is something that good readers do well (Share & Stanovich, 1995).

Recognition of the common letter combinations in one's native language is also automatized in the skilled reader. Good readers can recognize common English-letter combinations, such as *-kle*, *pre-*, and *-ing*, presumably because they have encountered these combinations many times during reading. This permits much more rapid decoding than occurs when an unknown word does not contain familiar letter combinations. Try reading these two words: *retuckable* and *ekuteracbl*. They both contain the same letters, but the first is easier than the second because it is composed of three familiar English-letter combinations while the second word's combinations are less familiar.

That readers rely more on letter-level cues than semantic-context cues to read a word does not mean that semantic-context cues are not important in processing words. In fact, they can be very important, *after the word has been recognized*. Read the following sentence: The duck could not be stopped from biting the boy, so his mother grabbed the bill! Now, read this sentence: The boy could not be stopped from using his money to buy the duck, so his mother grabbed the bill. How the word *bill* is interpreted depends heavily on semantic-contextual cues in this example (Phillip Gough, personal communication, June 1996). Although context does little to facilitate reading a word, it does much to facilitate understanding the meaning of the word once read.

One criticism of much of the work on letter-level and word-level processes is that such analyses do not put the focus on the reader as a meaning-maker. That criticism is valid to some extent, as will be made clear as this chapter proceeds, for much of skilled reading is getting meaning from sentences and paragraphs. Even keeping in mind the caveat that reading is more than word recognition, however, the active processing of sentences and paragraphs cannot occur unless the reader can recognize individual words reliably and efficiently. That is why learning to decode is so important.

GETTING THE GIST

Every text has many ideas in it (e.g., Clark & Clark, 1977; Kintsch, 1974). Consider the sentence, "John carefully nailed down the loose shingles on the roof" (Kintsch, 1982). There are four ideas in it: *John nails shingles, nailing is being done carefully, shingles are on the roof,* and *shingles are loose.* When good readers read such a sentence, they understand all of these ideas, although later they may remember only the main idea expressed in the sentence, "John nailed shingles."

Unless they have exerted great effort to memorize a text verbatim, people do not remember everything from a text they read. What people remember is the gist, which comprises the main ideas in the text (Kintsch & van Dijk, 1978; van Dijk & Kintsch, 1983). In long discourse, such as is found in a book, there are layers of main ideas: At the top level, there is an overall summary of the book; then, each chapter in the book has main ideas, as does each paragraph in each chapter. The lower level main ideas (e.g., paragraph-level) are integrated by the skilled reader to create the higher-level summaries (e.g., at the chapter and then book level; van Dijk & Kintsch, 1983, e.g., Chap. 2; Kintsch, 1988).

For example, suppose that you are beginning a paragraph-long text. The first sentence contains a number of ideas, with the reader coding the main idea of the sentence. This idea is held in active memory as the next sentence in the paragraph is read. Attempts are made to link the main idea from the first sentence to the ideas of the second sentence, with another main idea emerging from this synthesis, integrating the meanings expressed in the first two sentences of the paragraph.

Sometimes there will be a need for bridging inferences that reconcile the meaning of the previous sentence with the ideas in a new sentence—that is, to produce coherence between the sentence currently being read and the text read up until this point. These bridging inferences are derived largely from word knowledge the reader possesses. For instance, if a text about a worker pounding nails never mentions a hammer, the reader may infer "hammer" when the sentence, "The head slipped off," is encountered. Perhaps the resulting main idea would be, "The hammer broke while being used." By the end of the paragraph, good readers have implicitly generated a summary capturing the gist of the entire paragraph. (I emphasize *implicitly* at this point, for this process occurs automatically and unconsciously in the skilled reader.) Later, if the reader has to recall the paragraph, the most important ideas will be recalled (e.g., Kintsch & Keenan, 1973). The longer the retention interval between reading and recall, the fewer details are remembered (e.g., Kintsch & van Dijk, 1978). The recall data will reflect bridging inferences made during the original reading as well as some inferences made when the text is recalled.

Such inferences, again, are based on what the reader already knows; that is, memory for text typically reflects information in the text and the reader's knowledge of the world. For example, when I told my son the story of Dickens's *A Christmas Carol,* I told the entire book-length story in about 5 minutes, remembering just about everything I could in that period of time. What I remembered were the main ideas of the story, rather than what specific villagers said, or even the words of the four night visitors. During my telling of the tale, however, I mentioned that Tiny Tim had polio. I had to explain to my 9-year-old what polio was, since the disease is almost never encountered in contemporary America. Later, when he read the story, he pointed out to me that the story actually contained no information about the affliction that put Tiny Tim on crutches. What had occurred was that I had inferred at some point, probably during my original reading of the story or during one of the productions of the play that I have seen, that Tiny Tim was a polio victim. Memory of text is very personal because the reader's background knowledge plays a large role in determining the meaning constructed by the reader.

Good readers do not make inferences willy-nilly, however. They do not make associations to prior knowledge that is completely remote from the ideas in the current text. Instead, they make inferences that are needed to understand the text (McKoon & Ratcliff, 1992; van den Broek, 1994). Nonetheless, as good readers read a story, they often create an elaborate understanding of the world in which the story is taking place (e.g., Fletcher, 1994). One of the important roles of prior knowledge is that it allows people to have a very good understanding of a very large situation given relatively little information. Even in long novels, the author can describe in writing only the most important features of the story's setting and the most salient characteristics of the characters' personalities, and those readers with extensive prior knowledge are better able to fill in the gaps than those without such knowledge.

In summary, during normal beginning-to-end reading of a text, such as a story, the reader processes the individual ideas but remembers the gist. In processing the text and constructing the gist, prior knowledge plays an important role, permitting the generation of inferences required to understand the text. In some cases the inferences are elaborate, specifying complex situations. Although the model of reading discussed in this subsection has been studied most extensively with respect to narrative texts (i.e., stories), many of its main points apply to various types of expository texts as well (i.e., factual texts, such as articles concerned with a particular topic; e.g., Britton, 1994).

One of the reasons that people read is to know more—and indeed, people who read extensively are more knowledgeable than people who read less (Stanovich & Cunningham, 1993). The psycholinguists interested in how people learn from text have established how general knowledge of the world changes as a function of reading (e.g., Graesser, 1981; Graesser, Hoffman, & Clark, 1980; Kintsch, 1974; Kintsch & Keenan, 1973; Kintsch, Kozminsky, Streby, McKoon, & Keenan, 1975). The gist of what has been read is integrated with what the reader knew before reading the text (i.e., prior knowledge) to create new knowledge (e.g., Anderson & Bower, 1973). Thus, if you read a magazine article about the literacy crisis in America, you might implicitly construct a summary that includes the main ideas covered in the article. At a party tomorrow, you could rely on this summary alone to guide partial retelling of the article to a friend who might be interested in the literacy crisis. More importantly, however, your long-term knowledge of literacy might be changed by reading the article. Thus, 6 months from now, when someone makes a claim about literacy that conflicts with what was in the article, you can respond, "But I thought . . . ," going on to relate a general point from the article, perhaps no longer aware of where the information was acquired.

CONSCIOUS COMPREHENSION: VERBAL PROTOCOLS OF READING

Skilled readers tend to know a lot more about things in general than do unskilled readers, for skilled reading results in the development of extensive knowledge. Much of this knowledge creation occurs automatically as a function of reading and gistifying text. It can also involve more conscious processes, for meaning making during reading is not just automatic, implicit processing of text: it also involves much conscious, controlled processing.

Much has been learned about conscious, active comprehension processes by having good adult readers think aloud as they read. That is, researchers have asked adults to read text, interrupting them every so often to have them tell exactly what they are thinking and what they are doing as they read. Conscious decision making during reading is more obvious when readers read demanding, difficult texts. Thus, the texts read in verbal protocol studies often have been very demanding, requiring a good deal of thought for readers to understand the messages in them.

Wyatt et al.'s (1993) Study

Because my students and I carried out an ambitious study of skilled reading using verbal-protocol methods, I have some first-hand experience in this area (Wyatt et al., 1993). In that investigation, 15 professors from the University of Maryland thought aloud as they read articles that they had selected within their areas of expertise. Although each professor read a different article, and the professors and articles spanned a number of academic disciplines, there were important similarities that could be identified in their reading.

First, all of the readers were exceptionally active as they read:

• Based on information in the article being read and their prior knowledge of the topic of the article, the professors anticipated what might be said later in the article. They were very aware of when their predictions were on target versus when their predictions were in error.

• They looked for information that was relevant to their personal interests and personal goals in reading the article. Thus, the professor who was reading the article in preparation for writing a paper her- or himself looked for information that might be helpful in preparing her or his own paper. Information that was relevant to the professor's personal goal in reading the text was read more slowly than information considered not as important.

• Although the professors generally read the articles from first page to last, they also jumped ahead sometimes to look for information that they thought might be in the article, and sometimes they looked back for additional clarification about a point that seemed confusing at first. Thus, if a sentence that was just read made little sense, they might reread it, and they might look back a few paragraphs to find information (i.e., a critical point they must have missed previously) that might render the sentence sensible.

• The professors explained the ideas in the text to themselves, constructing summaries and reasoning about why what was stated in the text made sense, or, in some cases, did not make sense.

• The professors monitored their reading a great deal. That is, they were very aware of how difficult or easy the text was to read. They were aware of whether they already knew the ideas stated in the text or the text was covering new territory for them. And, as discussed previously, they were aware of just which portions of the text were most pertinent to their reading goals.

Second, and even more striking than all the activity that occurred during reading, the readers were extremely passionate as they read. They constantly evaluated what they were reading. This was possible because of their extensive prior knowledge. Thus, when the text included ideas near and dear to their hearts, they reacted positively, saying things like, "Right on," or "She's got it!" In contrast were those occasions when text contained ideas that clashed with the reader's thinking. Such ideas were sometimes greeted with exclamations of disgust (including profanity) or nonverbal reactions, such as giving the article "the raspberry." Throughout reading, the readers reported when they were interested and when they were bored. It was very clear that reading was anything but an affectively neutral experience for these readers.

Pressley and Afflerbach's (1995) Analysis of Skilled Reading

This think-aloud study that we conducted is one of about 50 think-aloud studies that have been published in scientific journals. The exact types of activities reported by readers as they read have varied from study to study, probably reflecting variation in the directions given to participants in different studies as well as the variety of different texts read in the various investigations.

Despite the variability across studies in procedures and materials read, when Peter Afflerbach and I reviewed all the studies that were published up until 1994, we were able to construct a summary of good reading that cut across the various investigations (Pressley & Afflerbach, 1995). The readers that my students and I studied were not unusual. Active reading is apparent in virtually every verbal protocol study in the research literature. Yes, there is evidence that some readers are much more active than others, but in general, consciously active reading seems to be common, especially among individuals who are known to be good readers. The conscious processing that is excellent reading begins before reading, continues during reading, and persists after reading is completed.

Before reading, good readers make certain that they know why they are reading the text and are clear about what they want to get from it (e.g., information about the role of the Indians in the French and Indian War, an understanding of what the professor who wrote this article is doing in her or his current research). Rather than simply diving into a text and beginning to read a piece from front to back, good readers often overview a text. During the overview, they are sensitive to the structure of the text, especially noting parts of the text that might contain information that is particularly relevant to their reading goal. Good readers make a reading plan in light of the information they obtained during the overview. The information gained during overviewing permits the good reader to gauge which parts of the text should be read first, which parts of text should be read more carefully than others, and which ones should not be read at all. The good reader begins to relate what is in the text to prior knowledge and to get a summary idea of what is in the text. Sometimes, overviewing reveals that the text is entirely irrelevant to the reader's goals (e.g., there seems to be nothing new in it about the role of the Indians in the French and Indian War). In that case, a good reader might decide not to read the text further.

Assuming the reader does think the text is worthwhile based on the overview, he or she begins to read from front to back, varying reading speed from section to section of the text, sometimes skimming and sometimes skipping sections. Sometimes the reader stops and rereads a segment or pauses to think about what was just said. The reader gives greater attention to information that is important relative to her or his reason for reading the text. Earlier predictions based on overviewing are updated based on the information encountered in text. New predictions about upcoming content are also made continuously as the text is processed. That is, the good reader draws conclusions throughout reading, although the conclusions remain tentative, subject to change as reading continues.

Throughout reading, the good reader is making conscious inferences as well as inferences that are unconscious and automatic. Good readers try to fill in information gaps in text, attempt to determine the meaning of unknown words, and relate ideas in text to their prior knowledge (e.g., "That's just like . . . "). They make inferences about the author, such as her or his intentions in writing the text, or the particular sources that the author used. Fiction readers are always making inferences about the intentions of characters in the story. Good readers consciously attempt to integrate ideas encountered in different parts of a text (e.g., how the actions of characters in a story are related to the larger story). When beginning a work of fiction, they think about the setting and how new characters relate to the setting. The setting is kept in mind as the action proceeds. Readers look for cause-and-effect connections between different parts of text (e.g., how one character's actions early in a story motivated another character's responses later in the story). In integrating ideas across text, a reader may review previous text or jump ahead.

Good readers make many interpretations as they read. Sometimes this is apparent in paraphrases (e.g., "So this myth is like the Exodus story . . . "). They form personal images of the events described in a text. If reading an expository text, they come up with summary comments (e.g., "What the author really wants to say in this chapter is . . . "). In making interpretations, prior knowledge plays a big role. Thus, a gender-stereotyped story written in the early-20th century gets a more sympathetic reading from an ardent feminist reader than a gender-stereotyped story written for the most recent issue of *The New Yorker*.

Processing of text does not conclude when the final word of an article, chapter, or book is read. Rather the good reader sometimes rereads sections or reskims parts that seemed especially important. The good reader might try to restate important ideas or construct a summary of the text to make certain the ideas in the text can be recalled later. Sometimes good readers make notes. They often continue to reflect on a text and what it might mean long after reading is concluded.

The monitoring processes that my students and I witnessed in our study of college professors reading articles (Wyatt et al., 1993) were also apparent in many other verbal protocol studies. Readers are consciously aware of many characteristics of text, from the author's style to the tone of the messages in the text. They are especially aware of whether they are understanding the text and whether such understanding is easy or requires considerable effort. When good readers detect problems, whether it is in understanding overall meanings in text or knowing the meaning of a particular word in a text, they do what they can to solve the problem.

Finally, just as evaluations were salient in the verbal protocols collected by Wyatt et al. (1993), they were salient in many other verbal protocol studies. Readers express feelings as they read. They consciously accept or reject the style of the text (e.g., quality of the writing) as well as the ideas expressed in the text.

CONCLUDING REFLECTIONS

There is a broad base of agreement among researchers that reading is about constructing meaning from text. After that agreement, there are differences of opinion about the nature of reading, although the differences can be resolved.

Bottom-Up versus Top-Down Processing

Some who have thought about meaning making during reading seem to think that meaning making occurs from the bottom up. For them, reading is about the processing of letters and words. Meaning making is sounding out the words, which are listened to by the mind. Indeed, there is a long history of distinguished research establishing that even when good readers read silently, there is something of a speech process involved. Sometimes, there is even silent speech (i.e., the reader literally says the words to her- or himself quietly). Sometimes the speech processes are not so complete, but, as words are read, information about the sounds of the words is activated in the mind, which seems to help the reader hold in memory the last few words that were read so that their meanings can be integrated to permit comprehension of the text (Carver, 1990, Chap. 4; Perfetti, 1985). The idea that reading involves decoding and listening comprehension, with readers listening to what they have decoded in order to understand the meanings conveyed by text (Gough, 1984), is a simple view of reading.

Others who think about meaning making during reading think that it occurs from the top down. That is, based on world knowledge, people have hypotheses about what the text is going to say and this prior knowledge goes far in explaining comprehension (Anderson & Pearson, 1994). There is plenty of evidence that what a text means varies from reader to reader, because text meaning is a joint product of the message the author intended to convey through the words placed in text and the reader's prior knowledge (e.g., Beach & Hynds, 1991; Rosenblatt, 1978). An important point is that good readers do not let their prior knowledge processing get out of control (e.g., Williams, 1993): Their understanding of a story is never so completely personal that a retelling would be unrecognizable by someone else reading the same story. Yes, the listener might have a different perspective on some of what happened in the story, but the essential story that both readers understood would be the same.

Between the bottom-up approach to reading and the top-down model, there is an intermediate position, which is that both bottom-up and top-down processes are involved in constructing meaning from text. Without a doubt, that is the most sensible conclusion that can be derived from the evidence reviewed in this chapter. The case that has been made here is that good readers process every single letter using efficient eye movements that involve fixation on most words. The case has also been made that the reader's mind is very active in constructing hypotheses about what a text might mean, generating inferences, based on prior knowledge, that are necessary in making meaning, and initiating strategies to locate portions of text that are especially likely to be informative. Bottom-up and top-down processing clearly interact as part of skilled reading. There cannot be one without the other if good reading is to occur (Rumelhart, 1994). They are in balance.

Does that mean that it will do no good to target educational efforts at either bottom-up or top-down processing alone? Not necessarily. In fact, there will be quite a bit of evidence considered in subsequent chapters that makes clear that targeting letter- and word-level processes sometimes can improve reading achievement, as can targeting comprehension strategies. Instruction in particular components can help on the road to excellent reading, which involves bottom-up and top-down thinking in interaction.

Analyses of Expert Reading That Leads to Ineffective Educational Interventions

I emphasize at this point that some conspicuous instructional intervention failures have resulted from past conceptions that compared expert reading to weaker reading. (I mention them at this juncture if for no other reason than to get them behind us.) For example, the eye movements of poor readers often differ from the eye movements of good readers, with left-to-right saccadic movement less apparent in poor readers, and poor readers less likely to fixate on words than spaces between words. This deficiency in poor readers has inspired efforts to train more efficient eye movements in poor readers, which sometimes have been successful in modifying fixations and saccades, but generally unsuccessful in affecting reading. A general conclusion emerging from research on the modification of eye movements is that dysfunctional eye movements do not cause poor reading but rather are a symptom of poor reading (see Gaddes, 1985, Chap. 8; also Rayner & Pollatsek, 1989, Chap. 11, for reviews).

A second example of ineffective instruction based on a flawed conception of expert reading is speed reading instruction. There is no doubt that many readers can be taught to skim rather than read, and this is what speed reading courses do. The problem is that when readers skim, their comprehension goes down, although not always on the tests used in speed-reading courses to prove to clients that they are comprehending. The tests often are very easy, involving questions that could have been answered without reading a passage. Consider the following example question (provided by Carver, 1990, p. 372):

Which one of the following least represents a folk society?
1. A group of people of similar ethnic backgrounds living close together in a city.
2. A group of survivors from a ship who land on a desert island.
3. The Aborigine of Australia.
4. The Pueblo Indians of the Southwestern United States.

Although you did not read the passage, I am confident that you selected the correct answer, number 2. Many who run speed reading programs would have you believe that being able to answer such a question after reading a passage about folk societies tells you something about your reading comprehension, when in fact what it tells about is prior knowledge. In short, there is no credible scientific evidence that teaching people to read quickly can succeed when comprehension is tested with demanding test items (Carver, 1990, Chap. 18). This does not negate, however, the point made earlier in this chapter that a state of high prior knowledge often enables skimming with high comprehension and efficient selective reading of text. That is, learning to be a skimmer can be a good thing when there is a need to cover a great deal of material related to areas of high prior knowledge.

As the discussion proceeds in these pages, there will be no more consideration of eye-movement training or the development of reading speeds of thousands of words per minute. There will be evidence presented, however, that improving some letter- and word-level decoding processes can improve reading, as can instruction in comprehension strategies that are matched to the comprehension processes involved in skilled reading.

SUMMARY

1. Skilled reading is a coordination of higher-order processes (e.g., comprehension) and lower-order processes (e.g., decoding). Getting meaning from text very much depends on efficient lower-order processing: good readers automatically recognize many words and efficiently decode unfamiliar words they encounter. Good readers process most words in the texts they read. Indeed, they seem to process most of the individual letters within words. The primary cues used to decode words are the letters, not the meaning of the text in which the words are embedded or the syntactic context in which an unfamiliar word is embedded.

2. When skilled readers read, they abstract the gist from text, getting the big ideas even though many details may not be recallable. Comprehension involves processing the ideas in text in light of one's own prior knowledge, with prior knowledge permitting readers to make many inferences as they proceed. One's knowledge, however, often changes as a function of reading.

3. Although much comprehension occurs implicitly, unconsciously, and almost automatically, much of comprehension involves conscious, active processing of text. The good reader can be active before reading (e.g., overviewing text and making predictions), during reading (e.g., updating predictions, constructing mental images), and after reading (e.g., constructing summaries, thinking about which ideas in text might be useful later). Good readers are both interpretive and evaluative, often reacting to the validity of ideas in text.

4. Understanding the nature of skilled reading provides perspectives on what reading instruction should accomplish. That expert readers are so proficient at word-level processes provides motivation for instruction that focuses on development of decoding. That excellent reading involves conscious comprehension processes motivates instruction that develops active comprehension habits.

5. That good readers do not seem to depend on meaning cues to decode words provides good reason to reject whole-language arguments that decoding instruction should emphasize orientation to meaning cues. By the conclusion of this book, it will be clear that advising children to attend first and foremost to meaning cues (e.g., to look at picture cues) to decode words is instructional advisement that belongs on the same scrap heap as eye-movement training. Meaning cues are critical, however, in appraising whether decoding was done properly: if the decoding makes no sense given the context, the good reader knows to go back and look at the word again. Context cues also help the skilled reader zero in on the intended meaning of words that have more than one definition.

6. Those who wish to teach reading well need to understand just what good reading is. Sound teaching of reading is aimed at developing readers who read as described in this chapter.

REFERENCES

Anderson, J. R., & Bower, G. H. (1973). *Human associative memory.* New York: Wiley.

Anderson, R. C., & Pearson, P. D. (1984). A schema-theoretic view of basic processes in reading. In P. D. Pearson (Ed.), *Handbook of reading research* (pp. 255–291). New York: Longman.

Beach, R., & Hynds, S. (1991). Research on response to literature. In R. Barr, M. L. Kamil, P. Mosenthal, & P. D. Pearson (Eds.), *Handbook of reading research,* (Vol. 2, pp. 453–489). White Plains, NY: Longman.

Britton, B. K. (1994). Understanding expository text: Building mental structures to induce insights. In M. A. Gernsbacher (Ed.), *Handbook of psycholinguistics* (pp. 641–674). San Diego: Academic Press.

Carver, R. P. (1990). *Reading rate: A review of research and theory.* San Diego: Academic Press.

Clark, H. H., & Clark, E. V. (1977). *Psychology and language.* New York: Harcourt, Brace, Jovanovich.

Fletcher, C. R. (1994). Levels of representation in memory for discourse. In M. A. Gernsbacher (Ed.), *Handbook of psycholinguistics* (pp. 589–607). San Diego: Academic Press.

Gaddes, W. H. (1985). *Learning disabilities and brain function* (2nd ed.). New York: Springer-Verlag.

Goodman, K. S. (1967). Reading: A psycholinguistic guessing game. *Journal of the Reading Specialist, 6,* 126–135.

Gough, P. D. (1983). Context, form, and interaction. In K. Rayner (Ed.), *Eye movements in reading* (pp. 203–211). New York: Academic Press.

Gough, P. B. (1984). Word recognition. In P. D. Pearson (Ed.), *Handbook of reading research* (pp. 225–254). New York: Longman.

Graesser, A. C. (1981). *Prose comprehension beyond the word.* New York: Springer-Verlag.

Graesser, A. C., Hoffman, N. L., & Clark, L. F. (1980). Structural components of reading time. *Journal of Verbal Learning and Verbal Behavior, 19,* 135–151.

Just, M. A., & Carpenter, P. A. (1980). A theory of reading: From eye fixations to comprehension. *Psychological Review, 87,* 329–354.

Kintsch, W. (1974). *The representation of meaning in memory.* Hillsdale, NJ: Erlbaum.

Kintsch, W. (1982). Text representations. In W. Otto & S. White (Eds.), *Reading expository material* (pp. 87–102). New York: Academic Press.

Kintsch, W. (1988). The role of knowledge in discourse comprehension: A construction-integration model. *Psychological Review, 95,* 163–182.

Kintsch, W., & Keenan, J. M. (1973). Reading rate and retention as a function of the number of propositions in the base structure of sentences. *Cognitive Psychology, 5,* 257–279.

Kintsch, W., Kozminsky, E., Streby, W. J., McKoon, G., & Keenan, J. M. (1975). Comprehension and recall as a function of content variables. *Journal of Verbal Learning and Verbal Behavior, 14,* 196–214.

Kintsch, W., & van Dijk, T. A. (1978). Toward a model of discourse comprehension and production. *Psychological Review, 85,* 363–394.

LaBerge, D., & Samuels, S. J. (1974). Toward a theory of automatic information processing in reading. *Cognitive Psychology, 6,* 293–323.

McConkie, G. W., & Hogaboam, T. W. (1985). Eye position and word identification during reading. In R. Groner, G. W. McConkie, & C. Menz (Eds.), *Eye movements and information processing* (pp. 159–192). Amsterdam: Elsevier/North-Holland.

McConkie, G. W., Zola, D., Blanchard, H. E., & Wolverton, G. S. (1982). Perceiving words during reading: Lack of facilitation from prior peripheral exposure. *Perception and Psychophysics, 32,* 271–281.

McKoon, G., & Ratcliff, R. (1992). Inference during reading. *Psychological Review, 99,* 440–466.

Perfetti, C. A. (1985). *Reading ability.* New York: Oxford University Press.

Pressley, M., & Afflerbach, P. (1995). *Verbal protocols of reading: The nature of constructively responsive reading.* Hillsdale, NJ: Erlbaum.

Rayner, K. (Ed.). (1992). *Eye movements and visual cognition: Scene perception and reading.* New York: Springer-Verlag.

Rayner, K., Inhoff, A. W., Morrison, R. E., Slowiaczek, M. L., & Bertera, J. H. (1981). *Journal of Experimental Psychology: Human Perception and Performance, 7,* 167–179.

Rayner, K., & Pollatsek, A. (1989). *The psychology of reading.* Englewood Cliffs, NJ: Prentice-Hall.

Rosenblatt, L. M. (1978). *The reader, the text, the poem: The transactional theory of the literary work.* Carbondale, IL: Southern Illinois University Press.

Rumelhart, D. E. (1994). Toward an interactive model of reading. In R. B. Ruddell, M. R. Ruddell, & H. Singer (Eds.), *Theoretical models and processes of reading* (4th ed., pp. 864–894). Newark, DE: International Reading Association.

Samuels, S. J. (1994). Word recognition. In R. B. Ruddell, M. R. Ruddell, & H. Singer (Eds.), *Theoretical models and processes of reading* (pp. 359–380). Newark, DE: International Reading Association.

Share, D. L., & Stanovich, K. E. (1995). Cognitive processes in early reading development: Accommodating individual differences into a model of acquisition. *Issues in Education: Contributions from Educational Psychology, 1,* 1–57.

Smith, F. (1971). *Understanding reading–A psycholinguistic analysis of reading and learning to read.* New York: Holt, Rinehart, & Winston.

Stanovich, K. E., & Cunningham, A. E. (1993). Where does knowledge come from? Associations between print exposure and information acquisition. *Journal of Educational Psychology, 85,* 211–229.

van den Broek, P. (1994). Comprehension and memory of narrative texts: Inferences and coherence. In M. A. Gernsbacher (Ed.), *Handbook of psycholinguistics* (pp. 539–588). San Diego: Academic Press.

van Dijk, T. A., & Kintsch, W. (1983). *Strategies of discourse comprehension.* New York: Academic Press.

Williams, J. P. (1993). Comprehension of students with and without learning disabilities: Identification of narrative themes and idiosyncratic text representations. *Journal of Educational Psychology, 85,* 631–641.

Wyatt, D., Pressley, M., El-Dinary, P. B., Stein, S., Evans, P., & Brown, R. (1993). Comprehension strategies, worth and credibility monitoring, and evaluations: Cold and hot cognition when experts read professional articles that are important to them. *Learning and Individual Differences, 5,* 49–72.

Ygge, J., & Lennerstrand, G. (Eds.). (1994). *Eye movements in reading.* Tarrytown, NY: Pergamon.

3

CHILDREN WHO
EXPERIENCE PROBLEMS
IN LEARNING TO READ

Some primary-grade students of normal intelligence experience difficulty in learning to read. Moreover, primary-grade difficulties in learning to read predict continuing reading difficulties throughout schooling (e.g., Francis, Shaywitz, Stuebing, & Fletcher, 1994; Satz, Taylor, Friel, & Fletcher, 1978; Spreen, 1978). Problems in reading during childhood also are predictive of poor reading during adulthood (Bruck, 1990, 1992; Finucci, Gottfredson, & Childs, 1985; Frauenheim & Heckerl, 1983; Schonhaut & Satz, 1983; Shaywitz et al., 1996; Spreen, 1988).

The most salient problem in learning to read is learning to decode. For example, poor readers have been documented to have difficulties segmenting words into their constituent sounds. Poor readers also experience a great deal of difficulty hearing and/or saying the sounds represented by the constituent letters of the word and blending the sounds to produce the word. *There are many, many analyses producing outcomes consistent with these findings* (e.g., Brady, Shankweiler, & Mann, 1983; Brady & Shankweiler, 1991; Bruck, 1990, 1992; Fletcher et al., 1994; Foorman, Francis, Fletcher, & Lynn, 1996; Goswami & Bryant, 1990; Gottardo, Stanovich, & Siegel, 1996; Gough, Ehri, & Treiman, 1992; Liberman, Shankweiler, Fischer, & Carter, 1974; Manis, Custodio, & Szeszulski, 1993; Mann, Liberman, & Shankweiler, 1980; Metsala, 1997; Rack, Hulme, Snowling, & Wightman, 1994; Shankweiler et al., 1995; Shankweiler, Liberman, Mark, Fowler, & Fischer, 1979; Share,

59

1995; Share & Stanovich, 1995; Snowling, Goulandris, & Defty, 1996; Stanovich, 1986, 1988; Stanovich & Siegel, 1994; Stone & Brady, 1995; Vellutino & Scanlon, 1982, 1987a, 1987b; Vellutino et al., 1996; Vellutino, Scanlon, Small, & Tanzman, 1991; Vellutino, Scanlon, & Tanzman, 1994).

If struggling beginning readers do not sound out words and blend the sounds specified by letters to produce words, what do such readers do instead? Weaker readers often rely much more on semantic–contextual cues to identify words than do skilled readers. That is, rather than trying to sound out an unfamiliar word, poorer readers rely on textual picture cues and clues to make a guess about the word's meaning (Corley, 1988; Goldsmith-Phillips, 1989; Kim & Goetz, 1994; Nicholson, 1991; Nicholson, Bailey, & McArthur, 1991; Nicholson, Lillas, & Rzoska, 1988; Perfetti, Goldman, & Hogaboam, 1979; Perfetti & Roth, 1981; Schwantes, 1981, 1991; Simpson, Lorsbach, & Whitehouse, 1983; Stanovich, West, & Freeman, 1981; West & Stanovich, 1978). Although such students might process the letters somewhat and use some letter-level information in making their guesses (e.g., constraining guesses to words beginning with p since the word begins with p), their processing of the letter cues is much less complete than it could be, with the picture and semantic–contextual cues given priority.

Strong beginning readers certainly could make use of context cues with respect to decoding, but they do not, nor do they need to do so. For anyone who can analyze words into their sounds and blend them, it makes little sense to rely on the semantic–contextual approach, for there are a number of problems with relying on semantic–contextual cues. One is that the semantic–contextual approach is much less certain to produce accurate decoding than sounding out words: a lot of the guesses are in error. A second problem is that when readers "read" words based on picture and other semantic–contextual cues, they are much less likely to make progress in transforming an unknown word into a sight word (e.g., Samuels, 1970). Thus, use of the semantic–contextual strategy negatively affects future reading by undermining the development of automatic word recognition. A third problem with relying on the semantic–contextual approach to decoding is that it is slow, and thus consumes a great deal of short-term cognitive capacity. For the average person, about seven chunks of information can be held in consciousness at any one time (Miller, 1956). Slow decoding eats up much of this short-term capacity in contrast to automatic decoding, which requires relatively little short-term capacity. When a great deal of capacity is required to decode, little is left over for comprehension and thus, comprehension suffers (LaBerge & Samuels, 1974).

The reason for reading is not to decode words but to get meaning from text. Comprehension, however, depends on word recognition skills, and thus, this discussion of comprehension begins with word-level comprehension failures in poor readers.

WORD-LEVEL COMPREHENSION FAILURES

Beyond being able to decode words by sounding them out, good readers can read many words without sounding them out. That is, although good readers can sound out an unfamiliar word, with additional exposures it becomes a sight word, one recognized automatically without the need to analyze and blend its component sounds. Such automaticity is crucial for children if they are to develop into skilled readers.

Why does automaticity matter? As discussed above, decoding does take place in short-term memory—that very limited capacity which is consciousness. In fact, decoding and comprehension compete for the available short-term capacity (LaBerge & Samuels, 1974). When a reader slowly analyzes a word into component sounds and blends them, a great deal of capacity is consumed, with relatively little left over for comprehension of the word, let alone understanding the overall meaning of the sentence containing the word and the paragraph containing the sentence. In contrast, automatic word recognition (i.e., recognizing a word as a sight word) consumes very little capacity, and thus, frees short-term capacity for the task of comprehending the word and integrating the meaning of the word with the overall meaning of the sentence, paragraph, and text. Consistent with this analysis, uncertain decoders comprehend less than more rapid, certain decoders (see Perfetti, 1985; Perfetti & Hogaboam, 1975; Perfetti & Lesgold, 1977, 1979).

Good readers are facile at word-level processing in other ways besides rapid and accurate decoding. When a good reader reads a word that has multiple meanings, she or he more quickly zeroes in on the correct meaning of the word in the given context than do weak readers. This is, in part, because good readers more efficiently suppress context-irrelevant meanings than do poor readers (Gernsbacher, 1990; Gernsbacher & Faust, 1990; Gernsbacher, Varner, & Faust, 1990; Merrill, Sperber, & McCauley, 1981). For example, the word *rock* differs somewhat in meaning depending on the context in which it occurs. When a good reader processes the sentence, "The thief lifted the rock from the jewelry case," he or she understands quickly that rock refers to a precious stone, and does not even think about other types of rocks or rock music. In contrast, weaker readers are more likely to think about the irrelevant meanings of *rock* when they encounter the word in the sentence. The failure of weaker readers to suppress irrelevant meanings of words is consistent with a more general inability of some struggling readers to suppress tangential (often bizarre) associations to material they are reading (McCormick, 1992; Purcell-Gates, 1991; Williams, 1993). The activation of irrelevant information interferes with processing, consuming the limited short-term capacity. That is, meaning-suppression failures create additional disadvantage for already disadvantaged readers.

Failures of Comprehension above the Word Level

Once poor readers can decode well enough to read texts, their problems often continue. Poor readers are less likely than good readers to make inferences linking ideas presented in text. Thus, Yuill and Oakhill (1991, Chap. 4) presented skilled and not-so-skilled 7- to 8-year-old readers passages such as the following:

> John had got up early to learn his spellings. He was very tired and decided to take a break. When he opened his eyes again the first thing he noticed was the clock on the chair. It was an hour later and nearly time for school. He picked up his two books, and put them in a bag. He started pedalling to school as fast as he could. However, John ran over some broken bottles and had to walk the rest of the way. By the time he had crossed the bridge and arrived at class, the test was over. (p. 71)

The most important finding in Yuill and Oakhill's work is that unskilled readers were much less likely to be able to answer inferential questions about such passages than skilled readers, even when the passages remained in front of them so that memory of the information was not a problem. Unskilled readers had more problems with questions such as, "How did John travel to school?", "What did John do when he decided to take a break?", "Why did John have to walk some of the way to school?", and "How do you know that John was late for school?" Yuill and Oakhill (1991) reported a number of outcomes consistent with the conclusion that unskilled and skilled child readers differ in their abilities to make inferences.

There are undoubtedly a number of factors contributing to such inferential failures. For example, inferential skills depend in part on the possession of prior knowledge related to text. Poor readers are often very deficient in their knowledge of the world relative to good readers, as reflected, for example, in vocabulary differences between good and poor readers (e.g., Ruddell, 1994). Good readers know more, in part, because they read more, and they get more out of each bit of reading they do (Cipielewski & Stanovich, 1992; Stanovich, 1986).

Inferential comprehension also depends, however, on knowing strategies and knowing when to use comprehension strategies (i.e., possessing metacognition about strategies). With respect to the latter, good child readers know more about how to read than do weaker child readers. For example, weak child readers are less likely than good child readers to recognize that they can reread, skim, selectively attend to text as they read, or test themselves over reading, depending on their purpose (e.g., Forrest-Pressley & Waller, 1984; Garner & Kraus, 1981–1982; Paris & Myers, 1981). Poor readers are less likely than good readers to recognize factors that can undermine their reading comprehension, such as inattention during reading or distraction (Paris & Myers, 1981). Children who are weak readers do not monitor their comprehension as well as good readers; thus, they are less aware of when they understand and when they do not—and in a worse position than good readers to make decisions about when additional efforts to comprehend are required (e.g., Garner, 1980).

These differences in metacognition are related to strategic differences between weak and strong child readers. For example, Owings, Petersen, Bransford, Morris, and Stein (1980) observed that weak grade-5 readers were less certain to vary their reading with difficulty of material than good grade-5 readers. Also, weak middle-school readers were less likely than good readers to look back in text for answers to questions that they did not know (Garner & Reis, 1981). In Phillips's (1988) think-aloud study of grade-6 reading, low proficiency readers were less likely to shift strategies when a comprehension difficulty was encountered, to attempt to verify their emerging interpretations of text meaning, and to empathize with messages in text. That is, Phillips observed that weak readers are less active when they read, leading to reduced comprehension of the material.

In summary, metacognitive theorists have noted differences among child readers in long-term knowledge about reading and how reading can be carried out, in monitoring of comprehension, and in active, strategic adjustments during reading. Metacognitive theorists explicitly believe that the differences in long-term metacognition and monitoring are causal factors in use of strategies (Flavell, Miller, & Miller, 1993), and thus in comprehension.

Summary

The most typical difficulty experienced by beginning readers is in learning to recognize words—to decode. Poor readers are more likely than good readers to attempt to "read" words by looking at pictures for cues or making a guess based on the meaning of the text. The result is many errors in reading. In addition, poor readers make less certain and rapid progress in developing automatic word-recognition skills. They also are less likely to understand individual words because they use capacity-demanding strategies for decoding (e.g., analyzing semantic-contextual cues, sounding out words that are sight-words for same-age good readers). Often poor readers fail to orient to the most contextually relevant meaning of a multiple-definition word.

The inability to decode also interferes with strategic functioning above the word level, because use of active comprehension strategies requires a great deal of short-term capacity. Because reading is difficult and comprehension uncertain for poor decoders, their knowledge base does not expand as certainly through reading as does the knowledge of good readers. There are strong associations between decoding skills and knowledge gained through reading of text (e.g., Cipielewski & Stanovich, 1992; Stanovich, 1986; Stanovich & Cunningham, 1993). This, of course, undermines future comprehension, for facility in comprehension very much depends on prior knowledge.

BIOLOGICAL DYSLEXIA

When a child experiences difficulties in learning to read, it is often tempting to explain it as a biological problem. Are there normally intelligent children who have biological differences that make it more difficult, or impossible, for them to learn to read, even in the context of intensive instruction that would be effective with most students of normal or above-average intelligence?

Biologically Determined Dyslexia versus Other Forms of Poor Reading

If a child of normal or superior intelligence receives intensive, high quality instruction and still fails to learn to read, there is reason to suspect developmental dyslexia—biologically determined reading disorder (e.g., Harris & Hodges, 1981). (There is another type of dyslexia, acquired dyslexia, which refers to difficulty in reading following a brain injury.) One hallmark of developmental dyslexia is that the affected individuals experience much more profound problems with reading and closely related language functions than with other academic and cognitive tasks.

Although most of the relevant analyses of biological dyslexia have been carried out with children, there is a growing body of evidence that for many weak adult readers of normal intelligence, there are language problems, particularly ones associated with decoding print into sound, that distinguish them from good readers (Bell & Perfetti, 1994; Elbro, Nielsen, & Petersen, 1994; Greenberg, Ehri, & Perin, 1997). What is particularly important to emphasize in these analyses is that language difficulties related to decoding have emerged as key in developmental dyslexia and reading difficulties over a number of other possibilities, including impairments in short-term memory, semantic processing, and syntactic processing skills (Lyon, 1995).

In contrast to the dyslexic reader is the garden-variety poor reader, whose difficulties in learning to read are consistent with other academic difficulties because of his or her generally low intelligence (Stanovich, 1988). The use of the term "garden-variety" emphasizes that poor reading due to generally low intelligence is more prevalent than developmental dyslexia. For caucasians, about 16% of the population has an IQ less than 85, with many such children experiencing reading difficulties because of low intelligence.

Dyslexia and garden-variety poor reading contrast with poor reading by children of normal intelligence and intact biology who are victims of poor instruction or educational neglect. However, it is often difficult or impossible to determine whether a student is developmentally dyslexic, a garden-variety poor reader, or a victim of poor teaching. Nonetheless, classification as dyslexic should occur only if it is known that general intelligence is at least average, and a variety of approaches to teaching reading have been attempted with the student.

Prevalence of Dyslexia

Experts differ in their estimates of the prevalence of biological dyslexia. The highest estimate that I have encountered is 20% (i.e., 20% of the population suffers from a biological difference that impairs reading; e.g., Shaywitz, 1996). Most experts, however, cite much lower figures, with many claiming that 1% or less of normally intelligent children are biologically impaired, and most informed estimates not exceeding 5% of the population (Hynd & Hynd, 1984). After a lot of reflection, my answer when I am asked for prevalence is, "It is closer to 1% than 20%. Many with well-informed opinions would be surprised if it were as high as 2% of the population."

A recently published analysis by Frank Vellutino and his associates (Vellutino et al., 1996) is one of the best bases for making an estimate of prevalence that I have encountered. From a total school population of 827 students in a suburban school district, the 9% who were falling behind the most during the grade-1 year, but who were of normal or superior intelligence (i.e., an IQ greater than 90), were enrolled in a daily tutoring program for 30 minutes a day. The tutoring consisted mostly of intensive phonics instruction. After one semester of remediation, only 3% of the original sample continued below the 30th percentile on a nationally normed test and only 1.5% of the original sample remained below the 15th percentile. That is, it is a very small percentage of students who cannot learn to read given intense decoding instruction. (Vellutino et al.'s study, which contained carefully designed control conditions, is but the first of the studies taken up in this book that demonstrate that many children who experience difficulties in learning to read in school can overcome them if given intensive tutoring; see Chapter 5.)

Individual Differences in the Verbal Processing Problems of Readers with Dyslexia

There are a variety of specific word-recognition problems that can underlie developmental dyslexia. Some with dyslexia experience difficulties in learning to decode rapidly, whereas others experience difficulties in doing so at all.

When students with dyslexia experience difficulties in recognizing words at all, even when permitted as much time as needed to decode, they are classified as decoding-accuracy disabled (e.g., Lovett, 1984). The most certain indicator of the decoding-accuracy deficit is the inability of children who have received intensive instruction in decoding to read phonologically regular pseudowords (e.g., *maglum, croleb*; Rack, Snowling, & Olson, 1992). Decoding pseudowords requires much knowledge of letter–sound relationships (Hogaboam & Perfetti, 1978). It is preferred as an indicator of decoding ability over reading of actual words because pseudowords could never have been encountered by the child before and hence must be decoded. They cannot be recognized as sight words.

In contrast to decoding-accuracy-disabled readers, some readers with dyslexia, often referred to as rate-disabled decoders, can accurately decode, but are very slow at it relative to classmates (e.g., Hogaboam & Perfetti, 1978). Maryanne Wolf (e.g., Wolf, Pfeil, Lotz, & Biddle, 1994; also Bowers & Swanson, 1991; Lovett, 1984), in particular, has argued that rate disability in decoding reflects a more general disability involving the speed of retrieval of linguistic information, as reflected, for example, in the relative slowness of some children to retrieve the names of things when presented pictures of them (see Wolf, 1986, 1991; also Denckla, 1972; Denckla & Rudel, 1976). In contrast, good readers respond quickly to the verbal symbols that constitute reading

(Perfetti, 1985). Such slowness in verbal processing, predictive of extreme difficulties in learning to read, can be detected in the early preschool years (e.g., McDougall, Hulme, Ellis, & Monk, 1994; Torgesen & Davis, 1996; Vellutino, Scanlon, & Spearing, 1995).

In short, some dyslexic readers can barely decode at all. Others can learn to decode with intensive instruction, but decoding is very slow, consistent with a speed deficit in linguistic retrieval abilities.

The Genetic Basis of Developmental Dyslexia

When a child experiences difficulties in learning to read, a family history of reading problems, unaccompanied by evidence of a family history of low intelligence, may be one reason to suspect developmental dyslexia. Clinicians have suspected for years that there is a genetic basis to developmental dyslexia. Recent research has succeeded in substantiating the hypothesis that developmental dyslexia can be inherited.

If a characteristic is genetically determined, its co-occurrence in identical twins should be more likely than its co-occurrence in fraternal twins, since the former share 100% of genes and the latter share only 50%. That, in fact, is the case with respect to reading difficulties (e.g., Bakwin, 1973; Decker & Vandenberg, 1985; DeFries, Fulker, & LaBuda, 1987), and especially with respect to the ability to read unfamiliar words (Olson, 1994). If genetics determines reading ability, there also should be a higher correlation between the reading abilities of adopted children and their biological parents than between adopted children and adopting parents: That is the case as well (Cardon, DiLalla, Plomin, DeFries, & Fulker, 1990).

Functional and Structural Differences in the Brains of Normal and Developmentally Dyslexic Readers

It is common for students experiencing severe problems learning to read to manifest a variety of problems in language functions, from basic perception of language to memory of language to development of syntax to comprehension skills (see Catts, 1989; Katz, Shankweiler, & Liberman, 1981; Liberman, Mann, Shankweiler, & Werfelman, 1982; Mann & Brady, 1988; Olson, Kliegl, Davidson, & Foltz, 1985; Sawyer & Butler, 1991; Stanovich, 1986; Vellutino, 1979). As early as two years of age, children who will later experience severe reading difficulties manifest differences in their use of language compared to those who will be normal readers: Their utterances are shorter and not as syntactically sophisticated; their pronunciations are not as good; they recognize fewer words. It is harder for the eventually developmentally dyslexic child to label common objects than it is for the eventually normally achieving reader (e.g., Scarborough, 1990).

In general, the left cerebral hemisphere plays a larger role in language processing than does the right hemisphere. Thus, it has not been surprising that modern imaging techniques, permitting detailed images of brain structures as well as dynamic images and records of brain activity during performance of tasks (e.g., reading), have provided a great deal of evidence of left hemisphere differences in structure and function between some poor readers and normal readers (Conners, 1971; Duffy & McAnulty, 1990; Fiez et al., 1995; Flowers, Wood, & Naylor, 1991; Galaburda, Sherman, Rosen, Aboitz, & Geschwind, 1985; Galin, 1989; Gross-Glenn et al., 1988; Harter, 1991; Hier, LeMay, Rosenberger, & Perlo, 1978; Jernigan, Hesselink, Sowell, & Tallal, 1991; Johnson & Myklebust, 1967; Larsen, Hoien, Lundberg, & degaard, 1990; Rumsey, 1996; Rumsey, Nace, & Andreason, 1995; Wood, Felton, Flowers, & Naylor, 1991). For example, some regions of the brain involved in reading tend to be smaller in reading disabled readers (Hynd & Semrud-Clikeman, 1989). In addition, the patterns of brain activity differ as dyslexics and normal readers read. In short, there are real anatomical and physiological differences between good and some poor readers.

Are There Visual–Perceptual Problems That Cause Reading Disabilities?

Vellutino (1979), in particular, made the first exceptionally strong case that dyslexia was the result of language deficits. This contrasted with the possibility that learning disabilities might be attributed to visual processing deficiencies, and was supported by many failed attempts to establish clear differences between learning disabled and nondisabled students with respect to many aspects of visual processing. Until recently, Vellutino's (1979) strong statement on the primacy of language difficulties in students with dyslexia has been unchallenged in most of the serious reading research community.

Even so, some researchers who study eye movements during reading, responded to Vellutino's (1979) book by continuing to reflect on unusual eye-movement patterns displayed by some dyslexics during reading (see Lovegrove, 1992). When normal readers read in a word-by-word fashion (see Chapter 2), there is rapid eye movement, with jumps (saccades), typically about six to nine characters in length, and fixations, typically about a quarter of a second in duration (Rayner & McConkie, 1976). When reading English, the normal saccadic movement is generally left to right, although there are also occasional right-to-left regressions. At the end of a line of normal reading, there is a smooth return, sweeping from right to left to the beginning of the next line of text.

In contrast to normal reading, which is more left to right than right to left, many dyslexics display what is referred to as the reverse-staircase pattern in their reading. It has been known since the early 20th century (Gray, 1917; Schmidt, 1917) that the return sweeps of some disabled readers are interrupted rather than smooth. Dyslexic readers also have been reported to make more and longer fixations during reading, more regressions (i.e., looking back) within a line of text, and more visual fixation regressions within individual words than normal readers (Pirozzolo, 1979).

Even though visual-processing differences between dyslexics and normals can be detected, the best informed researchers typically have not viewed them as the cause of dyslexia. If they were the cause, then successful efforts to modify eye movements should result in improved reading, but they do not (Pirozzolo, 1979, 1983). Rather than being the cause of poor reading, it seems that the difference in eye movements may be a result of poor reading: failures to decode and understand text cause regressions.

Even so, an important hypothesis in recent years has been that differences in visual-processing abilities between some dyslexics and normal readers really do reflect differences in fundamental spatial abilities. In particular, there are suspicions about differences between normal and dyslexic readers in the visual abilities responsible for the rapid pickup of information about the general shape of words (coarse perceptual information). Such processing occurs in peripheral vision and can affect saccadic movement (Fischer, 1992; Lovegrove, 1992). That is, some dyslexics have difficulty in processing rapidly presented visual information, particularly information embedded in rapid sequences of information (e.g., Gaddes, 1982; Galaburda & Livingstone, 1993; Lovegrove, Garzia, & Nicholson, 1990; Martin & Lovegrove, 1987). If reading is anything, it is rapid processing of sequences of information. Whether this perceptual difference is a cause or effect of dyslexia is not known at this time.

Another important new hypothesis about a fundamental physiological cause of some reading disabilities is emerging from the complicated pattern of data now in the literature pertaining to eye movement and rapid sequential processing. Livingstone, Rosen, Drislane, and Galaburda (1991; also Galaburda & Livingstone, 1993) believe that dyslexics may have atypical neural pathways linking the various parts of the visual system.

Additional research on these new hypotheses about perceptual differences between normal readers and individuals with dyslexia promises to shed light on the possibility that dyslexia may not be just a language disorder. Perhaps it is caused by a mix of language and visual perceptual problems or, alternatively, it is more a language disorder for some people with dyslexia and more a visual perceptual disorder for other people with dyslexia. Moreover, there are other related possibilities, including the possibilities that individuals with dyslexia might suffer from general difficulties (i.e., across a number of modalities rather than just in the visual modality) in rapid sequential processing of information (Farmer & Klein, 1995; Tallal, Miller, & Fitch, 1993) or general difficulties in making rapid discriminations between similar stimuli such as letters (Studdert-Kennedy & Mody, 1995). Thus, it may be that there are a variety of processing deficits that can result in dyslexia. This possibility has gained respectability in recent years (Martin, 1995), especially with the recognition that some of the possible causes of dyslexia (e.g., problems in rapid sequential processing of information) are much rarer than other deficiencies (e.g., language deficits; Rayner, Pollatsek, & Bilsky, 1995).

Summary

Some children who experience failures in learning to read do so because of generally low intelligence. Such failures are not puzzling to the research or education community: What is puzzling is when an otherwise normally intelligent, or even very intelligent child, fails to learn to read even after intensive efforts to teach him or her. That is developmental dyslexia.

A variety of biological pieces to the puzzle that is developmental dyslexia are now available. There is evidence of genetic determination of developmental dyslexia (Smith, Kimberling, & Pennington, 1991). There are certainly neurological differences between some people with reading difficulties and normal readers, especially with respect to parts of the brain implicated in the processing of language that are consistent with language differences between reading-disabled and normal readers. Even as the evidence continues to accumulate that developmental dyslexia typically involves verbal-phonological processing problems, there are new hypotheses emerging about the role of perception, and in particular, visual perception, in reading disabilities.

It is a tragic mistake to assume that initially poor reading necessarily implies a biological problem. A diagnosis of biologically caused dyslexia should only be reached after environmental deprivation has been ruled out (i.e., only after it is assured that the child was provided instruction about how to decode, something that is not certain in many contemporary classrooms). The most compelling evidence on this point comes from studies such as Vellutino et al.'s (1996) investigation, in which children who were experiencing difficulties in learning to read with normal classroom instruction came up to grade level quickly once intensive tutoring began.

Most children experiencing initial reading problems are not biologically dyslexic. For many, their problem is that they have not been taught how to decode text and/or how to construct meaning from text in ways that are efficient and effective. By the end of this book, I hope to have you convinced that with most children of normal intelligence, both decoding and comprehension are very teachable processes.

SUMMARY

1. The most salient problem for many poor readers is that they do not decode well. In Chapter 5, more evidence is presented that many children who have experienced difficulties in learning to read nonetheless benefit from systematic, intensive instruction in decoding, letter-sound associations, and the blending of such sounds to produce words. For many poor readers, their problem may be that they have never received such instruction or have received it in a watered-down fashion.

2. Poor readers often rely on semantic–contextual cues in an attempt to decode text. This reliance on semantic cues results in inaccurate decodings. It is also an approach that requires great effort, and hence, consumes much short-term capacity, leaving little for comprehension of words once they are decoded. Even when struggling readers succeed in decoding a word, they often fail to zero in on the one of its several definitions that would make sense in the semantic context in which the word occurs. Poor readers often activate irrelevant meanings of words they have decoded.

3. Poor readers often do not use efficient comprehension strategies to abstract meanings from text. They are less likely to possess prior knowledge that can be related to text content, and when they do possess it, they are less likely to use it appropriately to understand fully the ideas presented in text. When decoding is poor, students do not learn as much from texts as they would if their decoding were stronger.

4. In some cases, inability to read is caused by biological factors, with the two most conspicuous examples being people with low general intelligence and those suffering from developmental dyslexia. Biology probably does not account for anything like the majority of literacy

failures for individuals of normal intelligence, however. With normally intelligent children, dyslexia should not be ruled in as an explanation of reading failure until great efforts have been made to teach a student to read. If a student is of normal intelligence, the odds are very great that difficulties in learning to read are not developmental dyslexia but rather an environmental failure. One possibility is that the child has not experienced reading instruction that is systematic enough for him or her to learn how to read. Other possible environmental failures, however, will be considered in the next chapter, which takes up development during the preschool years. What happens during the preschool years affects children's subsequent success in learning to read in the primary years.

REFERENCES

Bakwin, H. (1973). Reading disability in twins. *Developmental Medicine and Child Neurology, 15,* 184–187.

Bell, L. C., & Perfetti, C. A. (1994). Reading skill: Some adult comparisons. *Journal of Educational Psychology, 86,* 344–355.

Bowers, P. G., & Swanson, L. B. (1991). Naming speed deficits in reading disability: Multiple measures of a single process. *Journal of Experimental Child Psychology, 51,* 195–219.

Brady, S., & Shankweiler, D. (Eds.). (1991). *Phonological processes in literacy.* Hillsdale, NJ: Erlbaum.

Brady, S., Shankweiler, D., & Mann, V. (1983). Speech perception and memory coding in relation to reading ability. *Journal of Experimental Child Psychology, 35,* 345–367.

Bruck, M. (1990). Word-recognition skills of adults with childhood diagnoses of dyslexia. *Developmental Psychology, 26,* 439–454.

Bruck, M. (1992). Persistence of dyslexics' phonological awareness deficits. *Developmental Psychology, 28,* 874–886.

Cardon, L. R., DiLalla, L. F., Plomin, R., DeFries, J. C., & Fulker, D. W. (1990). Genetic correlations between reading performance and IQ in the Colorado adoption project. *Intelligence, 14,* 245–257.

Catts, H. (1989). Defining dyslexia as a developmental language disorder. *Annals of Dyslexia, 39,* 50–64.

Cipielewski, J., & Stanovich, K. E. (1992). Predicting growth in reading ability from children's exposure to print. *Journal of Experimental Child Psychology, 54,* 74–89.

Conners, C. K. (1971). Cortical visual evoked response in children with learning disorders. *Psychophysiology, 7,* 418–428.

Corley, P. J. (1988). A developmental analysis of sentence comprehension abilities in good and poor readers. *Educational Psychologist, 23,* 57–75.

Decker, S. N., & Vandenberg, S. G. (1985). Colorado twin study of reading disability. In D. B. Gray & J. Kavanaugh (Eds.), *Biobehavioral measures of dyslexia* (pp. 123–135). Baltimore: York.

DeFries, J. C., Fulker, D. W., & LaBuda, M. C. (1987). Evidence for a genetic aetiology in reading disability of twins. *Nature, 329,* 537–539.

Denckla, M. B. (1972). Color naming deficits in dyslexic boys. *Cortex, 8,* 164–176.

Denckla, M. B., & Rudel, R. G. (1976). Rapid automatized naming (R. A. N.): Dyslexia differentiated from other learning disabilities. *Neuropsychologica, 14,* 471–476.

Duffy, F. H., & McAnulty, G. (1990). Neuropsychological heterogeneity and the definition of dyslexia: Preliminary evidence for plasticity. *Neuropsychologica, 28,* 96–103.

Elbro, C., Nielsen, I., & Petersen, D. K. (1994). Dyslexia in adults: Evidence for deficits in non-word reading and in the phonological representation of lexical items. *Annals of Dyslexia, 44,* 205–226.

Farmer, M. E., & Klein, R. M. (1995). The evidence for a temporal processing deficit linked to dyslexia: A review. *Psychological Bulletin and Review, 2,* 460–493.

Fiez, J. A., Tallal, P., Raichle, M. E., Katz, W. F., Miezin, F. M., & Petersen, S. E. (1995). PET studies of auditory and phonological processing: Effects of stimulus type and task condition. *Journal of Cognitive Neuroscience, 7,* 357–375.

Finucci, J. M., Gottfredson, L. S., & Childs, B. (1985). A follow-up study of dyslexic boys. *Annals of Dyslexia, 35,* 117–136.

Fischer, B. (1992). Saccadic reaction time: Implications for reading, dyslexia, and visual cognition. In K. Rayner (Ed.), *Eye movements and visual cognition: Scene perception and reading* (pp. 31–45). New York: Springer-Verlag.

Flavell, J. R., Miller, P., & Miller, S. (1993). *Cognitive development* (3rd ed.). Englewood Cliffs, NJ: Prentice-Hall.

Fletcher, J. M., Shaywitz, S. E., Shankweiler, D. P., Katz, L., Liberman, I.Y., Stuebing, K. K., Francis, D. J., Fowler, A. E., & Shaywitz, B. A. (1994). Cognitive profiles of reading disability: Comparisons of discrepancy and low achievement definitions. *Journal of Educational Psychology, 86,* 6–23.

Flowers, D. L., Wood, F. B., & Naylor, C. E. (1991). Regional cerebral bloodflow correlates of language processes in reading disability. *Archives of Neurology, 48,* 637–643.

Foorman, B. R., Francis, D. J., Fletcher, J. M., & Lynn, A. (1996). Relation of phonological and orthographic processing to early reading: Comparing two approaches to regression-based, reading-level-matched designs. *Journal of Educational Psychology, 88,* 639–652.

Forrest-Pressley, D. L., & Waller, T. G. (1984). *Cognition, metacognition, and reading.* New York: Springer-Verlag.

Francis, D. J., Shaywitz, S. E., Stuebing, K. K., & Fletcher, J. M. (1994). The measurement of change: Assessing behavior over time and within a developmental context. In G. R. Lyon (Ed.), *Frames of reference for the assessment of learning disabilities: New views on measurement issues* (pp. 29–58). Baltimore: Brookes.

Frauenheim, J. G., & Heckerl, J. R. (1983). A longitudinal study of psychological and achievement test performance in severe dyslexic adults. *Journal of Learning Disabilities, 16,* 339–347.

Gaddes, W. H. (1982). Serial order behavior: To understand it, a scientific challenge, an educational necessity. In W. M. Cruickshank & J. W. Lerner (Eds.), *Coming of age: Vol. 3. The best of ACLD* (pp. 87–107). Syracuse, NY: Syracuse University Press.

Galaburda, A., & Livingstone, M. (1993). Evidence for a magnocellular defect in developmental dyslexia. *Annals of the New York Academy of Science, 682,* 70–82.

Galaburda, A. M., Sherman, G. F., Rosen, G. D., Aboitz, F., & Geschwind, N. (1985). Developmental dyslexia: Four consecutive patients with cortical anomalies. *Archives of Neurology, 35,* 812–817.

Galin, D. (1989). EEG studies in dyslexia. In D. J. Bakker & H. van der Vlugt (Eds.), *Learning disabilities: Vol. 1. Neuropsychological correlates and treatment.* Amsterdam: Swets.

Garner, R. (1980). Monitoring of understanding: An investigation of good and poor readers' awareness of induced miscomprehension of text. *Journal of Reading Behavior, 12,* 55–64.

Garner, R., & Kraus, C. (1981–1982). Good and poor comprehenders differences in knowing and regulating reading behaviors. *Educational Research Quarterly, 6,* 5–12.

Garner, R., & Reis, R. (1981). Monitoring and resolving comprehension obstacles: An investigation of spontaneous text lookbacks among upper-grade good and poor comprehenders. *Reading Research Quarterly, 16,* 569–582.

Gernsbacher, M. A. (1990). *Language comprehension as structure building.* Hillsdale, NJ: Erlbaum.

Gernsbacher, M. A., & Faust, M. E. (1990). The role of suppression in sentence comprehension. In G. B. Simpson (Ed.), *Understanding word and sentence* (pp. 97–128). Amsterdam: North-Holland.

Gernsbacher, M. A., Varner, K. R., & Faust, M. E. (1990). Investigating differences in general comprehension skill. *Journal of Experimental Psychology: Learning, Memory, and Cognition, 16,* 430–445.

Goldsmith-Phillips, J. (1989). Word and context in reading development: A test of the interactive–compensatory hypothesis. *Journal of Educational Psychology, 81,* 299–305.

Goswami, U., & Bryant, P. (1990). *Phonological skills and learning to read.* London: Erlbaum.

Gottardo, A., Stanovich, K. E., & Siegel, L. S. (1996). The relationships between phonological sensitivity, syntactic processing, and verbal working memory in the reading performance of third-grade children. *Journal of Experimental Child Psychology, 63,* 563–582.

Gough, P. B., Ehri, L., & Treiman, R. (Eds.). (1992). *Reading acquisition.* Hillsdale, NJ: Erlbaum.

Gray, C. T. (1917). Types of reading ability as exhibited through tests and laboratory experiments. *Supplementary Educational Monographs, 1*(5), 1–191.

Greenberg, D., Ehri, L. C., & Perin, D. (1997). Are word reading processes the same or different in adult literacy students and 3rd–5th graders matched for reading level? *Journal of Educational Psychology, 89,* 262–275.

Gross-Glenn, K., Duara, R., Yoshii, F., Barker, W. W., Chen, J. Y., Apicella, A., Boothe, T., & Lubs, H. A. (1988). PET-scan reading studies of familial dyslexics [Abstract]. *Journal of Clinical and Experimental Neuropsychology, 10,* 34–35.

Harris, T. L., & Hodges, R. W. (Eds.) (1981). *A dictionary of reading and related terms.* Newark, DE: International Reading Association.

Harter, M. R. (1991). Event-related potential indices: Learning disabilities and visual processing. In J. E. Obrzut & G. W. Hynd (Eds.), *Neuropsychological foundations of learning disabilities: A handbook of issues, methods, and practice* (pp. 437–473). San Diego: Academic Press.

Hier, D. B., LeMay, M., Rosenberger, P. B., & Perlo, V. P. (1978). Developmental dyslexia: Evidence for a subgroup with a reversal of cerebral asymmetry. *Archives of Neurology, 35,* 90–92.

Hogaboam, T. W., & Perfetti, C. A. (1978). Reading skill and the role of verbal experience in decoding. *Journal of Educational Psychology, 70,* 717–729.

Hynd, G. W., & Hynd, C. R. (1984). Dyslexia: Neuroanatomical/neurolinguistic perspectives. *Reading Research Quarterly, 19,* 482–498.

Hynd, G. W., & Semrud-Clikeman, M. (1989). Dyslexia and brain morphology. *Psychological Bulletin, 106,* 447–482.

Jernigan, T. L., Hesselink, J. R., Sowell, E., & Tallal, P. A. (1991). Cerebral structure on magnetic resonance imaging in language- and learning-impaired children. *Archives of Neurology, 48,* 539–545.

Johnson, D., & Myklebust, H. R. (1967). *Learning disabilities: Educational principles and practice.* New York: Grune and Stratton.

Katz, R. B., Shankweiler, D., & Liberman, I. Y. (1981). Memory for item order and phonetic recoding in the beginning reader. *Journal of Experimental Child Psychology, 32,* 474–484.

Kim, Y. H., & Goetz, E. T. (1994). Context effects on word recognition and reading comprehension of poor and good readers: A test of the interactive-compensatory hypothesis. *Reading Research Quarterly, 29,* 178–188.

LaBerge, D., & Samuels, S. J. (1974). Toward a theory of automatic information processing in reading. *Cognitive Psychology, 6,* 293–323.

Larsen, J. P., Hoien, T., Lundberg, I., & degaard, S. (1990). MRI evaluation of the size and symmetry of the planum temporale in adolescents with developmental dyslexia. *Brain and Language, 39,* 289–301.

Liberman, I. Y., Mann, V. A., Shankweiler, D., & Werfelman, M. (1982). Children's memory for recurring linguistic and nonlinguistic material in relation to reading ability. *Cortex, 18,* 367–375.

Liberman, I. Y., Shankweiler, D., Fischer, F. W., & Carter, B. (1974). Explicit syllable and phoneme segmentation in the young child. *Journal of Experimental Child Psychology, 18,* 201–212.

Livingstone, M. S., Rosen, G. D., Drislane, F. W., & Galaburda, A. M. (1991). Physiological and anatomical evidence for a magnocellular deficit in developmental dyslexia. *Proceedings of the National Academy of Sciences of the U. S. A., 88,* 7943–7947.

Lovegrove, W. J. (1992). The visual deficit hypothesis. In N. N. Singh & I. L. Beale (Eds.), *Learning disabilities: Nature, theory, and treatment* (pp. 246–269). New York: Springer-Verlag.

Lovegrove, W. J., Garzia, R. P., & Nicholson, S. B. (1990). Experimental evidence for a transient system deficit in specific reading disability. *Journal of the American Optometric Association, 61,* 137–146.

Lovett, M. W. (1984). A developmental perspective on reading dysfunction: Accuracy and rate criteria in the subtyping of dyslexic children. *Brain and Language, 22,* 67–91.

Lyon, G. R. (1995). Toward a definition of dyslexia. *Annals of Dyslexia, 45,* 3–27.

Manis, F. R., Custodio, R., & Szeszulski, P. A. (1993). Development of phonological and orthographic skill: A 2-year longitudinal study of dyslexic children. *Journal of Experimental Child Psychology, 56,* 64–86.

Mann, V. A., & Brady, S. (1988). Reading disability: The role of language deficiencies. *Journal of Consulting and Clinical Psychology, 56,* 811–816.

Mann, V. A., Liberman, I. Y., & Shankweiler, D. (1980). Children's memory for sentences and word storage in relation to reading ability. *Memory and Cognition, 8,* 329–335.

Martin, F., & Lovegrove, W. (1987). Flicker contrast sensitivity in normal and specifically disabled readers. *Perception, 17,* 203–214.

Martin, R. C. (1995). Heterogeneity of deficits in developmental dyslexia and implications for methodology. *Psychonomic Bulletin and Review, 2,* 494–500.

McCormick, S. (1992). Disabled readers' erroneous responses to inferential comprehension questions: Description and analysis. *Reading Research Quarterly, 27,* 156–176.

McDougall, S., Hulme, C., Ellis, A., & Monk, A. (1994). Learning to read: The role of short-term memory and phonological skills. *Journal of Experimental Child Psychology, 58,* 112–133.

Merrill, E. C., Sperber, R. D., & McCauley, C. (1981). Differences in semantic encoding as a function of reading comprehension skill. *Memory and Cognition, 9,* 618–624.

Metsala, J. L. (1997). Spoken word recognition in reading disabled children. *Journal of Educational Psychology, 89,* 159–169.

Miller, G. A. (1956). The magical number seven, plus-or-minus two: Some limits on our capacity for processing information. *Psychological Review, 63,* 81–97.

Nicholson, T. (1991). Do children read words better in context or in lists? A classic study revisited. *Journal of Educational Psychology, 83,* 444–450.

Nicholson, T., Bailey, J., & McArthur, J. (1991). Context cues in reading: The gap between research and popular opinion. *Journal of Reading: Writing and Learning Disabilities, 7,* 33–41.

Nicholson, T., Lillas, C., & Rzoska, A. (1988). Have we been misled by miscues? *Reading Teacher, 42,* 6–10.

Olson, R. K. (1994). Language deficits in "specific" reading disability. In M. A. Gernsbacher (Ed.), *Handbook of psycholinguistics* (pp. 895–916). San Diego: Academic Press.

Olson, R. K., Kliegl, R., Davidson, B. J., & Foltz, G. (1985). Individual and developmental differences in reading disability. In G. E. MacKinnon & T. G. Waller (Eds.), *Reading research: Advances in theory and practice* (Vol. 4, pp. 1–64). Orlando, FL: Academic Press.

Owings, R. A., Petersen, G. A., Bransford, J. D., Morris, C. D., & Stein, B. S. (1980). Spontaneous monitoring and regulation of learning: A comparison of successful and less successful fifth graders. *Journal of Educational Psychology, 72,* 250–256.

Paris, S. G., & Myers, M. (1981). Comprehension monitoring, memory, and study strategies of good and poor readers. *Journal of Reading Behavior, 13,* 5–22.

Perfetti, C. A. (1985). *Reading ability.* New York: Oxford University Press.

Perfetti, C. A., Goldman, S. R., & Hogaboam, T. W. (1979). Reading skill and the identification of words in discourse context. *Memory and Cognition, 7,* 273–282.

Perfetti, C. A., & Hogaboam, T. (1975). The relationship between single word decoding and reading comprehension skill. *Journal of Educational Psychology, 67,* 461–469.

Perfetti, C. A., & Lesgold, A. M. (1977). Discourse comprehension and sources of individual differences. In M. A. Just & P. A. Carpenter (Eds.), *Cognitive processes in comprehension.* Hillsdale, NJ: Erlbaum.

Perfetti, C. A., & Lesgold, A. M. (1979). Coding and comprehension in skilled reading: Implications for reading instruction. In L. B. Resnick & P. Weaver (Eds.), *Theory and practice of early reading* (Vol. 1, pp. 57–84). Hillsdale, NJ: Erlbaum.

Perfetti, C. A., & Roth, S. F. (1981). Some of the interactive processes in reading and their role in reading skill. In A. M. Lesgold & C. A. Perfetti (Eds.), *Interactive processes in reading* (pp. 269–297). Hillsdale, NJ: Erlbaum.

Phillips, L. M. (1988). Young readers' inference strategies in reading comprehension. *Cognition and Instruction, 5,* 193–222.

Pirozzolo, F. J. (1979). *The neuropsychology of developmental reading disorders.* New York: Praeger.

Pirozzolo, F. J. (1983). Eye movements and reading disability. In K. Rayner (Ed.), *Eye movements in reading: Perceptual and language processes* (pp. 499–510). New York: Academic Press.

Purcell-Gates, V. (1991). On the outside looking in: A study of remedial readers' meaning-making while reading literature. *Journal of Reading Behavior, 23,* 235–253.

Rack, J., Hulme, C., Snowling, M., & Wightman, J. (1994). The role of phonology in young children learning to read words: The direct mapping hypothesis. *Journal of Experimental Child Psychology, 57,* 42–71.

Rack, J. P., Snowling, M. J., & Olson, R. K. (1992). The nonword reading deficit in developmental dyslexia: A review. *Reading Research Quarterly, 27,* 28–53.

Rayner, K., & McConkie, G. W. (1976). What guides a reader's eye movements? *Vision Research, 16,* 829–837.

Rayner, K., Pollatsek, A., & Bilsky, A. B. (1995). Can a temporal processing deficit account for dyslexia? *Psychonomic Bulletin and Review, 2,* 501–507.

Ruddell, M. R. (1994). Vocabulary knowledge and comprehension: A comprehension-process view of complex literacy relationships. In R. B. Ruddell, M. R. Ruddell, & H. Singer (Eds.), *Theoretical models and processes of reading* (4th ed., pp. 414–447). Newark, DE: International Reading Association.

Rumsey, J. M. (1996). Neuroimaging in developmental dyslexia: A review and conceptualization. In G. R. Lyon & J. M. Rumsey (Eds.), *Neuroimaging: A window on the neurological foundations of learning and behavior in children* (pp. 57–77). Baltimore: Brookes.

Rumsey, J. M., Nace, K., & Andreason, P. (1995). Phonologic and orthographic components of reading imaged with PET. *Journal of the International Neuropsychological Society, 1,* 180.

Samuels, S. J. (1970). Effects of pictures on learning to read, comprehension, and attitudes. *Review of Educational Research, 40,* 397–407.

Satz, P., Taylor, H. G., Friel, J., & Fletcher, J. M. (1978). Some developmental and predictive precursors of reading disabilities: A six-year followup. In A. L. Benton & D. Pearl (Eds.), *Dyslexia: An appraisal of current knowledge.* New York: Oxford University Press.

Sawyer, D. J., & Butler, K. (1991). Early language intervention: A deterrent to reading disability. *Annals of Dyslexia, 41,* 55–79.

Scarborough, H. S. (1990). Very early language deficits in dyslexic children. *Child Development, 61,* 1728–1743.

Schmidt, W. A. (1917). An experimental study in the psychology of reading. *Supplemental Educational Monographs, 1*(2), 1–123.

Schonhaut, S., & Satz, P. (1983). Prognosis for children with learning disabilities: A review of follow-up studies. In M. Rutter (Ed.), *Developmental neuropsychiatry* (pp. 542–563). New York: Guilford Press.

Schwantes, F. M. (1981). Locus of the context effect in children's word recognition. *Child Development, 52,* 895–903.

Schwantes, F. M. (1991). Children's use of semantic and syntactic information for word recognition and determination of sentence meaningfulness. *Journal of Reading Behavior, 23,* 335–350.

Shankweiler, D., Crain, S., Katz, L., Fowler, A., Liberman, A., Brady, S., Thornton, R., Lundquist, E., Dreyer, L., Fletcher, J., Stuebing, K., Shaywitz, S., & Shaywitz, B. (1995). Cognitive profiles of reading-disabled children: Comparison of language skills in phonology, morphology, and syntax. *Psychological Science, 6,* 149–156.

Shankweiler, D., Liberman, I. Y., Mark, L. S., Fowler, C. A., & Fischer, F. W. (1979). The speech code and learning to read. *Journal of Experimental Psychology: Human Learning and Memory, 5,* 531–545.

Share, D. L. (1995). Phonological recoding and self-teaching: Sine qua non of reading acquisition. *Cognition, 55,* 151–218.

Share, D. L., & Stanovich, K. E. (1995). Cognitive processes in early reading development: Accommodating individual differences into a model of acquisition. *Issues in Education: Contributions from Educational Psychology, 1,* 1–57.

Shaywitz, S. E. (1996). Dyslexia. *Scientific American, 275*(5), 98–104.

Shaywitz, S. E., Shaywitz, B. A., Pugh, K. R., Skudlarski, P., Fulbright, R. K., Constable, R. T., Bronen, R. A., Fletcher, J. M., Liberman, A. M., Shankweiler, D. P., Katz, L., Lacadie, C., Marchione, K. E., & Gore, J. C. (1996). The neurobiology of developmental dyslexia as viewed through the lens of functional magnetic resonance imaging technology. In G. R. Lyon & J. M. Rumsey (Eds.), *Neuroimaging: A window on the neurological foundations of learning and behavior in children* (pp. 79–94). Baltimore: Brookes.

Simpson, G., Lorsbach, T., & Whitehouse, D. (1983). Encoding contextual components of word recognition in good and poor readers. *Journal of Experimental Child Psychology, 35,* 161–171.

Smith, S. D., Kimberling, W. J., & Pennington, B. F. (1991). Screening for multiple genes influencing dyslexia. *Reading and Writing: An Interdisciplinary Journal, 3*, 285–298.

Snowling, M. J., Goulandris, N., & Defty, N. (1996). A longitudinal study of reading development in dyslexic students. *Journal of Educational Psychology, 88*, 653–669.

Spreen, O. (1978). Prediction of school achievement from kindergarten to grade five: Review and report of a follow-up study. *Research Monograph No. 33*. Victoria, BC, Canada: Department of Psychology, University of Victoria.

Spreen, O. (1988). *Learning disabled children growing up: A follow-up into adulthood.* New York: Oxford University Press.

Stanovich, K. (1986). Matthew effects in reading: Some consequences of individual differences in the acquisition of literacy. *Reading Research Quarterly, 21*, 360–407.

Stanovich, K. E. (1988). Explaining the differences between the dyslexic and the garden-variety poor reader: The phonological-core variable-difference model. *Journal of Learning Disabilities, 21*, 590–604.

Stanovich, K. E., & Cunningham, A. E. (1993). Where does knowledge come from? Specific associations between print exposure and information acquisition. *Journal of Educational Psychology, 85*, 211–229.

Stanovich, K. E., & Siegel, L. S. (1994). Phenotypic performance profile of children with reading disabilities: A regression-based test of the phonological-core variable-difference model. *Journal of Educational Psychology, 86*, 24–53.

Stanovich, K. E., West, R. F., & Freeman, D. J. (1981). A longitudinal study of sentence context effects in second-grade children: Tests of an interactive–compensatory model. *Journal of Experimental Child Psychology, 32*, 185–199.

Stone, B., & Brady, S. (1995). Evidence for phonological processing deficits in less-skilled readers. *Annals of Dyslexia, 45*, 51–78.

Studdert-Kennedy, M., & Mody, M. (1995). Auditory temporal perception deficits in the reading-impaired: A critical review of the evidence. *Psychonomic Bulletin and Review, 2*, 508–514.

Tallal, P., Miller, S., & Fitch, R. H. (1993). Neurobiological basis of the case for the preeminence of temporal processing. In P. Tallal, A. M. Galaburda, R. R. Linas, & C. von Euler (Eds.), *Temporal information processing in the nervous system: Special reference to dyslexia and dysphasia* (pp. 27–47). New York: New York Academy of Sciences.

Torgesen, J. K., & Davis, C. (1996). Individual difference variables that predict response to training in phonological awareness. *Journal of Experimental Child Psychology, 63*, 1–21.

Vellutino, F. R. (1979). *Dyslexia: Theory and research.* Cambridge, MA: MIT Press.

Vellutino, F. R., & Scanlon, D. M. (1982). Verbal processing in poor and normal readers. In C. J. Brainerd & M. Pressley (Eds.), *Verbal processes in children* (pp. 189–264). New York: Springer-Verlag.

Vellutino, F. R., & Scanlon, D. M. (1987a). Linguistic coding and reading ability. In S. Rosenberg (Ed.), *Advances in applied psycholinguistics* (Vol. 2, pp. 1–69). New York: Cambridge University Press.

Vellutino, F. R., & Scanlon, D. W. (1987b). Phonological coding, phonological awareness, and reading ability: Evidence from a longitudinal, experimental study. *Merrill–Palmer Quarterly, 33,* 321–363.

Vellutino, F. R., Scanlon, D. M., Sipay, E. R., Small, S. G., Pratt, A., Chen, R., & Denckla, M. B. (1996). Cognitive profiles of difficult-to-remediate and readily remediated poor readers: Early intervention as a vehicle for distinguishing between cognitive and experiential deficits as a basic cause of specific reading disability. *Journal of Educational Psychology, 88,* 601–638.

Vellutino, F. R., Scanlon, D. M., Small, S. G., & Tanzman, M. S. (1991). The linguistic basis of reading ability: Converting written to oral language. *Text, 11,* 99–133.

Vellutino, F. R., Scanlon, D. M., & Spearing, D. (1995). Semantic and phonological coding in poor and normal readers. *Journal of Experimental Child Psychology, 59,* 76–123.

Vellutino, F. R., Scanlon, D. M., & Tanzman, M. S. (1994). Components of reading ability: Issues and problems in operationalizing word identification, phonological coding, and orthographic coding. In G. R. Lyon (Ed.), *Frames of reference for the assessment of learning disabilities: New views on measurement issues* (pp. 279–324). Baltimore: Brookes.

West, R. F., & Stanovich, K. E. (1978). Automatic contextual facilitation in readers of three ages. *Child Development, 49,* 717–727.

Williams, J. P. (1993). Comprehension of students with and without learning disabilities: Identification of narrative themes and idiosyncratic text representations. *Journal of Educational Psychology, 85,* 631–641.

Wolf, M. (1986). Rapid alternating stimulus naming in developmental dyslexias. *Brain and Language, 27,* 360–379.

Wolf, M. (1991). The word-retrieval deficit hypothesis and developmental dyslexia. *Learning and Individual Differences, 3,* 205–223.

Wolf, M., Pfeil, C., Lotz, R., & Biddle, K. (1994). Towards a more universal understanding of the developmental dyslexias: The contribution of orthographic factors. In V. W. Berninger (Ed.), *The varieties of orthographic knowledge: I. Theoretical and developmental issues* (pp. 137–171). Dordrecht, The Netherlands: Kluwer Academic.

Wood, F., Felton, R., Flowers, L., & Naylor, C. (1991). Neurobehavioral definitions of dyslexia. In D. D. Duane & D. B. Gray (Eds.), *The reading brain: Biological basis of dyslexia.* Parkton, MD: York Press.

Yuill, N. M., & Oakhill, J. V. (1991). *Children's problems in text comprehension: An experimental investigation.* Cambridge, UK: Cambridge University Press.

4

◄◌►

THE DEVELOPMENT
OF LITERACY, Part 1

Before Reading Instruction Begins

Much that is relevant to the development of literacy occurs before a child first passes through the schoolhouse door. Among literacy researchers, it has become something of a truism to assert that literacy development begins at birth, with many opportunities for events in the home life of preschoolers that have implications for literacy development. These include game and play activities; interactions during meals; media viewed by children and their parents (e.g., watching of educational shows); outings (e.g., to the library); and reading, writing, and drawing (Baker et al., 1994). What should be emphasized is that the healthiest environments for the development of literacy during the preschool years are ones in which literate interactions are part of the natural fun of homelife. That is, the home that fosters preschooler emergent literacy is not school-like but rather playful, verbal, and stimulating in ways that are interesting to preschoolers (Sonnenschein et al., 1996). There are responsive relationships with adults. It is widely accepted by literacy researchers that the environment the preschool child experiences is a critical determinant of reading and writing abilities.

Literacy researchers studying the preschool years have been very much influenced by developmental psychology. The first section of this chapter takes up John Bowlby's theory of attachment and how the development of a secure attachment is critical to productive cognitive interactions between parents and children. The second section reviews briefly the theory of development proposed by Lev Vygotsky, who believed that many of the skills a child acquires reflect internalization of thinking first carried out by the child and adults in interaction. Then, the third section considers the emergent literacy skills, which have been studied closely by literacy researchers who are interested in the pre-school years. The chapter concludes with coverage of the development of a skill that seems to be especially important with respect to the development of beginning reading competence: the awareness that words are composed of sounds blended together (i.e., phonemic awareness).

A SECURE ATTACHMENT RELATIONSHIP AS A CONTEXT FOR LITERACY DEVELOPMENT

When parent–infant interactions go well, babies form strong emotional ties with their caregivers. The attached baby interacts extensively with the primary caregivers who become the primary adult attachment objects. Once attachment occurs, a baby does what it can to maintain proximity to primary caregivers, including crawling toward them, crying when they are out of sight, and clinging hard to them. John Bowlby (1969) provided a comprehensive theory about both the course of attachment and the biological and social mechanisms that account for attachment. The developmental course of infant–caregiver attachment has been studied extensively in the quarter-century since Bowlby's book first appeared, with Bowlby's perspective now enjoying a great deal of research support (e.g., Sroufe, 1996).

Perhaps the most important finding in the attachment literature is that the more responsive the adult, or rather, the more the adult is there to help when the baby needs help, the more secure the emerging attachment between infant and adult. When researchers have measured both parental sensitivity early in the first year of a baby's life and security of attachment later in the first year, they have found a clear association between them (Sroufe, 1996, Chap. 10). That is important with respect to other aspects of development, for the more secure the attachment, the more effective the parent is in helping the child to explore the world (Ainsworth, 1967; Schaffer & Emerson, 1964).

Security of Attachment and Later Development

Bowlby (1969) contended that secure attachment was a precursor of good mental health—that securely attached infants are more likely to be well-adjusted and sociable when they are older. One possible interpretation of a secure attachment during infancy is that it reflects the development of basic trust, whereas an insecure attachment reflects basic mistrust (e.g., Erikson, 1968). Basic trust in infancy is linked to later security and trust in interacting with others, which affects the quality of the interactions the child has. If social interactions matter in cognitive development, as I think that they do, then the child who has experienced secure attachment is going to benefit cognitively.

Particularly relevant here is the correlation between secure attachment during infancy and subsequent cognitive interactions with parents. For example, in a well-known study, Matas, Arend, and Sroufe (1978) demonstrated that secure attachment during infancy predicted the quality of problem solving undertaken by 2-year-olds and their mothers working together. The children, in interaction with their mothers, figured out how to get a lure from a long tube using two sticks. They also figured out how to weigh down the end of a lever with a block to raise candy through a hole in a Plexiglas box. How did this occur? The mothers of 2-year-olds who had been securely attached infants offered higher-quality support to their 2-year-olds during the problem-solving tasks. Problem solving was happier for the securely attached children compared to the less securely attached children, who more often rejected their mothers' suggestions, even aggressing against them when suggestions were offered. Others have replicated this result (Frankel & Bates, 1990).

In general, when there is a secure attachment, parental directions and support are more likely to be at an appropriate level, neither too little nor too much (Fagot & Kavanagh, 1993). That is, in emotionally secure parent–child dyads, parents provide support as needed but back off and permit the child to go it alone when that is possible (Borkowski & Dukewich, 1996; Moss, 1992).

Security of Attachment and Emergent Literacy Experiences

Attachment security is related to the quality of mother–child emergent literacy experiences during the preschool years. Dutch researchers Adriana Bus and Marinus van IJzendoorn (1988) observed 1½-year-olds, 3½-year-olds, and 5½-year-olds and their mothers as they watched *Sesame Street*, read a picture book together, and went through an alphabet book—all prototypical emergent literacy contexts. They also measured attachment as it is usually measured, by watching the interactions of infants when they are reunited with mother after a brief separation (Main, Kaplan, & Cassidy, 1985), with more securely attached infants happier on mother's return than less securely attached infants.

Consistently, the interactions during emergent literacy tasks were more positive for securely attached compared to less securely attached children. Securely attached children were more attentive and less easily distracted during emergent literacy interactions. Particularly critical with respect to the development of emergent literacy, secure dyads were more oriented to reading and reading-related skills during their interactions. The mothers of the securely attached children demanded more of their children, and the children met the demands.

Bus and van IJzendoorn (1995) studied a group of 3-year-olds who varied in the security of their attachments to their mothers. One important finding was that the frequency of reading that mothers reported doing with their children was related to security of attachment, with more securely attached children and mothers doing more reading together than less securely attached child–mother dyads. During the study, the researchers observed children and their mothers as they engaged in storybook reading. There was less engagement during reading when insecure dyads read than when securely attached children and mothers read with each other. The greater the insecurity, the more the children were inattentive, and the more the discussion digressed from the story. The less secure the attachment, the harder it seemed for the children to get the message of the text.

In short, security in attachment predicts healthy interactions as parents and children tackle intellectual challenges together, including reading with one another. Some children, however, are at substantially greater risk than others for not developing secure relationships with parents during infancy, because of their difficult temperaments, for example (Chess & Thomas, 1987; Thomas & Chess, 1977). Even in those cases, intervention can increase the likelihood of secure attachment and cognitively productive interactions. Parents can be taught to observe their children and be sensitive to them (e.g., Belsky, Rosenberger, & Crnic, 1995; van den Boom, 1994, 1995; van IJzendoorn, Juffer, & Duyvesteyn, 1995).

VYGOTSKY'S THEORY: INTELLECTUAL DEVELOPMENT THROUGH INTERNALIZATION OF INTERPERSONAL INTERACTION SKILLS

People learn from other people. Many researchers are now studying how interpersonal relationships contribute to the development of thinking and learning skills. Lev Vygotsky, who lived during the first third of the 20th century in what became the Soviet Union, has been the most influential theoretist in this arena.

Inner Speech and Thought

Vygotsky (1962) believed that for adults, *inner speech* was an important mechanism involved in thought. Inner speech is very different from outer speech, according to Vygotsky. Inner speech is abbreviated and fragmentary, with the meaning of complex thoughts captured in very few words and word fragments. It is speech that supports thought. You can get a feel for what is meant by inner speech by finding a somewhat complicated task to do, one that requires some thinking. Yesterday, for example, I repaired the part of my computer system file that controls the printer. As I worked, I thought to myself, "I wonder if the bundle bits might be damaged," which caused me to run a utilities program on the system files in order to repair any bundle bit damage. When that did not work, I thought to myself much faster than I could say it out loud, "Replace the system file." I did, and the printer function subsequently worked. As I reflected on what had gone on, I realized that my thoughts and inner speech were so intertwined that they were difficult to separate, just as Vygotsky (1962) had claimed.

Some extremely important research in Soviet psychology has focused on when people subvocalize (i.e., use inner speech to mediate performance) and when they do not. Subvocalization occurs when people work on problems that are challenging to them (Sokolov, 1975). For example, Sokolov substantiated that subvocalization occurs during reading, with the intensity of subvocalization varying with the difficulty of the text being read and with the task assigned to the reader (e.g., requiring the reader to attempt to memorize what is being read increases the intensity of subvocalization).

Development of Inner Speech

An important contribution by Vygotsky was a theory about how inner speech develops during childhood. During the first two years of life, thought is nonverbal. Speech plays a limited role in thought during the early stages of language development (i.e., beginning at about age 2). Then, children begin to manifest what has been called *egocentric speech* by developmental psychologists. That is, when preschoolers do things, they often talk to themselves about what they are doing. Vygotsky recognized the emergence of egocentric speech to be an important intellectual advance, with such speech beginning to influence what the child thinks and does. How many times does the parent of a preschooler hear, "I'm going to play with X," before she or he goes and plays with X? How many times does a parent hear, "I'm running to X," before the child runs to X? Often such utterances come when the preschooler is trying to figure out what to do.

Vygotsky carried out studies with preschoolers in which the preschoolers were given tasks that were complicated by some obstacle (e.g., when a colored pencil, or paper, or paint that was needed was missing). When difficulties occurred, the amount of egocentric speech was much greater than when preschoolers did the same tasks without obstacles.

Eventually, overt egocentric speech becomes covert and abbreviated. It can always become overt again if the child encounters a challenging problem. Recall from Chapter 2 that when skilled readers encounter very familiar words, reading of the words is automatic with little involvement of speech processes; speech processes involving sounding out a word only come into play with difficult words. This is consistent with the general principle advanced by Soviet theorists such as Vygotsky that speech is an important part of thinking, especially challenging thinking.

Contemporary literacy researchers are actively studying the development of children's use of speech during thinking. For example, Purdue University literacy researcher Beverly Cox (1994) observed self-regulatory speech in preschoolers as they attempted to construct and dictate a short story to an adult who wrote it down. As the children thought about what might be added next to the story, Cox heard them say things like, "Now, what did I do then?", "Think about what you say before you say it," and "That's it ... I think that's it." Such an observation is consistent with Vygotsky's and other developmental psychologists's observations (e.g., Kohlberg, Yaeger, & Hjertholm, 1968) that preschoolers use audible speech in order to organize their thinking.

Development of Thought in Social Interactions

The prominence of Vygotsky's thinking with respect to development has soared in the past twenty years, largely because of the translation of a work that proposed an explanation of the developments in thinking that were only described in his previously translated work (1962). In *Mind in Society*, Vygotsky (1978) made the case that interaction with others is a prime mover in the development of children's thinking abilities.

Development of Problem-Solving Skills

Adults often assist children with problems they are confronting. A child might not work through many problems without assistance, but with parental support makes fine progress. What goes on in these interactions is thinking, thinking that involves two heads. Years of participating in such interactions leads to their internalization by the child. That is, thought processes that were once interpersonal become intrapersonal. The most frequently reprinted Vygotskian quote captures this developmental progression:

> Any function in the child's cultural development appears twice, or on two planes. First, it appears on the social plane, and then on the psychological plane. First, it appears between people as an interpsychological category, and then within the child as an intrapsychological category. This is equally true with respect to voluntary attention, logical memory, the formation of concepts, and the development of volition. . . . Social relations or relations among people genetically underlie all higher functions and their relationships. . . . In their private sphere, human beings retain the functions of social interactions. (1978, pp. 163–164)

According to the Vygotskian perspective, cognitive development moves forward most certainly and completely if the child is in a world that provides assistance when the child needs it and can benefit from it. Such a responsive world is not intruding, however; rather, it provides support when the child needs it. When 2- or 3-year-olds can solve a problem themselves, appropriately responsive adults let the 2- and 3-year-olds do so. Any parent of a preschooler knows all too well the phrase, "I can do it myself!"; and when the child can, the parent honors that declaration. Of course, there are other tasks that 2- and 3-year-olds cannot perform, no matter how much assistance might be provided. A responsive social environment does not even try to encourage children to do such tasks and in fact, often discourages attempts at behaviors far outside the range of preschooler competence, as when, for example, a father physically lifts his son from the driver's seat of the car as the youngster urges the father to teach him to drive. (Think back to the research on attachment described earlier, with security of attachment linked to support from adults when children need it.)

Between the two extremes of tasks, the ones children can do autonomously and those they could never do, critical developmental interactions occur. That is, interactions that facilitate development are most likely with tasks that children only can do with adult help. The responsive social world provides assistance on these tasks that are within the child's *zone of proximal development*, according to Vygotskian theory. In fact, the zone is defined as behaviors beyond a child's level of autonomous functioning but within reach if assistance is provided. Children learn how to perform tasks appropriately within their zone by interacting with more competent and responsive others who provide hints and prompts to the child on an as-needed basis.

Thus, the responsive adult directs a child's attention to important dimensions of a problem, if the child seems not to be attending to those dimensions on her or his own. Sometimes the adult suggests a strategy to the child. Through doing the task with support, the child eventually can perform the task without assistance, having internalized the kinds of thinking that was previously supported by an adult. Without adult assistance, there are many forms of thinking that the child would not discover, either alone or in interaction with peers.

When adults assist in this fashion, they are said to *scaffold* a child (Wood, Bruner, & Ross, 1976), a metaphoric reference to the scaffold of a building under construction. It is an appropriate metaphor: The scaffolding on a building under construction provides supports when the new building cannot stand on its own. As the new structure is completed and becomes freestanding, the scaffolding is removed. So it is with scaffolded adult–child academic interactions. The adult carefully monitors when enough instructional input has been provided to permit the child to make progress toward an academic goal, and thus, provides support only when the child needs it. If a child catches on quickly, the adult's responsive instruction will be less detailed than if the child experiences difficulties with a task.

Development of Language Skills

As they use language during the preschool years, some children receive more scaffolding than do others. Lower-class children are less likely than middle- and upper-class children to be immersed in supportive communicative interactions (Bernstein, 1965). This is critical, since the development of oral communication skills during the preschool years is logically prerequisite to success in reading and writing (e.g., Snow, 1991). For example, two University of Kansas psychologists (Hart & Risley, 1995) documented a correlation between children's language interactions and their subsequent cognitive development. They observed 42 families carefully for $2\frac{1}{2}$ years, beginning when a child in the family was 7–9 months of age. During the observations, the researchers attempted to record everything that went on, using tape recorders and notes. The observations then were carefully coded and analyzed for the types of verbal interactions that occurred.

The outcomes in the study were very clear: There were large differences in the quality of language interactions as a function of social class. More high-quality verbal interactions were observed in professional homes than working-class homes, and more in working-class homes than welfare homes. The higher the socioeconomic level, the more the parents listened to their children, prompted children to elaborate their verbalizations, told their children what was worth remembering, and taught them how to cope with difficulties. These differences in the quality and quantity of verbal interactions were observed throughout the $2\frac{1}{2}$ years of observations, and they were pronounced: Whereas, on average, a child in a professional family experienced 4 million verbal utterances a year, a child in a welfare family experienced 250,000 utterances.

Based on such striking differences in input, it would be expected that there would be differences in outcomes, and there were. By the time the children were 3 years of age, those from professional homes knew much more vocabulary than children of working class parents, who knew more than the children of parents on welfare. However, because there were other differences between the homes of professional, working class, and welfare families, it was not possible in this study to be certain that the differences in language skills in the children were due to the linguistic interactions they experienced. Nonetheless, when the correlations obtained in this study are combined with evidence from other studies, there is a great deal of support for the conclusion that the quality of a child's verbal interactions is reliably related to linguistic and cognitive development.

In particular, responsive adults spend a great deal of time talking *with* their children about things that happened to the child, assisting the child in learning how to be tellers of their own memories. Judith Hudson (1990), a psychologist at Rutgers University, analyzed her own daughter Rachel's experiences in talking about the past and how those experiences increased Rachel's ability to describe events in her life. What was particularly critical were her many opportunities to talk about the past with Mom, through extended dialogues about the many things that had happened to Rachel. When Rachel had difficulties in remembering, Mom would prompt her, typically with questions.

Through experiencing such dialogues, Rachel learned how to talk about things that had happened to her. Consistent with the Vygotskian perspective, Hudson (1990) concluded that the important thinking skill of being able to describe events in one's life develops through social interaction. When the child could not structure recall of an event, the mother asked questions, providing a scaffold for the child's recollections. As Rachel became increasingly familiar with what should be told during recall of something that happened in the past, and began, in fact, to recall with greater completeness, adult scaffolding in the form of leading questions was reduced. Hudson's description of Rachel's progression from a teller of tales with assistance to an autonomous teller of tales is consistent with a variety of evidence that children's abilities to talk about their past depends on dialoguing experiences with supportive adults (Engel, 1986; Nelson, 1993a, 1993b; Pillemer & White, 1989; Ratner, 1980, 1984; Reese, Haden, & Fivush, 1993; Tessler, 1986).

Virtually everyone who thinks about reading believes that success in reading depends on language development. Thus, for the reading-education community, there is obvious significance to the finding that conversational experiences during the preschool years figure greatly in the development of cognitive and communication skills. The work of Hudson and her colleagues seems more significant than that, however. Hudson believes that supportive parent–child dialogical experiences not only promote the development of children's abilities to communicate about the past, but also increase their abilities to organize and understand their previous experiences (Nelson, 1996). Recall from previous chapters that prior knowledge based on experience is important in comprehending information presented in texts. Since children who have had rich and supportive dialogical experiences have better organized and more complete prior knowledge, they should be advantaged in comprehending what they read over children who have not had such experiences. Children who live in a richly responsive interpersonal world, who learn how to communicate with others, are going to be cognitively far ahead of other children.

EMERGENT LITERACY

For the most part, the discussion in this chapter thus far has emphasized general cognitive and language skills that support the development of literacy, with only limited discussion of research directly tapping the development of literacy skills per se. In fact, a great deal of literacy development occurs during the preschool years, so much so that the preschool years are often referred to as the period of emergent literacy (Clay, 1966, 1967) by reading theorists and researchers.

There has been a great deal of research directly focusing on emergent literacy. Literacy development begins before the first birthday, through, for example, experiences with plastic "bathtub" books filled with colorful pictures or from mothers and fathers who read nursery rhymes to their children as they rock them to sleep. These early beginnings expand into a rich array of literacy experiences, from scribbling letters to grandma to experiencing stories on grandma's lap. Environments that support emergent literacy include (1) rich interpersonal experiences with parents, brothers and sisters, and others; (2) physical environments that include literacy materials, from plastic refrigerator letters to storybooks to writing materials; and (3) high positive regard by parents and others for literacy and its development in children (Leichter, 1984; Morrow, 1997).

Put more concretely, in homes in which emergent literacy is fostered, children are exposed to paper-and-pencil activities, letters, and even printed words at an early age. Parents read to their children, and they help children as they attempt to read (e.g., by holding a book upright and pretending to read by recalling the story as they remembered it). Books and other reading materials are prominent in homes supporting emergent literacy (Briggs & Elkind, 1973; Clark, 1976; Durkin, 1966; King & Friesen, 1972; Morrow, 1983; Plessas & Oakes, 1964; Teale, 1978).

Storybook Reading

One activity which has high potential for fostering emergent literacy is storybook reading. There are strong and positive correlations between amount of storybook reading during the preschool years and subsequent vocabulary and language development, children's interest in reading, and early success in reading (Sulzby & Teale, 1991). Given their apparent power in stimulating children's literacy development, caregiver–child interactions during storybook reading have been studied in some detail.

At its best, storybook reading includes rich discussions and animated conversations between the reader and the child. The adult and child work out the meaning of the text, and they have a lot of fun doing it (Morrow, 1997). There is questioning, both by the adult and the child; there is modeling of dialoguing by the adult, with the child sometimes participating; the adult praises the child's efforts to get meaning from the pictures and print; the adult offers information to the child and responds to the child's reactions to text; and both adult and child relate what is happening in the text to their lives and the world around them (Applebee & Langer, 1983; Cochran-Smith, 1984;

Flood, 1977; Pellegrini, Perlmutter, Galda, & Brody, 1990; Roser & Martinez, 1985; Taylor & Strickland, 1986). A rich history of such interactions is predictive of subsequent success in literacy acquisition (Sulzby & Teale, 1991).

Scaffolding is prominent when storybook reading is going well— when it is engaging to the youngsters. Parents who are good at storybook reading encourage children to respond to readings and participate as much as possible in reading itself. They provide support as children need it, provide input that children can understand (e.g., DeLoache & DeMendoza, 1987). With increasing age through the preschool years, children are attentive to longer sections of text (Heath, 1982; Sulzby & Teale, 1987). As they gain experience reading story-books, adults and children have more complex discussions about text (Snow, 1983; Sulzby & Teale, 1987). Children who experience a lot of storybook reading are accustomed to interacting with an adult about story content; they are appropriately attentive during storybook read-ing, much more so than same-age children who have not experienced storybook reading (Bus & van IJzendoorn, 1988).

Some attention has been paid to differences in style of storybook reading and the effects of such variation on cognitive development. Children have better vocabulary development when they interact with adults who are skillful at eliciting verbal interactions from them during reading (e.g., Ninio, 1980; Pellegrini, Galda, Perlmutter, & Jones, 1994). There are also correlations between the degree to which parents elaborate on book content and success on literacy tasks in school (Heath, 1982). In short, not all storybook reading is ideal; the quality of storybook reading very much affects a child's cognitive development.

The correlations between quality of storybook reading and liter-acy development (Sulzby & Teale, 1991) prompted Grover Whitehurst and his colleagues at the State University of New York at Stony Brook (Whitehurst et al., 1988) to study whether it might be possible to improve parental skills during storybook interactions and thus, posi-tively affect the development of emergent literacy in children. The parents of 14 children between $1\frac{3}{4}$ years and 3 years of age partici-pated in a 1-month intervention designed to improve interactions between parents and children during storybook reading. Parents were taught to ask more open-ended questions and more questions about the functions and attributes of objects in stories as they read with their preschoolers. The parents were also given instruction about how to respond appropriately to their children's comments during story reading and how to expand on what the children had to say. The parents in the treatment group were also taught to reduce the amount of straight reading that they did, as well as to eliminate questions that the child could answer simply by pointing to something in an illustration. Fifteen other children and their parents, who served as control participants in the study, were encouraged to continue reading storybooks as they normally did with their children.

First, the intervention parents were able to learn to interact differently with their children during storybook reading, in ways that increased the qualities of interactions between the children and their parents. Although there had been no differences between intervention and control children at the beginning of the study with respect to language variables, there were clear differences favoring the intervention participants at the end of the month of treatment: At the end of the study, the intervention participants outscored the control subjects on a standardized measure of psycholinguistic ability and on two vocabulary tests. What was most striking in this study was that when the same measures were repeated 9 months later, the intervention subjects still had an advantage over the control participants, although the differences were not as large.

Notably, Whitehurst's group also has produced positive effects with storybook reading when Mexican children have been the intervention targets (Valdez-Menchaca & Whitehurst, 1992) and as part of a comprehensive day care intervention (Whitehurst et al., 1994). Whitehurst and his associates also have made progress in making their approach cost effective, developing videotapes that teach mothers how to interact with the preschoolers as they read stories (Arnold, Lonigan, Whitehurst, & Epstein, 1994). Others are also making progress in devising storybook reading interventions. For example, Crain-Thoresen and Dale (1995) taught preschool staff members to interact with children more actively during storybook reading. The targeted students then performed better on a variety of language measures, including a vocabulary test and an analysis of the length and complexity of utterances. Dickinson and Smith (1994) designed a similar intervention that produced similar effects. In short, by actively engaging preschoolers in discussions as part of storybook reading, adults can promote child language development: presumably, the earlier such experience begins, the better (Lonigan, Anthony, & Burgess, 1995).

Developing Rich Emergent Literacy Knowledge in Preschools

Neuman and Roskos (1997) recently provided an interesting analysis making clear just how extensive preschoolers' emergent literacy can be, at least when preschoolers experience an environment rich with emergent literacy learning opportunities. They studied 30 preschoolers who participated in a preschool with three play centers that permitted much emergent literacy activity: a post office, a restaurant, and a doctor's office. The children were observed over the course of 7 months.

What Neuman and Roskos (1997) found was that children learned the names and functions of a number of literacy objects in the play centers, including the following: envelopes, pencil, letter, mailbox, menu, bill, check, insurance card, and eye chart. They also learned how to do many literate things, including the following: getting stamps, putting together a letter, mailing a letter, addressing letters, delivering mail, taking a restaurant order, ordering from a menu, reviewing a restaurant bill, exchanging pleasantries over a meal, taking inventory at the restaurant, taking down information, giving prescriptions, signing in at the doctor's office, and describing medical emergency procedures. Neuman and Roskos (1997) also observed the use of some higher-order strategies similar to those used by older children as they read, write, and do things literate. These include seeking information, correcting and giving feedback to others, self-correcting, checking a literacy product against a standard (e.g., checking if letters in the post office are sorted the way that they should be sorted), and gathering up resources before beginning a task. In short, much literate behavior can be learned in a preschool classroom designed to foster emergent literacy activities.

Interpretational Controversies Regarding Emergent Literacy Experiences

From infancy, there are opportunities for adults and children to interact together with materials and activities related to reading and writing. Some children are more fortunate than others, participating in many more emergent literacy interactions than other children. The lucky children live in families in which literacy experiences are so common that they are family habits which are naturally extended to new family members, beginning shortly after their arrival from the hospital. That some preschoolers do not have consistent, excellent emergent literacy experiences has stimulated researchers such as Whitehurst, Neuman, and Roskos to begin to study ways of increasing interactions between parents, teachers, and children that promote emergent literacy. Their successes to date fuel enthusiasm for the possibility that many more children could be much better prepared for formal schooling by increasing the quality and quantity of literacy interactions during the preschool years.

In closing this section, however, I must admit that there is some variability in the interpretation of the emergent literacy research. For example, while there is agreement that storybook reading's effect on language and literacy development is not overwhelmingly large, some view the statistical associations produced to date as evidence of the power of storybook reading (Bus, van IJzendoorn, & Pelligrini, 1995; Dunning, Mason, & Stewart, 1994; Lonigan, 1994). That is, despite the many problems of measurement with preschool children (and there are many, not the least of which is the lower reliability of measurements on preschoolers compared to older children), the lack of statistical power in many studies (which reduces the likelihood of finding significant statistical associations), and great variability in the procedures from study to study, some researchers are impressed with the consistency of at least positive associations between activities like storybook reading and growth in emergent literacy. In contrast, others (Scarborough & Dobrich, 1994) examine the exact same correlations between storybook reading and emergent literacy, and write them off as small and potentially attributable to other factors, suggesting that perhaps the correlations between storybook reading and language and literacy achievement actually reflect other relationships (e.g., perhaps children more interested in things literate and/or those with higher verbal abilities are more likely to engage in storybook reading than children less interested and/or lower in ability). My own reading of the evidence is that there is much more reason to believe that early literacy interactions are important. I am especially struck by experimental work, such as that carried out by Whitehurst and his associates. Still, there is a need for much more research.

One possibility is that emergent literacy experiences may not be equally positive for all children. For example, when the studies of Adriana Bus and Marinus van IJzendoorn (1988, 1992, 1995) are read, it is striking that when children interact with parents with whom they are not securely attached, storybook reading is not the happy and engaging event that it can be when securely attached parents and children interact over books. It may very well be that such negative interactions over books may undermine interest in reading (Bus, 1993, 1994). We need to find this out, and then, of course, we must find out how more positive interactions can be encouraged between a preschooler and parent who have yet to develop a trusting relationship.

However positive a child's emergent literacy experiences, they rarely are sufficient for the development of one very important competency associated with successful beginning reading. I take up that competency in the next section.

PHONEMIC AWARENESS AND ITS
DEVELOPMENT THROUGH INSTRUCTION

Children who experience difficulties learning to read during the first several years of schooling often lack the critical competency that is phonemic awareness (e.g., Adams, 1990; Pennington, Groisser, & Welsh, 1993; Stanovich, 1986, 1988)—awareness that words are composed of separable sounds (i.e., phonemes) that are blended to produce words. There are varying degrees of phonemic awareness (Adams, 1990; Slocum, O'Connor, & Jenkins, 1993; Stahl & Murray, 1994, in press; Wagner, Torgesen, Laughon, Simmons, & Rashotte, 1993). Although there are some data-based differences of opinion among the various researchers studying phonemic awareness about the particular tasks that reflect less and more advanced forms of it, Marilyn Adams' (1990) conceptualization is generally valid. According to her, the most primitive form is simply having enough of an ear for sounds to remember rhyming words more easily than nonrhyming words. The child with this level of phonemic awareness can recall nursery rhymes with greater ease than the child who lacks this basic form of phonemic awareness (Maclean, Bryant, & Bradley, 1987). At the next level, the child can detect the odd word in a set of words, recognizing, for example, that *sod* is the odd word in the trio *can, dan, sod,* or that *mar* is odd in the set *bat, bax,* and *mar*. At a still higher level of awareness, the child can blend component sounds to form words, for example, when presented the sounds *m, ah* (i.e., short *a*), and *t,* producing the word *mat*. Even more advanced is the ability to segment a word into its sounds; the child at this level of awareness can report that *mat* is composed of the sounds *m, ah,* and *t*. Children at the highest level of awareness can split off individual sounds from intact words: for example, when asked to delete the *m* sound from *mat,* the child says *at*. Thus, phonemic awareness culminates when students can actively manipulate and play around with the sounds that compose words. I emphasize the playfulness in such manipulation, for whenever I have observed classrooms in which children are practicing blending, adding, deleting, and inserting sounds as part of phonemic-awareness instruction, they seem to be having a lot of fun.

One study more than any other has focused attention on phonemic awareness. Connie Juel (1988) followed a sample of 54 children as they progressed from grades 1 through 4, collecting a variety of reading and related measures as part of the study. The 23 Hispanic children, 14 African Americans, and 13 whites were all enrolled in the same school. One of the most striking findings in the study concerned continuing underachievement in reading: there was an 88% chance that if a child was having difficulty reading in grade 1, the child would still be having difficulty in grade 4. More importantly in this context, however, was that the best predictor of poor reading achievement in grade 1 was phonemic awareness: more advanced levels of phonemic awareness were required for a child to score highly in Juel's (1988) study. Especially striking, low phonemic awareness in grade 1 was highly predictive of continuing reading difficulties in grade 4.

This latter finding especially stimulated very hard thinking and many additional analyses by a number of researchers about phonemic awareness and how it relates to reading competence. Based on these analyses, it is now known that poor readers at all age levels often are less phonemically aware than same-age good readers (e.g., Pratt & Brady, 1988; Shaywitz, 1996). Children who lack phonemic awareness have a difficult time developing understanding of letter–sound relationships as well as learning to spell (Griffith, 1991; Juel, Griffith, & Gough, 1986). Since Juel, additional evidence has been produced that poor phonemic awareness at 4 to 6 years of age is predictive of reading difficulties throughout the elementary years (e.g., Bowey, 1995; Naslund & Schneider, 1996; Stuart & Masterson, 1992; Torgesen & Burgess, in press). The evidence that phonemic awareness difficulties in the elementary years are associated with reading difficulties has also been established more firmly in recent analyses, demonstrating even stronger relationships between phonemic awareness and reading ability than between other potentially important individual differences (i.e., rapid processing and naming of individual letters and numbers; Torgesen, Wagner, Rashotte, Burgess, & Hecht, 1997) and reading ability. An especially important finding is that more advanced forms of phonemic awareness (i.e., the ability to segment words into component sounds) are more predictive of reading ability than simpler forms (e.g., being able to detect rhymes; Nation & Hulme, 1997).

Lack of phonemic awareness seems to be the start of a vicious cycle. Deficiencies in phonemic awareness can undermine learning to decode, which in turn undermines reading a wide range of materials and comprehending what is read. The long-term result is less practice in reading and less exposure to information in text and thus, less development of higher-order reading competencies (e.g., ability to make sense of complex syntax) and world knowledge that can mediate understanding of text (Juel, 1988). This is the rich getting richer and the poor-getting-poorer story, what Stanovich (1986) referred to as the Matthew effect in reading.

For the most advanced levels of phonemic awareness to develop, formal instruction in reading seems essential (i.e., only a very small proportion of children develop the advanced levels of phonemic awareness in the absence of such instruction; e.g., Lundberg, 1991). Notably, the one emergent literacy experience that is predictive of phonemic awareness is parental teaching of letters and their sounds (Crain-Thoreson & Dale, 1992). Many parents, however, do not engage in such teaching, so that education that impacts phonemic awareness typically must occur in school. Thus, there is a need to provide phonemic awareness instruction to kindergarten and grade-1 children, if they are to develop it.

Instruction in Phonemic Awareness

Phonemic awareness can be developed through systematic practice in categorizing words on the basis of common beginning, middle, and end sounds. One of the first instructional studies of the development of phonemic awareness, conducted in England by Lynette Bradley and Peter Bryant (e.g., 1983) continues to be the best known.

An important principle emphasized in Bradley and Bryant's (1983) instruction was that the same word can be categorized in different ways on the basis of sound when it is in different sets of words. Thus, if *hen* is in a group of words that include *hat, hill, hair,* and *hand,* it would make sense to categorize all of these words together as starting with *h,* especially in contrast to other words starting with another letter (e.g., *b* words such as *bag, band, bat,* etc.). If *hen* were on a list with *men* and *sun,* however, these three words could be categorized as ones ending in *n.* If *hen* were on a list of words that included *bed* and *leg,* it would be possible to categorize the words as ones with *short e* in the middle.

The instruction in Bradley and Bryant (1983) took place over 40 10-minute sessions spread out over 2 years. During the first 20 sessions, 5- and 6-year-olds who initially lacked phonemic awareness were taught to categorize words on the basis of common sounds, using pictures of the objects (i.e., pictures of a *hen, men,* and a *leg*). For example, in one lesson a set of pictures representing the letter *b* was shown to the child, who named the objects. The child repeated the names, with the teacher urging the child to listen to the sounds. The child then was asked if he or she could hear a sound common to each word. This continued until the child could identify the common sound, with the adult providing help and hints if the child experienced difficulty doing this.

The sound identification task was repeated a number of times during training, with variations (e.g., presentation of *bus,* with the child required to pick out a picture starting with the same sound from an array of pictures; presentation of *bus,* with the direction to pick out pictures starting with a different sound than the one at the beginning of *bus*). Children were then given sets of pictures, asked to group them together on the basis of common sounds, and then required to justify their classifications. "Odd-one-out" was played, in which the child was required to eliminate a word starting with (or ending with or containing) a sound different than the other pictures in a set. Many such exercises were given for each sound (e.g., b), with the teacher moving on to a new sound only when the child seemed to be proficient with the sound previously introduced. Of course, as new sounds accumulated, the difficulty of tasks increased.

The 20 sessions with pictures were followed by 20 sessions with words, in which a child was required to determine whether words rhymed or began with the same sound (alliteration). After the child was proficient at this task, there were lessons on end sounds (e.g., odd-one-out exercises requiring elimination of the word ending in a sound different than the others). After the child could manage categorizing on the basis of final sounds, there was instruction of categorization based on middle sounds in words.

Pictures yielded to purely aural presentations in this training. Various discrimination exercises eventually gave way to production exercises, so that children had to recall words containing particular sounds in particular positions. In the latter half of the curriculum, children were required to spell words using plastic letters, with the teacher providing help as needed, up to and including spelling the word for the child. Spelling exercises included sets of words sharing common features. Thus, for a set involving *hat, cat,* and *rat,* an efficient strategy was simply to change the first plastic letter as each new word was requested. The saliency of many different sound patterns was illustrated with such spelling lists.

This training produced substantial gains in standardized reading performance (i.e., about a year's advantage) relative to a control condition in which children were trained to categorize pictures and words conceptually (e.g., *cat, bat,* and *rat* are all animals). The sound categorization trained students were even further ahead of control participants who had received no supplementary categorization training. Even more striking, however, were the results of a 5-year follow-up. Even though many of the control subjects had received substantial remediation during the 5 year interval following participation in the study, there were still striking reading advantages for students who had experienced the sound categorization training when they were in the primary grades (Bradley, 1989; Bradley & Bryant, 1991).

Since the appearance of the Bradley and Bryant (1983, 1985) study, there have been a number of well-controlled demonstrations that phonemic awareness can be developed in children with discernible effects on reading and learning to read. Thus, in Lundberg, Frost, and

Peterson (1988), classrooms of 6-year-olds were provided daily phonemic awareness training for 8 months (i.e. rhyming exercises; dividing words into syllables; and identifying phonemes, including segmenting words into phonemes and synthesizing phonemes into words). Control classrooms received no such training. Three years later, students in trained classrooms performed better on reading and spelling tasks than students in control classrooms.

Similarly, Ball and Blachman (1988) provided instruction to 5-year-olds. In the phoneme-awareness condition, kindergarten students met in small groups for 20 minutes, 4 days a week for 7 weeks. Students moved counters to represent the sounds in words, were exposed to letter names and their associated sounds, and performed categorization tasks like the ones used in Bradley and Bryant's work. In the language-activities control condition, students had vocabulary lessons, listened to stories, and practiced semantic categorization activities. They also received instruction in letter names and sounds that was identical to that provided to the phoneme awareness participants. There was also a no-instruction control condition in the study. The phoneme awareness group outperformed the two control groups on a word reading test, even though no word reading had been taught in the phoneme awareness condition. In followup studies with kindergarten students, the phoneme awareness treatment again produced superior word recognition and spelling compared to control performance (Ball & Blachman, 1991; Blachman, 1991; Tangel & Blachman, 1992, 1995).

Lie (1991) taught Norwegian grade-1 students to analyze new words with respect to their phonological structure. This training promoted reading and spelling in grade 2, compared to control students not receiving phonological training. Weaker readers benefited more from the training than did stronger students.

Cunningham (1990) compared two approaches to increasing the phonemic awareness of kindergarten and grade-1 children. One approach was "skill and drill," with emphasis on segmentation and blending of phonemes. In the second approach, there was discussion of the value of decoding and phonemic awareness and how learning to segment and blend phonemes could be applied in reading. This latter approach was metacognitively very rich, providing children with a great deal of information about when, where, and why to use the knowledge of phonemes they were acquiring. Although both forms of instruction were effective, the metacognitively rich instruction was more effective at the grade-1 level; that is consistent with the general perspective developed in this volume that instruction that increases children's awareness of when and where to use cognitive skills should result in more general and effective use of cognitive skills.

I have presented these results of true experimental evaluations of phonemic awareness training in some detail because these studies are very important. In general, regardless of the specific methods used to measure phonemic awareness or the specific comparison conditions (e.g., no-instruction controls or alternative instruction controls), pho-nemic awareness instruction has been successful in promoting phone-mic awareness (Murray, 1995). As just detailed, such instruction does much more, positively affecting subsequent reading achievement.

From those who are opposed to offering instruction aimed specifi-cally at promoting phonemic awareness I have heard that there is no causal evidence linking phonemic awareness and improved reading. That claim is simply not true. When there is an experimental manipu-lation of phonemic awareness instruction (i.e., some children receive it and some do not, with recipients determined by random assignment), there is a basis for making a causal claim about the effects of phonemic awareness instruction on subsequent reading achievement. In addition to the causal studies already discussed, interested readers should also see the work of Byrne and Fielding-Barnsley (1991, 1993, 1995); O'Connor, Jenkins, and Slocum (1995); Vellutino and Scanlon (1987); Williams (1980); and Wise and Olson (1995). When all of the relevant data are considered, the case that developing phonemic awareness between 4 and 6 years of age has powerful, positive effects on subsequent reading achievement is overwhelming. Learning to read is easier and more certain if the child has achieved a high level of phonemic awareness than if the child has not.

Unfortunately, many children do not receive phonemic awareness instruction. Sometimes the argument is made that because whole language involves much work with poetry, children in whole-language kindergartens receive sufficient exposure to tasks requiring phonemic awareness. Recall, however, that awareness of rhyme, which is the aspect of phonemic awareness that would seem to be most stimulated by poetry experiences, is only a rudimentary form of phonemic aware-ness.

Other times I have heard phonemic awareness instruction por-trayed as boring and unmotivating. Although I know of no formal studies on this point, I reiterate that I have been in many classrooms where such instruction takes place, and the kids really seem to have a ball playing with sounds. In my public lectures, I often ask the kindergarten and grade-one teachers who offer phonemic awareness instruction to identify themselves and ask them whether such instruc-tion is fun for the students or drudgery. Even before I reveal to them my perception of the situation, teachers who have tried such instruc-tion invariably report that the kids like it. If you need proof that phonemic awareness instruction can be a lot of fun, get hold of either *Daisy's Castle* or *DaisyQuest* (Blue Wave Software, now distributed through the Pro-Ed catalogue), two computer programs that develop phonemic awareness in a fantasy context, and really do what they claim to do (Barker & Torgesen, 1995; Foster, Erickson, Foster, Brinkman, & Torgesen, 1994). My son, Tim, delighted in these programs. Now, they are consistently on loan as colleagues' children tackle phonemic awareness, and the reports consistently come back that the programs are a huge hit.

In many cases, however, my hunch is that the reason teachers do not concern themselves with developing phonemic awareness is because they do not know how to develop it in children. (This surmise is based on the many questions I receive from the teachers about what phonemic awareness is, and how it can be developed in children.) There is a real need to heighten teachers' awareness about how phonemic awareness can be fostered in students.

Development of Phonemic Awareness through Reading

Just as development of phonemic awareness leads to improved reading, so does reading increase phonemic awareness (e.g., Goswami & Bryant, 1990): Among others, Wimmer, Landerl, Linortner, and Hummer (1991) and Perfetti (1992; Perfetti, Beck, Bell, & Hughes, 1987) have presented evidence that phonemic awareness is increased by reading, with the implication that reading-induced increases in phonemic awareness in turn influence subsequent development of reading competence. Again, the rich get richer by reading more!

I have heard whole language enthusiasts who are aware that phonemic awareness does increase through reading argue that that is the proof that instruction aimed specifically at the development of phonemic awareness, such as that detailed in the last subsection, is unnecessary. Consistent with whole language philosophy, they argue that phonemic awareness will develop from immersing the child in reading. Of course, there is a chicken-and-egg problem here, as the child who is initially low in phonemic awareness experiences more difficulties in learning to decode print (more about this in the next chapter) and hence is less able to read than other children and thus, benefits less from reading. I'm certain it is getting boring by now, but again, the rich get richer, with children high in phonemic awareness initially learning to read more certainly and thus, deriving greater benefits from opportunities to read.

The scientific community has made progress in cracking this chicken-and-egg dilemma, however, and although the specifics of the analyses are too detailed for presentation here, let it suffice to say that phonemic awareness seems to contribute more to learning to read than learning to read contributes to phonemic awareness (Wagner, Torgesen, & Rashotte, 1994; Wagner et al., 1997).

Phonemic Awareness Instruction and Whole Language

There is another set of data that are devastating to critics of phonemic awareness instruction. When activities that are explicitly intended to increase phonemic awareness are added to whole language classrooms, there are discernible benefits. In a study of Australian kindergarten instruction, Jillian Castle, Jacquelyn Riach, and Tom Nicholson (1994) manipulated the presence or absence of phonemic awareness instruction for kindergarten students experiencing a whole language program. They carried out two studies, one focusing on development of spelling skills and the other the development of ability to read words not seen previously. The phonemic awareness instruction involved two 20-minute sessions a week for 10 weeks. Control participants received supplementary instruction that involved development of skills not related to phonemic awareness. Although the effects were not large, there were greater gains in spelling skills and reading of pseudowords (i.e., invented words, which ensured that students had not seen them before) in the phonemic awareness training conditions than in the control conditions.

Although Castle et al. (1994) have offered the most carefully controlled insertion of phonemic awareness instruction into what were certainly whole language classrooms, there are other studies in which phonemic awareness has been added to classrooms. Thus, Byrne and Fielding-Barnsley (1991, 1993, 1995) reported long-term gains from adding phonemic awareness instruction to the preschool experiences of 4-year-olds (i.e., 12 half-hour sessions, once a week). Also, the kindergarten children in Blachman, Ball, Black, and Tangel (1994) had previously experienced instruction that was so incomplete with respect to development of skills that the children knew only two letters on average by the middle of the kindergarten year; adding 11 weeks of systematic phonemic-awareness instruction at the end of the year, however, did have an effect on the quality of children's invented spellings, with the trained children producing spellings much closer to the sound pattern of words than control participants. The trained children were also much more likely than controls to be able to spell words correctly.

In summary, when phonemic awareness instruction is added to educational environments in which little skills instruction is occurring, there are clear benefits for the students receiving it. Although the positive effects of phonemic awareness instruction in Castle et al.

(1994), which is the most easily interpreted of these studies with respect to whole language, were not large, they are apparent on several different measures. Moreover, the phonemic awareness instruction in Castle et al. (1994) was brief compared to other versions of phonemic awareness instruction, so that detection of effects in that experiment are notable. That the phonemic awareness instruction in Byrne and Fielding-Barnsley (1991) and Blachman et al. (1994) was also brief, but nonetheless produced positive effects compared to ongoing instruction that was weak in skills training, also encourages the conclusion that phonemic awareness instruction can be very potent.

Summary

Many kindergarten and grade-1 children lack the awareness that words are streams of sounds that can be disentangled, and that sounds can be assembled to produce words. They lack phonemic awareness, a metalinguistic insight that seems to be essential in learning to read. Fortunately, phonemic awareness can be developed through instruction, with clear benefits to subsequent acquisition of reading skills.

The strong associations between phonemic awareness and successfully learning to read have prompted much attention to this particular aspect of literacy development. The result has being increased knowledge about phonemic awareness and its development, so that now clear guidance can be offered to practicing kindergarten teachers about how to develop phonemic awareness in their students. Kindergarten is the right time for such instruction, since phonemic awareness is an important prerequisite to learning to decode, which is typically a key focus of grade-1 reading instruction.

I have heard the frequent claim that phonemic awareness can be developed by having children spend a great deal of time listening to and interacting with books that are filled with playfully varied speech sounds—for example, rhymes and alliterations. Even though I know of no study to prove this point, it is noteworthy that a list of books that could be used in this fashion has been compiled (e.g., Yopp, 1995). At a minimum, lots of such books in kindergarten provides lots of stimulus for students to think about the sounds of words.

SUMMARY

1. Throughout the 20th century, psychologists have studied the significance of the preschool years and the importance of the child's earliest social relationships. Bowlby (1969) and other developmentalists

came to understand the importance of a child's developing a trusting relationship with an adult early in life, typically the mother. Such a relationship is a context in which mother and child can explore new things together, including letters of the alphabet, words, and texts.

The interface between socioemotional development in infancy and the preschool years and cognitively oriented interactions with caregivers and others is being actively explored in the 1990s. The work of the Dutch group (e.g., Bus & can IJzendoorn, 1995), who have established that emergent literacy interactions are more certainly productive when mother and child are securely attached, is attracting great attention and undoubtedly will be followed up in Holland and elsewhere. An important implication of this research is that narrowly targeting literacy is unlikely to be an effective strategy for assuring the development of literate children. Rather, the message in the Dutch data is that every effort should be made to assure that mothers are responsive to their babies, for such responsivity is at the heart of secure attachment. Fortunately, researchers are identifying ways to stimulate parents to be more naturally responsive to their children, as parental responsivity is the key to the development of healthy parent–infant attachments.

Secure attachment is important for cognitive development because intellectual skills are developed in interaction with others, a perspective pioneered by Vygotsky a half-century ago and only now being explored in detail in the West. Vygotsky and other Soviet researchers have established the importance of speech in thinking and the organization of thinking; this is particularly important with respect to literacy.

2. Chapters 2 and 3 introduced the phonological processes involved in reading—that is, speech as a mediator of word recognition. In subsequent chapters, the case that speech mechanisms are critical in reading is elaborated. The important point at this juncture is that Vygotsky also made the case that the development of problem-solving skills involving speech occurs in interactions with others. According to the Soviets, the problem-solving dialogues that young children and adults engage in are internalized. From this perspective, there is very good reason for adults and children to spend time in verbal interaction around problems that are difficult for children.

3. At several points in this chapter, research has been reported in which parents are taught how to interact with their children so that parent–child interactions are healthier and more productive. Even brief interventions produce dramatic shifts in these studies. This work makes clear that parent–child interactions have a plasticity about them: parents who are not appropriately responsive to their children can learn to be more responsive. This also anticipates a theme that is reiterated throughout this book: some adult–child interactions are

more likely to promote the cognitive development of children than others. For example, an important characteristic of effective parent–child interactions that has been emphasized in this chapter is that the input must be at an appropriate level for the child. In healthy interactions, the adult does not demand too much or too little, but rather supports the child who is working on new competencies. This observation is consistent with a recurrent theme in the motivation literature that people are most motivated when they must try if they are to succeed, but if they try, the goal must not be so distant that it cannot be achieved. It is very motivating to be working at the boundary of one's competence: when this happens, competence expands. This is a point that has been reiterated repeatedly by theorists studying human motivation (e.g., White, 1959). It will come up again as the nature of effective reading instruction is explored further in the chapters that follow, especially in Chapter 8.

4. That natural parent–child interactions alone are typically not enough to prepare the child for success at beginning reading comes through especially clearly in the research on phonemic awareness. More positively, a great deal has been learned about how adults can interact with children in order to develop phonemic awareness in children—and it is not by just immersing children in reading and writing and things literate. Rather, it is through instruction that makes sense in light of our understanding of phonemic awareness that has been developed through careful research.

REFERENCES

Adams, M. J. (1990). *Beginning to read.* Cambridge, MA: Harvard University Press.

Ainsworth, M. D. S. (1967). *Infancy in Uganda: Infant care and the growth of love.* Baltimore: Johns Hopkins University Press.

Applebee, A. N., & Langer, J. A. (1983). Instructional scaffolding: Reading and writing as natural language activities. *Language Arts, 60,* 168–175.

Arnold, D. H., Lonigan, C. J., Whitehurst, G. J., & Epstein, J. N. (1994). Accelerating language development through picture book reading: Replication and extension to a videotape training format. *Journal of Educational Psychology, 86,* 235–243.

Baker, L., Sonnenschein, S., Serpell, R., Fernandez-Fein, S., & Scher, D. (1994). *Contexts of emergent literacy: Everyday home experiences of urban pre-kindergarten children* (Reading Research Report No. 24). Athens, GA, and College Park, MD: National Reading Research Center.

Ball, E. W., & Blachman, B. A. (1988). Phoneme segmentation training: Effect on reading readiness. *Annals of Dyslexia, 38,* 203–225.

Ball, E. W., & Blachman, B. A. (1991). Does phoneme segmentation training in kindergarten make a difference in early word recognition and developmental spelling? *Reading Research Quarterly, 26,* 49–66.

Barker, T. A., & Torgesen, J. K. (1995). The evaluation of computer-assisted instruction in phonological awareness with below average readers. *Journal of Educational Computing Research, 13,* 89–103.

Belsky, J., Rosenberger, K., & Crnic, K. (1995). The origins of attachment security: "Classical" and contextual determinants. In S. Goldberg, R. Muir, & J. Kerr (Eds.), *Attachment theory: Social, developmental, and clinical perspectives* (pp. 153–183). Hillsdale, NJ: Analytic Press.

Bernstein, B. (1965). *Class, codes, and control: Vol. 1. Theoretical studies toward a sociology of language.* London: Routledge & Kegan Paul.

Blachman, B. A. (1991). Phonological awareness: Implications for prereading and early reading instruction. In S. A. Brady & D. P. Shankweiler (Eds.), *Phonological processes in literacy: A tribute to Isabelle Y. Liberman* (pp. 29–36). Hillsdale, NJ: Erlbaum.

Blachman, B., Ball, E., Black, R., & Tangel, D. (1994). Kindergarten teachers develop phoneme awareness in low-income, inner-city classrooms: Does it make a difference? *Reading and Writing, 6,* 1–17.

Borkowski, J. G., & Dukewich, T. L. (1996). Environmental covariations and intelligence: How attachment influences self-regulation. In D. K. Detterman (Ed.), *Current topics in human intelligence: Vol. 5. The environment* (pp. 3–15). Norwood, NJ: Ablex.

Bowey, J. A. (1995). Socioeconomic status differences in preschool phonological sensitivity and first-grade reading achievement. *Journal of Educational Psychology, 87,* 476–487.

Bowlby, J. (1969). *Attachment and loss: Vol. 1. Attachment.* New York: Basic Books.

Bradley, L. (1989). Predicting learning disabilities. In J. Dumont & H. Nakken (Eds.), *Learning disabilities: Vol. 2. Cognitive, social, and remedial aspects* (pp. 1–18). Amsterdam, The Netherlands: Swets.

Bradley, L., & Bryant, P. E. (1983). Categorizing sounds and learning to read—a causal connection. *Nature, 301,* 419–421.

Bradley, L., & Bryant, P. (1985). *Rhyme and reason in reading and spelling* (International Academy for Research in Learning Disabilities Series). Ann Arbor: University of Michigan Press.

Bradley, L., & Bryant, P. (1991). Phonological skills before and after learning to read. In S. A. Brady & D. P. Shankweiler (Eds.), *Phonological processes in literacy: A tribute to Isabelle Y. Liberman* (pp. 37–45). Hillsdale, NJ: Erlbaum.

Briggs, C., & Elkind, D. (1973). Cognitive development in early readers. *Developmental Psychology, 9,* 279–280.

Bus, A. G. (1993). Attachment and emergent literacy. *International Journal of Educational Research, 19,* 573–581.

Bus, A. G. (1994). The role of social context in emergent literacy. In E. M. H. Assink (Ed.), *Literacy acquisition and social context* (pp. 9–24). New York: Harvester Wheatsheaf.

Bus, A. G., & van IJzendoorn, M. H. (1988). Mother–child interactions, attachment, and emergent literacy: A cross-sectional study. *Child Development, 59,* 1262–1272.

Bus, A. G., & van IJzendoorn, M. H. (1992). Patterns of attachment in frequently and infrequently reading mother–child dyads. *Journal of Genetic Psychology, 153,* 395–403.

Bus, A. G., & van IJzendoorn, M. H. (1995). Mothers reading to their 3-year-olds: The role of mother–child attachment security in becoming literate. *Reading Research Quarterly, 30,* 998–1015.

Bus, A. G., van IJzendoorn, M. H., & Pellegrini, A. D. (1995). Joint book reading makes for success in learning to read: A meta-analysis on intergenerational transmission of literacy. *Review of Educational Research, 65,* 1–21.

Byrne, B., & Fielding-Barnsley, R. (1991). Evaluation of a program to teach phonemic awareness to young children. *Journal of Educational Psychology, 83,* 451–455.

Byrne, B., & Fielding-Barnsley, R. (1993). Evaluation of a program to teach phonemic awareness to young children: A 1-year follow-up. *Journal of Educational Psychology, 85,* 104–111.

Byrne, B., & Fielding-Barnsley, R. (1995). Evaluation of a program to teach phonemic awareness to young children: A 2- and 3-year followup and a new preschool trial. *Journal of Educational Psychology, 87,* 488–503.

Castle, J. M., Riach, J., & Nicholson, T. (1994). Getting off to a better start in reading and spelling: The effects of phonemic awareness instruction within a whole language program. *Journal of Educational Psychology, 86,* 350–359.

Chess, S., & Thomas, A. (1987). *Origins and evolution of behavior disorders: From infancy to early adult life.* Cambridge, MA: Harvard University Press.

Clark, M. M. (1976). *Young fluent readers: What can they teach us?* London: Heinemann.

Clay, M. M. (1966). *Emergent reading behavior.* Unpublished doctoral dissertation. University of Auckland, NZ.

Clay, M. M. (1967). The reading behavior of five-year-old children: A research report. *New Zealand Journal of Educational Studies, 2,* 11–31.

Cochran-Smith, M. (1984). *The making of a reader.* Norwood, NJ: Ablex.

Cox, B. E. (1994). Young children's regulatory talk: Evidence of emerging metacognitive control over literary products and processes. *Reading and Writing Quarterly, 10.*

Crain-Thoreson, C., & Dale, P. S. (1992). Do early talkers become early readers? Linguistic precocity, preschool language, and emergent literacy. *Developmental Psychology, 28,* 421–429.

Crain-Thoresen, C., & Dale, P. S. (1995, April). *Parent vs. staff storybook reading as an intervention for language delay.* Paper presented at the biennial meeting of the Society for Research in Child Development, Indianapolis.

Cunningham, A. E. (1990). Explicit versus implicit instruction in phonemic awareness. *Journal of Experimental Child Psychology, 50,* 429–444.

DeLoache, J. S., & DeMendoza, O. A. P. (1987). Joint picturebook interactions of mothers and 1-year-old children. *British Journal of Developmental Psychology, 5,* 111–123.

Dickinson, D. K., & Smith, M. W. (1994). Long-term effects of preschool teachers' book readings on low-income children's vocabulary and story comprehension. *Reading Research Quarterly, 29,* 104–122.

Dunning, D. B., Mason, J. M., & Stewart, J. P. (1994). Reading to preschoolers: A response to Scarborough & Dobrich (1994) and recommendations for future research. *Developmental Review, 14,* 324–339.

Durkin, D. (1966). *Children who read early.* New York: Teachers College Press.

Engel, S. (1986). *Learning to reminisce: A developmental study of how young children talk about the past.* Unpublished PhD dissertation, Graduate Center, City University of New York, New York.

Erikson, E. (1968). *Identity: Youth and crisis.* New York: Norton.

Fagot, B. I., & Kavanaugh, K. (1993). Parenting during the second year: Effects of children's age, sex, and attachment classification. *Child Development, 64,* 258–271.

Flood, J. (1977). Parental styles in reading episodes with young children. *Reading Teacher, 30,* 864–867.

Foster, K. C., Erickson, G. C., Foster, D. F., Brinkman, D., & Torgesen, J. K. (1994). Computer administered instruction in phonological awareness: Evaluation of the *DaisyQuest* program. *Journal of Research and Development in Education, 27,* 126–137.

Frankel, K. A., & Bates, J. E. (1990). Mother–toddler problem-solving: Antecedents in attachment, home behavior, and temperament. *Child Development, 61,* 810–19.

Goswami, U., & Bryant, P. E. (1990). *Phonological skills and learning to read.* Hillsdale, NJ: Erlbaum.

Griffith, P. L. (1991). Phonemic awareness helps first graders invent spellings and third graders remember correct spellings. *Journal of Reading Behavior, 23,* 215–233.

Hart, B., & Risley, T. R. (1995). *Meaningful differences in the everyday experience of young American children.* Baltimore: Brookes.

Heath, S. B. (1982). What no bedtime story means: Narrative skills at home and school. *Language in Society, 11,* 49–76.

Hudson, J. A. (1990). Constructive processing in children's event memory. *Developmental Psychology, 26,* 180–187.

Juel, C. (1988). Learning to read and write: A longitudinal study of 54 children from first through fourth grades. *Journal of Educational Psychology, 80,* 417–447.

Juel, C., Griffith, P. L., & Gough, P. B. (1986). Acquisition of literacy: A longitudinal study of children in first and second grade. *Journal of Educational Psychology, 78,* 243–255.

King, E. M., & Friesen, D. T. (1972). Children who read in kindergarten. *Alberta Journal of Educational Research, 18,* 147–161.

Kohlberg, L., Yaeger, J., & Hjertholm, E. (1968). Private speech: Four studies and a review of theories. *Child Development, 39,* 691–736.

Leichter, H. P. (1984). Families as environments for literacy. In H. Goelman, A. Oberg, & F. Smith (Eds.), *Awakening to literacy.* Exeter, NH: Heinemann.

Lie, A. (1991). Effects of a training program for stimulating skills in word analysis in first-grade children. *Reading Research Quarterly, 26,* 234–250.

Lonigan, C. J. (1994). Reading to preschoolers exposed: Is the emperor really naked? *Developmental Review, 14,* 303–323.

Lonigan, C. J., Anthony, J. L., & Burgess, S. R. (1995, April). *Exposure to print and preschool-age children's interest in literacy.* Paper presented at the biennial meeting of the Society for Research in Child Development, Indianapolis.

Lundberg, I. (1991). Phonemic awareness can be developed without reading instruction. In S. A. Brady & D. P. Shankweiler (Eds.), *Phonological processes in literacy: A tribute to Isabelle Y. Liberman* (pp. 47–53). Hillsdale, NJ: Erlbaum.

Lundberg, I., Frost, J., & Peterson, O. (1988). Effects of an extensive program for stimulating phonological awareness in preschool children. *Reading Research Quarterly, 23,* 263–284.

Maclean, M., Bryant, P., & Bradley, L. (1987). Rhymes, nursery rhymes,, and reading in early childhood. *Merrill–Palmer Quarterly, 33,* 255–281.

Main, M., Kaplan, N., & Cassidy, J. (1985). Security in infancy, childhood, and adulthood: A move to the level of representation. In I. Bretherton & E. Waters (Eds.), Growing points of attachment theory and research. *Monographs of the Society for Research in Child Development, 50* (1–2, Serial No. 209), 66–104.

Matas, L., Arend, R. A., & Sroufe, L. A. (1978). Continuity of adaptation in the second year: The relationship between quality of attachment and later competence. *Child Development, 49,* 547–556.

Morrow, L. M. (1983). Home and school correlates of early interest in literature. *Journal of Educational Research, 76,* 221–230.

Morrow, L. M. (1997). *Literacy development in the early years: Helping children read and write* (3rd ed.). Englewood Cliffs, NJ: Prentice-Hall.

Moss, E. (1992). The socioaffective context of joint cognitive activity. In L. T. Winegar & J. Valsiner (Eds.), *Children's development within social context: Vol. 2. Research and methodology* (pp. 117–154). Hillsdale, NJ: Erlbaum.

Murray, B. A. (1995, December). *A meta-analysis of phoneme awareness teaching studies.* Paper presented at the National Reading Conference, New Orleans.

Näslund, J. C., & Schneider, W. (1996). Kindergarten letter knowledge, phonological skills, and memory processes: Relative effects on early literacy. *Journal of Experimental Child Psychology, 62,* 30–59.

Nation, K., & Hulme, C. (1997). Phonemic segmentation, not onset-rime segmentation, predicts early reading and spelling skills. *Reading Research Quarterly, 32,* 154–167.

Nelson, K. (1993a). Events, narratives, and memory: What develops? In C. A. Nelson (Ed.), *Memory and affect in development: Minnesota symposium on child psychology* (Vol. 26, pp. 1–24). Hillsdale, NJ: Erlbaum.

Nelson, K. (1993b). Explaining the emergence of autobiographical memory in early childhood. In A. F. Collins, S. E. Gathercole, M. A. Conway, & P. E. Morris (Eds.), *Theories of memory* (pp. 355–385). Hillsdale, NJ: Erlbaum.

Nelson, K. (1996). *Language in cognitive development: The emergence of the mediated mind.* New York: Cambridge University Press.

Neuman, S. B., & Roskos, K. (1997). Literacy knowledge in practice: Contexts of participation for young writers and readers. *Reading Research Quarterly, 32,* 10–32.

Ninio, A. (1980). Picture-book reading in mother–infant dyads belonging to two subgroups in Israel. *Child Development, 51,* 587–590.

O'Connor, R. E., Jenkins, J. R., & Slocum, T. A. (1995). Transfer among phonological tasks in kindergarten: Essential instructional content. *Journal of Educational Psychology, 87,* 202–217.

Pellegrini, A. D., Galda, L., Perlmutter, J., & Jones, I. (1994). *Joint reading between mothers and their head start children: Vocabulary development in two text formats* (Reading Research Report No. 13). Athens, GA, and College Park, MD: National Reading Research Center.

Pellegrini, A. D., Perlmutter, J. C., Galda, L., & Brody, G. H. (1990). Joint reading between black Head-Start children and their mothers. *Child Development, 61,* 443–453.

Pennington, B. F., Groisser, D., & Welsh, M. C. (1993). Contrasting cognitive deficits in attention deficit hyperactivity disorder versus reading disability. *Developmental Psychology, 29,* 511–523.

Perfetti, C. A. (1992). The representation problem in reading acquisition. In P. B. Gough, L. C. Ehri, & R. Treiman (Eds.), *Reading acquisition* (pp. 145–174). Hillsdale, NJ: Erlbaum.

Perfetti, C. A., Beck, I., Bell, L., & Hughes, C. (1987). Phonemic knowledge and learning to read are reciprocal: A longitudinal study of first grade children. *Merrill–Palmer Quarterly, 33,* 283–319.

Pillemer, D. B., & White, S. H. (1989). Childhood events recalled by children and adults. In H. W. Reese (Ed.), *Advances in child development and behavior* (Vol. 21, pp. 297–340). San Diego, CA: Academic Press.

Plessas, G. P., & Oakes, C. R. (1964). Prereading experiences of selected early readers. *Reading Teacher, 17,* 241–245.

Pratt, A. C., & Brady, S. (1988). Relation of phonological awareness to reading disability in children and adults. *Journal of Educational Psychology, 80,* 319–323.

Ratner, H. H. (1980). The role of social context in memory development. In M. Perlmutter (Ed.), *Children's memory: New directions for child development* (Vol. 10). San Francisco: Jossey-Bass.

Ratner, H. H. (1984). Memory demands and the development of young children's memory. *Child Development, 55,* 2173–2191.

Reese, E., Haden, C., & Fivush, R. (1993). Mother–child conversations about the past: Relations of style and memory over time. *Cognitive Development, 8,* 141–148.

Roser, N., & Martinez, M. (1985). Roles adults play in preschool responses to literature. *Language Arts, 62,* 485–490.

Scarborough, H. S., & Dobrich, W. (1994). On the efficiency of reading to preschoolers. *Developmental Review, 14,* 245–302.

Schaffer, H. R., & Emerson, P. E. (1964). Patterns of response to physical contact in early human behavior. *Journal of Child Psychology and Psychiatry, 5,* 1–13.

Shaywitz, S. E. (1996). Dyslexia. *Scientific American, 275*(5), 98–104.

Slocum, T. A., O'Connor, R. E., & Jenkins, J. R. (1993). Transfer among phonological manipulation skills. *Journal of Educational Psychology, 85,* 618–630.

Snow, C. E. (1983). Literacy and language: Relationships during the preschool years. *Harvard Educational Review, 53,* 165–189.

Snow, C. E. (1991). The theoretical basis of the Home-School Study of Language and Literacy Development. *Journal of Research in Childhood Education, 6,* 1–8.

Sokolov, A. N. (1975). *Inner speech and thought.* New York: Plenum.

Sonnenschein, S., Baker, L., Serpell, R., Scher, D., Fernandez-Fein, S., & Munsterman, K. A. (1996). *Strands of emergent literacy and their antecedents in the home: Urban preschoolers' early literacy development* (Reading Research Report No. 48). Athens, GA, and College Park, MD: National Reading Research Center.

Sroufe, L. A. (1996). *Emotional development: The organization of emotional life in the early years.* Cambridge, England: Cambridge University Press.

Stahl, S. A., & Murray, B. A. (1994). Defining phonological awareness and its relationship to early reading. *Journal of Educational Psychology, 86,* 221–234.

Stahl, S. A., & Murray, B. A. (in press). Issues involved in defining phonological awareness and its relation to early reading. In J. Metsala & L. Ehri (Eds.), *Word recognition in beginning reading.* Mahwah, NJ: Erlbaum.

Stanovich, K. E. (1986). Matthew effects in reading: Some consequences of individual differences in the acquisition of literacy. *Reading Research Quarterly, 21,* 360–407.

Stanovich, K. E. (1988). Explaining the differences between the dyslexic and the garden-variety poor reader: The phonological-core variable-difference model. *Journal of Learning Disabilities, 21,* 590–604.

Stuart, M., & Masterson, J. (1992). Patterns of reading and spelling in 10-year-old children related to prereading phonological abilities. *Journal of Experimental Child Psychology, 54,* 168–187.

Sulzby, E., & Teale, W. (1987). *Young children's storybook reading: Longitudinal study of parent–child instruction and children's independent functioning* (Final Report to the Spencer Foundation). Ann Arbor: University of Michigan Press.

Sulzby, E., & Teale, W. (1991). Emergent literacy. In R. Barr, M. L. Kamil, P. B. Mosenthal, & P. D. Pearson (Eds.), *Handbook of reading research* (Vol. 2, pp. 727–758). New York: Longman.

Tangel, D. M., & Blachman, B. A. (1992). Effect of phoneme awareness instruction on kindergarten children's invented spellings. *Journal of Reading Behavior, 24,* 233–261.

Tangel, D. M., & Blachman, B. A. (1995). Effect of phoneme awareness instruction on the invented spelling of first-grade children: A one-year follow-up. *Journal of Reading Behavior, 27,* 153–185.

Taylor, D., & Strickland, D. (1986). *Family storybook reading.* Exeter, NH: Heinemann.

Teale, W. H. (1978). Positive environments for learning to read: What studies of early readers tell us. *Language Arts, 55,* 922–932.

Tessler, M. (1986). *Mother–child talk in a museum: The socialization of a memory.* New York: City University of New York, Graduate Center.

Thomas, A., & Chess, S. (1986). The New York longitudinal study: From infancy to early adult life. In R. Plomin & J. Dunn (Eds.), *The study of temperament: Changes, continuities, and challenges.* Hillsdale, NJ: Erlbaum.

Torgesen, J. K., & Burgess, S. R. (in press). Consistency of reading-related phonological processes throughout early childhood. In J. Metsala & L. Ehri (Eds.), *Word recognition in beginning reading*. Mahwah, NJ: Erlbaum.

Torgesen, J. K., Wagner, R. K., Rashotte, C. A., Burgess, S., & Hecht, S. (1997). Contributions of phonological awareness and rapid automatic naming ability to the growth of word-reading skills in second- and fifth-grade children. *Scientific Studies of Reading, 1,* 151–185.

Valdez-Menchaca, M. C., & Whitehurst, G. J. (1992). Accelerating language development through picture book reading: A systematic extension to Mexican day care. *Developmental Psychology, 28,* 1106–1114.

van den Boom, D. C. (1994). The influence of temperament and mothering on attachment and exploration: An experimental manipulation of sensitive responsiveness among lower-class mothers and irritable infants. *Child Development, 65,* 1457–1477.

van den Boom, D. C. (1995). Do first-year intervention effects endure? Follow-up during toddlerhood of a sample of Dutch irritable infants. *Child Development, 66,* 1798–1816.

van IJzendoorn, M. H., Juffer, F., & Duyvesteyn, M. G. C. (1995). Breaking the intergenerational cycle of insecure attachment: A review of the effects of attachment-based interventions on maternal sensitivity and infant security. *Journal of Child Psychology and Psychiatry, 36,* 225–248.

Vellutino, F. R., & Scanlon, D. M. (1987). Phonological coding, phonological awareness, and reading ability: Evidence from a longitudinal and experimental study. *Merrill–Palmer Quarterly, 33,* 321–363.

Vygotsky, L. S. (1962). *Thought and language.* Cambridge, MA: MIT Press.

Vygotsky, L. S. (1978). *Mind in society: The development of higher psychological processes.* Cambridge, MA: Harvard University Press.

Wagner, R. K., Torgesen, J. K., Laughon, P., Simmons, K., & Rashotte, C. A. (1993). Development of young readers' phonological processing abilities. *Journal of Educational Psychology, 85,* 83–103.

Wagner, R. K., Torgesen, J. K., & Rashotte, C. A. (1994). The development of reading-related phonological processing abilities: New evidence of bi-directional causality from a latent variable longitudinal study. *Developmental Psychology, 30,* 73–87.

Wagner, R. K., Torgesen, J. K., Rashotte, C. A., Hecht, S. A., Barker, T. A., Burgess, S. R., Donahue, J., & Garon, T. (1997). Changing causal relations between phonological processing abilities and word-level reading as children develop from beginning to fluent readers: A five-year longitudinal study. *Developmental Psychology, 33,* 468–479.

White, R. W. (1959). Motivation reconsidered: The concept of competence. *Psychological Review, 66,* 297–333.

Whitehurst, G. J., Epstein, J. N., Angell, A. L., Payne, A. C., Crone, D. A., & Fischel, J. E. (1994). Outcomes of an emergent literacy intervention in Head Start. *Journal of Educational Psychology, 86,* 542–555.

Whitehurst, G. J., Falco, F. L., Lonigan, C. J., Fischel, J. E., DeBaryshe, B. D., Valdez-Menchaca, M. C., & Caulfield, M. (1988). Accelerating language development through picturebook reading. *Developmental Psychology, 24,* 552–559.

Williams, J. P. (1980). Teaching decoding with an emphasis on phoneme analysis and phoneme blending. *Journal of Educational Psychology, 72,* 1–15.

Wimmer, H., Landerl, K., Linortner, R., & Hummer, P. (1991). The relationship of phonemic awareness to reading acquisition: More consequence than precondition but still important. *Cognition, 40,* 219–249.

Wise, B. W., & Olson, R. K. (1995). Computer-based phonological awareness and reading instruction. *Annals of Dyslexia, 45,* 99–122.

Wood, S. S., Bruner, J. S., & Ross, G. (1976). The role of tutoring in problem solving. *Journal of Child Psychology and Psychiatry, 17,* 89–100.

Yopp, H. K. (1995). Read-aloud books for developing phonemic awareness: An annotated bibliography. *Reading Teacher, 48*(6), 538–543.

5

◄○►

THE DEVELOPMENT OF LITERACY, Part 2

Learning to Recognize Words

In this chapter I take up a topic that is at the center of the current debate about beginning reading instruction and has been the focal point of debates about beginning reading for a very long time (Chall, 1967): How should children be taught to recognize words as part of beginning reading instruction? For readers who have read Jeanne Chall's classic, *Learning to Read: The Great Debate,* there will be a sense of *déjà vu* about much of this chapter, for in general, Chall's conclusions from that book have endured. Today, more than ever, there is support for Chall's endorsement of code-emphasis (i.e., phonics-instructional) approaches to beginning reading over meaning-emphasis approaches, such as forms of whole language that play down the need for explicit (i.e., synthetic, systematic) decoding instruction. A great deal of research has taken place since Chall's book first appeared in 1967, and even since its update (Chall, 1983), with much of it supportive of Chall's positions. (For example, recall the word-level research reviewed in Chapter 2, documenting that very good readers sound out words, and the work reviewed in Chapter 3, making clear that for many struggling, beginning readers, their problem is that they cannot sound out words.) To be sure, new understanding has emerged from research since 1967, but I contend that most of those new findings are compatible with Chall's (1967) conclusions.

Nonetheless, many teachers identifying with the whole language approach have resisted explicit, systematic teaching of decoding. I believe that one reason this is so is that they have been convinced through the prominent whole language texts (see Chapter 1) that recognition of words is not as Chall depicted it. Perhaps the main motivation for this chapter is to inform the teaching community about the types of word-recognition instruction that are supported by research evidence.

In this chapter, I review first the progress made in understanding the developmental progression from not being able to read words at all to skillful reading of words. The remainder of the chapter is organized around the two main approaches to teaching word recognition that have been most supported in scientific analyses to date: teaching students to sound out words and teaching them to decode new words by analogy to words they already know—that is, by using familiar parts of words, parts of words encountered in other words they already know. I believe that these approaches are complementary. The evidence in support of these two approaches contrasts with the lack of support for word recognition which is focused more on semantic–contextual cues than graphemic–phonemic cues, the approach to word recognition favored in the whole-language texts reviewed in Chapter 1.

NATURAL DEVELOPMENT OF WORD RECOGNITION SKILLS

There is more than one way to recognize a word (see Ehri, 1991, which informs much of what follows, for elaborate discussion of this point), with some more sophisticated than others. In general, the more sophisticated a word recognition process, the later it appears in children's development of word recognition skills.

Logographic Reading

Many American 3-year-olds can "read" the trademark signs for McDonald's, Burger King, and Dunkin' Donuts. They are doing logographic reading (sometimes referred to as visual cue reading; e.g., Ehri, 1991), which involves using only salient visual characteristics of a display that includes a word to recognize the word rather than relying on letter–sound correspondences. There is an association for these children between the distinctive visual cue and the word. Thus, this generation of children often can read the word "Apple" on a computer or the same word on television when it is accompanied by the company's multicolored apple with a bite out of it; the word *Jell-O* has a memorable shape; *STOP* is read correctly by some children so long as it is in the middle of a red hexagon; many 5-year-olds can read the words *SCHOOL BUS* on the back of a large, yellow vehicle; and what 4- to 5-year-old has trouble decoding Disney's signature, even though it is written in script?

University of Texas psychologist Phil Gough (reported in Gough, Juel, & Griffith, 1992) presented 4- to 5-year-olds with four words to read, one on each of four flashcards. One of the flashcards had a blue thumbprint on it. The participants went through the deck of cards until they could say each word given its card. Then, came the interesting part. Could the children say the word that had been presented with the blue thumbprint if they were shown the word on a clean card devoid of the thumbprint? No. Could they say the word if they were shown just the blue thumb print? Yes. Gough et al. (1992) refer to this as selective association, which is another name for logographic reading or visual cue reading. Regardless of what it is called, it is the same process, and preschoolers typically can do it.

Although logographic reading is not real reading, it may play a role in facilitating real reading later on. Cronin, Farrell, and Delaney (1995) had children attempt to read logographs in context (e.g., "McDonald's" in the context of its logo, "Stop" on a stop sign). Some logos could be read by the children while others could not (e.g., "Zellers" on the Zellers sign). Then, the children were taught the same words as sight words. In general, words that children could read in the context of a logo were learned more quickly than words not read in the context of a logo. There were a variety of controls in the study, which led to the conclusion that learning to read a word in the context of a logo permitted transfer to learning to read the word outside of its logo context. Something was learned by the preschoolers in Cronin et al. (1995) about the words per se on logos!

Alphabetic Reading

Traditional decoding instruction emphasizes sounding out words using letter–sound relations. This mechanism is operative in both reading and writing well before the time when children know *all* of the letter–sound correspondences (e.g., Ehri & Wilce, 1985; Huba, 1984). For example, preschoolers who know some letter–sound correspondences use what they know to attempt invented spellings of familiar words. When readers know some letter–sound relationships, they also are capable of doing what Ehri (1991) refers to as phonetic cue reading, which is "reading" a word based on only a few of its letters. Ehri (1991) contrasts such phonetic cue reading with logographic reading using the following example:

> Logographic readers might remember how to read *yellow* by the "two sticks" in the middle (Seymour & Elder, 1986). In contrast, phonetic cue readers might see the two l's in *yellow*, hear their name in the pronunciation, and use this information to connect the spelling to the word in memory. (p. 391)

To be certain, however, such reading has its hazards. If the same letter cues are used for several words or if a cue used to decode some word is experienced in a new word, there may be mix-ups. For example, it is not uncommon for a child to misread a word as another similar word that is known to the child sharing common letters (e.g., *yellow* read for *pillow*; Ehri's [1991] interpretation of Seymour & Elder's [1986] data; Ehri & Wilce, 1987a, 1987b). And, of course, phonetic cue readers have a devil of a time if asked to learn a set of words that share letters (e.g., *pots, post, spot, stop*; Gilbert, Spring, & Sassenrath, 1977).

At some point after phonetic cue reading begins, a child comes to understand the alphabetic principle—"that all twenty-six of those strange little symbols that comprise the alphabet are worth learning and discriminating one from the other because [they stand] for . . . the sounds that occur in spoken words" (Adams, 1990, p. 245). Once this realization occurs, there are a number of specific decoding "rules" that must be acquired if the child is to read using the complete alphabet. Some are easy, for they require learning only one piece of information: The letter *b* is pronounced the same regardless of context, as are *d, f, l, n, r, v,* and *z*. Some letters are pronounced differently depending on other letters in the word; the most common example is that vowels are long if there is a final *e* in a syllable and short if there is not. Another example is that *c* is pronounced differently if followed by an *e* or an *i* than if followed by an *a, o,* or *u* (e.g., compare the pronounciation of the *c* sounds in *celestial, city, cat, cot,* and *cut*). In general, conditional rules (i.e., involving consideration of more than one letter to determine the sound of a particular letter) are acquired later than rules involving one letter–sound association (e.g., Venezky & Johnson, 1973). Eventually, young readers learn all of the letter–sound relationships, although there is much complex information to acquire (e.g., Gough et al., 1992):

> For only a minority of the letters (*b, d, f, l, n, r, v, z*) is it possible to identify the [sound] it represents. For the other 18, at least one additional letter must be identified before the identity of the word's first [sound] can be determined; in some cases, at least four more

letters are required (compare *chord* and *chore*). The vast majority of the letter–sound correspondences of . . . English . . . are context dependent. (Gough et al., 1992, p. 39)

In addition to learning the letter–sound associations, the beginning reader must learn how to use them to decode words, mapping the individual sounds represented by the letters of a word and blending the sounds. At first, such reading is only accomplished with very great effort. Indeed, it is a matter of years before it becomes very fluent and effortless. Long before that, however, individual words can be identified with relatively little effort.

Sight-Word Reading

I doubt that anyone reading this text has had to sound out a single word in this chapter, except perhaps for unfamiliar proper names such as Ehri. Every word in this text is in readers' sight vocabularies. There probably was a time, however, when you would have sounded out each and every word in this chapter. Conducting many trials of successfully sounding out a word, however, increases the connections between the letter patterns defining the word and the word in memory (Adams, 1990, Chap. 9; Ehri, 1980, 1984, 1987, 1992).

Thus, on initial exposure to a word like *frog*, a child sounds the word out. Such sounding out begins a process in which the connections between each letter and adjacent letters are strengthened (e.g., between *fr* and *og*) as are connections defining the entire sequence of letters and letter combinations in the word (strengthening of the connection between *fr* and *og*). Eventually the spelling is represented in memory as a unit consisting of *frog*. By repeated reading, there is also a strengthening of the connections between this visual stimulus and the conceptual understanding in long-term memory that defines a frog, so that eventually even the briefest exposure to the word *frog* elicits thoughts of a green, jumpy thing. For many beginning readers, there is rapid sight-word development of commonly encountered words.

Reading by Analogy to Known Words

Eventually, letter strings that occur in many different words are perceived as wholes (e.g., repeated co-occurrence of *i*, *n*, and *g* results eventually in *-ing* being perceived as a unit; Stanovich & West, 1989). Prefixes and suffixes are obvious examples, but there are other recurring combinations, many of which are root words (e.g., *-take*, *mal-*, *ben-*, *rog-*, *do-*). When such familiar letter patterns are encountered, it is not necessary to decode alphabetically. Rather, there is a direct connection with the sound sequence in memory.

When words can be read by sight and recurring letter chunks can be processed as wholes, what LaBerge and Samuels (1974; also Samuels, Schermer, & Reinking, 1992) dubbed as automatic reading, there are tremendous advantages for the reader. According to automaticity theory, two processes must occur for a reader to understand a word: (1) The word must be decoded, and (2) what is decoded must be comprehended. Both decoding and comprehension require use of short-term memory, that extremely limited resource that can be thought of as one's conscious attentional capacity. With only 7 ± 2 slots in short-term memory (at best), decoding operations and comprehension processes compete for only a little bit of capacity.

Alphabetic decoding requires a great deal of attention on the part of the reader. Walk into many grade-1 classrooms on any morning, and there will be children during round-robin reading who will have all of their mental energy and attention devoted to the task of sounding out the words when it is their turn to read. If all of their attentional capacity is consumed by decoding, there is nothing left over for comprehension. The result is that the word may be pronounced but not understood. One solution for the slow alphabetic decoder might be to decode first and then comprehend. The cost of this is enormous: Because decoding and comprehending are done in sequence, the phonological representation of the word must be held in short-term memory, which involves further reduction of capacity that is needed for comprehension. No matter how the alphabetic reader approaches the task, there is strain on short-term capacity.

Automatic sight-word reading and automatic recognition of commonly encountered word chunks (e.g., prefixes, suffixes, root words, frequently encountered combinations of letters such as *-ake* and *-op*), in contrast, require little effort or attention and thus, there is substantial mental capacity left over for comprehension (e.g., Baron, 1977). With experience in reading comes faster, more accurate, and less effortful reading (e.g., Horn & Manis, 1987). A paradox of slow, high-effort, alphabetic reading is that it is less certain to result in accurate decoding than fast, low-effort, automatic decoding via sight words and word chunks.

Once readers know a variety of word chunks, they are in a position to exploit the principle that words with the same spelling pattern often sound the same. Thus, a child who knows how to pronounce *beak* could make a good guess at *peak* the first time it is encountered simply by decoding by analogy (i.e., This is like *beak* only it starts with a *p*!). That same *beak*-word knower would have a fighting chance with *bean, bead,* and *beat* as well, using the analogy strategy. Adams (1990, pp. 210–211) provides the example of good readers quickly pronouncing the word *kail* to rhyme with *ail, bail, tail, Gail,* and *hail.* Each time a word with *-ail* in it is encountered and pronounced with the long *a* sound, the association between *-ail* and the long *a* sound is strengthened. Thus, when *kail* is encountered by someone who has had many exposures to the *-ail* and long *a* association, there is automatic activation of *kail* and the word is pronounced correctly almost without thinking.

For the most part, analogy has been considered an advanced strategy used only by adults or by children who have been reading awhile, with Australian researcher Herbert Marsh and his colleagues especially strong advocates of this position (e.g., Marsh, Desberg, & Cooper, 1977; Marsh, Friedman, Desberg, & Saterdahl, 1981; Marsh, Friedman, Welch, & Desberg, 1981). The case is made later in this chapter, however, that children can be taught to decode by analogy well before they might do so on their own.

Summary and Comment

There can be little doubt that when immersed in the word of language and print, there is some natural development of children's word reading skills. The holistic and insensitive visual pattern-matching that is logographic reading is only the start of a process that becomes the reading of every single letter and the construction of knowledge about commonly occurring letter patterns. That children naturally learn to sound out words and decode by analogy based on frequently encountered word chunks highlights that the instructional recommendations in this chapter only involve systematic elaboration and intensification of powerful, natural learning processes. When all of the learning to read is left to children's natural discovery of letter–sound associations and development of knowledge of word chunks, however, reading development is slower and less certain than it can be when children are taught to sound out words and/or decode by analogy. That is why the best informed reading researchers and educators focus so much attention on teaching beginning readers to decode, increasingly using the methods detailed in the remainder of this chapter.

TEACHING STUDENTS TO SOUND OUT WORDS

Many children can be taught to decode words by focusing on the sounds associated with individual letters and letter combinations and blending those sounds to produce a reading of the word. Once the word is read, the child will recognize it. Thus, once a child decodes "dog" by sounding it out, the child recognizes a word he or she has been hearing and using for several years. Since the child who is learning to read knows the meaning of many of the words in books appropriate for beginning readers, understanding of the word once it is decoded is likely.

The criticality of phonemic awareness as a beginning-reading competency becomes obvious in the context of the sounding-out strategy. As you will recall from the last chapter, phonemic awareness is the realization that words are composed of sounds. It would make no sense to a child lacking this insight to attend to the letters of a word and attempt to sound it out! That is, before instruction about sounding out a word can make any sense, it is essential that the child understand that words are amalgams of sounds.

In fact, there is research support for the claim that learning to decode depends on phonemic awareness. One study that is cited frequently regarding this point was conducted in Australia by Tunmer, Herriman, and Nesdale (1988) who observed that the first graders who were most certain to make progress in learning to decode were those who possessed phonemic awareness and knew the names of letters. Another frequently cited study making the same point was reported by Fox and Routh (1975), who found that 4-year-olds who could segment words into constituent phonemes benefited from decoding instruction involving the segmentation of words into constituent letters, the mapping of letters to sounds, and the blending of sounds. Four-year-olds who could not segment words into constituent phonemes did not benefit from such decoding instruction.

Beyond phonemic awareness, however, the child who is to sound out words needs to know more. A particularly important prerequisite to acquisition of decoding skills is knowledge of the associations between letters and the sounds they make.

Letter–Sound Associations

There is much that can be taught about letters. In recent generations, something that has been known by many, although not all, young children by the time they enter kindergarten is the names of letters. In part, this is due to intentional educational efforts by our society to teach the alphabet to all preschoolers, perhaps most prominently through *Sesame Street* (e.g., Anderson & Collins, 1988; Ball & Bogatz, 1970; Bogatz & Ball, 1971). In fact, it is now known that *Sesame Street* makes contributions to the development of literacy over and above family interactions and other sources of stimulation (e.g., Rice, Huston, Truglio, & Wright, 1990). The program does much to get preschoolers off to a good start.

Knowing letter names is not sufficient knowledge for learning to decode, however. Learning to analyze a printed word into component sounds followed by blending of those sounds requires knowledge of the letter–sound associations. Young readers need to learn about both the long and short vowel sounds as well as the sounds associated with the consonants. That is, they need to know various ways that *g* can sound when encountered in a word, as well as all the other consonants of the alphabet. Such instruction highlights that some letters sound the same regardless of the letters around them in a word (i.e., *b*, *d*, *l*, *n*, *r*, *v*, and *z* make the same sound regardless of the letter context in which they are embedded). Other letters sound different depending on context, for example, *c* is pronounced differently in *cut* than in *city*. Of course, the long vowel sounds occur when there is a final silent *e* in a syllable but often are short when there is not final *e*. In addition to learning the sounds associated with individual letters, good phonics instruction also covers the consonant digraphs (*sh*, *ch*, *th*, and *wh*) and the common consonant blends (e.g., *dr*, *bl*, *sk*, *sch*, and *tw*). In general, a lot of teaching about consonants and vowels and the sounds they make must take place if children are to learn how to decode words. There is some debate about exactly how many sounds there are in English, with a number between 43 and 46 most typically mentioned.

To be certain, there is a lot for children to learn when they are learning the associations between letters and sounds. The most common way of dealing with the very great memory demand is for the letter–sound associations to be taught over a long period of time, with many repetitions and many examples in the context of exercises and games involving letters and their sounds. (Cunningham, 1995, and Fox, 1996, are filled with suggestions about activities that build knowledge of letter–sound associations.) Of course, such activities are typically in the context of real reading and writing, which also permit many opportunities for use and review of the letter–sound associations.

Some researchers and educators who are aware of the memory demands involved in learning the initial letter–sound associations have gone farther, however. Ehri, Deffner, and Wilce (1984) created a set of pictorial memory aids for learning letter–sound associations (see Figure 5.1). Thus, for each consonant sound, children are presented a mnemonic picture that integrates the physical letter and a word beginning with the sound associated with the letter. Can you see the *h* in the picture of a house in the top portion of Figure 5.1? How about a *v* in the picture of a vase of flowers? I had a little trouble seeing the *y* in yak, but found the picture of a yak with a decidedly y-shaped head to be very memorable. The *w* in the wings of the butterfly took me a second to see at first, but after I figured it out, I almost always think of w when I see butterfly wings—even on real butterflies!! Ditto for the *g* in glasses.

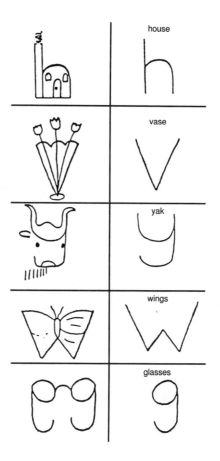

FIGURE 5.1. Mnemonic–pictorial aids for learning letter–sound associations. From Ehri, Deffner, and Wilce (1984). Copyright 1984 by the American Psychological Association. Reprinted by permission.

Ehri et al.'s (1984) approach is based on the well-established fact that even very young children can remember picture mnemonics (Pressley, 1977). Rather than simply assuming that this approach is effective because mnemonics generally work for young children, Ehri et al. (1984) conducted a well-controlled experiment, demonstrating clearly that the picture mnemonics really did increase the rate at which children learned letter–sound associations.

Unfortunately, Ehri et al. (1984) never did make their materials available commercially. Thus, individual classroom teachers who wish to use the picture–mnemonic approach are going to have to produce their own picture mnemonics. I have not tried it, but have talked to some teachers who have, and they tell me that with a little imagination, it is possible to produce memorable mnemonic pictures for all of the letter–sound associations in English.

Learning the letter–sound associations, which confers some intellectual power, is no small achievement. For example, Byrne and Fielding-Barnsley (1990, 1991) determined that preschoolers with phonemic awareness who also knew the letter–sound associations were very adept at decoding unfamiliar words compared to other preschoolers. Even so, there is much to be said for also teaching young readers how to blend the sounds of letters.

Blending Letter–Sound Correspondences

I suspect that as long as there have been teachers teaching students to read, there have been teachers teaching students to analyze words into component sounds and blend the sounds. This instructional approach and its effectiveness is well understood at the end of the 20th century, largely because of a distinguished mid-20th century analysis of beginning reading carried out by Jeanne Chall.

Chall's (1967/1983) Analyses and Summaries

Chall (1967/83) provided detailed original analyses and reviews of other analyses of the effectiveness of beginning reading instruction. One of the major conclusions of her review was that programs that included "synthetic phonics" instruction (sometimes referred to as systematic or explicit phonics instruction), in which the students are systematically taught letter–sound associations and how to blend the sounds made by letters to pronounce and recognize words, were more effective than other programs. There was a great diversity of findings supporting the conclusion that synthetic phonics instruction was more effective than alternatives.

- In reviewing studies dating back to 1912, Chall found evidence that synthetic phonics instruction produced word recognition and oral reading during grade 1 superior to look–say approaches, which emphasize students learning words as wholes rather than learning to decode via phonics. Although vocabulary and comprehension tended to be better in grade 1 with the look–say approach, students receiving synthetic phonics measures did better by the end of grade 2. Although look–say students seemed to read faster than synthetic phonics students, it was at the price of less accuracy.
  - Chall also found studies contrasting synthetic phonics instruc-

tion with what she termed intrinsic phonics instruction (sometimes referred to as analytic or implicit phonics). Intrinsic phonics teaching involves analyzing the sounds of known sight-words, although word analysis is played down in favor of semantic-context and picture cues as means for word recognition. (Notably, intrinsic phonics instruction seems to be closest to the phonics instruction that whole-language theorists claim to do as part of whole language.) Although these comparisons dated back to 1926, in fact, interest in the issue of whether synthetic or intrinsic phonics produced better readers was especially pronounced in the decade preceding Chall's (1967) text, largely because the most popular reading textbook series of the day used an intrinsic phonics approach. (That is what was going on in many classrooms that used Dick-and-Jane readers: Students learned to read whole words; once the whole words were acquired, they were analyzed into constituent sounds as part of instruction.) Studies comparing the intrinsic phonics approach with the synthetic phonics approach produced clear results. Oral word recognition was better for students taught with synthetic phonics than for students taught with intrinsic phonics. Spelling tended to be better for students instructed with systematic phonics, with this superiority holding across the elementary grades. Also, at least during the primary grades, the performance of synthetic phonics students on standardized vocabulary tests exceeded the performance of intrinsic phonics students. Although not quite as pronounced, the same pattern was observed for standardized comprehension.

• In analyzing the studies up through 1965, Chall (1967) found evidence that synthetic phonics was effective relative to alternatives for the broad range of abilities, from low-IQ to high IQ. Synthetic phonics seemed to be especially beneficial for low-IQ students, with Chall speculating that approaches that involve a great deal of induction, such as intrinsic phonics, might be too difficult for low-IQ students.

• In 1965–1966, the U.S. Office of Education conducted the *Comparative First Grade Studies*, which involved 27 comparative studies of the various methods used to teach grade-1 reading. Several analyses of these data resulted in the conclusion that code-based approaches to beginning reading instruction produced primary-grade reading which was superior to than other methods, particularly meaning-based methods of the day—the look–say, intrinsic-phonics approaches (Chall, 1983; Guthrie & Tyler, 1975).

• When Head Start was extended into the elementary grades as Follow Through, a variety of Follow Through models were tried. The outcomes produced by them were then contrasted in formal studies. Variations of Follow Through that included systematic phonics instruction (which involved direct instruction of phonics in a basal instructional program) produced superior performance on primary-level standardized tests than did alternative approaches (Abt Associates, 1977; Kennedy, 1978; Stallings, 1975). Chall (1983) interpreted these results as clear evidence favoring systematic phonics for children who are at risk for school failure because they are living in poverty.

  • Beginning in 1967, a number of laboratory studies of phonics instruction were carried out. In general, the critical dependent variable in these studies was ability to read words not seen before. Both teaching letter–sound associations and teaching of blending proved potent in these comparisons (Chall, 1983, Table I-1, p. 14).

  • From the appearance of *Learning to Read: The Great Debate* (1967) through the publication of the updated edition of the book (1983), there were a number of studies conducted in classrooms explicitly contrasting systematic, direct, synthetic phonics instruction with less systematic, indirect, implicit phonics instruction. Across a variety of measures of word recognition, oral reading, comprehension, vocabulary, and spelling, when there was a difference (and often, there was), it favored direct, synthetic phonics instruction over indirect, intrinsic approaches (Chall, 1983, Table I-2, pp. 18–20).

Adams's (1990) Analysis and Summary

The next really important book appraising the effectiveness of systematic phonics instruction was Marilyn Adams's (1990) *Beginning to Read*. She reviewed Chall's data analyses and conclusions for a new generation of readers. Beyond that, she also reviewed theory and evidence produced since Chall's book that was supportive of the case for systematic decoding instruction. For example, Adams (1990, Chap. 11) reviewed how modern basal programs cover phonics versus how they should do so based on contemporary evidence.

Adams also made the case that explicit decoding instruction is now understood to involve a number of different acquisitions.

  • Adams reviewed the evidence that kindergarten and grade-1 students often need to be taught the alphabetic principle: "one wants the students to understand that all twenty-six of those strange little symbols that comprise the alphabet are worth learning and discriminating one from the other because each stands for one of the sounds that occur in spoken words" (p. 245).

  • Adams established for her readers that students need to learn the physical representation of each letter. That is, they need to acquire the distinctive features of letters (Gibson, Gibson, Pick, & Osser, 1962;

Gibson & Levin, 1975). In doing so, they learn the difference between *P* and *R* as a single feature (i.e., the left-to-right downward diagonal in *R*) as well as the difference between *P* and *B* and *R* and *B* as single features (i.e., there is a fat rightward bulge in the bottom half of *B* that does not occur in *P* or *R*).

• Adams overviewed why students must learn the specific sounds that are associated with each letter and the common letter combinations in English (review Table 5.1), taking up the pros and cons of various orders of teaching the letter–sound correspondences (e.g., short versus long vowels first, consonants before vowels).

• Adams contended that students need much practice in learning to blend sounds, since reading a word consists both of analyzing the letter–sound correspondences and blending those correspondences to pronounce a word.

• Adams reviewed as well the case for teaching phonics rules, such as, "When there are two vowels side by side, the long sound of the first one is heard and the second is usually silent," "Words having double *ee* usually have the long *e* sound," and, "The two letters *ow* make the long *o* sound." She made a compelling case for not relying exclusively on phonics rules: First, none of the rules is entirely reliable, and second, learning the rules in no way can substitute for the complicated network of understandings about letter–sound correspondences that develops through learning the letter–sound correspondences and blending them to sound out words.

• Adams was emphatic that beginning reading instruction involves a great deal of reading words in real texts. Reading of actual texts makes clear to students why they are learning to decode individual words, and it should include many opportunities to apply the decoding skills being learned. Success in reading during the primary years depends on a heavy dose of reading texts that contain the letter–sound associations and combinations that the child's reading program teaches—that is, a heavy dose of so-called decodable texts (Juel & Roper/Schneider, 1985).

Thus, Adams's (1990) endorsement of the reading of texts from the beginning of reading instruction seems superficially consistent with whole language recommendations. The texts Adams favors, however, are ones emphasizing the graphemic–phonemic elements that the child knows at some level already (i.e., through instruction). Reading of such decodable texts is not favored by whole language theorists who want children to read authentic children's literature, which often includes many letter–sound combinations unfamiliar to the child. Indeed, the whole-language theorists have succeeded in nearly eradicating decodable texts from American classrooms. Even basal reading programs have far fewer decodable texts in the 1990s than they did in earlier eras, reflecting the response of many basal publishers to make their materials as consistent as possible with whole language principles (Hoffman et al., 1993). As such, they are much less consistent with the characteristics of excellent reading instructional materials based on the ideas developed in Adams (1990).

In short, Adams (1990) provided a powerful review of the evidence supporting the systematic teaching of phonics in beginning reading instruction, as well as a review of the scientific evidence supporting up-to-date phonics instruction. Adams also argued for such instruction on the basis of recent analyses of expert reading. She presented much evidence of letter- and word-level processing when skilled readers read, as reviewed briefly in Chapter 2 of this book.

In doing so, Adams (1990) explained to her readers how one of the foundational conclusions of the whole-language movement was simply not supported by data. That hypothesis, advanced first by Frank Smith and Kenneth Goodman (Goodman, 1972; Smith, 1971, 1973; Smith & Goodman, 1971), was that recognizing words in written context (i.e., in sentences, paragraphs, chapters, and/or whole texts) involves the coordinated use of semantic–contextual information (i.e., the meaning of the text up until a difficult-to-recognize word is encountered), syntactical information (i.e., the syntactical role of the difficult-to-recognize word as reflected by its position in a sentence), and graphophonemic cues (i.e., as represented by the letter sequence defining the word).

According to Smith and Goodman, readers know a great deal about language, about the meanings of words and the words that might appear in particular meaningful contexts. They also know a great deal about syntactical constraints and the syntactical roles that particular words can play in sentences. When encountering unknown words, according to Goodman, readers engage in a "psycholinguistic guessing game" (Goodman, 1967), combining semantic, syntactic, and graphophonemic cues in order to make a stab at the word.

The greatest problem with this hypothesis, as Adams (1990) detailed, is that it is not consistent with the data on skilled reading generated in the past several decades. For example, many different analyses have confirmed that skilled readers sound out words that they do not know (e.g., Barron, 1986; Patterson & Coltheart, 1987; Perfetti, Bell, & Delaney, 1988). Moreover, according to the psycholinguistic guessing-game thinking, eye movements should reveal that many words are being skipped over by the eyes. Certainly, there could be no way that individual letters could be processed given the speed of eye movements and the relatively large amount of time needed to process letters, at least as Frank Smith (1978, Chap. 2) conceived of the literature on eye movement and letter-level processing available at the time that Smith wrote his book.

In fact, the analyses of eye movements produced in the past two decades have made clear that most words are looked at during reading and that the individual letters in the words are processed (McConkie, Zola, Blanchard, & Wolverton, 1982; Rayner, Inhoff, Morrison, Slowiaczek, & Bertera, 1981; see Chapter 2 of this volume). Moreover, it is weaker readers rather than good readers who rely on context cues and, in doing so, often misread words (e.g., Byrne & Shea, 1979; Nicholson, 1991; Nicholson, Lillas, & Rzoska, 1988; Rayner & Pollatsek, 1989; Stanovich, 1980, 1986; Waterman & Lewandowski, 1993).

Even though Adams's (1990) made the case that good readers rely principally on word- and letter-level cues to read words, basal publishers and others abandoned materials that support the development of word- and letter-level skills. Even though it is poor readers who rely on semantic-and syntactic-context cues, largely because they are not proficient at using graphemic–phonemic cues to decode text, basal publishers and others had succumbed to the pressure from whole language to include many more predicable texts, texts that encourage and permit guessing of words on the basis of semantic and syntactic cues (Hoffman et al., 1993). That this is not as it should be has been further substantiated by research since Adams (1990).

Recent Research

Since Adams's (1990) book, there have been additional analyses supportive of the direct teaching of synthetic phonics, contrary to the most important assumptions of the whole language approach as represented in the writings of Goodman, Weaver, and like-minded curriculum specialists. There are three studies, in particular, that are very telling: at least, they are ones I find myself referring to often when I address educator groups concerned with beginning reading.

Nicholson (1991) directly confronted one of the pieces of evidence most frequently cited in support of the whole language approach to word recognition. In a study conducted by Kenneth Goodman (1965), students in grades 1 to 3 first read lists of words. Then, the children were presented the same words to read in meaningful text. The students made many more errors when they read the words out of context (i.e., when the words were in lists) than they did when the words were read in context. This, of course, is consistent with the hypothesis that reading will be facilitated when semantic- and syntactic-context cues are present (i.e., when words are read as part of text) compared to when words are read devoid of context cues (i.e., when words are read on lists). This finding has been used repeatedly to defend the whole-language practice of teaching students to recognize words by analyzing syntactic, graphemic–phonemic, and especially semantic cues.

Nicholson (1991) detected several very serious shortcomings in the Goodman (1965) study, however. First, no attention was paid in the Goodman (1965) investigation to the patterns of performance by good and poor readers. In addition, the participants always read the lists followed by reading of the words in context, and thus, there was the possibility that the improved performance in moving from list reading to reading in context might reflect some type of practice effect (i.e., the words in context had been seen before, on the lists).

In Nicholson (1991), students once again were asked to process words in lists and in context. In this study, however, the list–context order was manipulated, such that some participants read the lists first, and others read the words in context first. Moreover, there was systematic analysis of reading as a function of the grade of participants and their reading abilities relative to other students (i.e., good, average, weak). The outcomes in this study were anything but consistent with Goodman's (1965) results:

- Some readers did benefit from reading the words in the sentence context: Namely, poor readers at each age-level and average 6- and 7-year-olds.
- In contrast, a positive effect on reading was obtained in sentence context for good 6-year-old readers and average 8-year-olds only when reading words in sentence contexts followed reading words in list, consistent with the practice effect explanation of the original Goodman (1965) finding.
- There was no positive effect derived from reading words in context for good 7- and 8-year-old readers. Indeed, when the 8-year-old good readers did sentence-context reading first, they did better on reading of the words in list format.

In short, Nicholson's (1991) results are consistent with the conclusion that semantic contexts aid weaker, younger readers, but are not helpful for better, older readers. Thus, teaching children to attend to semantic-context cues is teaching them to use an immature strategy associated with poorer reading. In contrast, good readers can read based on graphophonemic cues alone.

The other recent analyses (Foorman, Francis, Novy, & Liberman,

1991; Lovett, Ransby, Hardwick, Johns, & Donaldson, 1989; Lovett et al., 1994) that I frequently point to as supportive of Chall's (1967/1983) and Adams's (1990) conclusions were instructional studies. These studies provided supportive evidence of the importance of synthetic phonics instruction as conceived of by Chall (1967)—that is, instruction focusing on letter–sound associations and the blending of letters and sounds to produce words.

Foorman et al. (1991) examined the reading development of grade-1 students enrolled in one of two types of programs. Half the students were experiencing instruction driven by a basal series that emphasized reading words in meaningful context. The meaningful-context cues were emphasized as critical in deciding what an unknown word might be, and relatively little instruction was given in sounding out words in order to recognize them. The other students were enrolled in a program emphasizing letter–sound associations and the blending of sounds to produce whole words. The students experiencing the two programs were matched for socioeconomic status, with the participants all coming from lower-middle to middle-class populations in an urban area. By the end of the year, students who were enrolled in the classes experiencing synthetic phonics instruction were reading and spelling words better than the participants in the classrooms emphasizing the use of semantic context cues during decoding.

Maureen Lovett and her associates focused their attention on students experiencing extreme difficulties in learning to read. The participating students in that work were so far behind in reading that they had been referred to the Hospital for Sick Children, Lovett's home institution, for potential diagnoses and treatment. Lovett et al. (1989) succeeded in improving the decoding of very weak readers between ages 9 and 13 through intensive instruction in letter–sound analyses and blending (i.e., tutoring in very small groups of children), which also improved student performance on a measure of standardized reading comprehension. Lovett et al. (1994) also succeeded in teaching such students to decode using phonological analysis and blending, and again, performance on a standardized comprehension measure showed improvement compared to a control condition. What is especially impressive in these studies was how well controlled they were, with control participants also enrolled in treatment conditions to evaluate placebo effects. When combined with some other analyses (e.g., Francis, Shaywitz, Stuebing, Shaywitz, & Fletcher, 1996; Shaywitz, Escobar, Shaywitz, Fletcher, & Makuch, 1992), there is increasing evidence that many children who fall behind in beginning reading are not qualitatively different from other readers, but rather require intense, systematic decoding instruction in order to learn to read. Confidence in the instructional conclusions offered by Lovett's group is heightened by the fact that other research teams have also reported that students who experience difficulties in learning to read benefit from intensive systematic phonics instruction (e.g., Alexander, Anderson, Heilman, Voeller, & Torgesen, 1991; Manis et al., 1993; Olson, Wise, Johnson, & Ring, 1997; Torgesen & Burgess, in press; Torgesen et al., 1996; Vellutino et al., 1996).

I close this section by explicitly addressing a claim I have sometimes heard from opponents of explicit decoding instruction (i.e., synthetic or systematic phonics). They say, "All right, so some kids who are experiencing difficulties learning to read do need it, but it really does no good for other students." There are a number of ways to challenge that claim, but I like a recent analysis by Fielding-Barnsley (1997). Her study included 32 children who came to kindergarten extremely well-prepared for beginning reading. Their preschool experiences had brought them to a high level of phonemic awareness and high alphabetic knowledge. Half of the children in the study were taught ten words at the beginning of kindergarten, with the instruction emphasizing sounding out the words and highlighting word parts (e.g., the common part of *pam* and *am*). The ten words were the following: *am, pam, sat, mat, splat, pal, lap, slam, lamp,* and *tam.* The other children learned the words using a whole word approach. (Remember the approach that predominated in the Dick-and-Jane readers.) In both conditions, the teaching took place over about six weeks, with a few minutes a day devoted to teaching of the words.

There were dramatic differences favoring the students who had been taught using decoding as opposed to whole word. First, the decoding-instructed students read and wrote the taught words better than did the whole word-instructed students. There were even more dramatic effects, however, with respect to reading novel words which included the letters and word parts of the words taught (e.g., *at, pat, sam, tap*), and pseudowords (e.g., *ap, lat, tal*). The students taught using decoding instruction greatly outperformed the whole word-instructed students. Decoding instruction prepares students to tackle words they have never seen before, even when they are well prepared for beginning reading.

Summary

There has been a great deal of research in the past several decades on the positive effects of teaching early reading competencies. The case is strong that explicit efforts to teach the alphabet, letter–sound associations, and sounding out of words (i.e., analysis of words into component sounds which are blended) make a positive impact on progress in early reading. In contrast to the consistently positive evidence associated with synthetic-phonics approaches, there has been little support for intrinsic-phonics approaches (sometimes referred to as analytic-phonics or whole-word approaches) or for the approaches to decoding favored in whole language (i.e., ones involving emphasis on analysis of semantic–contextual and syntactic cues). Indeed, perhaps the most disturbing conclusion that comes from this research is that teaching children to decode by giving primacy to semantic and syntactic cues over graphemic–phonemic cues is equivalent to teaching them to read the way weak readers read!

The work on synthetic phonics instruction conducted throughout this century has succeeded in clarifying what works and what does not work in developing word recognition skills. Every primary teacher in the country needs to think hard about the research evidence that was covered in this section. As I say that, I also feel some regret that so much of the recent research attention on explicit decoding instruction (often delivered as intensive tutoring) has focused on students experiencing difficulties in learning to read. The good news is that such instruction does improve the reading of many students who have had difficulties learning to read with regular classroom instruction. One piece of bad news is that not much is known about how modern versions of synthetic phonics work with normally achieving students. Another is that such instruction is not revealing about how explicit phonics instruction can occur within the context of other elements of literacy instruction. More positively, there are studies like Fielding-Barnsley (1997) in which students who were in good shape for beginning reading instruction benefited from explicit decoding instruction. In addition, Chapter 6 discusses how some teachers are balancing explicit skills instruction and immersion in whole-language activities, such as writing and reading of literature.

I must emphasize, however, that in fairness to Chall (1967/1983) and Adams (1990), the point must be made that they have been in favor of balanced instruction all along. They made many clear statements in their books about the need for synthetic phonics instruction in a much larger program involving a great deal of reading of various types. It was never only phonics *or* only whole language (or any other alternative) with either of these careful thinkers. That reductionistic dichotomy came about as whole-language advocates attempted to make a case for their approach. As will become obvious in Chapter 6, there have been many calls for balancing of skills and whole language. I think that my friend Lesley Morrow, a reading professor at Rutgers, was the first to refer to balanced instruction as the radical middle. It has become that because of the polemics of recent years, but the truth is that Chall defined the radical middle 30 years ago.

TEACHING STUDENTS TO READ NEW WORDS BY ANALOGY TO KNOWN WORDS

Recall from the discussion of skilled reading in Chapter 2 that good readers know and use word parts to decode unfamiliar words. Moreover, as reviewed earlier in this chapter, as children encounter common root words, prefixes, and suffixes again and again, they come to treat such word parts as wholes, no longer requiring letter-by-letter analysis and sounding out in order to recognize and pronounce them (e.g., Ehri, 1992; Leslie & Calhoon, 1995). By the middle-elementary grades, there are clear differences between good and poor readers in their use of word chunks (e.g., Bowey & Hansen, 1994; Bowey & Underwood, 1996; Leslie & Calhoon, 1995): it is likely that good readers process words more at the level of frequently encountered word chunks than single phonemes much of the time (Scarborough, 1995). There is even some evidence that there are differences in word-part awareness and knowledge during kindergarten and grade one that are predictive of reading competence during the primary and later elementary years (Badian, 1993, 1994, 1995; Carlisle, 1994; Cunningham & Stanovich, 1993). For example, early competence in selecting the exact match of a short word (e.g., *drop*) from among four possibilities (i.e., *droq, drop, borq, brop*) is predictive of reading comprehension in the later elementary grades (Badian, 1995).

That commonly encountered word chunks are used to decode by good readers, and increasingly by children as they increase in reading skill, has suggested to some that word chunks should be highlighted and taught to children in beginning reading. After all, by age 4, children can detect the separate syllables in multisyllable words (Liberman, Shankweiler, Fisher, & Carter, 1974). They can also detect the onsets and rhyming parts (i.e., *rimes,* defined as a vowel with subsequent consonants; e.g., *-at* in *bat, cat,* and *hat*) of words. Thus, they can detect the rime *-ealth* in *health, stealth,* and *wealth,* identifying as well the onset sounds of *h-, st-,* and *w-* (Goswami, in press). Beyond detecting onsets and rimes, 5-year-olds can decode new words by analogy to rhyming words, at least when the rhyming relationship is very obvious. Thus, if a 5-year-old sees the word *beak,* and hears it pronounced with the word remaining in full view, he or she often can decode words like *peak,* *weak,* and *speak* (Goswami, 1986, 1988). At first, only rimes can be used to decode by analogy. As children's reading improves over the course of the first year are able to use parts of rimes (e.g., the *-ea* in *-eak*) in a similar fashion (Goswami, 1993, in press).

Teaching Word Families

How can children be taught to use word parts for decoding? One way is to teach "word families." It is not at all unusual to observe a group of grade-1 children constructing a list of all the words they can think of that end in *-ade, -eeze,* or *-isk.* In many classrooms, once teacher and students have constructed such a list on a big piece of paper, the list joins a display of other lists of word families based on word endings. Endings appearing in ten or more English words are contained in Table 5.1. Most of the word family endings are rimes—they require only a beginning consonant sound to make a word. Some, however, end in a vowel sound, such as *-aw* or *-ay.* Thus, it is more accurate to say that the word family endings in Table 5.1 are phonograms rather than rimes (Fry, Kress, & Fountoukidis, 1993). The word endings that occur most frequently are the ones learned first by students (Leslie & Calhoon, 1995), and logically, seem like likely candidates to be emphasized in instruction.

When I have observed the word-family approach in primary-level classrooms, it is almost always in the context of very strong synthetic phonics instruction. That makes a great deal of sense since good readers do blend individual sounds and word parts they know (i.e., root

TABLE 5.1. Common Word Families in English

-ab	-amp	-ear (short *e*)	-ice	-ip	-out
-ace	-ank	-eat	-ick	-it	-ow (*know*)
-ack	-ap	-ed	-id	-ob	-ow (*cow*)
-ad	-ar	-ee	-ide	-ock	-ub
-ade	-are	-eed	-ies	-od	-uck
-ag	-ark	-eek	-ig	-og	-uff
-ail	-ash	-eep	-ight	-oke	-ug
-ain	-at	-eet	-ile	-old	-um
-ake	-ate	-ell	-ill	-one	-ump
-ale	-ave	-ell	-im	-ong	-ung
-all	-aw	-end	-ime	-oop	-unk
-am	-ay	-ent	-in	-op	-ush
-ame	-aze	-ess	-ine	-ope	-ust
-an	-eak	-est	-ing	-ore	-ut
-ane	-eal	-et	-ink	-orn	-y
-ang	-eam	-ew	-int	-ot	

Note. Based on List 47 in Fry et al. (1993).

words, phonograms, prefixes, and suffixes). A little thought to the task of generating all the words that end with -ade (bade, fade, jade, made, wade, blade, glade, grade, shade, spade, trade), for example, will make it obvious that to construct such a list, as well as to be able to say the words on the list, requires knowledge not only of the rime but also of the sounds made by the onsets, as well as understanding of blending. Thus, it is not surprising that only children who already have some knowledge of phonological decoding skills are able to decode by analogy (Ehri & Robbins, 1992; Peterson & Haines, 1992) or at a minimum know a good many letter–sound associations (Walton, 1995). When encountering a word that shares a rime with another word known by the child, the young reader using the analogy strategy sound outs the phonemic onset and blends it with the rime (Bruck & Treiman, 1992).

Word ID Program[*]

The best developed decoding-by-analogy program that I have encountered was developed at Benchmark School, a school serving children who have difficulties in learning to read in the context of regular schooling. The program was devised by the school's instructional leader, Irene Gaskin, in collaboration with Professors Linnea Ehri (Graduate Center, City University of New York), Patricia Cunningham (Wake Forest University), and Richard Anderson (University of Illinois). They dubbed their approach the "Word ID" program (Gaskins, Gaskins, Anderson, & Schommer, 1994; Gaskins, Gaskins, & Gaskins, 1991, 1992).

At the heart of the program are 120 key words that capture the key spelling patterns associated with the six English-language vowels. In addition, there also are key words for the two sounds of g (e.g., girl, giraffe) and the two sounds of c (e.g., can, city). Some word parts that always sound the same (e.g., -tion) are taught as wholes. All of the keywords in the program are summarized in Table 5.2.

Thus, to decode the word dispatcher, the Word ID user would learn to identify a key word for each syllable of the word. For the first syllable, dis-, the key word this could be used, since the vowel i is followed by a consonant. For the second syllable, -patch-, the keyword could be cat, since the a in -patch- is followed by a consonant. For the final syllable (-er), her would apply. Thus, the student, who is also learning the simple consonant–sound associations of English plus the digraphs and consonant

---

*The entire Word ID program can be purchased from Benchmark School (2107 N. Providence, Media, PA 19063).

TABLE 5.2. Benchmark School Word Identification/Vocabulary Development Program: Key Patterns

a	e	i	o	u	y
grab	he	hi	go	club	my
place	speak	mice	boat	truck	baby
black	scream	kick	job	glue	gym
had	year	did	clock	bug	
made	treat	slide	frog	drum	
flag	red	knife	broke	jump	
snail	see	pig	old	fun	
rain	bleed	right	from	skunk	
make	queen	like	on	up	
talk	sleep	smile	phone	us	
all	sweet	will	long	use	
am	tell	swim	zoo	but	
name	them	time	good		
champ	ten	in	food		
can	end	find	look		
and	tent	vine	school		
map	her	king	stop		
car	yes	think	for		
shark	nest	ship	more		
smart	let	squirt	corn		
smash	flew	this	nose		
has		wish	not		
ask		it	could		
cat		write	round		
skate		five	your		
brave		give	scout		
saw			cow		
day			glow		
			down		
			boy		

g			g = i
girl	grab		gym
go	dragon		giraffe
bug	glow		

c = k			c = s	
can	club		city	excitement
corn	discover		princess	centipede

an i mals	drag on
con test	ex cite ment
crea ture	pres i dent
choc o late	ques tion
dis cover	re port
thank ful	un happy
va ca tion	

Reprinted by permission of the Benchmark School and Irene Gaskins.

blends, would know the sequence of vowel sounds and would then be able to sound out the word. Thus, rather than *this-cat-her* being pronounced, the student would sound out the word *dispatcher*.

Because students are taught to self-verbalize their thinking as they apply the strategy, consistent with an approach to strategy teaching that often works with children (Meichenbaum, 1977), you might hear something like the following from a young Benchmark student confronted with a word like *dispatcher*:

> I can tell by looking at this word that it has three vowel sounds, therefore I know it will have three chunks. The three common English parts I see in this word are divided here. The spelling pattern, or the vowel and what comes after it, in the first chunk is -*is*. The word that I know with the same spelling pattern is *this*. The spelling pattern or the vowel and what comes after it in the second chunk is -*at*. The word I know with the same spelling pattern is *cat*. The spelling pattern for the third chunk is -*er* with the word I know with this spelling pattern being *her*. The word is *dispatcher*. (adapted from Gaskins et al., 1995, p. 343)

Similarly, when Benchmark students are presented a word like *caterpillar*, they can sound out an approximate pronounciation through analogy with the component words *cat, her, will,* and *car*.

The program extends over several years at Benchmark. First, a variety of exercises are used to develop student understanding of the spelling patterns in the key words. Five new key words are introduced at a time, with 5 days of lessons aimed at developing mastery of the words, including practice using the key words to decode other words. After the key words are mastered, lessons in their use continue. During these lessons, teachers model use of the key words to decode. Students review words learned previously in the Word ID program, and they practice decoding new words—with many exercises included in the instruction to produce overlearning of the key words and decoding using them. I have watched many Benchmark students use the Word ID approach: By the middle-elementary grades, most of the students can use the memorized key words with ease to decode multisyllable words they have not encountered previously.

What is especially striking, however, is that from the introduction of the program to children in their first year at Benchmark, Word ID lessons do much more than teach children to decode. When key words are introduced, children learn the meanings of the key words, which are also used as part of story writing. The lessons include reading of patterned books. Students hear and read good literature every day they are enrolled at Benchmark. The Benchmark approach is anything but a decoding skill-only approach; rather, Word ID is embedded in ongoing instruction and used to empower children so that they can participate fully in writing and in reading of real literature.

The development and evaluation of the program has a fascinating history (see Gaskins et al., 1995), beginning with Irene Gaskins's analyses of the particular reading problems of students at the Benchmark School. This led to an initial version of the program, which was tried in a few classrooms at the school. With evidence of improved decoding, spelling, and vocabulary development in those classrooms, the approach was extended. Across-school implementation, however, did not mean that the approach was employed completely and faithfully in every Benchmark classroom. The natural classroom variations in the implementation of the program permitted an important evaluation of it. Richard Anderson and his then-student colleague Marlene Schommer analyzed reading achievement as a function of complete implementation of the program, and found a striking relationship: the more teachers spent time encouraging and assisting students in the use of the Word ID approach as they read, the better the reading in the classroom. That is, simply providing the Word ID lessons was not as powerful as supplementing the lessons with a great deal of support in applying the lessons. (Make note of this finding, for there is plenty of evidence in the chapters that follow that a key ingredient in effective beginning-reading instruction is such scaffolding [Wood, Bruner, & Ross, 1976] of student performance—that teachers who provide support as their students attempt to use skills taught in formal lessons are especially effective teachers.)

Many reading researchers believe that an especially good measure of decoding ability is pseudoword reading—that is, being able to read items that have the structural characteristics of real words but are not real words. Such words could not be known by the reader through previous exposure, but must be decoded. Anderson and Schommer found that the greater the implementation of the Word ID program in a Benchmark program, the better the students' reading of pseudowords.

The Benchmark faculty and the external university faculty monitored difficulties with the program, refining it until it could be taught efficiently in the classroom and be used efficiently by students. The program became especially well-known when it was featured in a videotape produced and distributed by the Center for the Study of Reading at the University of Illinois. Although Gaskins and her colleagues never published the program commercially, they have made it available to any school district that wants it for the cost of reproducing the materials. They have had many takers. Regardless of where I talk in the United States, it is likely that I will be asked about the Word ID program.

Such visibility caught the attention of some prominent reading education researchers who were particularly interested in the impact of the Word ID approach compared to synthetic phonics approaches. I know of two such evaluations to date; both of which provide evidence that the effects of Word ID and synthetic phonics instruction are roughly comparable in developing the decoding skills of beginning readers (DeWitz, 1993; Lovett et al., 1994). Lovett et al.'s study was especially notable because it involved teaching students who experienced a great deal of previous difficulties in learning to read—much like Benchmark students. The results of Word ID instruction are consistent with other evidence that teaching children to decode by analogy to known words is effective in developing young readers who can decode words they have not seen before (e.g., Ehri & Robbins, 1992; Peterson & Haines, 1992). This holds true even for students who have experienced previous difficulties in reading, and even when the shared word chunks are contained in words that are more complex than the simple onset-plus-rime structure (e.g., van Daal, Reitsma, & van der Leu, 1994).

The Need for Decoding-by-Analogy Instruction

If children can learn to read either with synthetic phonics or word analogy, is there really a need for both approaches? For a very long time, reading clinicians have believed that there are some children who experience difficulties with letter-by-letter analysis and blending but who are able to learn whole words and syllables. Indeed, Irene Gaskins's initial motivation for developing the Word ID approach was her perception that many of the Benchmark students really struggled with synthetic phonics. On the other hand, clinicians have also believed that there are children who are quite good at analyzing the individual sounds of words and blending them but who fail to develop word-chunk and sight-word knowledge. Those children are better at decoding using a synthetic phonics approach than with an analogy approach (Berninger, 1995).

In support of this possibility, there now is evidence that some primary-level students rely more on synthetic phonics to decode while others are more reliant on an analogy approach (Berninger, Yates, & Lester, 1991; Byrne, Freebody, & Gates, 1992; Freebody & Byrne, 1988). That is, some weaker readers learn to recognize words more easily if they are presented as wholes without making their phonemic composition salient (Wise, 1992). Nonetheless, no one has yet succeeded in providing a good study demonstrating that some children who have a tough time with synthetic phonics do much better with an analogy approach such as Word ID, nor has anyone succeeded in demonstrating that some children who have a tough time with an analogy approach do better with synthetic phonics.

To date, short-term direct comparisons favor sounding out of words over decoding by analogy (Bruck & Treiman, 1992; Wise, Olson, & Treiman, 1990). Employing only one approach to the exclusion of the other, however, is the wrong way to think about synthetic phonics and analogies approaches with respect to most children's development as readers. Good readers do analyze and blend individual sounds, but they also make use of word chunks (Berninger, 1994, Chap. 4; Ehri, 1992). Although the dynamics are not completely understood, good readers induce word-chunk regularities as they sound out words; moreover, they learn more about the sounds of individual letters and letter combinations while experiencing those sounds as part of word chunks (e.g., Thompson, Cottrell, & Fletcher-Flinn, 1996). Given all this, what makes most sense for beginning reading instruction is to encourage children to analyze and blend individual sounds while at the same time teaching them to make use of word parts during decoding. Although I have seen very good teachers who take this approach, I must admit that at this time it is not well understood how to obtain the advantages of synthetic phonics instruction *and* analogy instruction. Researchers such as Gaskins, Ehri, and the Benchmark School faculty, interested in teaching children to decode by analogy, are now hard at work attempting to update their instruction so that it combines the synthetic phonics and analogy approaches to decoding instruction.

Thus, as Benchmark students learn their key words, they are being taught how to analyze the key words into individual sounds. The key words are used to provide a great deal of instruction about the key letter–sound associations and letter combinations that commonly occur in English. The students spend a great deal of time stretching out the pronunciations of the keywords in order to hear their constituent sounds. They are taught to look at the visual patterns in words and to be sensitive that some letter patterns occur in a number of words. In short, as the Word ID program has matured, it has come to include more about sounding out words, blending the ideas from phonics and decoding by analogy approaches (Gaskins, Ehri, Cress, O'Hara, & Donnelly, 1997). (As is discussed in Chapter 6, one of the most prominent approaches to tutoring primary students experiencing reading difficulties, Reading Recovery®, also teaches students both to attend to word chunks and to sound out words.)

My own intuition, consistent with the direction of Gaskins and her Benchmark colleagues, is that decoding instruction will work best if there is flexibility, especially for children who might really have problems with synthetic phonics or with using analogies to decode words. Thus, what I envision in the future is phonics instruction that teaches not only analysis and blending of sounds of words, but also that there are big chunks of words that do not need to be analyzed and blended every time. By providing lots of opportunities for students to experience the major recurring word parts (i.e., frequent letter patterns, such as phonograms, prefixes, and suffixes), they should come to be automatically recognized.

If the reading clinicians are right, and I'm betting that they are, flexibility in decoding instruction is especially important for students who might experience difficulties with analyzing and blending or in learning word chunks. For students experiencing the former problem, instruction should focus more on the word chunks and use of analogies to decode words. For students experiencing the latter problem, downplaying word families and word chunks in favor of analyzing and blending would make sense. In short, what is needed is decoding instruction that is powerful for all, accommodating individual differences in students rather than being one-size-fits-all instruction. Working out the specifics of such instruction is going to be challenging but, I suspect, will pay off in improved beginning reading instruction.

CONCLUDING COMMENTS

The goal of reading is not to decode words but to understand the messages conveyed in text. When readers are not skilled in word recognition, however, comprehension is low. A consistent characteristic of poor readers is that they have difficulties in decoding words, with this factor more than any other accounting for their low comprehension (e.g., Ehrlich, Kurtz-Costes, & Loridant, 1993). There is very good reason for researcher attention to word-level processes and identification of instructional methods to increase word recognition. Arguments that development of word recognition skills should not be paramount in beginning-reading instruction must ignore a great deal of data to the contrary.

Among scholars who have carefully and respectfully studied all of the evidence on early word recognition, there is agreement, at least with respect to the big conclusions that are the focus in this chapter. There is a consensus among scientifically oriented reading researchers that teaching children to sound out words and to use commonly encountered word chunks (e.g., root words, prefixes, suffixes) makes more sense than teaching them to orient to meaning-related cues in order to recognize words. There is little support for approaches to word recognition favored by those who believe that word recognition is more a psycholinguistic guessing game (e.g., Goodman, 1967) than analyzing and blending the component sounds of words.

I like to think about word-recognition instruction in Vygotskian terms (see Chapter 4). When adults and children work together to sound out words and decode words by recognizing word chunks, they probably are engaging in the early stages of an internalization process, one in which the child learns how to use speech to decode words. One of Vygotsky's main messages is that the mind develops in interactions with others, interactions involving a lot of dialogue in which adults and children work on problems together. Learning to read should likewise develop in interaction with others, so that reading strategies that the adult scaffolds dialogically, such as those involved in decoding, will potentially be internalized by the child. (The tutoring provided by the likes of Lovett and her associates, Vellutino and his colleagues, and at Benchmark School reveals substantial scaffolding of students in the Vygotskian sense of the term.)

According to the Soviets, inner speech, including the inner speech that mediates word recognition, has its origins in social interactions between children and adults who introduce them to the most important problem-solving strategies that children need to acquire. When an adult models the sounding out of words and then assists the child who at first must sound out words with great effort, it is the beginning of an internalization process, one that is decidedly social. In this way, the adult passes on to another generation a powerful set of tools that humans invented in order to read print.

Will the information presented in this chapter be translated into general practice in the near future? I hope so, but there are challenges ahead. One of the greatest difficulties is that many primary teachers do not understand enough about phonics or commonly encountered word chunks in order to implement either a synthetic phonics program or a decoding-by-analogy approach. For example, Moats (1994) administered a survey of phonics knowledge to experienced teachers of reading. She found that formal knowledge of phonics was low. For example, only 10–20% of the teachers were able to identify consonant blends in written words: many thought that the *tch* in *stretch* and the *bt* in *doubt* were consonant blends. None could identify a consonant digraph (e.g., *wh, ch, th*). Only 21% seemed to know what an inflected verb was. Only 27% could identify the morphemes (i.e., the smallest meaningful units, such as root words, prefixes, suffixes, etc.) in a word. The only item on the survey that was answered correctly by the majority of the teacher concerned identification of the number of syllables in words. If teachers are to teach phonics to students, they must understand phonics first and well. Otherwise, they will not be able to explain phonics principles, select effective examples of phonics applications, or be able to recognize the bases for student errors and offer appropriate remediation (Moats, 1994).

One reason that knowledge of word-recognition processes is so low is that teacher-education programs have not been teaching the information about language that teachers need to know. When implicit phonics programs predominated in the marketplace, there was little incentive to offer teacher-education students instruction in synthetic phonics. With the rise of whole language, there was exceptionally active opposition to teaching beginning teachers about phonics as detailed in Chapter 1. I cannot tell you how many teachers have told me that they would like to incorporate more word-level skills, such as sounding out and teaching decoding-by-analogy, but they simply do not know how to begin. I suspect that hybrid approaches, such as the new versions of Benchmark Word ID, are going to seem even more challenging because they not only require teachers to understand the value of teaching students to sound out and to decode by analogy at the same time, they also require knowledge of the procedures to do so.

Even when teachers are willing to teach word-level skills, the materials available to them often are not very informative about decoding instruction at its best. Quite frankly, many phonics programs I have seen are dreadful (although there are exceptions), not much more than a collection of skill sheets and drills, providing little information to teachers about the skills that should be developed. There are two trade books on the market that I especially like as starting points for the teacher who wants to improve decoding instruction in her or his classroom. Teachers have told me that they have found these two references useful in understanding the word recognition process and how word-recognition can be taught. One is Patricia M. Cunningham's (1995) *Phonics They Use: Words for Reading and Writing.* The other is Barbara J. Fox's (1996) *Strategies for Word Identification.*

As the evidence accumulates in favor of the instruction documented in this chapter, whole language opposition to it seems to intensify. The case made by opponents of the word-recognition instruction summarized in this chapter is that if children are taught how to systematically recognize words, somehow the benefits of whole language will be lost. The argument is that in primary reading, it is either phonics or whole language: teaching phonics emphasizes the parts of language, thus precluding whole-language experiences. As it turns out, phonics and whole-language practices can coexist, and indeed complement one another. Exceptionally effective primary teachers balance systematic skills instruction, including word recognition, with immersion in real literature and student writing. I make the case in the next chapter that such teaching is better employment of effective and attractive primary-level reading instruction than what is recommended in doctrinaire textbooks on whole language that have predominated in primary teacher-preparation courses in recent years.

I have spent much of this past year in Madison, Wisconsin, watching teachers who are doing a good job of teaching their students to decode. They are teaching their students to look for the major parts of words and to use their knowledge of word parts to sound out words. As much as they are urging the primacy of phonological processing and use of word chunks in decoding, they also consistently encourage their students to make certain that the decoded word makes sense. Thus, if a child is given the sentence, "The boy kicked a goal," accompanied by a picture of a boy kicking a football held by another boy, the child might sound out, "The boy kicked a goat." It would not be unusual to hear the teacher remark, "Does that make sense?" The teachers I have been watching are encouraging the students to make use of a variety of cues, consistent with whole language emphases, but, consistent with the work on decoding, they are encouraging students to rely more on sounding words out, including through recognition of word parts for the initial decoding. Context cues are then used to decide if the word as sounded out really makes sense.

The idea of giving letter and word chunk cues priority in word recognition, and then using semantic–contextual cues to check decodings based on sounding out, is one shared by some with distinguished reputations in teaching beginning reading (e.g., Clay, 1991). Indeed, the Madison, Wisconsin, teachers I have been studying found the inspiration for their instruction in Clay's writing.

SUMMARY

1. Ehri (e.g., 1991) has proposed a general developmental progression in learning to recognize words. Preschoolers can first recognize logographs before they can do alphabetic reading, which begins even before the child knows all the letter–sound associations. Experience in sounding out particular words results in frequently encountered words becoming sight words, no longer requiring alphabetic decoding. Letter strings that occur frequently in words, including root words, phonograms, prefixes, and suffixes, come to be perceived as units, no

longer needing to be sounded out when encountered in a new word. At this point, new words can often be decoded by analogy to words known by the reader (e.g., knowing *beak,* the child can read *peak*). There are some researchers, such as Goswami, who believe that reading by analogy may come in earlier than Ehri proposes, so the progression proposed by Ehri is currently being researched rather than considered indisputable fact.

2. There is a great deal of support for the efficacy of synthetic phonics instruction. Chall's (1967) book is a summary of the first wave of evidence, which has continued to accumulate since its publication. Synthetic phonics instruction involves learning the letter–sound associations and blending the sounds specified by a word's letters in order to produce the word.

3. The success in using synthetic phonics to teach beginning readers to recognize words contrasts with lower success rates for analytic phonics approaches involving less systematic instruction of phonics (i.e., on an as-needed basis).

4. An alternative to emphasizing the decoding and blending of individual sounds is to teach students to decode by analogy. This approach requires teaching students a large number of word parts that then can be used to read by analogy. Both traditional "word family" approaches and the Benchmark School Word ID program involve decoding by analogy.

5. Good readers decode by analysis and blending and also by analogy, and thus, there is hard thinking going on about how to teach beginning readers to use both approaches. A possibility is that each approach is better for some readers. Although there is not much firm evidence in favor of this position, it seems likely that especially effective decoding instruction would be flexible enough to permit students to use the approach or approaches that work for them.

6. In contrast to the substantial data base in favor of synthetic phonics instruction and the growing data base in support of decoding by analogy, there is very little support for teaching students to decode by orienting primarily to semantic– and syntactic–contextual cues as opposed to graphemic–phonemic cues. That is, there is very little support to decoding as favored by whole-language enthusiasts.

7. Even so, research on how to teach decoding is an extremely active area of research at present. One important hypothesis that deserves a great deal of attention is that a very effective way to teach decoding is to teach students to attend to letter-level, phonological cues first, blending individual letter sounds and word parts, and then to check their decoding by determining its sensibility in light of semantic-context and syntactic cues.

REFERENCES

Abt Associates. (1977). *Education as experimentation: A planned variation model: Volume IV-B. Effects of follow through models.* Cambridge, MA: Abt Books.

Adams, M. J. (1990). *Beginning to read.* Cambridge, MA: Harvard University Press.

Alexander, A., Anderson, H., Heilman, P. C., Voeller, K. S., & Torgesen, J. K. (1991). Phonological awareness training and remediation of analytic decoding deficits in a group of severe dyslexics. *Annals of Dyslexia, 41,* 193–206.

Anderson, D. R., & Collins, P. A. (1988). *The impact on children's education: Television's influence on cognitive development* (Office of Research Working Paper No. 2). Washington, DC: U.S. Department of Education, Office of Educational Research and Improvement.

Badian, N. A. (1993). Phonemic awareness, naming, visual symbol processing, and reading. *Reading and Writing: An Interdisciplinary Journal, 5,* 87–100.

Badian, N. A. (1994). Preschool prediction: Orthographic and phonological skills, and reading. *Annals of Dyslexia, 44,* 3–25.

Badian, N. A. (1995). Predicting reading ability over the long term: The changing roles of letter naming, phonological awareness and orthographic processing. *Annals of Dyslexia, 45,* 79–96.

Ball, S., & Bogatz, G. A. (1970). *The first year of "Sesame Street": An evaluation.* Princeton, NJ: Educational Testing Service.

Baron, J. (1977). Mechanisms for pronouncing printed words: Use and acquisition. In D. LaBerge & S. J. Samuels (Eds.), *Basic processes in reading: Perception and comprehension* (pp. 175–216). Hillsdale, NJ: Erlbaum.

Barron, R. W. (1986). Word recognition in early reading: A review of the direct and indirect access hypotheses. *Cognition, 24,* 93–119.

Berninger, V. W. (1994). *Reading and writing acquisition: A developmental neuropsychological perspective.* Madison, WI: Brown & Benchmark.

Berninger, V. W. (1995). Has the phonological recoding model of reading acquisition and reading disability led us astray? *Issues in Education: Contributions from Educational Psychology, 1,* 59–63.

Berninger, V. W., Yates, C., & Lester, K. (1991). Multiple orthographic codes in reading and writing acquisition. *Reading and Writing: An Interdisciplinary Journal, 3,* 115–149.

Bogatz, G. A., & Ball, S. (1971). *The second year of "Sesame Street": A continuing evaluation.* Princeton, NJ: Educational Testing Service.

Bowey, J. A., & Hansen, J. (1994). The development of orthographic rimes as units of word recogntion. *Journal of Experimental Child Psychology, 58,* 465–488.

Bowey, J. A., & Underwood, N. (1996). Further evidence that orthographic rime usage in nonword reading increases with word-level reading proficiency. *Journal of Experimental Child Psychology, 63,* 526–562.

Bruck, M., & Treiman, R. (1992). Learning to pronounce words: The limits of analogies. *Reading Research Quarterly, 27,* 374–398.

Byrne, B., & Fielding-Barnsley, R. (1990). Acquiring the alphabetic principle: A case for teaching recognition of phoneme identity. *Journal of Educational Psychology, 82,* 805–812.

Byrne, B., & Fielding-Barnsley, R. (1991). Evaluation of a program to teach phonemic awareness to young children. *Journal of Educational Psychology, 83,* 451–455.

Carlisle, J. F. (1994). Morphological awareness and early reading achievement. In L. B. Feldman (Ed.), *Morphological aspects of language processing.* Hillsdale, NJ: Erlbaum.

Chall, J. S. (1967). *Learning to read: The great debate.* New York: McGraw-Hill.

Chall, J. S. (1983). *Learning to read: The great debate* (updated ed.). New York: McGraw-Hill.

Clay, M. M. (1991). *Becoming literate: The construction of inner control.* Portsmouth, NH: Heinemann.

Cronin, V., Farrell, D., & Delaney, M. (1995, April). *Environmental print facilitates word reading.* Paper presented at the biennial meeting of the Society for Research in Child Development, Indianapolis.

Cunningham, A. E., & Stanovich, K. E. (1993). Children's literacy environments and early word recognition skills. *Reading and Writing: An Interdisciplinary Journal, 5,* 193–204.

Cunningham, P. M. (1995). *Phonics they use: Words for reading and writing* (2nd ed.). New York: HarperCollins.

Dewitz, P. (1993, May). *Comparing an analogy and phonics approach to word recognition.* Paper presented at the Edmund Hardcastle Henderson Round-table in Reading, Charlottesville, VA.

Ehri, L. C. (1980). The development of orthographic images. In U. Frith (Ed.), *Cognitive processes in spelling* (pp. 311–338). London: Academic Press.

Ehri, L. C. (1984). How orthography alters spoken language competencies in children learning to read and spell. In J. Downing & R. Valtin (Eds.), *Language awareness and learning to read* (pp. 119–147). New York: Springer-Verlag.

Ehri, L. C. (1987). Learning to read and spell words. *Journal of Reading Behavior, 19,* 5–31.

Ehri, L. C. (1991). Development of the ability to read words. In R. Barr, M. L. Kamil, P. B. Mosenthal, & P. D. Pearson (Eds.), *Handbook of reading research* (Vol. 2, pp. 383–417). New York: Longman.

Ehri, L. C. (1992). Reconceptualizing the development of sight word reading and its relationship to recoding. In P. B. Gough, L. C. Ehri, & R. Treiman (Eds.), *Reading acquisition* (pp. 107–143). Hillsdale, NJ: Erlbaum.

Ehri, L. C., Deffner, N. D., & Wilce, L. S. (1984). Pictorial mnemonics for phonics. *Journal of Educational Psychology, 76,* 880–893.

Ehri, L. C., & Robbins, C. (1992). Beginners need some decoding skill to read words by analogy. *Reading Research Quarterly, 27,* 12–27.

Ehri, L. C., & Wilce, L. S. (1985). Movement into reading: Is the first stage of printed word learning visual or phonetic? *Reading Research Quarterly, 20,* 163–179.

Ehri, L. C., & Wilce, L. S. (1987a). Does learning to spell help beginners learn to read words? *Reading Research Quarterly, 18,* 47–65.

Ehri, L. C., & Wilce, L. S. (1987b). Cipher versus cue reading: An experiment in decoding acquisition. *Journal of Educational Psychology, 79,* 3–13.

Ehrlich, M.-F., Kurtz-Costes, B., & Loridant, C. (1993). Cognitive and motivational determinants of reading comprehension in good and poor readers. *Journal of Reading Behavior, 25,* 365–381.

Fielding-Barnsley, R. (1997). Explicit instruction in decoding benefits children high in phonemic awareness and alphabet knowledge. *Scientific Studies of Reading, 1,* 85–98.

Foorman, B., Francis, D., Novy, D., & Liberman, D. (1991). How letter–sound instruction mediates progress in first-grade reading and spelling. *Journal of Educational Psychology, 83,* 456–469.

Fox, B. J. (1996). *Strategies for word identification: Phonics from a new perspective.* Englewood Cliffs, NJ: Prentice-Hall.

Fox, B., & Routh, D. K. (1975). Analyzing spoken language into words, syllables, and phonemes: A developmental study. *Journal of Psycholinguistic Research, 4,* 331–342.

Francis, D. J., Shaywitz, S. E., Stuebing, K. K., Shaywitz, B. A., & Fletcher, J. M. (1996). Developmental lag versus deficit models of reading disability: A longitudinal, individual growth curves analysis. *Journal of Educational Psychology, 88,* 3–17.

Freebody, P., & Byrne, B. (1988). Word-reading strategies in elementary school children: Relations to comprehension, reading time, and phonemic awareness. *Reading Research Quarterly, 23,* 441–453.

Fry, E. B., Kress, J. E., & Fountoukidis, D. L. (1993). *The reading teacher's book of lists.* Englewood Cliffs, NJ: Prentice-Hall.

Gaskins, I. W., Ehri, L. C., Cress, C., O'Hara, C., & Donnelly, K. (1997). Procedures for word learning: Making discoveries about words. *Reading Teacher, 50,* 312–327.

Gaskins, R. W., Gaskins, I. W., Anderson, R. C., & Schommer, M. (1995). The reciprocal relationship between research and development: An example involving a decoding strand for poor readers. *Journal of Reading Behavior, 27,* 337–377.

Gaskins, R. W., Gaskins, J. C., & Gaskins, I. W. (1991). A decoding program for poor readers—and the rest of the class, too! *Language Arts, 68,* 213–225.

Gaskins, R. W., Gaskins, J. C., & Gaskins, I. W. (1992). Using what you know to figure out what you don't know: An analogy approach to decoding. *Reading and Writing Quarterly, 8,* 197–221.

Gibson, E. J., Gibson, J. J., Pick, A. D., & Osser, H. A. (1962). A developmental study of the discrimination of letter-like forms. *Journal of Comparative and Physiological Psychology, 55,* 897–906.

Gibson, E. J., & Levin, H. (1975). *The psychology of reading.* Cambridge, MA: MIT Press.

Gilbert, N., Spring, C., & Sassenrath, J. (1977). Effects of overlearning and similarity on transfer in word recognition. *Perceptual and Motor Skills, 44,* 591–598.

Goodman, K. S. (1965). A linguistic study of cues and miscues in reading. *Elementary English, 42,* 639–642.

Goodman, K. S. (1967). Reading: A psycholinguistic guessing game. *Journal of the Reading Specialist, 6,* 126–135.

Goodman, K. S. (1972). Orthography in a theory of reading instruction. *Elementary English, 49,* 1254–1261.

Goswami, U. (1986). Children's use of analogy in learning to read: A developmental study. *Journal of Experimental Child Psychology, 42,* 73–83.

Goswami, U. (1988). Orthographic analogies and reading development. *Quarterly Journal of Experimental Psychology, 40,* 239–268.

Goswami, U. (1993). Toward an interactive analogy model of reading development: Decoding vowel graphemes in beginning reading. *Journal of Experimental Child Psychology, 56,* 443–475.

Goswami, U. (in press). The role of analogies in the development of word recognition. In J. Metsala & L. Ehri (Eds.), *Word recognition in beginning reading.* Mahwah, NJ: Erlbaum.

Gough, P. B., Juel, C., & Griffith, P. L. (1992). Reading, spelling, and the orthographic cipher. In P. B. Gough, L. C. Ehri, & R. Treiman (Eds.), *Reading acquisition* (pp. 35–48). Hillsdale, NJ: Erlbaum.

Guthrie, J. T., & Tyler, S. J. (1975). Cognition and instruction of poor readers. *Journal of Reading Behavior, 10,* 57–78.

Hoffman, J. V., McCarthey, S. J., Abbott, J., Christian, C., Corman, L., Curry, C., Dressman, M., Elliot, B., Maherne, D., & Stahle, D. (1993). *So what's new in the new basals?: A focus on first grade* (Reading Research Report No. 6). Athens, GA, and College Park, MD: National Reading Research Center.

Horn, C. C., & Manis, F. R. (1987). Development of automatic and speeded reading of printed words. *Journal of Experimental Child Psychology, 44,* 92–108.

Huba, M. E. (1984). The relationship between linguistic awareness in prereaders and two types of experimental instruction. *Reading World, 23,* 347–363.

Juel, C., & Roper/Schneider, D. (1985). The influence of basal readers on first grade reading. *Reading Research Quarterly, 20,* 134–152.

Kennedy, M. M. (1978). Findings from the Follow Through planned variation study. *Educational Researcher, 7*(6), 3–11.

LaBerge, D., & Samuels, S. J. (1974). Toward a theory of automatic information processing in reading. *Cognitive Psychology, 6,* 293–323.

Leslie, L., & Calhoon, A. (1995). Factors affecting children's reading of rimes: reading ability, word frequency, and rime-neighborhood size. *Journal of Educational Psychology, 87,* 576–586.

Liberman, I. Y., Shankweiler, D., Fisher, F. W., & Carter, B. (1974). Reading and the awareness of linguistic segments. *Journal of Experimental Child Psychology, 18,* 201–212.

Lovett, M. W., Borden, S. L., DeLuca, T., Lacerenza, L., Benson, N. J., & Brackstone, D. (1994). Treating the core deficits of developmental dyslexia: Evidence of transfer of learning after phonologically- and strategy-based reading training programs. *Developmental Psychology, 30,* 805–822.

Lovett, M. W., Ransby, M. J., Hardwick, N., Johns, M. S., & Donaldson, S. A. (1989). Can dyslexia be treated? Treatment-specific and generalized treatment effects in dyslexic children's response to remediation. *Brain and Language, 37,* 90–121.

Manis, F. R., Custodio, R., & Szeszulski, P. A. (1993). Development of phonological and orthographic skill: A 2-year longitudinal study of dyslexic children. *Journal of Experimental Child Psychology, 56,* 64–86.

Marsh, G., Desberg, P., & Cooper, J. (1977). Developmental strategies in reading. *Journal of Reading Behavior, 9,* 391–394.

Marsh, G., Friedman, M., Desberg, P., & Saterdahl, K. (1981). Comparison of reading and spelling strategies in normal and reading-disabled children. In M. P. Friedman, J. P. Das, & N. O'Connor (Eds.), *Intelligence and learning* (pp. 363–367). New York: Plenum.

Marsh, G., Friedman, M., Welch, V., & Desberg, P. (1981). A cognitive–developmental theory of reading acquisition. In G. E. MacKinnon & T. G. Waller (Eds.), *Reading research: Advances in theory and practice* (Vol. 3, pp. 199–221). New York: Academic Press.

McConkie, G. W., Zola, D., Blanchard, H. E., & Wolverton, G. S. (1982). Perceiving words during reading: Lack of facilitation from prior peripheral exposure. *Perception and Psychophysics, 32,* 271–281.

Meichenbaum, D. (1977) *Cognitive behavior modification.* New York: Plenum.

Moats, L. C. (1994). The missing foundation in teacher education: Knowledge of the structure of spoken and written language. *Annals of Dyslexia, 44,* 81–102.

Nicholson, T. (1991). Do children read words better in context or in lists? A classic study revisited. *Journal of Educational Psychology, 83,* 444–450.

Nicholson, T., Lillas, C., & Rzoska, A. (1988). Have we been misled by miscues? *Reading Teacher, 42,* 6–10.

Olson, R. K., Wise, B., Johnson, M., & Ring, J. (1997). The etiology and remediation of phonologically based word recognition and spelling disabilities: Are phonological deficits the "hole" story? In B. Blachman (Ed.), *Foundations of reading acquisition* (pp. 305–326). Mahwah, NJ: Erlbaum.

Patterson, K. E., & Coltheart, V. (1987). Phonological processes in reading: A tutorial review. In M. Coltheart (Ed.), *Attention and performance XII: The psychology of reading.* London: Erlbaum.

Perfetti, C. A., Bell, L. C., & Delaney, S. M. (1988). Automatical (prelexical) phonetic activation in silent word reading: Evidence from backward masking. *Journal of Memory and Language, 27,* 1–22.

Peterson, M. E., & Haines, L. P. (1992). Orthographic analogy training with kindergarten children: Effects of analogy use, phonemic segmentation, and letter–sound knowledge. *Journal of Reading Behavior, 24,* 109–127.

Pressley, M. (1977). Imagery and children's learning: Putting the picture in developmental perspective. *Review of Educational Research, 47,* 586–622.

Rayner, K., Inhoff, A. W., Morrison, R. E., Slowiaczek, M. L., & Bertera, J. H. (1981). *Journal of Experimental Psychology: Human Perception and Performance, 7,* 167–179.

Rayner, K., & Pollatsek, A. (1989). *The psychology of reading.* Englewood Cliffs, NJ: Prentice-Hall.

Rice, M. L., Huston, A. C., Truglio, R., & Wright, J. (1990). Words from "Sesame Street": Learning vocabulary from viewing. *Developmental Psychology, 26,* 421–428.

Samuels, S. J., Schermer, N., & Reinking, D. (1992). Reading fluency: Techniques for making decoding automatic. In S. J. Samuels & A. E. Farstrup (Eds.),

What research has to say about reading instruction (pp. 124–144). Newark, DE: International Reading Association.

Scarborough, H. S. (1995, April). *The fate of phonemic awareness beyond the elementary school years.* Paper presented at the biennial meeting of the Society for Research in Child Development, Indianapolis.

Seymour, P. H. K., & Elder, L. (1986). Beginning reading without phonology. *Cognitive Neuropsychology, 3,* 1–36.

Shaywitz, S. E., Escibar, M. D., Shaywitz, B. A., Fletcher, J. M., & Makuch, R. (1992). Evidence that dyslexia may represent the lower tail of a normal distribution of reading ability. *New England Journal of Medicine, 326,* 145–150.

Smith, F. (1971). *Understanding reading: A psycholinguistic analysis of reading and learning to read.* New York: Holt, Rinehart & Winston.

Smith, F. (1973). *Psycholinguistics and reading.* New York: Holt, Rinehart & Winston.

Smith, F. (1978). *Reading without nonsense.* New York: Teachers College Press.

Smith, F., & Goodman, K. S. (1971). On the psycholinguistic method of teaching reading. *Elementary School Journal, 71,* 177–181.

Stallings, J. (1975). Implementation and child effects of teaching practices in Follow Through classrooms. *Monographs of the Society for Research in Child Development, 40*(7–8, Serial No. 163).

Stanovich, K. E. (1980). Toward an interactive compensatory model of individual differences in the development of reading fluency. *Reading Research Quarterly, 16,* 32–71.

Stanovich, K. (1986). Matthew effects in reading: Some consequences of individual differences in the acquisition of literacy. *Reading Research Quarterly, 21,* 360–407.

Stanovich, K. E., & West, R. F. (1989). Exposure to print and orthographic processing. *Reading Research Quarterly, 24,* 402–433.

Thompson, G. B., Cottrell, D. S., & Fletcher-Flinn, C. M. (1996). Sublexical orthographic–phonological relations early in the acquisition of reading: The knowledge sources account. *Journal of Experimental Child Psychology, 62,* 190–222.

Torgesen, J. K., & Burgess, S. R. (in press). Consistency of reading-related phonological processes throughout early childhood. In J. Metsala & L. Ehri (Eds.), *Word recognition in beginning reading.* Mahwah, NJ: Erlbaum.

Torgesen, J. K., Wagner, R. K., Rashotte, C. A., Alexander, A., Lindamood, P. C., Rose, E., & Conway, T. (1996). *Prevention and remediation of phonologically based reading disabilities.* Paper presented at The Spectrum of Developmental Disabilities XVIII: Dyslexia, Baltimore MD.

Tunmer, W. E., Herriman, M. L., Nesdale, A. R. (1988). Metalinguistic abilities and beginning reading. *Reading Research Quarterly, 23,* 134–158.

van Daal, V. H. P., Reitsma, P., & van der Leu, A. (1994). Processing units in word reading by disabled readers. *Journal of Experimental Child Psychology, 57,* 180–210.

Vellutino, F. R., Scanlon, D. M., Sipay, E. R., Small, S. G., Pratt, A., Chen, R., & Denckla, M. B. (1996). Cognitive profiles of difficult-to-remediate and readily remediated poor readers: Early intervention as a vehicle for distinguishing between cognitive and experiential deficits as a basic cause of specific reading disability. *Journal of Educational Psychology, 88,* 601–638.

Venezky, R. L. (1976). *Theoretical and experimental bases for teaching reading.* The Hague: Mouton.

Walton, P. D. (1995). Rhyming ability, phoneme identity, letter–sound knowledge, and the use of orthographic analogy by prereaders. *Journal of Educational Psychology, 87,* 587–597.

Waterman, B., & Lewandowski, L. (1993). Phonologic and semantic processing in reading-disabled and nondisabled males at two age levels. *Journal of Experimental Child Psychology, 55,* 87–103.

Wise, B. W. (1992). Whole words and decoding for short-term learning: Comparisons on a "talking-computer" system. *Journal of Experimental Child Psychology, 54,* 147–167.

Wise, B. W., Olson, R. K., & Treiman, R. (1990). Subsyllabic units in computerized reading instruction: Onset-rime versus postvowel segmentation. *Journal of Experimental Child Psychology, 49,* 1–19.

Wood, S. S., Bruner, J. S., & Ross, G. (1976). The role of tutoring in problem solving. *Journal of Child Psychology and Psychiatry, 17,* 89–100.

6

◄o►

THE DEVELOPMENT OF LITERACY, Part 3

Expert Primary-Level Teaching of Literacy Is Balanced Teaching

with RUTH WHARTON-McDONALD and JENNIFER MISTRETTA HAMPSTON

In the early 1990s, we spent a great deal of time thinking about the fact that we see many children experience difficulties in elementary reading as early as grade 1. Although not all of the research summarized in the previous chapters was available in the early 1990s, enough did exist for us to understand that development of phonemic awareness and decoding skills were key in beginning reading. We were also aware, however, that many teachers were committed to whole language, and they believed it was affecting competencies beyond the word level. We had been in enough primary-level classrooms filled with literature and writing to know that there was much that was attractive about such instruction. Moreover, we had seen classrooms which seemed to be doing quite a bit of word-level skills instruction while simultaneously immersing children in literature and rich language arts experiences. We had enough memories then of lots of students seeming to read fairly well in these classrooms to know that success in learning to read was common in the 1990s. Unfortunately, there were also visits to grade-1 classrooms in which students were struggling. We decided that we wanted to know what distinguished the more successful primary classrooms from the less successful ones we had seen, believing that such knowledge was essential to have a fully informed opinion about what should be occurring in elementary language-arts classrooms.

As cognitively oriented researchers, we were aware that cognitive psychologists had devoted much effort to understanding how professionals do what they do, investigating radiologists reading X-rays and airline pilots dealing with emergencies, among others (Chi, Glaser, & Farr, 1988; Ericsson & Smith, 1991; Hoffmann, 1992). The typical tactic in such research was to compare expert professionals to novice professionals. Awareness of this literature stimulated an important insight in the summer of 1992, as one of us (M.P.) reflected on the various texts he had been reading about what primary-level reading instruction should be like.

Most of his reading that summer was in books considered foundational by the whole language educator community, volumes chock full of pedagogical suggestions. What occurred to him as he read them, however, was that, for the most part, the various recommendations were being made at something of a distance from primary-level teaching. Most of the books were written by professors of education. As someone who knew many professors of education, and who knew the expert–novice studies, M.P.'s gut reaction was that to ask professors of curriculum and instruction about how to teach elementary reading was somewhat akin to asking airline executives and aeronautical engineers how to fly a plane. In the case of flying, such a strategy would result in a lot of information about what could go on in the cockpit, but much of it would be wrong and many important nuances would be missing. Expert pilots have what is known as conditional knowledge: They know very well about when to make which decisions during a flight, with years of experience resulting in very detailed understanding about when particular tactics work and when others should be tried. Nobody else, including airline executives and aeronautical engineers, has access to such information, which develops only through years of experience flying an airplane.

It seemed to M.P. that the education professors writing the whole-language texts knew a great deal about instructional theory and certainly affect instruction through their research, writing, and influence on teacher education, but, nonetheless, they had little if any experience in the pilot's seat of American education. They were not the ones who planned and executed days and weeks and months of primary-grades experiences for students, and hence, they were in less-than-an-ideal position to know how curriculum and pedagogy mix.

That perspective could only be gained by being in primary classrooms for long periods of time.

Based on these reflections and experiences, it seemed to us that to know the nature of effective primary-level reading instruction, the best bet was to study and interact with effective primary-level teachers. We have done much of that since 1992 to develop an informed perspective on what should be occurring in elementary classrooms in order to maximize the likelihood that students learn to read.

A SURVEY STUDY OF OUTSTANDING PRIMARY-LEVEL READING TEACHERS

In order to get a running start in the pursuit of an understanding of outstanding primary-level teaching, Pressley and his associates Joan Rankin and Linda Yokoi (1996) decided to attempt to gather a great deal of data in a fairly short time. To do this, they selected a sample of elementary language-arts supervisors throughout the United States and asked them to identify their very best kindergarten, grade-1, and grade-2 teachers, ones who were exceptional in promoting literacy achievement in students. Once these exceptional teachers were nominated, they were contacted by mail and simply asked to describe in an open-ended fashion the 10 most important elements of their teaching. When all of the responses to this question were catalogued, it came to more than 400 individual practices that the teachers claimed occurred as part of their teaching. It was clear at this point in the study that primary-level classrooms are very busy places!

Pressley, Rankin, and Yokoi (1996) did not stop there, however. For each of the elements of instruction specified in response to the open-ended query, they developed a question that could be responded to on a quantitative scale, with all of the questions then placed on a questionnaire. Consider the following sample questions, all of which appeared on the questionnaire:

Do you use "big books"? (Answered on a "never" to "several times a day" scale.)

After a story, do you ask students "comprehension questions"? (Answered on a "not at all" to "all stories" scale.)

What percentage of the material read by your students is outstanding children's literature? . . . written at a "controlled" reading level? . . . written to provide practice in phonetic elements and/or patterns? . . . high-interest, low-vocabulary materials?

Which of the following extension activities do you use regularly, occasionally, or never? arts/crafts with print attached, cooking activities, dramatics or puppet plays, drawing or illustrating stories, movement activities, field trips, games.

Are home/parents involved in your reading instruction for good readers? . . . average readers? . . . weaker readers?

The questionnaire was then mailed to the teachers who had responded to the open-ended question. Most of them responded once again. The teachers described their classrooms, indicating in their responses that their classrooms involved a complex articulation of components.

Literate Environment

Virtually all of the teachers reported that they identified, at least to some extent, with whole-language and language-experience approaches. They reported that they attempted to create a literate environment in the classroom, including in-class library, display of student work, and display of chart stories and poems. These classrooms were portrayed as rich with stories being told, read, and reread. Learning centers dedicated to development of listening, reading, and writing were typical.

The teachers reported daily practice of reading and writing, with limited practice of skills in isolation, such as with worksheets or workbooks. Even so, the teachers also reported that they made certain that unmastered skills—including phonics, letter recognition, and spelling—were experienced repeatedly by students, often in the context of other reading and writing activities.

The teachers reported that they overtly modeled literacy skills and strategies, as well as positive attitudes toward literacy. They expressed concern with the individual literacy achievement of students, monitoring student needs, giving mini-lessons and reteaching as needed. Reading and writing were portrayed as individually guided on a student-by-student basis.

Many different types of reading were reported as occurring in these classrooms, including students reading along with teacher, echo and choral reading, shared reading, students reading aloud with others, daily silent reading, student rereading of books and stories, and reading homework (e.g., teachers sending books home and asking parents to listen to children read). Many different types of material were read, including outstanding children's literature, big books, chart poems and stories, picture books, and patterned and predictable books. Reading often included author studies, involving the reading of several books by distinguished children's authors and illustrators. The teachers reported limited reading of basals, materials at a controlled reading level, chapter books, and expository materials.

The teachers indicated that literacy instruction was integrated with the rest of the curriculum. As part of this, extension experiences were reported as common, including arts and crafts, illustrating activities, and games. In short, these expert teachers presented their classrooms as places in which literacy development occurred throughout the day, connected both to formal curriculum and less formal activities.

Teaching of Reading

There was a lot of concern with the development of reading skills, not only in context, when such instruction was needed and made sense, as favored in whole language, but also using decontextualized approaches (e.g., games, spelling tests). The teachers reported developing many particular competencies as part of their reading instruction, including skills prerequisite to reading (e.g., auditory and visual discrimination; attending and listening skills), concepts of print (e.g., concept of a word, parts of a book), letter recognition, the alphabetic principle (i.e., letters code the sounds in words), letter–sound associations, punctuation, decoding strategies (using context and picture cues, sounding out words using letter–sound knowledge), sight words and vocabulary, spelling, text elements (e.g., cause-and-effect relations, theme/main idea, character analysis), comprehension strategies (especially prediction and visualization), and critical thinking skills (including brainstorming, categorization, and recalling details).

Writing

Consistent with the whole language identification of these teachers, a great deal of writing was also reported. The teachers reported that they employed story and journal writing. Writing occurred in response to pictures, wordless picture books, and stories. Shared writing activities were implemented, including the class dictating stories to the teacher, who served as scribe. The teachers also reported encouraging students to write at home.

Teachers taught the writing process, including planning, making drafts, and revising. Once revised, students often published their writing in these classrooms, sometimes on the computer.

Writing was viewed as connected to reading in a number of ways.

An important one was through students reading aloud to classmates and the teacher the stories they had written.

Qualitatively Similar Instruction Regardless of Ability

The teachers were emphatic that the same types of materials and activities were experienced by all students regardless of ability. That is not to say, however, that they did not report making adjustments in response to individual reader ability. The teachers claimed to be more explicit and extensive in their teaching of some prereading, letter-, and word-level skills with weaker readers. That is, they seemed to believe, contrary to whole-language philosophy, that weaker students would not develop the skills needed to be literate simply through immersion in the literate environment that was their classroom. Consistent with this concern, the teachers reported providing more guidance during reading and writing instruction with weaker readers than with good ones.

Motivation

The teachers were clearly concerned with motivating their students to do literate things. In general, their perspective on motivation was consistent with standard whole-language thinking. They reported attempting to motivate literacy by reducing risks for students attempting literate activities, setting an exciting mood, and encouraging students to believe they can be readers and writers.

Grade-Level Shifts in Teaching

By including kindergarten, grade-1, and grade-2 teachers, it was possible to have a window on grade-level shifts during the primary years in effective literacy instruction. Not surprisingly, some instructional practices were reported as decreasing with increasing grade level and others were reported as increasing moving from kindergarten to grade 2.

Practices Decreasing with Advancing Grade Level

With advancing grade level, the teachers reported fewer signs and labels in their classrooms and less use of learning centers. Letter-recognition drills and singing of the alphabet song occurred less often. So did teaching *focusing* on the alphabetic principle, letter–sound associations, and simple concepts of print (e.g., concept of a "letter," directions of print). There was less teacher rereading of stories, shared big book reading, and reading of chart stories and poems with advancing grade level. Picture, patterned, and controlled-reading-level books declined in frequency of use. Writing together (e.g., students dictating stories to teachers) declined. There were fewer parent conferences.

Practices Increasing with Advancing Grade Level

With increasing grade level, there was more round-robin reading reported and more reading aloud in general by individual students. There was also more silent reading, of, for example, chapter books. Basals were reported as more frequent as students advance through the primary years.

Consistent with whole language, increased emphasis on using syntactic cues to decode was reported. On the other hand, so was increased teaching of phonics rules, sounding out, and orthographic analysis for decoding. Sight word and spelling drills increased, as did spelling tests. There was more teaching of vocabulary. The teaching of comprehension strategies increases with advancing grade, including teaching students to activate prior knowledge, generate questions during reading, find main ideas, and summarize. Teaching of critical thinking skills increased, including webbing and identification of causes and effects.

There was more writing of stories and more writing in response to reading. Punctuation was emphasized more during writing. The writing process was emphasized more as well, with greater planning, revising, and publishing. Writing portfolios were reported as increasing in saliency with increasing grade level.

Accountability

The teachers reported extensive monitoring of their students, including comprehension checks (e.g., questions following a reading, student retelling of stories heard or read, student retelling with story strips or pictures), writing portfolios, and reading portfolios. The teachers also reported regular conferences with parents and frequent communications with home as part of accountability.

Summary

The teachers in this study, who had been identified as effective by their supervisors, reported school days packed with all types of reading and writing. Most critically, from the perspective of this book, great balance was reported in the instruction offered to students. Consistent with the recommendation of a number of educators and theorists (e.g., Adams, 1990; Cazden, 1992; Delpit, 1986; Duffy, 1991; Fisher & Hiebert, 1990; McCaslin, 1989; Pressley, 1994; Stahl, McKenna, & Pagnucco, 1994), the teachers in this study depicted their classrooms as integrating the attractive features of whole language with explicit skills instruction. For example, although they claimed to be immersing students in literacy experiences, they also reported extensive and explicit teaching through modeling, explanation, and mini-lesson reexplanations, especially with respect to decoding and other skills (e.g., punctuation mechanics, comprehension strategies). Explicit teaching of letter-level and decoding skills, as well as elementary writing skills, was reported as especially frequent for students experiencing difficulties in learning to read and write.

There were many reasons for confidence in the survey data. One was that there was little variability in the opinions offered. Another was that the data were orderly in ways that would be expected (Harris & Sipay, 1990) if the teachers were being honest in their reports. Thus, teachers who claimed to be exclusively whole language were, in fact, less likely to endorse practices not endorsed by pure whole-language theorists, such as out-of-context decoding instruction. Also, there were reported decreases in instructional practices that should decrease between kindergarten and grade 2 (e.g., letter-level skills), and there were reported increases in instructional practices that should increase between kindergarten and grade 2 (e.g., spelling).

Even though such data were closer to actual teaching than the musings of a curriculum professor sitting at her or his word processor, nonetheless, they were farther removed from actual teaching than desirable. Thus, we followed the survey with studies of grade-1 teaching that involved much more observation. The survey study was a good starting point, however; nothing that follows in this chapter contradicts the reports provided by the responses of the effective teachers who responded to the survey.

AN OBSERVATIONAL STUDY OF OUTSTANDING AND MORE TYPICAL GRADE-1 LITERACY TEACHERS

The first challenge in studying outstanding teachers is to find them. Thus, in setting out to study outstanding grade-1 teaching (Wharton-McDonald, Pressley, & Hampston, in press; Wharton-McDonald et al., 1997), we asked language arts supervisors in the Albany, New York, area to nominate teachers. To be able to determine what was unique about outstanding teaching, we also asked the supervisors to identify teachers who were more typical of the grade-1 teachers in their district. The supervisors made a case for each teacher's participation, based on observations of teaching, indications of students' literacy achievement (e.g., reading test achievement, written products), and parental feedback. In autumn 1994, we began to observe 10 teachers, 5 considered outstanding by their supervisors and 5 considered more typical. (One nominated outstanding teacher dropped out during the course of the study for personal reasons.)

Although we respected the supervisors' judgments, we were also determined to find out for ourselves during the course of the study which of the teachers produced exceptional achievement. Thus, as our observation progressed, we were particularly attentive to possible indications of achievement.

In the end, three types of information were identified as measures of the effectiveness of teaching:

1. Every 10 to 15 minutes, the observer would look around the classroom and calculate percentage of students attentively engaged in academic activities. The classrooms varied with respect to this dimension: some were characterized by consistently high engagement, even when the teacher was not present or attending to the class, while others were more variable in engagement.

2. Reading level was defined by the difficulty levels of books that students were reading at the end of the year. There was wide variation between the classes by the end of the year, ranging from ones in which most students seemed to be working regularly with texts that were at or above grade level to others in which many students were regularly reading books intended for low or middle grade-1 reading.

3. Writing was appraised by examining the stories and essays that children wrote. In some classrooms, typical compositions were several pages long, reflecting knowledge of a variety of writing conventions, good spelling, and appropriate punctuation. The writing in these classrooms often reflected real coherence in expression, with a single topic developed over the pages of writing. At the other extreme were classrooms in which writing typically was less than a page long—usually two to three sentences. In these classrooms, topical development and mechanics typically were much less impressive.

By the conclusion of the study, which involved at least 10 observations of each teacher and two in-depth interviews of each participant, the researchers agreed that there were really three clusters of teachers. In three classrooms, student engagement was typically high, reading levels were at or above grade level, and writing was relatively coherent and sophisticated. Three classrooms were at the other extreme, with much more variable, and often low, engagement, and more modest indications of reading and writing achievement. Three classrooms were in the middle.

The researchers developed a model of each teacher's teaching. Then, they compared and contrasted the nine teachers to develop an understanding of aspects of instruction that were common across classrooms as well as aspects of instruction that distinguished the three best teachers from the other six.

Commonalities in Instruction across Classrooms

The nine classrooms, in fact, did have much in common, with the following characteristics observed in at least seven of nine classrooms:

- They were positive places, led by caring teachers.
- There was little competition.
- There were classroom routines, and thus, much of the time, students just knew what they were supposed to be doing.
- There was a variety of teaching configurations—whole and small group instruction, cooperative learning, and independent work.
- Teachers mixed direct skills instruction (i.e., of decoding, punctuation, capitalization, spelling) and whole language-type activities. Skills instruction was sometimes accompanied by worksheets, coexisting with whole language practices, such as the extensive use of trade books, teacher modeling a love of reading, and process writing.
- All teachers recognized the importance of parental participation in children's literacy development.

In summary—particularly important in the context of this book—there was some balancing of skills instruction and whole-language activities in all of the classrooms we observed.

Unique Characteristics of the Three Outstanding Teachers

As indicated earlier, student engagement was consistently high in the best three classrooms, compared to the much more variable engagement in the other six classrooms. There were a number of aspects of the teaching that contributed to this difference in student involvement:

- The best teachers in the sample were masterful classroom managers. They were so good, in fact, that classroom management was hardly noticeable. In the best classrooms, students were busy and appeared to be happy, with virtually no misbehavior observed. The worst that happened in these classrooms was off-taskedness, which typically ended quickly as the teacher moved in to get the student back on task, quietly and positively.

• The top three teachers were also skillful managers of the human resources available to them. Thus, resource teachers who "pushed in" to these classrooms were always busy providing instruction and assistance to students. In contrast, resource teachers often were underused by the more typical teachers—for example, they would spend a great deal of time on the periphery of the classroom with nothing to do as the classroom teacher conducted a whole group lesson.

• There was a high density of instruction in the best classrooms—that is, there was always something to keep the children engaged. Mornings in the best classrooms seemed jam-packed compared to more relaxed paces in the other classrooms.

• Activities connected with one another. Reading materials connected to writing topics, and literacy instruction tied to content instruction. For example, one of the outstanding teachers integrated her lessons on nutrition, a required part of the grade-1 science curriculum for the district, with readings such as Judith Barrett's *Cloudy with a Chance of Meatballs,* which motivated writing of balanced menus in the style of the children's book.

• In the best classrooms, the activities were consistently academically rich, in comparison to academically vacuous activities that were often observed in other classrooms. For example, in one of the more typical classrooms, there was a great deal of copying. In another of the more typical classrooms, much of the literacy instruction was devoted to "sharing" discussions not related to what the children were reading or to other academic content.

• In general, there was more going on—in terms of both activities and objectives covered—in the more outstanding classrooms than in the typical classrooms.

• The classrooms with outstanding teachers were filled with the message that students can and will learn. These teachers were determined that their students would develop as readers and writers. In contrast, there was more willingness by the more typical teachers to believe lack of student progress simply reflected the students' unreadiness to read and write.

• In the outstanding classrooms, every student was reinforced for her or his achievements. Each of the three best teachers beamed at the progress being made by weak students in particular.

• Literacy instruction in the top three classrooms was exceptionally well balanced with respect to the elements of whole language—reading of outstanding literature, writing—and the explicit teaching of skills. Reading, writing, and skills instruction were very well integrated in these classrooms. Although there were lessons dedicated specifically to certain skills, the skills instruction observed in the three best classrooms in this study was anything but decontextualized. The skills lessons were filled with reminders about how the skills related to the children's writing and their reading. Moreover, the children had many opportunities to use the skills as they read and wrote. As one of the outstanding teachers described it, teaching beginning reading "is a fine balance between immersing the child in whole language and teaching through . . . sounds, going back to using skills. . . . If you don't have a balance, it's kind of like trying to fit a square through a circle. It doesn't work. You don't connect with everyone if you don't use a variety of [teaching] strategies." In contrast to the integrated, balanced approach displayed by teachers in the top group, the other teachers tended to present instruction which was either heavily skills-based or heavily whole language, or they attempted to combine the two approaches but did so in a disjointed or inconsistent way. Thus, one teacher in the middle group whose instruction was heavily influenced by the whole-language philosophy also had a weekly spelling program based on basic decoding skills. Students learned to spell word families and practiced words each week but were not necessarily expected to be responsible for their spelling words when they wrote stories or compositions in their journals.

There were several more typical classrooms in which the teachers were determined to be as consistent as possible with whole language, including the downplaying of skills instruction. These classrooms just did not work as well as the three best classrooms: boredom was often very easy to detect, and end-of-the-year achievement in reading and writing was not as apparent. We also had two classrooms in which skills were paramount. These classrooms did not work either, as boredom was easy to spot, and reading and writing achievement in these classrooms was not even close to the end-of-the-year performances we observed in the best classrooms.

• One of the reasons that the students were busy, happy, and learning in the three best classrooms was that they received help as they needed it. The three best teachers were exceptionally active in scaffolding students' learning (Wood, Bruner, & Ross, 1976), providing hints and prompts when students faltered, whether during whole group instruction or one-on-one interactions. Students received assistance as they attempted to read challenging texts and as they drafted and revised what they wrote. The assistance often involved prompting students to use the skills they were learning. For example, on the day before Valentine's Day, one teacher managed to insert mini-lessons on shapes and phonemic awareness as she introduced an art project:

T: Miss _____ thinks of things when she thinks of Valentine's Day, too, and I wrote them down. What shape did I write them on? (*students are quiet*) Is it a square? A circle? A rectangle? A triangle? What shape is it?

S1: A heart.

T: Can anyone try to spell "heart"?

S2: H-E-A-R-T.

T: My goodness. If I wanted to use my sounds to spell heart, what would I start with?

S3: H.

T: And what would it end with?

S3: T.

T: So right away, you know some of the letters in "heart."

• Given many such opportunistic reviews, it was clear that the best teachers viewed skill development as they viewed all of reading and writing: as involving long-term construction of knowledge about how to read and write. At the same time, these teachers were not so committed to developmental educational models that they did not use worksheets or provide practice opportunities for some skills.

• The instruction and help that was given to children in the best classrooms did not make the children dependent on the teachers, however. Rather, self-regulation was most common in the three best classrooms. Students in these classrooms often worked independently or with other children. The best teachers developed students who could do much of what was required of them without adult assistance. The children were engaged in productive learning, regardless of whether the teacher saliently monitored them.

• The best teachers were highly aware both of their practices and of the purposes which drove those practices. There was nothing haphazard about literacy instruction in these classes. This was in contrast to some of the other teachers who justified some frequently observed activities as giving the children something to do while the teacher worked with small groups. Busy work was just not a concept in the thinking of the outstanding teachers.

The observers were struck that despite the commonalities between the outstanding classrooms (summarized in Table 6.1), every classroom in this study had its own personality, including the three headed by the best teachers. Thus, it is tough to illustrate outstanding teaching by

TABLE 6.1. Distinguishing Characteristics of the Best Teachers in the Wharton-McDonald, Pressley, and Hampston (in press) Study

- Masterful classroom management.
- High density of instruction and activity.
- Reading, writing, and other instruction well integrated.
- Good balancing of whole language and explicit skills instruction.
- High expectations that students would learn.
- Extensive use of scaffolding.
- Consistent encouragement of self-regulation.

describing the work of any one outstanding teacher. Still, we think that by considering in greater detail the teaching of one outstanding teacher, the complexity of an outstanding grade-1 class will be clearer.

Andy's Teaching

One of the three outstanding teachers in Wharton-McDonald et al. (in press) was a middle-aged male named Andy. He typically wore a sports shirt and jeans, rarely wearing a tie. His principal described him as looking like "a giant teddy bear," an accurate characterization except no teddy bear was ever so animated, ever so aware of the strengths and needs of the children in his contact, nor ever so able to build on student strengths as he addressed their needs. Andy's classroom was an extremely attractive world. One student said it all, when he said to himself one day, "I wish I lived here." Andy never criticized students. Typical was the following type of remark when things got a little out of hand: "I hear productive talk, but how about a little softer." He always intervened positively to get students back on task or to correct behavior. Thus, when a student was off task during an observation, Andy said, "Kenny, why don't you read your essay with Mark?" Kenny and Mark then read together with enthusiasm, with Mark providing revision feedback to Kenny. (All students' names are changed here to protect their privacy.)

When other adults entered the classroom, nothing stopped. Andy efficiently and quickly dealt with outside adults, never missing a step in his teaching as he did so. Attention to students more to the exclusion of visiting adults was a characteristic of all three of the best teachers, while more typical teachers were much more willing to attend to visiting adults. Interestingly, when the outstanding teachers did divert their attention to visitors, their students just kept at their work. In contrast, students in the other classrooms in the study were more likely to go off task if the teacher's attention was diverted from them.

Student engagement was invariably high in Andy's class, with students attentive during their whole group and small group lessons and working hard when on their own. The students started reading and writing on their own as soon as they arrived in the classroom. Moreover, their time was mostly spent on actual reading and writing, with very little time devoted to activities such as illustrating stories they had written. In other classrooms in this study, we observed much more art, often involving time-consuming, difficult-to-manage materials, such as paste or silhouette tracings. Such difficult-to-manage materials never entered Andy's classroom. In short, time was spent well, largely because the students managed themselves, with the environment set up so that their attentions were not diverted to solving problems like getting enough paste without getting it everywhere.

Why were Andy's students so self-regulated? Andy strongly encouraged self-regulation, regularly praising students for making decisions and taking responsibility. There were lots of comments like, "Some of you already had the words in alphabetical order before I told you to do so. Good." Each group of desks had a bin of easy reading books, with students making their own choices about which ones to read. On their own, students selected books from the "Reading Is Fundamental" project that were related to ongoing themes in the class. Andy taught his students to read "inside your heads." He encouraged students to monitor whether what they were reading was making sense and to reread when it did not. Before writing, Andy urged students to attend to mechanics themselves, although mechanics were, in fact, checked by the teacher as part of his monitoring of writing. The classroom included a writing checking chart so that students could begin to check their own writing and begin revision rather than wait for the teacher. Students practiced a variety of simple thinking skills—comparing, contrasting, and summarizing. These skills occurred in the context of other activities: For example, students were encouraged to plan, an important critical thinking skill, as part of their end-of-basal projects.

Although students were good at working on their own, there also was a lot of cooperation in this classroom, with kids checking each others' work and helping one another work through difficult materials. Andy assigned weaker readers to stronger partner readers. Children worked together on important projects. Students helped one another, just as they were often helped themselves by peers and by Andy.

Andy provided extensive scaffolding for students when they experienced difficulties, inserting many mini-lessons appropriate to the problems of particular students. Tasks given to students were always within their reach, at least with scaffolding: Andy is a *master* hinter. He monitored what his students were understanding during group discussions and provided helpful prompts to assist in their understanding of elusive concepts. For example, when group members were having difficulty differentiating the habitats of ducks and chickens, Andy pondered aloud to himself, "I wonder if it might have something to do with dealing with water." Andy checked on his students individually as they worked at their seats, providing help as needed. For example, when a student had difficulties with spelling a word during writing, Andy prompted the student to think about the sounds in the word. There were lots of comments like, "Shawn, is that the way we used those letters when we did the other words? Think about it." Shawn went on to spell the word correctly.

Andy first sought out students most likely to be having problems. The weaker kids were never scapegoated, however. Rather, Andy went out of his way to maintain their participation in the class in ways that were decidedly honorable. For example, when it was time for students to read their essays aloud to the class, the weaker students sat at a table near Andy so he could support their reading. The table had several other seats, each of which were occupied only by bidding from other members of the class. Sitting near Andy was seen as special for the students in his class, with no stigma ever attached to any student who spent time interacting with the teacher.

Excellent literature was extremely important in Andy's class, with student writing typically involving responses to high-quality stories and trade books. If one wanted to make an edited tape of outstanding whole language experiences, it could be done using footage from Andy's classroom. Consistent with whole language, there was extensive reading of trade books, with much attention to and discussion of distinguished children's authors (e.g., the author of the month). *Weekly Reader* was read. There were many types of reading, from choral reading aloud to partner reading to silent reading.

There was lots of discussion of what had been read. Andy asked a lot of questions, not simply to assess students' knowledge of a reading, but to begin conversations. In these discussions, students did a lot of explaining, with Andy constantly using follow-up questions to draw out students' conceptions of things. Andy's subsequent questions typically reflected consideration of previous answers, sending the message that what the students said about the reading was important. Yes, Andy often elaborated on the students ideas, but the students' voices and ideas were always honored.

Consistent with whole language, there was lots of writing, with clear reading–writing connections in Andy's classroom (e.g., rewrite in your own words a story just heard). This writing instruction covered macrostructural characteristics of stories—for example, clear emphasis on having a beginning, middle, and ending—and a title. It involved writing and revision as a function of conferencing with the teacher. There was also some peer conferencing, with students responding in writing to what they read by following four steps: read, think, tell neighbor, write.

Anything but consistent with whole language, however, Andy's class included systematic coverage of a basal. He liberally used stories from other basals, especially when they related to content themes. That Andy was not married to whole-language philosophy comes through in many other ways as well. In this classroom, skills instruction intelligently complemented the reading of authentic literature and student writing. There was extensive phonics instruction, both in formal lessons and on-line as part of mini-lessons. Simple phonics rules were taught (such as that the "bossy final e" caused the vowel preceding it to say its name). This occurred in the context of spelling instruction with, for example, lists of words that exemplified particular phonics principles. During the reading of a story, there was often discussion of words with particular characteristics (e.g., a word with a "short o" sound). During small group lessons, there often were word analysis activities, such as finding the little words in big words. Workbook pages sometimes complemented instruction, when Andy believed the students could benefit from such work.

Andy consciously stimulated students to think as they did skill activities, often requiring explanations from them. There were lots of exchanges like this one during a whole-group alphabetizing activity:

Andy: Why did you put *whale* before *woman*?

Tommy: Both start with a *w* but I used the second letter. *h* comes before *o,* so whale before woman.

A: That's right. . . . Your group has been learning how to alphabetize using the second letter. . . . This one is tricky because one letter in it can have two different sounds.

Eddy: Huge (*pronounced correctly*).

A: Why is it tricky?

E: Because *g* and have hard *g* or soft *g* sound.

A: That's right. Sometimes *g* can say [makes hard *g* sound] and sometimes [makes soft *g* sound]. So that's why this word needs a little extra practice.

Andy and his students talked a lot about what was in the books they were reading, how the ideas in their readings related to other ideas being covered in the curriculum, and how to use basic reading skills. There was dialoguing all day in this classroom.

There also was explicit attention to vocabulary development in Andy's classroom. Consistent with the thinking of whole language advocates, new vocabulary words encountered in stories were discussed by Andy and the students. These discussions were supplemented, however, with many sight words posted around the room. There were sight word drills. Resource teachers provided more explicit and extensive instruction to weaker students.

There were strong ties across the curriculum, with the gardening theme in the spring, for example, being represented in reading, writing, and a class science activity—as well as in students' self-selected reading from sources such as the "Reading Is Fundamental" books. Easy reading of books about plants continued for well after the unit on gardening was completed. Such integration was observed with respect to other themes as well, including the hatching of chickens in the late spring as the students' entrée to sex education. Literature, science, and values came together enthusiastically as students read about chickens and discussed the biology that permitted the birth of 12 chickens in their classroom. Students wrote on their own about the incubation process, but they also worked together to prepare a news story celebrating their 100% hatching success. Given the detailed student planning that went into the construction of the hatching process and the monitoring of the eggs—just like good readers and writers check to make certain everything is right—the hatching success was unsurprising. Connections were everywhere in Andy's teaching, creating an exciting classroom. We will remember for a long time the students who just had to share what they had written about the hatching chickens because they were so proud of the hatching project and what they wrote about it.

Andy fostered a strong *home–school* connection through homework (e.g., spelling) that he carefully monitored. Students were encouraged to take home challenging stories to read with a parent in the evening. When students talked about doing something academic with a parent, Andy noted and praised it publicly. Before vacation breaks, Andy sent home a packet of homework and a letter to parents to encourage them to work with their students over the break, including writing in their journals.

Although Andy was superb at adjusting his teaching in reaction to student needs, the magnificent orchestration that was a day in Andy's classroom did not simply happen. Andy did a lot of *planning,* with the result a rich classroom day.

Weeks and months of such days paid off, for at the end of the year, every student was writing at least three sentences in response to writing assignments, and most of the students were writing a full page or more. Their ideas were well connected in most compositions and were related to topical coverage in the class. Their printing was excellent, as was capitalization and punctuation. The students' writing reflected understanding of line and page conventions. There were some invented spellings, but many words were spelled correctly.

By June, all students except one were reading at least in the 1:5 basal reader. Most students in the class had read through all of the grade 1 basals and seemed comfortable in doing so. Quite a few students were reading second-grade trade books and in middle second-grade basal readers.

As we watched Andy's teaching in the context of visiting the more typical classrooms in the Wharton-McDonald et al. (in press) study, we could not help but think how fortunate his students were. What a difference it made for those children to experience Andy's classroom versus one of the more typical ones in the sample. As we thought about that, we also kept in the forefront of our minds that in soliciting classrooms for the study, we had emphasized to language arts supervisors that we did not want any weak grade-1 classrooms, that what we were interested in was outstanding classrooms and others that were solid grade-1 experiences. We had emphasized to the language arts supervisors that the typical classrooms should be ones that the school district would certainly be comfortable in showing to the public. Thus, the contrast between what happened in Andy's class and what happened in the weakest of the classrooms in the sample we studied probably underestimates the full range of experience of grade-1 students. Many children in American grade-1 classrooms do not get what Andy's students get; many do not even get close!

Concluding Comments

When the survey study that was summarized earlier in this chapter was reviewed for publication, one of the criticisms of it was that the list of instructional practices cited by the respondents was simply too long to be credible. The observations made by Wharton-McDonald et al. (in press) confirmed, however, that most of the instructional practices cited in the survey do occur in the classrooms of competent first grade literacy teachers—most critically, in the three best classrooms that Wharton-McDonald et al. (in press) observed. One way to think about instruction is with respect to its elements. This was the focus of the survey and the description of the Wharton-McDonald et al. (in press) data provided here. There is another way to think about the complicated nature of grade-1 instruction, however, that is also revealing about how the out-standing classrooms compare to the more typical classrooms.

The children entering grade 1 are vastly different in their prepa-ration for the instruction they will encounter there. Some enter with a history of rich emergent literacy experiences, and hence, they have very well developed language and communication competencies compared to less fortunate classmates. Some enter with advanced phonemic awareness, able to manipulate sounds in words up to and including the demands required by Pig Latin! Others, however, have much more rudimentary phonemic awareness, perhaps understanding that some words rhyme but little more. Sometimes there are children who are not even that far along in development of phonemic awareness. The elements of instruction that occur in the grade-1 classroom must meet the needs of all of these children, and that is no small task.

A key mechanism for teaching students in grade 1 so as to be sensitive to their individual needs is for the teacher to monitor students and provide scaffolding. Sometimes the scaffolding is in the form of differentiating task demands for students. For example, we certainly observed occasions when our excellent teachers encouraged the best writers to compose a couple of pages about a topic but in the next instant stroked one of the weakest writers for producing a couple of sentences. More often the scaffolding consisted of reminding students about how skills they were learning might help in a particular situation. By providing more frequent and intense scaffolding for students who were struggling, the excellent teachers were able to run classrooms in which all students experienced pretty much the same curriculum while at the same time receiving instruction appropriate to their needs and progress. The three best teachers made scaffolding a centerpiece of the instructional day and were always helping their students learn.

In contrast, scaffolding was not as prominent or frequent in the other classrooms. Indeed, the needs of the students did not seem to be as prominent in many of these classrooms, with the teachers more often focused on their curriculum than on the students. For example, both of the extreme whole language teachers talked to us a great deal about whole language, both during the formal interviews and on the run. In many ways, they seemed to believe that dedication to whole language would result in their students being readers and writers. We also observed greater attention to outside adults in the more typical classrooms, with teachers often diverting their attention from their students to deal with adults who came to the door or entered the classroom for some reason. In contrast, the excellent teachers rarely missed a beat in teaching their students as they dealt with the outside adult with a quick aside. The best classrooms we observed were as decidedly student centered as they were balanced with respect to skills and whole-language instruction.

In closing this discussion, we cannot help but emphasize the academic engagement that was so manifest in the best classrooms observed by Wharton-McDonald et al. (in press). Yes, the balanced instructional approach probably had something to do with it, but we attribute a great deal of the engagement to the excellent teachers' management skills. Their whole group lessons were always well planned, and materials were ready to use when they were needed. This contrasted with the hunt for materials that was so often observed in more typical classrooms. Perhaps even more critical, however, was that students in the best classrooms were asked to do tasks that were much more academic than anything else. For example, in all classrooms in the study, writing often was accompanied by art activities. In the more typical classrooms, the art often required more time and effort than the writing: students spent long amounts of time getting paste out of the paste jar and agonizing to cut out some weird shape (e.g., a cup with a handle with a finger hole, a silhouette of George Washington). This was never the case in the outstanding classrooms, where students were not given complicated tasks when art accompanied writing. Students' time was better spent.

We also emphasize in closing that students in the best classrooms typically wrote about what they had read, and they read further to develop their writing topics—all of which often was connected to social studies or science content. Concepts encountered on one day were related to concepts encountered on other days. Cross-curricular connections could not be missed during any visit to one of the top three classrooms in the Wharton-McDonald et al. (in press) study.

Even in the best classrooms, however, there are students who experience extreme difficulties. Increasingly in America's primary grades, when reading is not going well, it has meant providing children with a particular form of instructional intervention, taken up next.

READING RECOVERY®

Many grade-1 students make little progress in learning how to read, and are at long-term risk for academic difficulties. An important program aimed at such children was developed by New Zealand educator, Marie Clay (e.g., 1985). It involves daily one-teacher, one-child sessions for 10 to 20 weeks, with each session lasting approximately 30 to 40 minutes. The goal is to help these students catch up with peers. The starting assumption is that students may be learning too narrow a range of strategies for dealing with print and may not be flexible in their use of the strategies they have acquired. For example, students may attempt to sound out every word, when in fact a variety of strategies (see the earlier discussion in this section) can be applied during the identification of words in texts.

Much of Reading Recovery consists of teaching students strategies, which are defined by Clay (1985; Pinnell, 1989) as the processes required for reading, including the following:

- Reading left to right on a page.
- Using a return sweep rather than a slow return from the right-hand side of the page to the left side.
- Monitoring whether what is being read makes sense.
- Using cross checks on meaning-making processes, as illustrated by the following:

> A reader might use one kind of information to predict a word but will check that prediction by using another source of information. For example, glancing at a picture of the Billy Goats Gruff going across a bridge, a young reader might predict the word "water" in the text. Checking the print, however, the reader might notice that the word "stream" is not visually consistent with that prediction. This cross-checking may lead to a self-correction or other indication from the child of an awareness of a discrepancy. (Pinnell, 1989, p. 166)

- Searching for cues to meaning from pictures, language structures, and visual cues in print.
- Rereading when meaning is unclear.
- Self-correction rather than waiting for teacher correction of errors.

The emphasis on strategies in Reading Recovery comes through in quotes such as the following:

> Attention of teacher and child must be on strategies or operations—mental activities initiated by the child to get messages from a text. If the teacher becomes involved in teaching items rather than strategies—particular letter–sound correspondences or sight vocabulary words, for example, rather than the strategy of checking a word that would make sense in the context against the information in the print—the prospect of accelerated learning is seriously threatened. Letter–sound correspondences and spelling patterns are learned, but in the course of reading and, especially, writing meaningful text, RR teachers praise children for generative strategies, not for items learned. (Clay & Cazden, 1990, p. 208)

There is a common structure to each Reading Recovery lesson:

1. First the child rereads two or more short, familiar books.
2. Then the child reads a book introduced the day before, while the teacher keeps track of errors that are made. (This provides baseline information; the goal is to have the child eventually reading the book with 90% accuracy on subsequent days as part of step 1.)
3. The child does a letter identification exercise which involves plastic letters that attach to a metal board. (Once children know letters, this step is deleted or other decoding or vocabulary teaching is substituted.)
4. The child composes and writes out a story.
5. The child reassembles the story after the teacher cuts it up into pieces.
6. A new book is introduced and read by the child.

There is a great deal of teacher monitoring throughout the Reading Recovery process to assure that the child's particular problems are the focus of instruction, with the child's reading extensively observed and assessed before instruction even begins (Marks et al., 1994). The interaction that goes on around composing and reading of the new books is definitely scaffolded, with the student receiving hints and support as needed (Clay & Cazden, 1990). For example, during writing, the teacher calls attention to the sounds of words and spelling patterns by urging the student to listen carefully to words that will be written, prompting the child to write out a new word several times so that it will be memorable, praising progress, and so on. Consistent with Clay's (1991) perspective that reading instruction should develop inner control (i.e., internalized use of strategies taught to children), such support is phased out as the child is able to function independently (Wong et al., 1994), but additional support is provided following success with earlier texts and tasks as more challenging ones are presented. Conceptually, we find Clay's (1991) description of reading instruction as the development of inner control to be appealing: It is similar to other ideas about internalization of cognitive processes such as those offered by Vygotsky (1978).

We also are taken by Clay's positions on the importance of visual processing of words and attention to word sounds and parts. Clay (1991) argues for teaching children to attend carefully to words, analyzing the words into parts that can be sounded out, but also emphasizes that the decodings that result should be cross-checked with other information (i.e., syntactic and semantic–contextual cues) to determine whether the word as decoded makes sense. As indicated in Chapter 5, Clay has an appealing idea about how multiple cues can be used and coordinated, but there is a real need for research carefully evaluating her ideas about word recognition.

Why Are Educators Enthused about Reading Recovery?

Extremely visible evaluations of Reading Recovery were conducted in both New Zealand and in Ohio, and publicized by Reading Recovery enthusiasts (see Pinnell, 1989). They made the claim that most Reading Recovery students catch up with their classmates; more impressively, 2 or 3 years later, Reading Recovery enthusiasts reported that their students were reading pretty much like other students.

The Ohio group has been extremely active in training new Reading Recovery teachers, sending them back to their school districts to promote the approach. Those trained Reading Recovery teachers typically have convinced their districts to invest heavily in the development of new Reading Recovery teachers and to use the Reading Recovery approach.

What Are the Concerns about Reading Recovery?

Critics, however, point to the cost of one-to-one tutoring for a third to half of a schoolyear. A typical Reading Recovery teaching load is four students at a time, meaning that the teacher will deal with 12 students a year. This typically works out to $3,000 to $4,000 per student who receives Reading Recovery, which is, of course, in addition to the costs of the student's regular education. Doubts are especially intense when less expensive approaches to one-to-one tutoring, such as parental tutoring, also seem to have the potential to encourage inner-controlled reading in primary students who are experiencing difficulties (e.g., Mudre & McCormick, 1989).

The costs of Reading Recovery might be more palatable if it consistently delivered what its enthusiasts claim—that most Reading Recovery students leave the program at grade level and stay at grade level for the remainder of their education. Increasingly, there is reason to doubt that that is true, and prominent and well-respected analysts of early reading instruction concur that the long-term positive effects of Reading Recovery may not be as great or as certain as enthusiasts would like (Hiebert, 1994; Shanahan & Barr, 1995). Quite frankly, we would have been shocked if it were otherwise: Typically, when at-risk children receive educational interventions, the treatment effect is most pronounced immediately after the intervention has ended (e.g., effects of cognitive stimulation of at-risk infants during the first three years of life, Brooks-Gunn et al., 1995; effects of Head Start on IQ, Cicarelli et al., 1969). In general, the best approach for keeping students who are at-risk for academic difficulties on track is to provide consistent supplementary instruction for them (e.g., Campbell & Ramey, 1994). Reading interventions are somewhat analogous to sustained medical treatments, because being at risk for intellectual difficulties is a chronic condition, not a temporary state. To date, there is no quick and easy inoculation to prevent academic disabilities.

Finally, Reading Recovery enthusiasts represent their approach as the best approach to remediating reading difficulties. That claim is rather easily challenged, with a variety of one-to-one tutoring approaches, especially at the primary levels, producing striking positive effects on early reading (see Shanahan & Barr, 1995; Slavin, Karweit, & Wasik, 1994; Wasik & Slavin, 1993). Some of the most convincing findings, reviewed in Chapters 3 and 5, were those conducted by Lovett and her associates (Lovett, Ransby, Hardwick, Johns, & Donaldson, 1989; Lovett et al., 1994; see Chapter 5 of this volume) and the study by Vellutino et al. (1996; see Chapter 3 of this volume). Recent work on intense decoding instruction also has identified the possibility that Reading Recovery might have greater impact if it were to include even more explicit decoding instruction than usually occurs during Reading Recovery. For example, Iversen and Tunmer (1993) produced quicker improvement when Reading Recovery was complemented with more explicit instruction about phonology and decoding than when students experienced only Reading Recovery which places greater emphasis on decoding using word parts followed by checking through use of semantic–contextual cues.

In addition to the possibility that other one-to-one approaches produce benefits that are similar to, or even greater than, those associated with Reading Recovery, there is growing evidence that small-group tutoring, which is much less expensive than one-to-one tutoring, can also be very effective at the primary level (e.g., Hiebert, Colt, Catto, & Gury, 1992), including, for example, the Word ID Program that has been developed at Benchmark School (Gaskins, Gaskins, Anderson, & Schommer, 1995; Gaskins, Gaskins, & Gaskins, 1991, 1992; see Chapter 5 of this volume).

Not surprisingly, given the attention during Reading Recovery to letter- and sound-level cues, some who identify with whole language-type perspectives have responded to it unfavorably, contending that the program addresses only a small part of what literacy development should be (e.g., Barnes, 1996; Dudley-Marling & Murphy, 1997). Enthusiastic Reading Recovery teachers have responded that Reading Recovery lessons are only part of the child's day, part of the balance of instruction the child is receiving, albeit a very important part for the child experiencing reading failure in the primary years (Browne, Fitts, McLaughlin, McNamara, & Williams, 1996). Personally, we find the case that benefits can be derived from individual tutoring such as occurs in Reading Recovery to be more convincing than arguments that there is something wrong with a few minutes of daily instruction that is highly structured and more attentive to the basic skills of reading than other more abstract goals (e.g., emphasizing children's interpretations of what they read, honoring interpretations based on the diversity of sociocultural experiences that children bring to the classroom). Those who criticize the structure of Reading Recovery lessons miss one of the most striking features of Reading Recovery lessons, which we have observed personally: Reading Recovery students seem to get a charge out of the lessons. Although it may be hard for some whole language enthusiasts to accept that there can be joy for children in anything except immersion in literature and unstructured and undemanding opportunities to compose, experiencing success in Reading Recovery lessons seems to be a source of joy for students. Our perceptions on this point are shared by others who have a great deal of experience in Reading Recovery (Browne et al., 1996).

In summary, there is support for one-to-one tutoring when beginning reading goes awry, whether that tutoring is Reading Recovery or an alternative involving intense emphasis on the most challenging of early reading competencies, which typically is learning to decode. There are no magic bullets, including Reading Recovery, that cure problems in learning to read, however, although work on Reading Recovery has been revealing about what can be helpful in early reading remediation. Work on Reading Recovery also has stimulated the development of alternatives. More positively, much more is known now about beginning reading and how to inculcate it than was known even a decade ago. Reading research is paying off in the American schoolplace.

CONCLUDING REFLECTIONS

As this book goes to press, we are following up the Wharton-McDonald et al. (in press) study with other researchers, observing grade-1 classrooms in five sites across the nation (upstate New York; New Brunswick, New Jersey; Dallas–Fort Worth, Texas; Madison, Wisconsin; and Oakland, California). At each site, we are observing teachers who have been nominated as outstanding in producing student literacy achievement and others who have been nominated as producing more typical achievement for their district. Although the data are only now being collected, it seems certain based on ongoing observations that many of the Wharton-McDonald et al. (in press) conclusions will hold up. For example, there can be no missing the fact that whenever a classroom is highly engaged, the classroom is well managed, with a high density of academic activities. Again, the more engaging classrooms also seem to be more balanced with respect to skills and whole language.

One criticism of this line of research is that when others have looked at teachers who are supposed to be outstanding (e.g., Wendler, Samuels, & Moore, 1989), they have failed to find much difference in those classrooms. Why are our results so different? We think the reason is that the criteria in our observational studies are so high in order for a teacher to be deemed an outstanding teacher. Achievement, defined as consistent academic engagement that translates into superior reading and writing by the end of the academic year, must be clear in the classroom.

Balance Is a Commonplace Idea

The radical middle proposed here is only radical in contrast to the extreme whole-language and phonics positions that have defined the recent debates about beginning reading instruction. There are a number of scholars before us (e.g., Adams, 1990; Cazden, 1992; Chall, 1967/1983; Delpit, 1986; Duffy, 1991; Fisher & Hiebert, 1990; McCaslin, 1989) who have proposed that the most sensible beginning-reading curriculum should be a balance of skills development and authentic reading and writing. The unique contribution of the work of our group is in demonstrating that that is really what good teachers do.

It has not been lost on us that the current work is offensive to both extremist sides of the current great debates. The first time we presented the Wharton-McDonald et al. (in press) data at a professional conference, one prominent whole-language advocate stormed out of the session, and we later received reports that the individual had characterized the results of the study as "dangerous." On the other side, after discussing these results with a state school board, several members of the audience were agitated that there was not a phonics-first tone in our conclusions. There can be no doubt that, based largely on the types of data summarized in this chapter, we have come to the conclusion that both sides in the current great debate are wrong, that excellent elementary instruction is much more than the beginning reading instruction that either of the extreme groups holds dear.

As we were conducting the studies described in this chapter, Pressley was working on an edited book on balanced elementary-literacy instruction (McIntyre & Pressley, 1996). In that volume, a variety of individuals in elementary language-arts instruction articulated visions of balance, always based on teachers they had studied. In all cases, skills and whole-language instruction were occurring in classrooms. One could not miss, however, that some of the chapters included much more emphasis on up-front, systematic coverage of skills (akin to synthetic phonics as Chall, 1967/1983, defined it, in the case of beginning reading), and others emphasized much more instruction on an as-needed basis (akin to implicit phonics as Chall, 1967/1983, defined it, or analytic phonics). As a result, Pressley (1996) concluded that the jury is still out on the exact nature of balancing that works.

Was that conclusion a cop-out? We don't think so. When Chall's (1967/1983) analyses are examined, it is clear that there is great variability in classrooms offering both synthetic and analytic phonics instruction. In some classrooms, analytic phonics works pretty well; indeed, one of the three outstanding teachers in the Wharton-McDonald et al. (in press) study seemed more like an analytic phonics teacher than a synthetic phonics teacher, with most of her teaching of letter–sound associations and blending contexted in lessons focusing on literature and writing. We suspect that there are some really talented analytic phonics teachers who are consistently and busily monitoring their students for the skills instruction they need, and providing it many times a day. However, the great variability within the analytic phonics classrooms means that sometimes analytic phonics instruction does not work. Having seen some really unbalanced skills-instruction classrooms in which engagement was very low, we know that analytic phonics alone does not lead to high reading achievement. In light of all of these data, we believe that the key to high achievement in decoding is extensive coverage of skills (and at primary level, decoding skills in particular) and scaffolding of student application of those skills. That said, synthetic phonics generally produces a better outcome than analytic phonics. Thus, if one is not already an extremely skilled analytic phonics teacher, it makes more sense to attempt synthetic phonics than analytic phonics. We feel especially strongly about this in light of our examination of phonics packages that have been designed to be used in the context of a balanced program. The best of them are synthetic phonics programs.

No matter how good the phonics instruction is, however, we emphasize that phonics instruction alone will not be enough to produce excellent literacy in students. The whole-language components stimulate elements of literacy development not affected by decoding instruction alone, such as vocabulary development, writing competence, and positive attitudes toward reading and writing (e.g., Freppon, 1991; Graham & Harris, 1994; Morrow, 1990, 1991, 1992; Morrow, O'Connor, & Smith, 1990; Neuman & Roskos, 1990, 1992; Robbins & Ehri, 1994). It makes good sense based on the various empirical analyses now available to develop primary-level instruction that is rich in skills instruction and whole language immersion.

Technology and the Promise of Richer Home–School Connections

We did not fail to notice that most of the primary classrooms that we observed were attempting to connect with home, to stimulate activities in the home that would complement what was going on in school. There is growing evidence that increasing literacy activities at home can make a difference in literacy acquisition. For example, Morrow and Young (1997) carried out an experiment in which families in the treatment condition were encouraged to carry out at home literacy activities mirroring those occurring in their primary-level students' classrooms during the day. The families were urged to do more storybook and magazine reading, vocabulary development based on words in the home environment, and journal writing with children. The inner-city African American and Latino children in the treated condition were reading and writing better at the end of the study than control students.

The possibilities for stimulating literacy interactions at home seem especially great when it is recognized that there is a media explosion occurring which provides possibilities at home that were not possible previously. For example, all new televisions in the United States have the capacity for captioning, so that children can watch captioned television, something that improves reading and vocabulary development (Koskinen, Wilson, Gambrell, & Neuman, 1993; Koolstra, van der Voort, & van der Kamp, 1997). In addition, with the increasing availability of children's books on tape, there are many more opportunities to stimulate children to listen to books at home, including listening as they read (Koskinen et al., 1995). In addition, with more and more homes having access to computers, there are opportunities for children increasingly to experience electronic texts. There are no ends to the types of interactions that children might be able to experience with electronic texts, including texts that talk, texts that permit immediate elaboration of ideas currently on the screen, and texts that can be cut and pasted easily (Reinking, 1994). As electronic wizardry becomes cheaper, the ways that literacy development at home and school can connect will expand greatly.

Teacher Education

Finally, we are watching the outstanding teachers in order to have some idea about what competencies need to be developed in beginning teachers. Although our thinking on this point is not yet complete, there are definitely some notions that seem undeniable. The education of excellent primary-level teachers should be balanced to include much of whole-language philosophy and methods, but also other important traditions as well. Beyond simply teaching potential primary teachers about phonics, we think it makes sense to give them an excellent overview of the contemporary linguistics that supports language-skills instruction. Young teachers need to know about the English sound system as well as child language development, including descriptions and explanations of grammatical development. They also need background in cognitive development and cognition and instruction, since those disciplines are doing much to define contemporary primary-level literacy instruction. For example, the cognitive developmentalists and psychologists have clarified the nature of phonemic awareness and its significance in development (see Chapter 4). Process writing has been much informed by information-processing analysis of the composition process as involving planning, drafting, and revising (Pressley with McCormick, 1995a, or 1995b, Chap. 15). Beyond the exhortations of the whole-language theorists for teachers to use fine literature in their classrooms, teachers need to have an extensive background in, and an understanding of, the excellent children's literature that exists.

And what in whole language should be eliminated? First, we should eliminate all the antiskills sentiment and the argument against systematic skills instruction and decontextualized skills practice. There just is no support for these positions; indeed, there is a good deal of evidence to the contrary. For example, there is plenty of evidence that synthetic phonics instruction does work. That good teachers are able to balance whole language and skills is more than enough evidence that skills and whole language are not logically incompatible. Second, the inaccurate psycholinguistic arguments in whole language should be dispensed with. Arguments that reading and writing develop analogously to oral language are not supportable based on what is now known about reading and writing, and such arguments should be dropped. No one with an informed understanding about the development of reading and writing believes that they develop as oral language does. Whereas learning to read and write are conscious, intentional processes, oral language development is for the most part anything but intentional. Oral language typically is acquired from immersion in a speaking community, while reading and writing simply do not develop that way. Third, the political analyses should go. If conservatives favor skills instruction in the elementary curriculum, they certainly are not alone.

In recent decades, it has been fashionable for colleges and universities to dispense with elementary education as a major in favor of having students major in an arts and sciences area, assigning education courses needed for certification as a supplement. One reason for this is that the traditional elementary education curriculum involves many methods courses, which are viewed by many in academia as academically undemanding. We think it is time to rethink the possibility of elementary education as a major, this time emphasizing the conceptual knowledge that an elementary teacher needs to have in order to understand excellent elementary curricula. We can imagine an elementary education curriculum that would include courses in cognitive and social development, cognition and instruction, educational psychology (especially those aspects relevant to classroom management and assessment), linguistics, and children's literature. We would also want to see courses that cover the conceptual foundations of elementary arithmetic, social studies, and science. Having reviewed the literatures related to all of these areas (see Pressley with McCormick, 1995a, 1995b), we can state with some confidence that there is much in the conceptual realm that the aspiring elementary teacher could learn.

The capstone for such an education would be internship in the classroom of a really outstanding teacher. For the most part, student teaching in the past has sent potential teachers out to classrooms that have not been selected for excellence but rather for willingness to admit student teachers. It seems to us that a much better way to go would be to use the knowledge that is now being developed about outstanding elementary teaching to identify those teachers who should be shepherding the next generation into the profession.

One objection to this might be that there are not nearly enough really excellent elementary teachers to handle the very great demand for student teaching experience. The solution to that is easy: Train fewer teachers. With a half dozen or so teachers now being trained in order to produce one career teacher (Goodlad, 1994), there is a lot of waste in the system. Rather than training so many, become more selective about who should be allowed to become a teacher. One possibility which we find appealing is to select individuals for teacher training like professional sports teams select athletes: An individual gets a shot at the pros only after demonstrating some talent in the amateur ranks. We need to think about the many ways that young people could demonstrate potential talent for teaching before they are admitted to teacher education. Perhaps a strong track record as a child care worker or a tutor or camp counselor would be telling. How talent might be spotted early and used as a basis for selection for teacher education seems to us to be something that should be researched carefully.

In the end, there will be excellent primary-level education in American classrooms when there are excellent primary-level teachers delivering such instruction. We suspect that there are some personal individual differences that predispose a person to be a good primary-level teacher, probably including high energy as well as great commitment to children. But good elementary instruction is more than that. It requires extensive knowledge about the nature of language, modern conceptions of learning to read and write, and thorough understanding of children's literature and other primary-level content. Such knowledge can be taught in teacher education programs. When it is, teachers leave their undergraduate years knowing that teaching is largely about supporting child learners as they construct understandings of reading and writing. The good primary-level teacher understands that her or his lessons are only a start on the knowledge construction process, for example, with a great deal of scaffolding required before students come to own the skills (e.g., word-recognition competencies) that are at the heart of learning to read.

SUMMARY

1. Outstanding primary-level literacy teachers (defined by their positive effects on the literacy achievement of their students) balance elements of whole language (e.g., immersion in authentic literature and writing experiences) and systematic skills instruction. Excellent primary-level literacy education involves the complex articulation of many specific elements, often including both use of skills in context and decontextualized skills experiences.

2. Outstanding primary-level literacy instruction is engaging, as a simple metric reveals: Every 10 or 15 minutes, calculate the proportion of students who are academically engaged—doing something involving reading, writing, or closely related activities. In effective classrooms, most students are so engaged much of the time.

3. Explicit teaching of skills is the beginning of a constructivist process for young learners. It gives them a good start, but it is only that. As children attempt to use and adapt knowledge they are taught (e.g., of letter–sound associations), their understanding of it deepens. The opportunities to apply skills during real reading and writing

provide especially rich constructivist experiences, which is why balancing of whole language and skills teaching makes so much sense compared either to extreme anti-skills-instruction whole language or skills instruction-first approaches.

4. The balanced approach advocated here is consistent with the thinking of many research-oriented scholars in reading.

5. Many students who experience difficulties in learning to read in the grade-1 classroom can benefit from programs like Reading Recovery. Even so, students whose reading improves as a function of intensive tutoring may require much more support if they are to continue to succeed in school.

REFERENCES

Adams, M. J. (1990). *Beginning to read.* Cambridge, MA: Harvard University Press.

Barnes, B. L. (1996). But teacher you went right on: A perspective on Reading Recovery. *Reading Teacher, 50,* 284–292.

Brooks-Gunn, J., McCarton, C. M., Casey, P. H., McCormick, M. C., Bauer, C. R., Bernbaum, J. C., Tyson, J., Swanson, M., Bennett, F. C., Scott, D. T., Tanascia, J., & Meinert, C. L. (1995). Early intervention in low-birth-weight premature infants: Results through age 5 years from the Infant Health and Development Program. *Journal of the American Medical Association, 272*(16), 1257–1262.

Browne, A., Fitts, M., McLaughlin, B., McNamara, M. J., & Williams, J. (1996). Teaching and learning in Reading Recovery: Response to "But teacher you went right on." *Reading Teacher, 50,* 294–300.

Campbell, F. A., & Ramey, C. T. (1994). Effects of early intervention on intellectual and academic achievement: A followup study of children from low income families. *Child Development, 65,* 684–698.

Cazden, C. (1992). *Whole language plus: Essays on literacy in the United States and New Zealand.* New York: Teachers College Press.

Chall, J. S. (1967). *Learning to read: The great debate.* New York: McGraw-Hill.

Chall, J. S. (1983). *Learning to read: The great debate* (updated ed.). New York: McGraw-Hill.

Chi, M. T. H., Glaser, R., & Farr, M. J. (Eds.). (1988). *The nature of expertise.* Hillsdale, NJ: Erlbaum.

Cicarelli, V., et al. (1969). *The impact of Head Start: An evaluation of the effects of Head Start on children's cognitive and affective development.* Athens, OH: Westinghouse Learning Corporation, Ohio University.

Clay, M. M. (1985). *The early detection of reading difficulties: A diagnostic survey with recovery procedure.* Portsmouth, NH: Heinemann.

Clay, M. M. (1991). *Becoming literate: The construction of inner control.* Portsmouth, NH: Heinemann.

Clay, M. M., & Cazden, C. B. (1990). A Vygotskian interpretation of Reading

Recovery. In L. C. Moll (Ed.), *Vygotsky and education: Instructional implications and applications of sociohistorical psychology* (pp. 206–222). Cambridge, England: Cambridge University Press.

Delpit, L. D. (1986). Skills and other dilemmas of a progressive black educator. *Harvard Educational Review, 56*, 379–385.

Dudley-Marling, C., & Murphy, S. (1997). A political critique of remedial reading programs: The example of Reading Recovery. *Reading Teacher, 50*, 460–468.

Duffy, G. G. (1991). What counts in teacher education? Dilemmas in educating empowered teachers. In J. Zutell & S. McCormick (Eds.), *Learner factors/teacher factors: Issues in literacy research and instruction: Fortieth yearbook of the National Reading Conference* (pp. 1–18). Chicago: National Reading Conference.

Ericsson, K. A., & Smith, J. (Eds.). (1991). *Toward a general theory of expertise.* Cambridge, England: Cambridge University Press.

Fisher, C. W., & Hiebert, E.H. (1990). Characteristics of tasks in two approaches to literacy instruction. *Elementary School Journal, 91*, 3–18.

Freppon, P. A. (1991). Children's concepts of the nature and purpose of reading in different instructional settings. *Journal of Reading Behavior, 23*, 139–163.

Gaskins, R. W., Gaskins, I. W., Anderson, R. C., & Schommer, M. (1995). The reciprocal relationship between research and development: An example involving a decoding strand for poor readers. *Journal of Reading Behavior, 27*, 337–377.

Gaskins, R. W., Gaskins, J. C., & Gaskins, I. W. (1991). A decoding program for poor readers—and the rest of the class, too! *Language Arts, 68*, 213–225.

Gaskins, R. W., Gaskins, J. C., & Gaskins, I. W. (1992). Using what you know to figure out what you don't know: An analogy approach to decoding. *Reading and Writing Quarterly, 8*, 197–221.

Goodlad, J. F. (1994). *Teachers for our nation's schools.* San Francisco: Jossey-Bass.

Graham, S. & Harris, K. R. (1994). The effects of whole language on children's writing: A review of literature. *Educational Psychologist, 29*, 187–192.

Harris, A. J., & Sipay, E. R. (1990). *How to increase reading ability: A guide to developmental and remedial methods.* New York: Longman.

Hiebert, E. H. (1994). Reading Recovery in the United States: What difference does it make to an age cohort? *Educational Researcher, 23*(9), 15–25.

Hiebert, E. H., Colt, J., Catto, S., & Gury, E. (1992). Reading and writing of first-grade students in a restructured Chapter 1 program. *American Educational Research Journal, 29*, 545–572.

Hoffmann, R. R. (1992). *The psychology of expertise: Cognitive research and empirical AI.* New York: Springer-Verlag.

Inhelder, B., Sinclair, H., & Bovet, M. (1974). *Learning and the development of cognition.* Cambridge, MA: Harvard University Press.

Iversen, S., & Tunmer, W. E. (1993). Phonological processing skills and the reading recovery program. *Journal of Educational Psychology, 85*, 112–120.

Kohlberg, L., & Mayer, R. (1972). Development as the aim of education: The Dewey view. *Harvard Educational Review, 42*, 449–496.

Koolstra, C. M., van der Voort, T. H. A., & van der Kamp, L. J. T. (1997).

Television's impact on children's reading comprehension and decoding skills: a 3-year panel study. *Reading Research Quarterly, 32,* 128–152.

Koskinen, P. S., Blum, I. H., Tennant, N., Parker, E. M., Straub, M., & Curry, C. (1995). *Have you heard any good books lately?: Encouraging shared reading at home with books and audiotapes* (Instructional Resource No. 15). Athens, GA, and College Park, MD: National Reading Research Center.

Koskinen, P. S., Wilson, R. M., Gambrell, L. B., & Neuman, S. B. (1993). *Captioned video and vocabulary learning: An innovative practice in literacy instruction* (Instructional Resource No. 3). Athens, GA, and College Park, MD: National Reading Research Center.

Lovett, M. W., Borden, S. L., DeLuca, T., Lacerenza, L., Benson, N. J., & Brackstone, D. (1994). Treating the core deficits of developmental dyslexia: Evidence of transfer of learning after phonologically- and strategy-based reading training programs. *Developmental Psychology, 30,* 805–822.

Lovett, M. W., Ransby, M. J., Hardwick, N., Johns, M. S., & Donaldson, S. A. (1989). Can dyslexia be treated? Treatment-specific and generalized treatment effects in dyslexic children's response to remediation. *Brain and Language, 37,* 90–121.

Marks, T. A., O'Flahaven, J. F., Pennington, L., Sutton, C., Leeds, S., & Steiner-O'Malley, J. (1994). *A study of two first-grade teachers "roaming around the known" with their students* (Reading Research Report No. 9). Athens, GA, and College Park, MD: National Reading Research Center.

McCaslin, M. M. (1989). Whole language: Theory, instruction, and future implementation. *Elementary School Journal, 90,* 223–229.

McIntyre, E., & Pressley, M. (Eds.). (1996). *Balanced instruction: Strategies and skills in whole language.* Norwood, MA: Christopher–Gordon.

Morrow, L. M. (1990). Preparing the classroom environment to promote literacy during play. *Early Childhood Research Quarterly, 5,* 537–554.

Morrow, L. M. (1991). Relationships among physical designs of play centers, teachers' emphasis on literacy in play, and children's literacy behaviors during play. In J. Zutell & S. McCormick (Eds.), *Learner factors/teacher factors: Issues in literacy research and instruction*: *Fortieth yearbook of the National Reading Conference* (pp. 127–140). Chicago: National Reading Conference.

Morrow, L. M. (1992). The impact of a literature-based program on literacy achievement, use of literature, and attitudes of children from minority backgrounds. *Reading Research Quarterly, 27,* 251–275.

Morrow, L. M., O'Connor, E. M., & Smith, J. K. (1990). Effects of a story reading program on the literacy development of at-risk kindergarten children. *Journal of Reading Behavior, 22,* 255–275.

Morrow, L. M., & Young, J. (1997). Parent, teacher, and child participation in a collaborative family literacy program: The effects of attitude, motivation, and literacy achievement. *Journal of Educational Psychology, 89,* 736–742.

Mudre, L. H., & McCormick, S. (1989). Effects of meaning-focused cues on underachieving readers' context use, self-corrections, and literal comprehension. *Reading Research Quarterly, 24,* 89–113.

Neuman, S. B., & Roskos, K. (1990). The influence of literacy-enriched play settings on preschoolers' engagement with written language. In J. Zutell &

S. McCormick (Eds.), *Literacy theory and research: Analyses from multiple paradigms* (pp. 179–188). Chicago: National Reading Conference.

Neuman, S. B., & Roskos, K. (1992). Literacy objects as cultural tools: Effects on children's literacy behaviors in play. *Reading Research Quarterly, 27,* 203–225.

Pinnell, G. S. (1989). Reading recovery: Helping at-risk children learn to read. *Elementary School Journal, 90,* 161–183.

Pressley, M. (1994). Commentary on the ERIC whole language debate. In C. B. Smith (Moderator), *Whole language: The debate* (pp. 155–178). Bloomington, IN: ERIC/REC.

Pressley, M. (1996). Concluding reflections. In E. McIntyre & M. Pressley (Eds.), *Balanced instruction: Strategies and skills in whole language* (pp. 277–286). Norwood, MA: Christopher-Gordon.

Pressley, M., with McCormick, C. B.(1995a). *Advanced educational psychology for educators, researchers, and policymakers.* New York: HarperCollins.

Pressley, M., with McCormick, C. B. (1995b). *Cognition, teaching, and assessment.* New York: HarperCollins.

Pressley, M., Rankin, J., & Yokoi, L. (1996). A survey of instructional practices of primary teachers nominated as effective in promoting literacy. *Elementary School Journal, 96,* 363–384.

Reinking, D. (1994). *Electronic literacy* (Perspectives in Reading Research No. 4). Athens, GA, and College Park, MD: National Reading Research Center.

Robbins, C., & Ehri, L. C. (1994). Reading storybooks to kindergartners helps them learn new vocabulary words. *Journal of Educational Psychology, 86,* 54–64.

Shanahan, T., & Barr, R. (1995). Reading Recovery: An independent evaluation of the effects of an early instructional intervention for at-risk learners. *Reading Research Quarterly, 30,* 958–996.

Slavin, R. E., Karweit, N. L., & Wasik, B. A. (1994). *Preventing early school failure: Research, policy, and practice.* Boston: Allyn & Bacon.

Stahl, S. A., McKenna, M. C., & Pagnucco, J. R. (1994). The effects of whole language instruction: An update and reappraisal. *Educational Psychologist, 29,* 175–186.

Vellutino, F. R., Scanlon, D. M., Sipay, E. R., Small, S. G., Pratt, A., Chen, R., & Denckla, M. B. (1996). Cognitive profiles of difficult-to-remediate and readily remediated poor readers: Early intervention as a vehicle for distinguishing between cognitive and experiential deficits as a basic cause of specific reading disability. *Journal of Educational Psychology, 88,* 601–638.

Vygotsky, L. S. (1978). *Mind in society: The development of higher psychological processes.* Cambridge, MA: Harvard University Press.

Wasik, B. A., & Slavin, R. E. (1993). Preventing early reading failure with one-to-one tutoring: A review of five programs. *Reading Research Quarterly, 28,* 178–200.

Wendler, D., Samuels, S. J., & Moore, V. K. (1989). The comprehension instruction of award-winning teachers, teachers with master's degrees, and other teachers. *Reading Research Quarterly, 24,* 382–401.

Wharton-McDonald, R., Pressley, M., & Hampston, J. M. (in press). Outstanding literacy instruction in first grade: Teacher practices and student achievement. *Elementary School Journal.*

Wharton-McDonald, R., Pressley, M., Rankin, J., Mistretta, J., Yokoi, L., & Ettenberger, S. (1997). Effective primary-grades literacy instruction = balanced literacy instruction. *Reading Teacher, 50,* 518–521.

Wong, S., Groth, L., O'Flahaven, J., Gale, S., Kelley, G., Leeds, S., Regetz, J., & Steiner-O'Malley, J. (1994). *Characteristic teacher student interaction in Reading Recovery lessons.* College Park, MD: National Reading Research Center.

Wood, S. S., Bruner, J. S., & Ross, G. (1976). The role of tutoring in problem solving. *Journal of Child Psychology and Psychiatry, 17,* 89–100.

7

-<o>-

THE DEVELOPMENT OF LITERACY, Part 4

The Need for Increased Comprehension Instruction In Upper-Elementary Grades

with RUTH WHARTON-McDONALD

$\mathbf{S}$ome readers might be wondering how they could be so far along in a book dedicated to elementary literacy instruction with so little yet said about anything beyond grade 3. One of the main reasons for this is that intense researcher interest in emergent literacy and the renewed great debates about the nature of beginning reading have led to much more research attention to the preschool and primary grades in recent years. Nonetheless, there is good reason to think about the upper-elementary grades and to worry about the instruction that is occurring there. In particular, much more could be done to promote comprehension abilities in contemporary elementary schools. Before discussing this, however, it is necessary to provide some information about what is going on in the upper-elementary grades.

THE NATURE OF LITERACY INSTRUCTION IN GRADES 4 AND 5

In 1995–1996, we and some colleagues (Pressley, Wharton-McDonald, Hampston, & Echevarria, in press) decided to study the nature of literacy instruction in grades 4 and 5, because they are often the final 2 years of elementary school. We carried out the grade-4 and -5 study much as we had conducted the observational study of grade-1 instruction reported in Chapter 6. We observed 10 classrooms in upstate New York over the course of a year, all of which were selected by the participating school districts as very solid classrooms. In addition to the observations, two in-depth interviews with each teacher were conducted to clarify the instruction that was observed and to gain understanding of the teacher's intentions in teaching the way she or he did.

Background

We expected to find quite complex instruction in the upper grades:

1. The grade-1 study had made it clear that literacy teaching is a complex articulation of components. It made sense that instruction at the upper end of the elementary years would be at least as complex.

2. In addition, however, we had conducted a survey of grade-5 teachers from across the nation who were nominated as outstanding in the promotion of literacy achievement in their classrooms (Pressley, Yokoi, Rankin, Wharton-McDonald, & Hampston, 1997). The methodology for that survey was much like the methodology in the primary-grades survey: the teachers first responded to a few open-ended questions about the elements of their teaching, and then the elements mentioned by the teachers were examined in a quantitative questionnaire requiring teachers to indicate the frequency of each element of instruction in their classroom.

Consistent with the results obtained at the primary level, the sample of nominated-outstanding grade-5 teachers reported that their instruction balanced many components, including whole-language experiences and skills instruction. The various components that entered into the instructional mix included the following:

- Extensive reading at the heart of language arts instruction.
- Diverse grouping patterns (e.g., whole-group instruction, small-group instruction, cooperative learning experiences, individual reading).
- Teaching of both word-level and higher-order (e.g., comprehension, critical thinking) skills and processes.
- Development of student background knowledge.
- Regular instruction in writing, including lower-order mechanical

skills and higher-order composition skills (e.g., planning, drafting, revising as a process).

- Extensive evaluation of literacy competencies using diverse assessments.
- Integration of literacy and content-area instruction.
- Efforts to promote student motivation for reading and writing.

As was the case at the primary level, we felt that even though the survey was informative about some of the diversity of experience in the upper-elementary grades, it did not provide the type of in-depth understanding that comes from getting to know a number of individual classrooms. It did, however, sensitize us somewhat to what we should be looking for in the classrooms in the observational study.

Results of the Observational Study

What emerged from the observational study was a much more complicated set of results than came out of the survey research. Basically, we observed some practices that were common across classrooms, but we also observed many dimensions of difference. In what follows, we detail both, and comment on several other findings that were very important and somewhat unexpected.

Commonalities across Classrooms

There were some instructional practices that we observed in at least 8 of 10 classrooms. Because virtually all of these practices were also represented on the survey of exceptionally strong grade-5 teachers from across the nation, we suspect that the following can be found in some way, shape, or form in most grade-4 and -5 classrooms in the United States:

- Some class discussions driven by teacher questioning, with student responses evaluated by the teacher
- Literature-driven reading instruction
- Direct instruction in specific skills
- One-to-one mini-conferences with students
- Reading of trade books—in particular, novels
- Opportunities for students to select reading materials
- Teacher read-alouds
- Expressed belief in the importance of reading comprehension at this level of instruction
- Teacher activation of students' prior knowledge

- Exercises emphasizing reading comprehension
- Independent reading time
- Writing of connected text on at least a weekly basis
- Use of the writing process model and instruction in its components (i.e., planning, drafting, and revising long compositions)
- Connections between reading, writing, and content area coverage (e.g., readings related to a social studies theme inspiring writing of stories related to the theme)
- Use of procedural facilitators for writing assignments (e.g., worksheets reminding students of the parts of a story)
- Teaching of writing mechanics
- Use of computers for writing of final drafts
- Worksheets (teacher-made and commercial)
- Book projects
- Spelling exercises and tests
- Explicit vocabulary instruction
- Homework

In short, in keeping with the grade-5 survey, which reported a balancing of whole language (i.e., reading of literature, writing) and skills-instruction components, we observed such balancing in the classrooms in upstate New York. Even so, our sense as we watched these classrooms was that they were very different from one another, with the differences at the grade-4 and -5 level much more pronounced than the differences we had observed in primary-level classrooms.

Dimensions of Difference

Because we became aware very early in the study that the classrooms we were watching differed dramatically from one another, we were sensitive throughout most of the study to the many differences that existed. In the end, the differences could be clustered in five groups, pertaining to differences in classroom management, reading, writing, word-level skills, and academic engagement.

The teachers varied tremendously in their *class management.* For example, in some classes, every day was pretty much the same, while there was much day-to-day and week-to-week variability at the other extreme. Some teachers used classic behavior management tactics well, and others used them hardly at all. Grouping varied from predominantly whole-group to predominantly individualized instruction, with just about everything in between also observed. An exceptionally important dimension of difference among classrooms was the extent to which student progress was monitored and responded to in an appropriate fashion. Some teachers were very aware of their students and provided assignments that matched student needs and competencies, while others were less concerned with such monitoring and tailoring of work. The classrooms also varied in the extent to which they were driven by concern with external standards (e.g., preparing for state tests) versus concern for student improvement. In addition, whereas some classrooms included a high density of activity, others were relaxed. Homework varied from skills practice to authentic reading and writing.

There were substantial differences in the *amount of reading* in each class and *variability in types of reading* (e.g., Did the teacher cover all of the main genres?), although much reading of novels was observed. There were many different ways that reading could connect with the content-area curriculum, from well-planned units relating to important curricular themes to generally haphazard comments made by the teacher relating ideas in current readings to social studies and science concepts.

There was great variability as to how much *writing* occurred, from being the focus of literacy instruction to being quite a small part of it. Students in most classes did narrative writing. Although planning, drafting, and revising occurred in all classes, the classes varied in the extent of their commitment to the process, from consistent use of and great reflection on planning, drafting, and revising to much more implicit use of the writing process. There were differences in how mechanics were covered as well, from substantial reflection on rhetorical devices used by authors of works the students were reading to coverage of mechanics on worksheets.

There was great variation between classrooms in the extent to which *word-level skills* was emphasized. The amount of vocabulary instruction varied from class to class (e.g., in some classes, there were published lists with tests, whereas others focused on discussion of words encountered in readings). Spelling instruction and tests occurred in all classrooms, although the sources of the words varied (e.g., published lists, words encountered in reading), as did the amount of drilling and the extent to which spelling and vocabulary instruction were connected (i.e., from being completely independent to vocabulary words being the spelling words).

Student engagement varied considerably from classroom to classroom, as defined by the percentage of students typically involved in academic activities. In some classes, engagement was usually high. In others, it was much more variable.

Different Core Emphases

Each classroom had at its core some particular emphases around which the curriculum was organized and presented. These core sets of activities, while observed in every classroom, differed somewhat from one classroom to the next. The most common emphases included reading of trade books and writing, which were related through thematic connections, although as summarized in Table 7.1, each classroom really did have a unique orientation.

TABLE 7.1. Central Emphases for Each Classroom in the Pressley et al. (in press) Study of Grade-4 and -5 Classrooms

Classroom	Emphasis
1	Trade book reading and process writing, with thematic connections; reader response to literature; encourages self-regulation including through use of modified reciprocal teaching as students respond to literature in small groups.
2	Reader response to novels consistent with a current theme; writing process instruction with emphasis on self-regulated writing, reading, and studying.
3	Reading of trade books, with connections to writing; heavy emphasis on process writing and self-regulation of reading, writing, and behavior.
4	Basal reading and teacher question-driven discussion of basal selections; isolated skills instruction; quiet seatwork.
5	Content strongly emphasized, including current events; heavy emphasis on vocabulary acquisition and acquisition of factual knowledge; process writing; explicit skills instruction; whole-group teacher question-driven discussions and individual seat work.
6	Cooperative exploration; theme-driven instruction; lots of reading of trade books; skills instruction, which is not tied to theme/current readings.
7	Reading–writing–content integration, with many activities relating to trade book currently being read by class; extensive discussions driven by teacher questions.
8	Reading trade books; skills instruction with worksheets.
9	Process writing; reading of trade books; reading–writing–content instruction connections.
10	Teacher reading of literature to class; student reading of trade books; writing with process instruction and teaching of mechanics; clear reading–writing–content instruction connections.

Instruction That Was Not Happening.

In some classrooms, there were aspects of the instruction that we found to be very disturbing. For example, we observed explicit comprehension instruction only rarely, despite a great deal of research in the past two decades on how to promote children's comprehension of what they read (Pearson & Fielding, 1991). Indeed, the situation seemed to be much as Durkin (1978–1979) described it two decades ago, with a great deal of *testing* of comprehension but very little *teaching* of it. (See the next section of this chapter, if you are not familiar with Durkin's work.)

A twist on this situation, however, was that the comprehension tasks now being given to students did seem to be informed by the comprehension process research of the past two decades. It was not uncommon, for example, for students to be asked to respond to short-answer questions requiring them to summarize what they read, identify confusing points in a text, construct questions pertaining to a text, or predict what might be next in a text. That is, they were asked to respond to questions constructed around the cognitive processes involved in skilled comprehension (i.e., summarizing, monitoring confusion, self-questioning, predicting based on prior knowledge). However, there was little evidence that students were being taught to self-regulate comprehension processes *as* they read, and in some classrooms, there was no evidence that they were being taught the active comprehension processes validated in the last two decades. In general, students were provided with opportunities to practice comprehension strategies, but were not actually taught the strategies themselves nor the utility value of applying them.

It also was striking how little teaching of self-regulation occurred. Rather than teaching students how to become self-regulated learners, the teachers seemed to expect that the behaviors would develop naturally, if students were given enough independent assignments.

Summary

The 10 grade-4 and -5 classrooms observed by Pressley et al. (1997) varied greatly. In general, the teachers heading these classrooms tended to emphasize a few aspects of literacy development in their classroom, with the core instructional emphases varying from classroom to classroom. Despite the great variability between classrooms, it was possible to find some commonalities. An important commonality was a mixture of literature and whole writing experiences and skills instruction, consistent with the balance model developed in this book.

That there was balance is not to say that we felt the instruction we observed was as good as it could be. Specifically, self-regulation was actively encouraged in only a few of the classrooms, and the lack of comprehension process instruction was especially striking, given the widespread assumption that development of comprehension skills is a key activity in the upper-elementary grades (e.g., Chall, 1983; Harris & Sipay, 1990).

FOUNDATIONS OF MODERN COMPREHENSION INSTRUCTION

Since 1990, when Marilyn Adams's book, *Beginning to Read,* reviewed in detail the letter-level and word-level processing skills that young readers must acquire, reading researchers and educators have focused their attention on the processes surrounding children's acquisition of decoding skills. One reason is that the dominant approach to beginning reading education in the United States, whole language (e.g., Weaver, 1994), has been suspected of not developing decoding skills in students (Smith, 1994). Even so, regardless of whether instructional orientation is whole-language or skills-inculcation, there is a broad base of agreement that the most important goal of reading education should be to develop readers who can derive meaning from texts.

One of the reasons that researchers have focused on word recognition is because of their belief that word decoding is *the* bottleneck in the meaning-getting process. Of course, when children cannot decode at all, there is no chance of comprehension. When they can decode only with effort, decoding competes with comprehension efforts for the limited capacity available for processing of text (i.e., the 7 ± 2 chunks of short-term memory; Miller, 1956), so that effortful decoding consumes capacity that might otherwise be used to understand text. With increasing automaticity of decoding, there is freeing up of capacity which permits greater comprehension of what is being read (LaBerge & Samuels, 1974). According to the LaBerge and Samuels model, if decoding is automatized, comprehension at the word level is more or less taken care of. Although we agree that word-level comprehension is facilitated by automatic decoding, there is no doubt that comprehension beyond the word level requires much, much more.

There has been a great deal of research in the past two decades on how to increase the reading comprehension of elementary-level students, selectively discussed in the next section of this chapter. Most of this work is concerned with teaching students to use comprehension strategies. In this section we explore the various reasons that researchers focused on the teaching of comprehension strategies as a means to improve comprehension. This work on strategies instruction did not occur in a vacuum; rather, it reflected many converging efforts.

Awareness of the Need for Comprehension Instruction

In a landmark study, Dolores Durkin (1978–1979) raised the consciousness of the reading education community about the need for comprehension instruction. She observed grade-3 through -6 classrooms and students, watching for comprehension instruction during reading and social studies, but seeing little of it. Instead of teaching students how to comprehend, teachers were assessing comprehension, asking students questions about material they had just read. Durkin's study did much to stimulate researchers to study comprehension as a process and identify ways to increase comprehension.

Study Skills Instruction as the Norm

In the 1970s, the conventional way of thinking about increasing comprehension was through study skills instruction. Such instruction often boiled down to teaching of strategies, such as reflecting on prior knowledge related to a reading, restudying difficult portions of passages, visualizing, and summarizing (Forrest-Pressley & Gilles, 1983). One of the most systematic and well known approaches was the SQ3R approach (Robinson, 1946), involving survey of text, question-generation in advance of reading based on text headers, reading, reciting the text, and reviewing. The problem with all of the study skills approaches was that there was little or no evidence that they really worked (e.g., Tierney, Readence, & Dishner, 1980). That is, there was no convincing proof that the great effort required to execute SQ3R paid off in equivalent benefits (Johns & McNamara, 1980). Although the study skills developers had not done the research and development required to hone their procedures so that they worked well (i.e., provided substantial benefits for the effort expended), the study strategies approaches made it sensible to think about teaching strategies as a way to increase comprehension.

Theories of Meaning Representation That Stimulated Research on Specific Types of Strategies Instruction

In the late 1970s and early 1980s, there was much new theorizing about how meaning is represented in the mind and how mental representations of meaning determine comprehension of complex ideas, such as those represented in text. The various representational theories stimulated hypotheses about the nature of effective comprehension strategies instruction.

For example, Walter Kintsch of the University of Colorado and his associate van Dijk (1978; also van Dijk & Kintsch, 1983) developed a theory about how skilled readers construct representations of the main ideas of text (macropropositions, to use their terminology). Their work inspired studies on teaching students how to summarize texts in order to make them more memorable, producing quite a bit of evidence that elementary students could generate good summaries (e.g., Doctorow, Wittrock, & Marks, 1978; Taylor, 1982).

Canadian cognitive psychologist Allan Paivio (e.g., 1971, 1986; Clark & Paivio, 1991) proposed that knowledge is composed of complex associative networks of verbal and imaginal representations. This led to work on how children could be induced to construct mental images that would increase their memories of text content (Levin, 1973; Pressley, 1976). In general, these studies showed that when children were taught to construct mental images representing the content of texts, there was increased memory (e.g., as tested by literal, short-answer questions) and understanding (e.g., as tested by questions tapping inferences that could be made during reading of the text) compared to when same-age students read as usual (Pressley, 1977).

Several theorists proposed that stories have conventional structures: a beginning, including information about the time, setting, and characters in the story; an initiating event, setting a goal or leading to a problem; a series of attempts to achieve the goal or overcome the problem; achievement of the goal or resolution of the problem; and character reactions to the resolution (e.g, Mandler, 1984; Stein & Glenn, 1979). Children, especially weak readers, can be taught to attend to story grammar elements as they read, leading to increases in their comprehension and memory of stories (e.g., Short & Ryan, 1984).

Without a doubt, the most prominent representational theory among reading researchers and educators during the late 1970s and early 1980s was schema theory, as specified by Richard Anderson and David Pearson (1984) at the Center for the Study of Reading. A schema integrates a number of commonly co-occuring concepts into an orderly representation. For example, the schema for the christening of a ship includes its purpose—to bless the ship. It includes information about where it is done (i.e., in dry dock), by whom (i.e., a celebrity), and when it occurs (i.e., just before the launching of a new ship). The christening action is also represented (i.e., breaking a bottle of champagne that is suspended from a rope). Schema activation can dramatically affect comprehension, inferences, attention allocation, and memory of what is read: thus, schema theorists advocated encouraging students to activate, in several ways, their prior knowledge while reading, by making predictions about text content before reading, relating information encountered in text to prior knowledge, and asking themselves questions about the reasons for the relations specified in text (Anderson & Pearson, 1984).

In summary, representational theorists in the 1970s and early 1980s believed that if children failed to understand and remember text, the problem might have been that they were not constructing complete representations of the ideas coded in the text. Their solution was to encourage students to construct fuller representations through instruction, using strategies for enhancing mental representations of texts—strategies that could be applied before, during, and after reading (Levin & Pressley, 1981).

Verbal Protocols of Skilled Reading

As discussed in Chapter 2, many verbal protocol studies of reading were carried out in the 1970s and 1980s. It became apparent in these think-aloud studies that skilled readers used cognitive strategies as they read, including strategies favored by the representational theories—summarizing, constructing images, attending to story grammar elements, and relating to prior knowledge (Pressley & Afflerbach, 1995). This work made apparent that teaching students to use comprehension strategies was to teach them to read as exceptionally skilled readers do.

Emergence of Metacognitive Theory

An approach known as metacognitive theory was developed in the 1970s. Metacognition is cognition about cognition (Flavell, 1977). It plays an important regulatory role in cognition: Knowing that one can retain more of what one reads by creating a summary of it is important metacognitive knowledge—conditional knowledge (Paris, Lipson, & Wixson, 1983) about summarization. Such knowledge can inform a student how to proceed when confronted with text containing ideas that must be remembered. That is, metacognition increases the likelihood of long-term, appropriate use of strategies (for reviews, see Pressley, Borkowski, & O'Sullivan, 1984, 1985).

Both Flavell (1977) and Flavell and Wellman (1977) offered analyses of how metacognition might regulate cognitive strategies in various task situations. That many strategies were definitely teachable became well established during this era as well (Pressley, Heisel, McCormick, & Nakamura, 1982), although it also became obvious that long-term use of taught strategies only occurred when strategies instruction was metacognitively embellished (e.g., information about the usefulness of a trained strategy was included in instruction; e.g., Borkowski, Levers, & Gruenenfelder, 1976; Cavanaugh & Borkowski, 1979; Kennedy & Miller, 1976). Metacognitive theory, implicating strategies as critical in effective thinking, was thriving, borne out by the first analyses and tests of it.

Vygotskian Theories about the Development of Internalized Cognitive Competence

Vygotsky's (1978) theory of cognitive development became prominent in the late 1970s and early 1980s. Recall from Chapters 4 and 6 Vygotsky's view that interactions between adults and children that are critical to cognitive development occur with tasks that are within the child's *zone of proximal development,* tasks which the child can do only with assistance. Vygotsky's perspective on the zone did much to stimulate developmentally oriented researchers and educators to embrace the teaching of cognitive skills which are not fully developed in children, but which could develop with adult support—such as comprehension strategies. In particular, developmentalists felt that development of cognitive skills might be consistent with Vygotsky's (1962) theory that skills once done with others come to be internalized as self-directed inner speech.

One prominent developmentalist who thought this was Canadian Donald Meichenbaum (e.g., 1977), who formulated an extremely visible position about how adults could interact with children to encourage their acquisition and autonomous use of new cognitive skills. Like Vygotsky (1962), Meichenbaum believed that speech-for-self began as interpersonal, overt speech between adults and children, the adult role highly directive at first, but gradually fading as children increasingly internalized directive speech. By the middle 1970s, there were a number of American analyses suggesting that the development of self-directive speech plays an important role in the development of children's self-regulation (e.g., Kohlberg, Yaeger, & Hjertholm, 1968; Patterson & Mischel, 1976; Wozniak, 1972).

Thus, in the late 1960s and early 1970s, Meichenbaum hypothesized that children could learn a variety of cognitive skills if they were taught simultaneously to use self-speech to direct their use of the cognitive skills they were acquiring (e.g., Meichenbaum & Goodman, 1969). Meichenbaum's general approach can be illustrated by a study by Bommarito and Meichenbaum (reported by Meichenbaum & Asarnow, 1979). They taught comprehension strategies to middle-school students who could decode but were experiencing difficulties understanding what they read. Instruction began with an adult modeling self-verbalized regulation of comprehension strategies: looking for the main idea, attending to the sequence of important events in a story, and attending to how characters in a story feel and why they feel the way they do, among others.

The students saw the adult read, and heard the following verbalizations:

> Well, I've learned three big things to keep in mind before I read a story and while I read it. One is to ask myself what the main idea of the story is. What is the story about? A second is to learn important details of the story as I go along. The order of the main events or their sequence is an especially important detail. A third is to know how the characters feel and why. So, get the main idea. Watch sequences. And learn how the characters feel and why. . . . While I'm reading I should pause now and then. I should think of what I'm doing. And I should listen to what I'm saying to myself. Am I saying the right things? Remember, don't worry about mistakes. Just try again. Keep cool, calm, and relaxed. Be proud of yourself when you succeed. Have a blast. (Meichenbaum & Asarnow, 1979, pp. 17–18)

By the end of six training sessions, the students were self-verbalizing covertly, as control was gradually transferred to them over the course of the sessions. Did the self-verbalization instruction affect reading comprehension? Yes: There was greater pretest-to-posttest gain on a standardized comprehension test among these students than for control condition participants. That is, the researchers concluded that adults could advance the cognitive development of children through scaffolded teaching of important cognitive processes.

Reader Response Theory

Thus far, we have made the case that in the late 1970s and early 1980s, there were lots of pieces of cognitive psychology supporting the teaching of comprehension strategies. For comprehension instruction to make sense and be acceptable to the reading-education community, most of whom do not identify principally with cognitive psychology, it had to be consistent with traditions embraced by reading educators. As it turned out, teaching of comprehension strategies was consistent with an exceptionally important language-arts perspective.

Language-arts educator Louise Rosenblatt (1938) made the then-radical proposal that the meaning of a text will vary somewhat from reader to reader. Like Vygotsky, Rosenblatt would be discovered anew in the late 1970s, in her case with the 1978 publication of her book, *The Reader, the Text, the Poem*. The reader response theory defined by that book had an enormous impact on the language arts education community. It legitimized the teaching of active and interpretive reading (e.g., Clifford, 1991).

According to reader-response theory, interpretive variability occurs because the meaning of a text involves a transaction between a reader, who has particular perspectives and prior knowledge, and a text, which can affect different readers in different ways (e.g., Beach & Hynds, 1991; Rosenblatt, 1978). Readers sometimes form impressions of characters in stories, and frequently relate their personal and cultural experiences to events encountered in text. As part of responding to text, readers sometimes explain events in a text to themselves. Often they form vivid images. In short, language arts theorists and educators viewed as reader responses the processes that psychologists considered to be comprehension strategies. Reader response has been acceptable to the language arts community since the late 1970s. This means the cognitive psychologists and the language arts specialists had the same idea of prompting child readers to be more active as they read.

RECIPROCAL TEACHING

By the late 1970s and early 1980s the stage was set for research on teaching elementary students to use comprehension strategies as they read. The diverse elements in this mixture came together at the University of Illinois Center for the Study of Reading. The Center was the intellectual home for Dolores Durkin, whose work established the need for comprehension strategies instruction. A great deal of important work was carried out there: Several young scholars at the Center would put together a summary of study skills (Tierney, Readance, & Dishner, 1980); important work on individual comprehension strategies was conducted including work on summarization (Brown & Day, 1983), imagery (Anderson & Hidde, 1971), and prior knowledge activation (Anderson & Pearson, 1984). Reader response was known to the Center group, if for no other reason than the National Council of Teachers of English was headquartered at Illinois, with scholars such as Alan Purves frequently interacting with the Center group.

The scholars who would bring it all together, however, would be Annemarie Palincsar and Ann Brown. Their landmark study of reciprocal teaching (1984) had a great impact on interest in comprehension strategies instruction.

Reciprocal teaching (Palincsar & Brown, 1984) involves teaching comprehension strategies in the context of a reading group. Students are taught to make predictions when reading, to question themselves about the ideas in text, to seek clarifications when confused, and to summarize content. The adult teacher initially explains and models these strategies for students, but quickly transfers responsibility to the members of the group, with individual students taking turns leading the reading group.

During a reciprocal teaching lesson, one student is assigned the role of group leader, supervising the group's generation of predictions, questions, and summaries as reading proceeds. The group leader also solicits points that need to be clarified and either provides clarifications or elicits them from other group members. The group interactions are cooperative, and the adult teacher provides support on an as-needed basis only. That is, the adult teacher provides scaffolding: enough support so that the group makes progress but not so much support as to stifle students' active self-direction of their reading and comprehension.

Brown and Palincsar (1989) summarized a typical discussion of text in a reciprocal teaching group:

> The dialogue leader begins the discussion by asking a question on the main content and ends by summarizing the gist. If there is disagreement, the group rereads and discusses potential candidates for question and summary statements until they reach consensus. Summarizing provides a means by which the group can monitor its progress, noting points of agreement and disagreement. Particularly valuable is the fact that summarizing at the end of a period of discussion helps students establish where they are for tackling a new segment of text.
>
> Attempts to clarify any comprehension problems that might arise are also an integral part of the discussion. And, finally, the leader asks for predictions about future content. Throughout, the adult teacher provides guidance and feedback tailored to the needs of the current discussion and his or her respondents. (p. 413)

Reciprocal teaching is chock full of good things, according to cognitive views of learning and development (Brown & Palincsar, 1989). First of all, students are presented with multiple models of cognitive processing: The teacher models and explains. Every day the group comes together and executes a sequence of strategies well matched to the processes required to understand text; thus, peers in the group are continuously modeling reasoning about text. With respect to the learning of content, students are led to make the types of elaborations and inferences that should facilitate learning of text—that is, predictions, inferences required as part of question generation and elaboration, and summarization. The discussions permit various points of view to be aired and require students to justify and back up their claims. These discussions permit review and commentary about the strategies being learned and the content being covered. Thus, reciprocal teaching offers opportunities to learn new content as it offers opportunities to learn how to process new content.

A major assumption of reciprocal teaching is that by participating, students will eventually internalize use of the four strategies practiced in the group. That is, the processing that was once carried out between persons in the group will come to be carried out within the individual students, consistent with the Vygotskian perspective that individual cognitive development develops from participation in social groups.

Reciprocal teaching has shortcomings, however. Many reciprocal teaching lessons involve a preponderance of literal questions and little in the way of evidence that students are monitoring their comprehension. This is obvious from a lack of clarification questions in many reciprocal teaching lessons. Because reciprocal teaching emphasizes a gradual reduction of teacher support, there are often long pauses in lessons, with students fumbling because the teacher is uncertain whether to enter into the conversation and provide input. With respect to performance on standardized comprehension tests, the effects of reciprocal teaching are not particularly striking, with an average effect size of 0.3 *SD*, although it is more successful when there is more direct teaching of the four comprehension strategies (Rosenshine & Meister, 1994). Contemporary comprehension strategies instruction involves more direct explanation than reciprocal teaching.

DIRECT EXPLANATION OF COMPREHENSION STRATEGIES AND MORE: TRANSACTIONAL COMPREHENSION STRATEGIES INSTRUCTION

In 1984, Michigan State researchers Laura Roehler and Gerald Duffy proposed an important model of teaching that begins with teacher explanations. At the heart of it is a process that they referred to as mental modeling, which is showing students what a strategy is and how to apply a strategy by thinking aloud (Duffy & Roehler, 1989). The teacher introducing mental imagery as a comprehension strategy using Roehler and Duffy's (1984) approach might tell students about how good readers sometimes make pictures in their heads that are consistent with the ideas in a story. Then, the teacher might begin to read a story aloud to the students, stopping from time to time to explain the images she or he is constructing of what was going on in the story. Students would then try the strategy, monitored by the teacher, who would provide additional explanations and modeling as needed. Feedback and instruction are reduced as students become more and more comfortable with the strategic process being taught. The information provided to students during practice depends very much on the particular problems the students encounter and the particular ways that their understanding is deficient. Reinstruction and reexplanations occur, as well as follow-up mental modeling. The teacher responds to specific student needs, sometimes offering an elaboration of student understanding up until that point. That is, instruction is scaffolded according to the Duffy and Roehler approach.

Duffy et al. (1987) produced an extremely well-designed study of the effects of direct-explanation strategy instruction on grade-3 reading, with 10 groups of weak readers assigned randomly to the direct explanation condition, and 10 control groups receiving their usual instruction. Duffy et al. (1987) taught grade-3 teachers to explain directly the strategies, skills, and processes that are part of skilled grade-3 reading, as the study continued over the course of an entire academic year. The teachers were taught first to explain a strategy, skill, or process, and then to mentally model use of it for students. Then came guided student practice, in which the students initially carried out the processing overtly so that the teacher could monitor their use of the new strategy. Assistance was reduced as students became more proficient. Teachers encouraged transfer of strategies by reviewing when and where the strategies being learned might be used. Teachers cued use of the new strategies when students encountered situations where the strategies might be applied profitably, regardless of when these occasions arose (i.e., scaffolding continued throughout the school day). Cuing and prompting continued until students autonomously applied the strategies they were taught.

By the end of the year, students in the direct-explanation condition outperformed control students on standardized measures of reading, including a measure of reading achievement given the year after the direct-explanation intervention had been administered. These results had a profound effect on the reading-education community. Direct explanation as defined by Duffy et al. (1987) was subsequently used by many educators as a starting point as they implemented comprehension strategies instruction in their own schools.

Descriptive Studies of Transactional Comprehension Strategies Instruction

We studied several places where teaching of comprehension strategies was developed and implemented in light of the Roehler and Duffy (1984) model. Because the instruction we studied involved so much more than direct explanation, we felt that a different term was needed to describe it, one more inclusive of all that occurs during such teaching. In particular, we wanted a summary term that better captured the dynamic give-and-take between teachers and students that typifies classrooms employing strategies instruction. The descriptive label, "transactional strategies instruction," thus seemed appropriate from three different perspectives. Recall Rosenblatt's (1978) reader response position that meaning is not in text alone or in the reader's head alone but rather is constructed by readers as they consider text content in light of their previous knowledge and experiences. Such meaning construction, termed transactional by Rosenblatt, was certainly emphasized in the instruction described here, as students were encouraged to use strategies such as prediction, visualization, and summarization to create personalized interpretations and understanding of text.

The term "transactional" was also appropriate for a second reason, however. Most comprehension strategies instruction occurred in small reading groups involving a teacher and students reading texts together, applying comprehension strategies as they did so. In the developmental psychology literature (e.g., Bell, 1968), the term transactional is used to refer to interactions in which the child's actions in part determine the behaviors of adults in the child's world. Consistent with that use of the term transactional, teachers' reactions in the instruction detailed here were determined largely by the reactions of the students. Teachers responded to student interpretations and difficulties: If a student offered a good summary, the teacher might prompt elaboration of the summary; if the student's summary was difficult for the teacher to understand, she or he might prompt rereading or reconsideration of the text. What happened in transactional strategies instructional groups was determined largely by the reactions of students to teachers and to other students.

The strategies instruction described in what follows was transactional in yet a third sense. Organizational psychologists (e.g., Hutchins, 1991) in particular have been concerned with the types of solutions produced during group problem solving as compared with individual problem solving: Groups invariably produce interpretations that no one individual in the group would have produced. Group interpretations following this pattern were prominent during the comprehension strategies instruction we watched. The group used the strategies they were learning as interpretational tools, producing impressive interpretations of text.

To summarize, there were three senses in which the classroom strategies instruction we observed was transactional: (1) Meaning was determined by heads employing strategies as they processed the text; (2) how one head reacted was largely determined by what other heads in the group were doing, thinking, and saying; and (3) the meaning that emerged as teachers and students together used strategies to read and comprehend a text was the product of all of the heads in the group. Instruction was transactional in all of these senses largely because of extremely intelligent assistance to students during strategies instruction. Direct explanation of strategies was followed by sensitive scaffolding of their use by students in small groups.

Benchmark School Studies

Pressley's initial studies on comprehension strategies instruction were conducted at Benchmark School in Media, Pennsylvania, which is dedicated to the education of high ability students who experience difficulties learning to read in the first two years of schooling. Even though the Benchmark students are at great risk for long-term school failure, most emerge after 4–7 years well prepared to return to regular education. Virtually all Benchmark graduates complete high school, and many attend college. Because much of the Benchmark approach involves teaching students to use cognitive strategies to accomplish reading and other literacy tasks, the school seemed like a perfect place to do an initial investigation of effective strategies instruction: Reading strategies are taught in primary through middle school, with students encouraged to use them across the curriculum.

One study was an interview study of the faculty (Pressley, Gaskins, Cunicelli, et al., 1991). The 31 academic teachers at Benchmark were asked 150 questions about their instruction, each requiring an objective answer (e.g., a response on a Likert scale) but also permitting any additional input the responding teacher might wish to provide. Up to 5 hours of face-to-face interviews permitted ample opportunity for teachers to provide detailed explanations, based on their extensive experience, of what they believed about strategies instruction as well as why they believed it.

Generalizing across the 31 teachers, there were many points of agreement, including the following:

• The Benchmark teachers strongly endorsed direct explanation and modeling as essential components of effective strategies instruction. Many observations at Benchmark confirmed that such explanations were used during small and large group instruction and as part of one-to-one tutoring and reinstruction. Teachers reported that their initial explanations and modeling were more complete than later explanations and modeling, although the faculty members, especially the more experienced ones, were emphatic that explanations and modeling should continue for a long time after introduction of strategies.

- Extensive practice in use of strategies was endorsed by the teachers, as was extensive guidance and feedback in response to student needs during such practice. Even so, the teachers admitted that it is often difficult to diagnose the specific problems experienced by students, and a challenge to devise remediation. The teachers were aware that students did not learn strategies quickly: facile use of strategies across a wide range of tasks and materials occurred only after extensive practice, which included struggling to adapt strategies to a wide range of academic problems.

- Teaching of strategies and their application was reported as occurring across the curriculum, consistent with our frequent observations of Benchmark teachers encouraging strategies use in many different contexts.

- The teachers considered it essential to provide extensive information to students about when and where to apply the strategies they were learning, as well as information about the learning benefits produced by use of strategies.

- The teachers recognized that transfer of the newly acquired strategies to new academic tasks and contents was anything but automatic; rather, it required extensive teaching about when strategies might be applied as well as practice applying strategies across a number of situations.

- The teachers were emphatic that only a few strategies could be introduced at a time. In accordance with this, in-depth instruction of strategies over months and years was the preferred approach to teaching at Benchmark. Their view was that students developed strategic repertoires over the course of their years in the school—strategies instruction was definitely not seen as a quick fix.

- Although cognitive in their orientation, the teachers also recognized the need for explicit reinforcement of student efforts and successes in applying strategies and accomplishing difficult academic tasks. Feedback to students was considered essential. It was seen as especially important to follow students' success with positive feedback as a means of keeping students motivated. The teachers were well aware that their students had already experienced several years of school failure and believed that students' Benchmark successes needed to be rewarded in order to offset the damage produced by the previous failures.

- The Benchmark teachers believed they should develop students who were habitually reflective and good planners. Strategies instruction was seen as a way of accomplishing this higher-order goal.

Pressley, Gaskins, Cunicelli, et al. (1991) presented the same questions that had been given to the Benchmark teachers to a sample of 9 nationally known researchers in strategies instruction, distinguished investigators who had extensive hands-on experience in implementing long-term strategies instruction at their home institutions. What was striking was the high congruence between the responses of the Benchmark teachers and this researcher sample. Extensive experience with strategies instruction seems to produce perceptions of it which are consistent with the thinking of the Benchmark teachers.

Two additional studies at the school provided even more detailed understanding of how Benchmark teachers do what they do. One was a case study of the instruction in one Benchmark classroom during spring semester of 1990 (Pressley, Gaskins, Wile, Cunicelli, & Sheridan, 1991). The focal strategy taught there was the generation of an outline of the major ideas in each text, which would include information about causes and effects coded in the text, temporal sequences, compare and contrast information, and simple descriptions. Teaching of these strategies was thoroughly integrated with the teaching of content, with focal strategies instruction occurring during reading, writing, and social studies as teachers and students interacted to create maps. For example, semantic maps were generated by students as they planned writing assignments as part of social studies. Social studies homework often required semantic mapping.

Consistent with teachers' claims in the interview study, explanations and modeling of the semantic mapping strategy was more extensive and explicit early in the instruction. After several months, given a one-line direction from the teacher (e.g., "Make a map of what's in this text") , students often began to map the meaning of a text. The teachers provided assistance to students on an as-needed basis, often giving gentle hints about how specific relationships in a text might be represented in a semantic map.

Instruction in other strategies did not stop when semantic mapping was introduced. Rather, teachers modeled and explained use of semantic mapping in conjunction with other strategies. For example, the strategies of activating prior knowledge, predicting, seeking clarification, and summarizing were all prompted frequently during lessons intended primarily to provide new information about semantic mapping as a strategy.

We had an important insight at Benchmark that cognitive strategies were being taught as methods to encourage interpretations, which we define as the construction of personally significant understanding. The teachers in the Pressley, Gaskins, Wile, et al. (1991) case study taught their students that no two semantic maps should be alike and that each student's map should reflect reactions to the content of the text.

Interpretive activities were especially apparent in analyses of Benchmark classroom dialogues produced by Gaskins, Anderson, Pressley, Cunicelli, and Satlow (1993) who studied the strategy instruction lessons of six teachers at Benchmark. Three lessons were analyzed for each teacher in Gaskins et al. (1993): one when a new focal strategy was introduced, the second somewhat later, and a third considerably later than that. The discourse in these classrooms was much different from the discourse in conventional classrooms in typical schools: Many repeated cycles consisting of a teacher asking a question, a student responding, and the teacher evaluating the response (i.e., IRE cycles involving teacher initiation, student response, and teacher evaluation), ordinarily observed in many classroom studies (see Cazden, 1988; Mehan, 1979), were not found in the Benchmark data. Instead, the teachers engaged in interactive dialogues with their students 88% of the time in what Gaskins et al. (1993) referred to as process–content cycles: The teacher used content as a vehicle to stimulate application and discussion of strategies. When students made comments during discussions, Benchmark teachers did not attempt to evaluate their responses but rather encouraged the students to elaborate on them— encouraging students to further process the content using strategies. The goal was to encourage student understanding of content through strategic processing. Thus, a teacher might ask a student to summarize a passage. Once the summary is offered, the teacher might ask the student if any images come to mind while reading the text, or encourage the student to liven up the summary by relating it to prior knowledge (e.g., "Do you think most people would ask Bob Cratchet to work on Christmas Eve?"; "Do your parents have to work on Christmas Eve?").

An extremely important finding in the Gaskins et al. (1993) investigation was the identification of events that occurred often in many lessons:

- Students were provided instruction about how to carry out the strategies.
- Teachers modeled the focal strategies (and sometimes use of other strategies as well).
- Students practiced strategies, with teacher guidance and assistance provided on an as-needed basis.
- The focal strategy for a lesson and the focal curriculum content for the day were identified for students early in the lesson.
- Information was presented about why the focal strategy (and

sometimes nonfocal strategies as well) was important; often teachers provided anecdotal information about how strategies had helped them.
- Information about when and where strategies apply was conveyed to students.

In summary, when Benchmark teachers were interviewed, when they were observed, and when their discourse was analyzed thoroughly, it was easy to discern direct explanations about, and modeling of, strategies, followed by student practice that was guided and assisted by teachers who carefully monitored student attempts to use strategies, offering help when needed. Elementary content coverage was not displaced in favor of strategies instruction; rather, strategies were applied as students learned elementary content.

A Comprehension Strategies Instructional Program in a Maryland County

As it turned out, Benchmark School was not the only place where such instruction took place. We extensively studied comprehension strategies programs that were developed and implemented in one Maryland county school district. The comprehension instruction in that county occurred around high-quality texts, often in reading groups small enough to encourage exchanges between all students about interpretations of text, imaginal reactions to content, and summaries. When strategies were initially introduced (i.e., in grade 1 or 2), lessons often focused on individual strategies. For example, there were several weeks of students making predictions, predictions, and more predictions followed by weeks of students visualizing, visualizing, and visualizing. Once students were familiar with the strategies, the lessons emphasized coordinated use of strategies, although this required a great deal of teacher prompting, which continued for months and sometimes years. Eventually, by the third year of participation in such instruction, students could meet in groups and carry out strategic processes in a self-directed fashion—that is, teacher prompting and cuing was much less pronounced than it had been in previous years.

El-Dinary, Pressley, and Schuder (1992; also Pressley et al., 1992) summarized the comprehension instruction they observed in this county:

- Students were provided instruction about how to carry out the strategies emphasized in curriculum. Usually this was re-explanation of strategic processes which were somewhat familiar to the students, amounting to a recasting of the strategies in new terms.

- Teachers modeled use of the comprehension strategies that were taught.
- Students practiced strategies, with teacher guidance and assistance provided on an as-needed basis. Prompts were often in the form of questions suggesting additional strategic processing or possible ways to extend or expand an interpretation.
- Information was presented about why the focal strategy (and sometimes nonfocal strategies as well) was important. Teachers often provided anecdotal information about how strategies had helped them.
- Students were often required to model and explain use of the comprehension strategies.
- Information about when and where strategies could be applied was conveyed to students. The positive effects of strategies were continuously pointed out to them.
- Sophisticated processing vocabulary (e.g., terms like "predictions," "clarifications," "validation of predictions," and "summaries") were used frequently.
- Flexibility in strategy use was apparent, with teachers emphasizing how different students might apply strategies in different ways to the same content.
- Teachers sent the message that student thought processes mattered.

Of course, these behaviors were apparent at Benchmark as well. Both settings had developed strategies instruction involving a great deal of direct explanation and mental modeling, consistent with Roehler and Duffy's (1984) recommendations. In both settings, students and teachers talked aloud a great deal about their thinking processes (i.e., did mental modeling). They shared their interpretations of texts in an open and generally relaxed group context. Coordination of strategies was emphasized in both programs, with students engaging in years of practice in such coordination.

Concluding Comment

In these two settings, educators who were aware of the comprehension strategies research literature selected from that literature the strategies and methods that made the most sense to them in light of their years of experience. They were particularly impressed with the work of Gerald Duffy, Laura Roehler, and their associates (e.g., Duffy et al.,

1987; Duffy, Roehler, & Herrmann, 1988) on direct explanation of strategic processes. Duffy and Roehler's perspective on direct explanation—including mental modeling and subsequent guided practice of students—is the most influential to date about how to teach strategic processes in classrooms.

Explaining strategies to students, showing them how to use strategies, and helping them as they attempt to apply strategies as part of in-school practice seemed sensible to these educators. Although these were all studied in the basic research literature, transactional strategies instruction goes well beyond anything presented in it. The transactional strategies instruction described here evolved as teachers worked with it. Credit the educators with this intervention, which really does affect student achievement, although basic research provided great impetus and guidance for initial efforts.

Validation of Transactional Strategies Instruction

There have been three studies conducted in which transactional strategies instruction has been evaluated in a carefully controlled fashion. Taken together, their outcomes support the conclusion that transactional strategies instruction can promote reading instruction beginning in grade 2 and continuing into high school.

Brown, Pressley, Van Meter, and Schuder (1996)

Brown et al. (1996) was a year-long quasi-experimental investigation of the effects of transactional strategies instruction on grade-2 children's reading. Five grade-2 classrooms receiving transactional strategies instruction were matched with grade-2 classrooms taught by teachers who were well regarded as language-arts teachers but who were not using a strategies instruction approach. In each classroom, a group of readers who were low achieving at the beginning of grade 2 were identified. It was the changes in reading achievement in these students that was carefully studied by Brown et al. (1996).

In the fall, the weak students in the strategies instruction classrooms and the weak readers in the control classrooms did not differ on standardized measures of reading comprehension and word attack skills. By the spring, however, there were clear differences on these measures, favoring the transactional strategies instruction classrooms. In addition, there were differences favoring the strategies-instructed students on strategies use measures as well as interpretive measures (i.e., strategies-instructed students made more diverse and richer interpretations of what they read than controls).

One of the most compelling differences between Brown et al.'s (1996) transactional strategies instruction students and control students was a demonstration that the students who had learned strategies acquired more content from their daily lessons. We emphasize as well that it was not that the control students did not improve over the course of the year. They did, but students experiencing transactional strategies instruction improved significantly more.

Collins (1991)

Cathy Collins (1991) improved comprehension in grade-5 and -6 students by providing a semester (3 days a week) of comprehension strategies lessons. Her students were taught to predict, seek clarification when uncertain, look for patterns and principles in arguments presented in text, analyze decision making that occurs during text processing, solve problems (including the use of backward reasoning and visualization), summarize, adapt ideas in text (including rearranging parts of ideas in text), and negotiate interpretations of texts in groups. Although the strategies-instructed students did not differ from controls before the intervention with respect to standardized comprehension performance, there was a 3-*SD* difference between treated and control conditions on the posttest, a very large effect for the treatment.

Anderson (1992)

Valerie Anderson (see also Anderson & Roit, 1993) conducted a 3-month experimental investigation of the effects of transactional strategies instruction on reading-disabled students in grades 6 through 11. Students were taught comprehension strategies in small groups, with nine groups of transactional strategies students and seven control groups. Although both strategies-instructed and control students made gains on standardized comprehension measures during the study, the gains were greater in the trained group. Anderson (1992) also collected a variety of qualitative data supporting the conclusion that reading for meaning improved in the strategies-instructed condition: For example, strategies instruction increased students' willingness to read and attempt to understand difficult material, collaborate with classmates to discover meanings in text, and react to and elaborate upon text.

Concluding Comment

Doing research on long-term interventions such as transactional strategies instruction is very difficult, requiring that researchers make careful measurements in a number of classrooms over a long period of time. As far as policymakers are concerned, however, the gold standard is that an educational intervention make a difference with respect to performance on standardized tests. What was striking in these validations was that a semester to a year of transactional strategies instruction made definitive impact on standardized tests but also made differences that were captured by other measures.

Having spent a great deal of time in classrooms in which transactional strategies instruction occurs, and in many other classrooms as well, we can say without hesitation that daily life is very different in classrooms based on the transactional strategies instruction model than it is in other classrooms. Most noticeable is that there is really intelligent discussion of readings occurring in the transactional strategies instruction classes, with the students using the strategies they are learning in conversations about readings. In these conversations, they make predictions about what will happen in the story. They talk about the parts of readings that are confusing, and about ways to overcome those confusions. The children offer summaries of what they read permitting differences in interpretation. The students in these classrooms have come to expect differences, since they know that the meaning of a text is a function of both what is in the text and what the reader knew before reading the text.

In the typical classroom which does not involve strategy instruction, most talk occurs in a participation structure in which the teacher asks questions and the students answer them (e.g., Mehan, 1979). That definitely does not occur in transactional strategies instruction classrooms. There, the students have learned how to talk about text without being prompted by the teacher to do so. The teacher never prompts students by saying, "Now, it's time for a prediction," or "Can someone think of a good question to ask about this part of the story?" Rather, if the teacher needs to prompt at all, she merely prompts the students to be active, asking students to decide for themselves what they should be doing to understand the text. Prompts like, "What might you do here?," or, "I was wondering how you were thinking about this portion of the text," are common. The teacher prompts students to choose to think. There is considerable evidence that the opportunities to participate in such student-driven dialogues are highly motivating to students, enabling them to think of plenty of questions to ask about text and plenty of ways to relate to one another about the ideas in text (e.g., Almasi & Gambrell, 1994).

Transactional strategies instruction is about the development of self-regulation, developing students who, on their own, cause the comprehension strategies that excellent readers use. Return to Chapter 2 and review the comprehension processes used by excellent readers. Those processes—prediction, questioning, making images, seeking clarification, and constructing summaries—are exactly the processes that are taught as strategies by transactional strategies instruction teachers. Exceptionally skilled readers use these on their own, and thus, the transactional strategies instruction teacher does not want to be cuing students to use any specific strategy. Rather, the transactional strategies instruction teacher consistently sends the message that students should be active during reading, choosing their own activities and strategies. If self-regulation is anything, it is choosing to be cognitively active, and transactional strategies instruction is all about teaching students to choose active reading over passive reading and to decide for themselves which strategic processes to use when they confront challenging texts.

Concerning the way strategies instruction stimulates cognitive activity, we cannot resist the temptation to point out that even when very insensitive analyses are employed, as when national data bases of questionnaire data are analyzed, there are clear relationships between cognitive strategies instruction and the reported frequencies of reading (Guthrie, Schafer, Wang, & Afflerbach, 1993). Even more intriguing is evidence in the Guthrie et al. (1993) analysis that part of the reason for the increased reading when comprehension strategies are taught is that it leads to more dialogue about what was read. There is plenty of reason to teach comprehension strategies in elementary school, and we suspect that there will be more evidence documenting that students receiving such instruction read better, read more, talk more, and talk more intelligently about what they read.

CONCLUDING REFLECTIONS

We have spent a great deal of time in upper-grades elementary classrooms in the last 8 years. Most classrooms we have seen have included a great deal of teacher direction and student passivity. There is very little teaching of students to be self-regulative or to comprehend texts. There is a great deal of reading, the implicit theory being that if children simply read, read, and read, they will become skilled comprehenders. Massive reading does increase fluency, and thus, there is something to be said for having students read a great deal in order to increase comprehension.

Good comprehension, however, is not just word-level processing. It involves abstracting the big ideas in a text, the macrostructure, as Kintsch and van Dijk (1978) refer to it. Sometimes, good readers construct images capturing the big ideas expressed in a text as well as critical details. The ideas expressed in text are understood in terms of, and related to, prior knowledge by the skilled reader.

There is no reason to believe that elementary students naturally discover that they should use such processes to understand text. Indeed, quite the contrary, there is substantial evidence that many students can make it to college without learning the active comprehension processes used by skilled readers (Pressley & Afflerbach, 1995). More positively, there is substantial evidence that elementary students can learn to comprehend actively—they can learn to predict, question, make mental images, seek to clarify confusions, and summarize as they read.

Consider some of the grade-4, -5, and -6 classrooms we have studied in recent years that were headed by teachers who decided to emphasize comprehension and to teach their students to use comprehension strategies consistently. All of the evidence pertaining to the effectiveness of this approach is positive. Beyond the numbers, however, there is a real excitement in classes in which comprehension processing is being taught. By the end of the year, small groups of children will be using the strategies while they do pair reading. When individual children retell stories they have read, it is not just a spitting back of information in the text; rather, it is interpretive, reflecting the cognitive activities that occurred during reading.

Why is such instruction not more common? For one, many teachers do not understand comprehension as active reading—nor as active predicting, questioning, imagining, seeking clarifications, summarizing, and interpreting. One of the most interesting reflections that we have heard again and again from teachers who have become teachers of comprehension strategies is that they did not really know how to read actively until they learned about the comprehension strategies model and began to teach students to use comprehension strategies.

Another reason that this form of teaching is not more common is that it leads to classroom interactions that are very different from the norm. In typical classrooms, teachers control most interactions, asking questions that students then answer. The goal with comprehension strategies instruction, however, is to teach students to take over their own reading and thinking: When teachers and students read texts together, the teacher is not asking questions but rather participating in a real conversation. The students make predictions, talk about the questions that occur to them as they read, report the images they get during reading, discuss parts of text that are hard to understand, and generate interpretations, including summary interpretations. After the early stages of comprehension strategies instruction—that is, after the teacher is no longer introducing the strategies—the teacher's role in the conversation is limited to prompting students to be active in deciding how they might process the text at this point. Throughout classroom life, the teacher is also supposed to model strategies use to make clear to students how the comprehension strategies the students are learning can be usefully adapted across many different types of reading. Such mental modeling is not always easy for many teachers. (See Pressley & El-Dinary, 1997, for an elaboration of the challenges of comprehension strategies teaching.)

A final reason that comprehension strategies teaching is not more widespread is that constructivist educators, including many whole-language types, send the message that processes that are taught rather than discovered are not natural strategies. Our reply is that the explanations and mental modeling the teacher provides are just a starting point, and that students actively discover much about the usefulness and adaptability of comprehension strategies as they attempt to do them. From our perspective, good teaching is constructivist in that it sets students to exploring in productive directions. As students in transactional strategies instruction classrooms use strategies together, there is plenty constructive discovery going on. Long-term strategies use seems to result in individual students internalizing active cognitive processing during reading; the proof of the pudding is better reading when measured in a number of different ways across studies. There is much to be said for encouraging many more teachers to define their elementary classrooms as classrooms in which students learn to use comprehension strategies constructively, practicing them with other students with the many types of reading that can be encountered in the elementary curriculum.

At this point in the lecture that inspired this book, M.P. would always ask the audience to think back to the expert reading described in Chapter 2 and ask them, "Isn't that what you want for your students?" He would continue:

> "If you start to teach your students to read that way, something wonderful is going to happen to you. You are going to become a more active reader yourself. But there's more! As you read wonderful stories and books with your students, you are going to experience a myriad of student responses that you never dreamed possible. If you do not believe it, read an article by Rachel Brown and Lynn Coy-Ogan (1993) which discussed the differing interpretations of Maurice Sendak's *Where the Wild Things Are* offered by three different groups of students in Lynn's classes. Your class-

room is going to become more interesting for everyone in it, including you."

SUMMARY

1. Similar to the primary grades, instruction in grades 4 and 5 involves a balancing of skills instruction and more authentic reading and writing. Although there are many commonalities across grade-4 and -5 classrooms, there are also many optional emphases, with each classroom seeming to have a core of practices that define its emphasis.

2. Although development of comprehension ability is a widely-agreed upon goal of literacy instruction, it rarely is offered as systematically as it could be in the elementary grades. This is especially striking in the 1990s, given many different lines of evidence which support the teaching of comprehension strategies to elementary students.

3. Reciprocal teaching is perhaps the best known of the comprehension-instructional efforts developed and evaluated by researchers. This approach consists of students learning to use prediction, questioning, seeking clarification, and summarization by working in small groups, with the members of the group taking turns leading the group through the strategic processes. We think reciprocal teaching was an important first step in teaching students a repertoire of comprehension strategies, but it was no more than that, as more flexible, long-term teaching has now been developed and validated by educators and researchers.

4. Transactional strategies instruction begins with teacher explanations and modeling of strategies, with scaffolded student practice in strategies application following over a long period of time. Much of the practice takes place in small reading groups, which involve a great deal of student conversations, rich in student reports of how they are applying strategies in their interpretations of texts being read by the group. Long-term participation in such groups is intended to produce internalization of the strategic processes. To date, the consistently positive effects of transactional strategies instruction demonstrated in validations are consistent with the interpretation that such instruction is producing such internalization. The record of the positive effect of transactional strategies instruction on standardized tests in well-controlled studies is quite striking, but so are the qualitative benefits produced by such instruction.

5. The most common strategies included in transactional strategies instruction are (a) predicting, (b) questioning, (c) constructing

mental images representing text content, (d) seeking clarifications, (e) responding to text based on prior knowledge, (f) summarizing, and (g) interpreting. Young readers who participate in such instruction are being taught to use the comprehension processes reported by exceptionally skilled readers, as detailed in Chapter 2.

REFERENCES

Adams, M. J. (1990). *Beginning to read.* Cambridge, MA: Harvard University Press.

Almasi, J. F., & Gambrell, L. B. (1994). *Sociocognitive conflict in peer-led and teacher-led discussions of literature* (Reading Research Report No. 12). Athens, GA, and College Park, MD: National Reading Research Center.

Anderson, R. C., & Hidde, J. L. (1971). Imagery and sentence learning. *Journal of Educational Psychology, 62,* 526–530.

Anderson, R. C., & Pearson, P. D. (1984). A schema-theoretic view of basic processes in reading. In P. D. Pearson (Ed.), *Handbook of reading research* (pp. 255–291). New York: Longman.

Anderson, V. (1992). A teacher development project in transactional strategy instruction for teachers of severely reading-disabled adolescents. *Teaching and Teacher Education, 8,* 391–403.

Anderson, V., & Roit, M. (1993). Planning and implementing collaborative strategy instruction for delayed readers in grades 6–10. *Elementary School Journal, 94,* 121–137.

Beach, R., & Hynds, S. (1991). Research on response to literature. In R. Barr, M. L. Kamil, P. Mosenthal, & P. D. Pearson (Eds.), *Handbook of reading research* (Vol. 2, pp. 453–489). White Plains, NY: Longman.

Bell, R. Q. (1968). A reinterpretation of the direction of effects in studies of socialization. *Psychological Review, 75,* 81–95.

Borkowski, J. G., Levers, S., & Gruenenfelder, T. M. (1976). Transfer of mediational strategies in children: The role of activity and awareness during strategy acquisition. *Child Development, 47,* 779–786.

Brown, A. L., & Day, J. D. (1983). Macrorules for summarizing texts: The development of expertise. *Journal of Verbal Learning and Verbal Behavior, 22,* 1–14.

Brown, A. L., & Palincsar, A. S. (1989). Guided, cooperative learning and individual knowledge acquisition. In L. B. Resnick (Ed.), *Knowing, learning, and instruction: Essays in honor of Robert Glaser* (pp. 393–451). Hillsdale, NJ: Erlbaum.

Brown, R., & Coy-Ogan, L. (1993). The evolution of transactional strategies instruction in one teacher's classroom. *Elementary School Journal, 94,* 221–233.

Brown, R., Pressley, M., Van Meter, P., & Schuder, T. (1996). A quasi-experimental validation of transactional strategies instruction with low-achieving second grade readers. *Journal of Educational Psychology, 88,* 18–37.

Cavanaugh, J. C., & Borkowski, J. G. (1979). The metamemory–memory "connection": Effects of strategy training and maintenance. *Journal of General Psychology, 101,* 161–174.

Cazden, C. B. (1988). *Classroom discourse: The language of teaching and learning.* Portsmouth, NH: Heinemann.

Chall, J. S. (1983). *Stages of reading development.* New York: McGraw-Hill.

Clark, J. M., & Paivio, A. (1991). Dual coding theory and education. *Educational Psychology Review, 3,* 149–210.

Collins, C. (1991). Reading instruction that increases thinking abilities. *Journal of Reading, 34,* 510–516.

Doctorow, M., Wittrock, M. C., & Marks, C. (1978). Generative processes in reading comprehension. *Journal of Educational Psychology, 70,* 109–118.

Duffy, G. G., & Roehler, L. R. (1989). Why strategy instruction is so difficult and what we need to do about it. In C. B. McCormick, G. Miller, & M. Pressley (Eds.), *Cognitive strategy research: From basic research to educational applications* (pp. 133–154). New York: Springer–Verlag.

Duffy, G., Roehler, L., & Herrmann, G. (1988). Modeling mental processes helps poor readers become strategic readers. *Reading Teacher, 41,* 762–767.

Duffy, G. G., Roehler, L. R., Sivan, E., Rackliffe, G., Book, C., Meloth, M., Vavrus, L. G., Wesselman, R., Putnam, J., & Bassiri, D. (1987). Effects of explaining the reasoning associated with using reading strategies. *Reading Research Quarterly, 22,* 347–368.

Durkin, D. (1978–1979). What classroom observations reveal about reading comprehension instruction. *Reading Research Quarterly, 15,* 481–533.

El-Dinary, P. B., Pressley, M., & Schuder, T. (1992). Becoming a strategies teacher: An observational and interview study of three teachers learning transactional strategies instruction. In C. Kinzer & D. Leu (Eds.), *Forty-first Yearbook of the National Reading Conference* (pp. 453–462). Chicago: National Reading Conference.

Flavell, J. H. (1977). *Cognitive development.* Englewood Cliffs, NJ: Prentice–Hall.

Flavell, J. H. , & Wellman, H. M. (1977). Metamemory. In R. V. Kail & J. W. Hagen (Eds.), *Perspectives on the development of memory and cognition* (pp. 3–33). Hillsdale, NJ: Erlbaum.

Forrest-Pressley, D. L., & Gilles, L. A. (1983). Children's flexible use of strategies during reading. In M. Pressley & J. R. Levin (Eds.), *Cognitive strategy research: Educational applications* (pp. 133–156). New York: Springer–Verlag.

Gaskins, I. W., Anderson, R. C., Pressley, M., Cunicelli, E. A., & Satlow, E. (1993). Six teachers' dialogue during cognitive process instruction. *Elementary School Journal, 93,* 277–304.

Guthrie, J. T., Schafer, W., Wang, Y. Y., & Afflerbach, P. (1993). *Influences of instruction on amount of reading: An empirical exploration of social, cognitive, and instructional indicators* (Reading Research Report No. 3). Athens, GA, and College Park, MD: National Reading Research Center.

Harris, A. J., & Sipay, E. R. (1990). *How to increase reading ability: A guide to developmental and remedial methods.* New York: Longman.

Hutchins, E. (1991). The social organization of distributed cognition. In L. Resnick, J. M. Levine, & S. D. Teasley (Eds.), *Perspectives on socially shared cognition* (pp. 283-307). Washington, DC: American Psychological Association.

Johns, J. C., & McNamara, L. P. (1980). The SQ3R study technique: A forgotten research target. *Journal of Reading, 23,* 705–708.

Kennedy, B. A., & Miller, D. J. (1976). Persistent use of verbal rehearsal as a function of information about its value. *Child Development, 47,* 566–569.

Kintsch, W., & van Dijk, T. A. (1978). Toward a model of discourse comprehension and production. *Psychological Review, 85,* 363–394.

Kohlberg, L., Yaeger, J., & Hjertholm, E. (1968). Private speech: Four studies and a review of theories. *Child Development, 39,* 691–736.

LaBerge, D., & Samuels, S. J. (1974). Toward a theory of automatic information processing in reading. *Cognitive Psychology, 6,* 293–323.

Levin, J. R. (1973). Inducing comprehension in poor readers: A test of a recent model. *Journal of Educational Psychology, 65,* 19–24.

Levin, J. R., & Pressley, M. (1981). Improving children's prose comprehension: Selected strategies that seem to succeed. In C. M. Santa & B. L. Hayes (Eds.), *Children's prose comprehension: Research and practice* (pp. 44–71). Newark, DE: International Reading Association.

Mandler, J. M. (1984). *Stories, scripts, and scenes: Aspects of schema theory.* Hillsdale, NJ: Erlbaum.

Mehan, H. (1979). *Social organization in the classroom.* Cambridge, MA: Harvard University Press.

Meichenbaum, D. (1977). *Cognitive behavior modification.* New York: Plenum.

Meichenbaum, D., & Asarnow, J. (1979). Cognitive–behavioral modification and metacognitive development: Implications for the classroom. In P. C. Kendall & S. D. Hollon (Eds.), *Cognitive–behavioral interventions* (pp. 11–35). New York: Academic Press.

Meichenbaum, D., & Goodman, J. (1969). Reflection-impulsivity and verbal control of motor behavior. *Child Development, 40,* 785–797.

Miller, G. A. (1956). The magical number seven, plus-or-minus two: Some limits on our capacity for processing information. *Psychological Review, 63,* 81–97.

Paivio, A. (1971). *Imagery and verbal processes.* New York: Holt, Rinehart & Winston.

Paivio, A. (1986). *Mental representations: A dual-coding approach.* New York: Oxford University Press.

Palincsar, A. S., & Brown, A. L. (1984). Reciprocal teaching of comprehension-fostering and monitoring activities. *Cognition and Instruction, 1,* 117–175.

Paris, S. G., Lipson, M. Y., & Wixson, K. K. (1983). Becoming a strategic reader. *Contemporary Educational Psychology, 8,* 293–316.

Patterson, C. J., & Mischel, W. (1976). Effects of temptation-inhibiting and task-facilitating plans on self-control. *Journal of Personality and Social Psychology, 33,* 209–217.

Pearson, P. D., & Fielding, L. (1991). Comprehension instruction. In R. Barr, M. L. Kamil, P. B. Mosenthal, & P. D. Pearson (Eds.), *Handbook of reading research* (Vol. 2, pp. 815–860). New York: Longman.

Pressley, G. M. (1976). Mental imagery helps eight-year-olds remember what they read. *Journal of Educational Psychology, 68,* 355–359.

Pressley, M. (1977). Imagery and children's learning: Putting the picture in developmental perspective. *Review of Educational Research, 47,* 586–622.

Pressley, M., & Afflerbach, P. (1995). *Verbal protocols of reading: The nature of constructively responsive reading.* Hillsdale, NJ: Erlbaum.

Pressley, M., Borkowski, J. G., & O'Sullivan, J. T. (1984). Memory strategy instruction is made of this: Metamemory and durable strategy use. *Educational Psychologist, 19,* 94–107.

Pressley, M., Borkowski, J. G., & O'Sullivan, J. T. (1985). Children's metamemory and the teaching of memory strategies. In D. L. Forrest-Pressley, G. E. MacKinnon, & T. G. Waller (Eds.), *Metacognition, cognition, and human performance* (pp. 111–153). New York: Academic Press.

Pressley, M., & El-Dinary, P. B. (1997). What we know about translating comprehension strategies instruction research into practice. *Journal of Learning Disabilities, 30,* 486–488.

Pressley, M., El-Dinary, P. B., Gaskins, I., Schuder, T., Bergman, J., Almasi, L., & Brown, R. (1992). Beyond direct explanation: Transactional instruction of reading comprehension strategies. *Elementary School Journal, 92,* 511–554.

Pressley, M., Gaskins, I. W., Cunicelli, E. A., Burdick, N. J., Schaub-Matt, M., Lee, D. S., & Powell, N. (1991). Strategy instruction at Benchmark School: A faculty interview study. *Learning Disability Quarterly, 14,* 19–48.

Pressley, M., Gaskins, I. W., Wile, D., Cunicelli, B., & Sheridan, J. (1991). Teaching literacy strategies across the curriculum: A case study at Benchmark School. In J. Zutell & S. McCormick (Eds.), *Learner factors/teacher factors: Issues in literacy research and instruction: Fortieth yearbook of the National Reading Conference* (pp. 219–228). Chicago: National Reading Conference.

Pressley, M., Heisel, B. E., McCormick, C. G., & Nakamura, G. V. (1982). Memory strategy instruction with children. In C. J. Brainerd & M. Pressley (Eds.), *Progress in cognitive development research: Vol. 2. Verbal processes in children* (pp. 125–159). New York: Springer–Verlag.

Pressley, M., Wharton-McDonald, R., Hampston, J. M., & Echevarria, M. (in press). The nature of literacy instruction in ten grade-4 and -5 classrooms in upstate New York. *Scientific Studies of Reading.*

Pressley, M., Yokoi, L., Rankin, J., Wharton-McDonald, R., & Hampston, J. (1997). A survey of the instructional practices of grade-5 teachers nominated as effective in promoting literacy. *Scientific Studies of Reading, 1,* 145–160.

Robinson, F. P. (1946). *Effective study* (2nd ed.). New York: Harper & Row.

Roehler, L. R., & Duffy, G. G. (1984). Direct explanation of comprehension processes. In G. G. Duffy, L. R. Roehler, & J. Mason (Eds.), *Comprehension instruction: Perspectives and suggestions* (pp. 265–280). New York: Longman.

Rosenblatt, L. M. (1938). *Literature as experience.* New York: Progressive Education Association.

Rosenblatt, L. M. (1978). *The reader, the text, the poem: The transactional theory of the literary work.* Carbondale, IL: Southern Illinois University Press.

Rosenshine, B., & Meister, C. (1994). Reciprocal teaching: A review of nineteen experimental studies. *Review of Educational Research, 64,* 479–530.

Short, E. J., & Ryan, E. B. (1984). Metacognitive differences between skilled and less-skilled readers: Remediating deficits through story grammar and attri-bution training. *Journal of Educational Psychology, 76,* 225–235.

Smith, C. B. (Moderator) (1994). *Whole language: The debate.* Bloomington, IN: ERIC/REC.

Stein, N. L., & Glenn, C. G. (1979). An analysis of story comprehension in elementary school children. In R. O. Freedle (Eds.), *New directions in discourse processing* (Vol. 2). Norwood, NJ: Ablex.

Taylor, B. M. (1982). Text structure and children's comprehension and memory for expository material. *Journal of Educational Psychology, 74,* 323–340.

Tierney, R. J., Readence, J. E., & Dishner, E. K. (Eds.). (1980). *Reading strategies and practices: Guide for improving instruction.* Boston: Allyn & Bacon.

van Dijk, T. A., & Kintsch, W. (1983). *Strategies of discourse comprehension.* New York: Academic Press.

Vygotsky, L. S. (1962). *Thought and language.* Cambridge, MA: MIT Press.

Weaver, C. (1994). *Reading process and practice: From socio-psycholinguistics to whole language.* Portsmouth, NH: Heinemann.

Wozniak, R. (1972). Verbal regulation of motor behavior: Soviet research and non-Soviet replications. *Human Development, 15,* 13–57.

Vygotsky, L. S. (1978). *Mind in society: The development of higher psychological processes.* Cambridge MA: Harvard University Press.

8

◄◉►

MOTIVATION
AND LITERACY

In the early 1990s, when the National Reading Research Center was planned, the organizers conducted a national survey of teachers that asked their opinions about the most pressing issues confronting education. One concern was much more prominent than any other in the responses: The teachers were emphatic that maintaining student academic motivation was a major challenge that needed to be addressed by any center concerned with promoting the reading achievement of students. In response to that input from teachers, the National Reading Research Center focused on the promotion of student engagement in literacy (O'Flahavan, Gambrell, Guthrie, Stahl, & Alvermann, 1992).

A great deal about academic motivation was learned during the tenure of the National Reading Research Center. Some of the most important findings related to motivation are covered in this chapter. For example, the Center was able to establish that the main reason that teachers were concerned about motivation was that they recognized that motivation to read is connected to good grades (Sweet & Guthrie, 1994). Other important discoveries were the many facets of student motivation that can affect reading (Wigfield & Guthrie, 1995; Wigfield, Guthrie, & McGough, 1996; Wigfield, Wilde, Baker, Fernandez-Fein, & Scher, 1996). These include the following:

- *Reading self-efficacy*: Believing that one can read well affects commitment to reading.
- *Reading challenge*: How challenging a book is for a reader at a

228

particular competence level can impact on whether the book will be read.

- *Reading curiosity*: Students are more likely to read about topics that are interesting to them.
- *Aesthetically enjoyable reading topics*: Some things are read because they are fun to read.
- *Importance of reading*: Recognition that reading is important can affect motivation to read and to be a good reader.
- *Reader recognition*: Being recognized as a good reader can affect motivation to read.
- *Reader grades*: Grades earned for reading can affect motivation to read.
- *Reading competition*: Being a better reader than others can motivate reading and working at becoming a better reader.
- *Social reasons for reading*: Opportunities to read with family and friends can affect motivation to read.
- *Compliance*: Students sometimes read to fulfill academic obligations (e.g., assignments).
- *Reading work avoidance*: There are factors that certainly reduce the likelihood of reading (e.g., difficult words in text, too-complicated stories).

The Center's work must be reported in the context of many other analyses of student motivation that have been conducted in the past two decades. This research activity, including the work of the National Reading Research Center, permits much more complete understanding of student motivation for reading and the determinants of that motivation than was possible in the past.

It will become clear as the chapter proceeds that academic motivation is a fragile commodity. Although kindergarten and grade-1 children arrive at school expecting to do well, and are enthused about school and academic tasks, expectations often diminish as students go through school. For academic motivation to remain high, students must be successful and perceive that they are successful. Perhaps it is not surprising that students who have a difficult time in school experience declining academic motivation. More surprising is that the policies of most elementary schools are such that most students will experience declining motivation, perceiving that they are not doing well, at least compared to other students.

More positively, much is being learned about how to reengineer school so that high academic motivation is maintained. Some of the most important ideas about how to maintain student motivation will be taken up in the second half of the chapter. When the messages in the latter half of this chapter are combined with the messages in the first half, it will be clear that more is now known about how to keep students motivated than is being done to motivate students in contemporary schools.

THE DECLINE OF ACADEMIC MOTIVATION DURING THE ELEMENTARY YEARS

Humans are born intrinsically motivated to learn and improve their performances. This is transparent to anyone who has watched a child trying to learn to walk. Indeed, developmental psychologists have made a good case that young children have great motivation to explore their world and that such exploration is important in stimulating mental and physical development (White, 1959).

Despite a motivated start on life, intrinsic motivation often declines during the elementary years (Eccles, 1993; Eccles & Midgley, 1989; Harter, 1990; Stipek & Mac Iver, 1989). As children proceed through elementary school, they generally value school less: they are less interested in school and what is studied in school (e.g., Eccles & Midgley, 1989; Eccles et al., 1989; Wigfield, 1994; Wigfield & Eccles, 1992; Wigfield, Eccles, Mac Iver, Reuman, and Midgley, 1991).

Academically, kindergarten and grade-1 children believe they can do anything. If you ask them whether they are going to learn to read, they are certain of it (e.g., Entwisle & Hayduk, 1978). Moreover, even after failure, they remain confident that next time they will do better (Clifford, 1975, 1978, 1984; Parsons & Ruble, 1977; Phillips, 1963; Pressley & Ghatala, 1989; Stipek & Hoffman, 1980). Although grade-1 students who are experiencing difficulties in reading understand it is a difficult task, confidence in their competence to read remains high (Chapman & Tunmer, 1995). In contrast, students in grades 5 and 6 are much less confident that they will meet teacher and parent expectations with respect to academic achievement. They are much more aware of their failures than their successes (Kloosterman, 1988). Students in grades 5 and 6 often believe they are doing worse than they are (e.g., Juvonen, 1988). The weaker the student, the more pessimistic the self-appraisal and the less enthused the student is about academic activities (e.g., Renick & Harter, 1989).

Georgia Southern University professor Michael McKenna and his associates (McKenna, Ellworth, & Kear, 1995) have most clearly documented the declines in student attitudes about reading. They surveyed more than 17,000 elementary students in grades 1 through 6 from across the United States. The survey contained 10 questions assessing how students felt about reading as a recreational activity (e.g., "How do you feel about spending free time reading?" "How do feel about going to a bookstore?"). It also included 10 questions assessing students academic attitudes about reading (e.g., "How do you feel about reading your school books?" "How do you feel when it is time for reading class?"). The students provided a rating for each question on a 1 (very negative) to 4 (very positive) scale.

For both boys and girls, for all ethnic and racial groups, and for all ability levels, there were clear declines in the positive attitudes of students toward reading, both recreational and academic. Yes, girls were more positive than boys, and the declines in attitude were not as consistent for high-ability readers as for other students. Even so, what was most striking in the data was that no matter how the researchers looked at them, attitudes toward reading were relatively high in grade 1, with student indifference toward reading the norm by grade 6.

Perhaps most disturbing is the fact that by the middle grade-school years, some children are really down on reading. When Gambrell and her National Reading Research Center colleagues (Gambrell, Codling, & Palmer, 1996; Gambrell, Palmer, Codling, & Mazzoni, 1996) administered a reading motivation inventory to grade-3 and grade-5 students, they found nontrivial proportions of children who claimed they would rather clean their rooms than read (17% of respondents), expected to spend little time reading when they grew up (14%), and felt that people who read are boring (10%). There is reason for concern when children are so turned off by an activity as important as reading.

Developmental and educational psychologists carried out in-depth analyses of some of the reasons for the declines in positive academic attitudes and motivation during the elementary years. There are several contributing factors, each of which is reviewed in what follows. These factors coalesce so that declining academic motivation with advancing grade level is inevitable for many students, at least given the nature of contemporary schooling.

Developmental Shifts in Attributions about the Causes of Performance

Different people explain their successes and failures in different ways. When some people experience success or failure, they explain the outcome as due to personal effort. That is, a success is attributed to trying hard, while a failure is explained as reflecting lack of effort. Alternatively, successes and failures can be explained in terms of abilities: Such people might reason that, "I succeeded because I am naturally smart, being born with a high IQ," or "I cannot read well because I was born with dyslexia." Sometimes people explain successes or failures in terms of task characteristics. For example, a student who did well on a test might believe it was because the test was easy, and a student who did poorly might blame the failure on the test being too difficult. Finally, some believe that what happens to them is determined by luck, with successes due to good luck and failures due to bad luck.

Of all these explanations—effort, ability, task difficulty, and luck—the only one that is under personal control is effort. Thus, if you believe that you succeeded on a task because of high effort, there is reason to exert effort in the future. If you think that your failure reflects insufficient effort, the route to future success is to do more and try harder, and effort attributions are consistently associated with high effort in the future (Weiner, 1979). In contrast, there is nothing a person can do about inherited abilities, the difficulty of tasks, or luck; thus, individuals who believe their academic outcomes depend on ability, task difficulty, or luck have little or no motivation to try hard in the future.

One of the reasons that children's motivations decline is that as children mature during the grade-school years, the ways that they explain their performance outcomes change. Kindergarten and grade-1 students do not differentiate between effort and ability. Thus, young children typically attribute their successes to effort. Moreover, whenever they exhibit effort, they believe their effort reflects high ability. Thus, if they fail but expended high effort, they leave the task still believing they have high ability because they exerted effort! In short, 6- and 7-year-olds typically believe that they can succeed by trying hard (Nicholls, 1978, 1990).

With increasing age during the elementary years, children differentiate effort and ability. Thus, by the end of the elementary years, children understand that if two people expend the same amount of effort, the one who is more successful probably has higher ability. Moreover, by the end of the grade-school years, students are explaining successes and failures more in terms of ability than effort. Successes are considered to be indications of high ability and failures to be indications of low ability.

Of course, such attributions are much less motivating than the effort attributions of younger children. When a person believes that ability determines performance, there is no motivation for exerting effort, since effort does not matter. That children increasingly believe their failures are due to low ability probably goes far in explaining their decreasing motivation to tackle academic tasks.

Young Students and Their Attributions as They Try to Learn to Read

Learning to decode and recognize words is a very challenging task for some children. Children can make a lot of mistakes along the way. The first-grade child is not as likely to be discouraged by such mistakes as a child in grade 4 who is struggling to learn decoding. After all, for the grade-1 child, trying hard is what counts. In contrast, the grade-4 child has come to believe that having to try harder on a task that others accomplish with much less effort is a sign of low ability. Thus, for the grade-4 child still struggling with decoding as classmates read with ease, there is plenty of reason to conclude that one does not have the ability to read. Such a conclusion would undermine the student's expenditure of effort in learning how to decode. This is one reason that the first grader struggling to read is much more likely to be influenced by teacher and parent urgings to try harder than is an older child. From a motivational perspective, it makes no sense to expect that if children do not learn to read on their own in grades 1 or 2, they will learn later, when they are ready. The motivation to exert the effort to learn to read will never be greater than it is during the primary years. The older the struggling reader, the more the struggle will be interpreted as reflecting low ability with the child unmotivated to learn to read.

Children with Learning Disabilities

The role of attributions in motivating academic efforts has been studied, especially in children with learning disabilities. Learning disabled children are much more likely than their normally achieving classmates to believe that their academic performances are determined by ability (Jacobsen, Lowery, & DuCette, 1986; Pearl, 1982). Yes, there are exceptions: some learning-disabled children continue to believe that they can do better by trying hard. Continuing to believe that effort matters probably makes a difference for these children. Such low achievers who believe they can control their academic progress through effort, in fact, do achieve at higher levels than low achievers who believe their low achievement reflects low ability (Kistner, Osborne, & LeVerrier, 1988).

Often I speak to groups of special educators, and when I do, I always ask the audience the following question: "What if you talk with a grade-5 or -6 learning disabled student about how they are doing in school and ask the student to explain why he or she is having problems in school? What do such children say?" Every audience provides the same answer: "The kid says, 'It's because I'm stupid.' " Years of school failure result in students concluding that their academic achievement is not controllable, that they do not have the ability to do well academically. They have come to *expect* academic failure. Developmental studies show that such attributions are very different from the attributions these children made when they were younger, when they believed that effort might help them make progress.

What is going on here? How does a spirited 6-year-old who knows he can learn to read become a 10-year-old who believes that reading is something that he cannot accomplish? (No sexism implied here, for young boys are much more likely than young girls to experience difficulties in learning to read.) The child's continued failures lead to negative affect (Covington & Omelich, 1979a) and decreasing expectancies for future success (Covington & Omelich, 1979b). That classmates are experiencing success following their efforts does not help; in fact, it probably intensifies the struggling student's feelings of personal incapacity (Covington, 1987). Learned helplessness—that is, the belief that nothing one does can lead to success—develops in such a situation (Dweck, 1987). Doing nothing can actually be therapeutic for such children, for at least failure following lack of effort does not lead to the conclusion that one is stupid. In that case, learning-disabled children can more easily convince themselves that they do not do well in reading because they are not interested enough to try (Covington & Omelich, 1981, 1984). Is it any surprise that children with reading disabilities often seem passive in school? Trying gets them nowhere; not trying permits an explanation of failure that is not as damaging to their self-esteem as failure follows effort.

Recall the argument made in Chapter 3 that children who experience difficulties in learning to decode could and would learn if they were taught using an approach different than the one experienced in school. Failing to make progress in decoding during grade 1 may not seem frustrating to the child because the grade-1 child is so willing to persist. Such willingness to persist wanes as the child matures and comes to understand that she or he is making little progress, and eventually interprets this as an indication of low ability. Not intervening when children are experiencing initial reading difficulties is setting students up for additional failure and diminishing self-esteem. School days filled with failure are school days filled with the lesson that, "You are stupid." That the grade-1 child is not much ruffled by failures is no reason not to intervene, for it will not be long before that same child is interpreting failures as indications of a lack of ability. Once children come to the conclusion that they lack ability with respect to reading, there is little or no reason for them to make additional efforts to learn to read, and hence, interventions at that point must also be targeted at increasing the child's academic self-esteem. Reading difficulties that might have been addressed in grade 1 through simple decoding instruction become much more serious, now that the once vital child seems helpless. Waiting to intervene makes no sense from the perspective of attribution theory.

Other Factors Affecting Attributions

The belief that efforts pay off is affected by histories of success and failure, the former encouraging the continuing belief in effort and the latter causing students to doubt their own abilities. Other factors play a role as well. Teachers and parents can encourage effort attributions. They can make children aware of how their personal successes are tied to their efforts (Schunk, 1991). Parents' and teachers' awareness of their power to be persuasive about the role of effort in success is the main reason that effective educational environments, such as the ones considered in previous chapters, always include the repeated message that effort matters.

Teachers and parents can also help to develop in children an understanding of intelligence that is very different from the theory that intelligence is determined by genes and thus unmodifiable. The message can be sent to students that ability is not a fixed entity, but is, rather, changeable. Psychologist Carol Dweck and her colleagues (e.g., Dweck & Leggett, 1988; Henderson & Dweck, 1990) have proposed that a critical determinant of achievement motivation is whether a person believes that intelligence is fixed biologically, and hence neither malleable nor affected by environmental variables. Dweck describes people who believe that intelligence is fixed as possessing an "entity" theory of intelligence: Such people believe intelligence is a thing that one either has in great quantity or does not. In contrast, those who think intelligence is modifiable subscribe to an "incremental" theory of intelligence.

Dweck has found that the particular view of intelligence held by an individual has a powerful impact on his or her achievement behavior. Entity theorists are oriented toward seeking positive evaluations of their abilities and avoiding negative evaluations. Such a perspective can be damaging when negative feedback occurs, as it inevitably does in school. Such students are likely to interpret failures as indications of low intelligence, and hence, be discouraged by failures. In contrast, incremental theorists are much more oriented toward increasing their abilities, believing that daily efforts lead to small gains, all of which can add up to substantially higher intelligence when effort is persistent over the long term. Such students keep trying when obstacles occur because they see obstacles as a natural part of the learning process.

In short, students who are entity theorists are more likely to experience negative emotion when confronted with failure, believing that failure signals low ability, and allowing that belief to undermine future attempts at academic tasks. Indeed, the entity theorist may be so motivated to avoid additional evidence of low ability that she or he will not engage again in a task that has been associated with failure in the past. Incremental theorists experience much less negative affect in response to failure, interpreting the failure as part of the improvement process, which motivates high persistence.

As long as there is success, there is little difference in the behaviors of entity and incremental theorists. It is when failure occurs that the differences in their outlooks become apparent, with the entity theorists much more at risk for believing they are helpless when they experience difficulties during challenging tasks, leading to low persistence and task avoidance. Incremental theorists just keep plugging away following a failure.

It is for these reasons that effective classrooms always include the following messages:

- Trying hard fosters achievement and intelligence.
- Failure is a natural part of learning.
- Being best is not what school is about; getting better is.

Every teacher and parent can send the messages that people get smarter by trying hard, that part of getting smart is bouncing back from failures, and that school is about becoming better, not becoming best. Given the tendency of children to explain their performances in terms of ability, there is plenty of reason to do everything possible to encourage students to believe that effort attributions are the way to go when explaining performance.

Summary

Primary-grades children have much more faith in effort than do students in the later grades. This provides great motivation for accomplishing complicated tasks, such as learning to read. When grade-1 children experience frustration, their effort attributions support the expenditure of additional efforts. In contrast, older children are more likely to make ability attributions than effort attributions, so that failures are no longer seen as indications of insufficient effort but as indications of low abilities. Failures followed by attributions of low abilities leads to reduced motivation for the frustrating activity. Thus, grade-1 students are more likely to be motivated to continue with challenging tasks than are grade-3 students.

Worse yet is when the grade-3 student is confronted with a task that is difficult for her or him but was accomplished several years earlier by most other grade-3 children. Thus, the grade-3 student who has not yet learned to read interprets his or her failures to date as strong evidence of a lack of ability to read, undermining attempts to make additional efforts to learn to read. There is no reason to believe, based on attributional theory, that a high motivation to learn to read will be maintained for children who go through grades 1 and 2 without acquiring the basic reading skills that they need.

Researchers have done a good job of establishing the value of encouraging students to continue to make attributions as they did when they were in grade-1, and to believe that academic success depends on effort. Even more generally, psychologists have determined that academic motivation is more likely to be encouraged if students come to believe that intelligence itself is the result of effort rather than the reflection of innate ability. A lot of input about the value of effort is necessary, however, because with increasing grade level, the implicit message in the classroom is that effort is not what matters—that there are the smart and the not-so-smart.

Grade-Level Differences in Classroom Reward Structures

Intrinsic academic motivation is killed off by academic failures. An important reason that such failures are more devastating with increasing grade level is that competition between students accelerates during the elementary years.

Competition is a way of life in many classrooms. There is grading on the curve, so that only a very few students can receive the highest grades. Worse yet, grades are often public and salient in the classroom, as when students "call in" their grades as the teacher marks them in the grade book or when students retrieve their papers from the "graded bin." Finding one's own paper in such bins results in exposure to the grades of many other students in the class. Thus, each student in a class knows how she or he is doing relative to others.

Many societal forces support such competitiveness. How many parents respond to their children's report card by asking how "So-and-so" did, followed by remarks about how it would be nice if their son or daughter were like "So-and-so"? Local papers carry news about academic achievements in the school, for example, publishing the names of students earning straight A's.

One result of this obsession with identifying who is smart and, implicitly, who is not is to undermine the academic motivation of many children. Classroom competition and evaluation foster what John Nicholls (1989) referred to as ego involvement. Success in the competitive classroom (especially relative to peers) implies high intellectual capacity (i.e., that one is smart, which is ego enhancing) while failure implies low capacity (which is ego diminishing). Since most students will not end up doing "best" in the class, feelings of failure, self-criticism, and negative self-esteem occur often (Ames, 1984). Many students come to expect that they will not earn top grades or be reinforced as much as other students. Such a system has high potential for undermining effort when success is not certain (e.g., with new task demands), for trying and failing leads to feelings of low ability.

One likely reason that there is a clear decline in academic motivation from the early primary to the later elementary grades is that comparative evaluations are less frequent and salient in the early primary years than in the later primary and middle grades (Harter, Whitesell, & Kowalski, 1992; Stipek & Daniels, 1988). With increasing age, children are more aware of the competitiveness in their classrooms (see Harter et al., 1992; also Schmidt, Ollendick, & Stanowicz, 1988) and of the implications of not succeeding. What is certain, based on research (e.g., Wigfield, 1988), is that by the middle-elementary years, paying attention to how one does compared to others affects perceptions of one's own competency, expectancies about future success and thus, potentially, school performance.

Life in Noncompetitive Classrooms

The problems produced by classroom competitiveness are especially apparent when competitive classrooms are compared with ones that are not so competitive. In some classrooms, rather than rewarding students for being better than one another, students are rewarded for doing better than they did previously. They are rewarded for personal improvement on academic tasks. John Nicholls referred to such classrooms as fostering task involvement. Nicholls and his colleague Terri Thorkildsen (e.g., 1987) studied 30 grade-5 classrooms ranging in ego and task involvement. They found that work avoidance was much more commonly reported in ego-involved (competitive) classrooms than in task-involved (noncompetitive) classrooms. The students in the task-oriented classrooms believed that success in school depended on interest, effort, and attempting to learn, whereas the students in the ego-involved classrooms believed that success depended on being smarter than other kids and trying to beat out other students. That is, whether grade-5 students continued to believe in effort, as they had when they were younger, or in ability as a determinant of performance depended on the reward structure of the classroom.

Task-oriented classrooms are much more likely to keep students interested in and committed to school than are ego-oriented classrooms (Nicholls, 1989). The problem is that many more classrooms are ego-involved than task-involved. Far too often, the goal is to get better grades than the ones earned by peers rather than to learn (e.g., Ames, 1992; Blumenfeld, 1992). Many other classrooms are structured so as to encourage expectations of failure (i.e., relative to other students) rather than success. This has big consequences for students.

For example, Susan Nolen (1988) assessed whether grade-8 students were task- or ego-oriented. In addition, Nolen assessed students' use of particular strategies for reading and understanding textbook material. Although both task- and ego-oriented students used superficial strategies for processing text (e.g., reading the whole thing over and over), the task-oriented students were much more likely than the ego-oriented students to endorse and use strategies that involved deeper processing of text (e.g., trying to see how this fits with what I've learned in class). The type of sophisticated reading that should be fostered in students occurred more often in the noncompetitive classrooms.

Mainstreaming

The effects of classroom competitiveness are also striking when the fate of students with learning difficulties is considered. In recent years, there has been a national movement to eliminate special classrooms for students experiencing academic difficulties, having them receive their education in regular classrooms. By the middle elementary grades, mainstreaming means placement into a competitive classroom in which failure relative to others is virtually assured for the child with learning difficulties. A similar situation occurs with respect to the education of English-as-a-Second-Language students. Such students often enter competitive classrooms far behind the other students. The competitive nature of the classrooms guarantees failure relative to other students, with potentially devastating impact on the motivation of the students who were disadvantaged from the outset. Whenever a class includes a mix of abilities and preparation levels, classroom competition virtually guarantees that many students will experience failure, potentially impacting most negatively on the academic self-esteem and motivation of at-risk students.

From a motivational perspective, if school must be competitive, placing at-risk students in classrooms with other at-risk students has advantages. A student may have more positive perceptions about his or her own academic ability and better school performance (measured in some absolute way) if enrolled in a low- rather than a high-ability class, because what one thinks about one's own ability is determined with reference to the students in one's class. Social comparisons with classmates can motivate additional effort (e.g., when one is at the top of a low-ability class) or undermine effort (e.g., when one is near the bottom of a high-ability class; e.g., Marsh, 1987). Of course, better yet for such students would be to place them in noncompetitive classes, where they would be given good grades for improving. However, the reality is that most schools in America are going to remain competitive for the foreseeable future. If that is the case, mainstreaming has great potential to undermine the motivation of the students who are mainstreamed.

Consequences of Success

So far in this section, the concern has been with the negative effects of rewards on those who do not often receive them in classrooms. As it turns out, classroom rewards can undermine the intrinsic motivation of those who receive the rewards. When students receive tangible rewards for activities that are intrinsically interesting to them, their intrinsic interest in the activity can decline. Thus, when teachers begin to reward behaviors that had been intrinsically rewarding, they may undermine students' interest in those activities in the future when rewards are not available. This is known as the overjustification effect, with students coming to believe that they are engaging in rewarded activities for the reward they are receiving rather than because of the intrinsic value of the activity (Lepper, Keavney, & Drake, 1996). Once rewarded, they begin to justify their behavior to themselves, making the case to themselves that they are carrying out the behavior because of the tangible reward. The person who does something in the absence of reward can only explain his or her behavior to her or himself in terms of personal interest in the activity.

McLoyd (1979) provided an apt demonstration of the overjustification effect with respect to reading. Children read high-interest books, some receiving a reward for doing so. McLoyd observed that when students could read on their own without the possibility of reward, those who had not received rewards for reading did more reading than those who previously received rewards for doing it. There is very good reason to suspect that students who are reading and writing for "points" given by a teacher or for high grades may not be as highly motivated to read in the absence of teacher rewards than they would have been had they participated in instruction in which classroom rewards for performance were not so salient.

I am often asked about the implications of the overjustification effect for reading reward programs such as the one sponsored by Pizza Hut. The answer is that it depends on the kid. For children who are already motivated to read, providing extrinsic rewards has the potential to undermine their intrinsic motivation to read. For children who are not motivated to read, such programs can motivate reading that would not otherwise occur. I urge teachers to use such programs with unmotivated students but to refrain from using tangible incentive programs with students who are already reading for the fun of it.

Summary

One of the reasons that, with increasing grade level, children increasingly tend to believe that ability determines achievement is that classrooms are more competitive with advancing grade level. Competitive classrooms foster the attribution that ability is what matters, thus undermining student academic motivation. It does not have to be that way, however: It is possible to structure classrooms so that students are graded on improvement rather than in comparison to other students. In such classrooms, there seems to be greater academic motivation and more sophisticated reading. The problem is that there are too few such classrooms, for the competitive classroom model thrives in contemporary America. America is a nation of competitive classrooms, which are structured so that most children will experience failure relative to other children.

A further complication is that rewards, such as grades, can undermine students' intrinsic motivations. Recall from the survey conducted by McKenna et al. (1995) that many children are intrinsically motivated to read in the early grades but that the motivation of even the top students declines. This occurs even though top students are being rewarded with high grades for doing well! Whenever the emphasis on grades is high enough that students can convince themselves that they are reading only to obtain a high grade or other tangible reward, there is danger of undermining whatever intrinsic motivation a student might have (Sweet & Guthrie, 1996).

One of the strengths of primary-grades classrooms is that they are more likely to be organized along cooperative principles. The increasing shift to competitiveness during the later primary (i.e., increasingly in grades 2 and 3 compared to kindergarten and grade 1) and middle elementary years comes at a time when students' thinking abilities mature in ways that increase their notice of their own achievements relative to others.

Developmental Differences in Making of Social Comparisons

Young children tend not to compare themselves much with others, especially with respect to psychological characteristics such as intelligence, reading ability or extent of prior knowledge. Yes, preschool children can and do compare the tangible goodies they have with the tangible goodies another child has (Ruble, Boggiano, Feldman, & Loebl, 1980): "I have more orange juice than you." "Do not!" "Do too!" But they do not make much of differences or similarities in performance on academic tasks. Thus, a grade-1 student who feels badly because she or he is having difficulty with two-column addition is unlikely to feel better if the teacher reminds the student that all the other kids in the class are experiencing the same difficulty. With increasing age during the elementary-grade years, students become concerned with their academic standing relative to others (Ruble, 1983). Again, because for most students, there will be others around who are doing better, the increasing focus on comparing one's own achievement with that of classmates has increasing potential for leading to negative conclusions about one's own ability. Such conclusions can then translate into reduced motivation to achieve.

Summary

Academic intrinsic motivation declines with increasing grade level. Why? It is probably due to shifts in information-processing abilities and proclivities as well as characteristics of American schooling as an institution.

With respect to information processing, there is an increasing tendency with increasing age during the elementary grades to make achievement comparisons with others. For many children, this means increasing recognition that their performances are not as good as the performances of other students. There are also developmental shifts in attributional tendencies. Although preschoolers and early elementary-grade students do not interpret academic difficulties as indications of low ability, the tendency to do so increases with age. The greater the effort required to obtain academic success, the more likely it is to encourage an inference of low ability with increasing grade level. In short, developmental shifts in information processing lead to developmental shifts in expectations about future success and failure.

These shifts favoring student inferences about low ability occur in the context of schooling that increasingly emphasizes competition with increasing grade level. Despite the healthiness of sending the message that intelligence is incremental, school is an institution that often signals that intelligence is fixed, something a student either has or does not have (Ames, 1992). This is very discouraging for many students who do not do well in such a competitive environment. The bad attitudes that many high school students have about school seem very justified given such an institutional climate. School has shaped them to expect academic failure.

My view is that changing the motivational structure of schooling should be a high priority in education reform. In the meantime, individual teachers and parents can do their part by repeatedly sending the message to children that effort counts and that an excellent mind is built a little bit at a time through academic effort. Reward children for growth, not for outperforming others. As is elaborated in the rest of this chapter, reading researchers have identified a number of more specific ways to maintain and increase the motivation of children for reading.

INCREASING STUDENT MOTIVATION FOR LITERACY

The research in the past two decades on student motivation has heightened awareness that students often are not motivated to read or learn to read better. This awareness has energized efforts to identify ways to increase student motivation. Admittedly, most of what is described here has not been researched so thoroughly that any of the recommendations can be given with great confidence. As a whole, however, the research community has identified a variety of methods with the potential for increasing student motivation for reading, each of which is conceptually sensible, if not yet fully validated. Teachers who use the methods described in this section will be on the cutting edge of educational motivation, although I expect that edge to be sharpened somewhat in the next few years as more evaluation data on the various techniques reviewed here accumulates.

The methods described in this section range from individual components of literacy instruction (e.g., interesting materials, attribution retraining) to entire redefinitions of the literacy program (e.g., concept-oriented instruction, whole language). The discussion proceeds from research on individual components to approaches intended to redefine literacy instruction completely.

Attribution Retraining

That the attributions of many low-achieving children are dysfunctional (i.e., the students attribute their failures to uncontrollable ability factors and hence are not motivated to exert academic effort; e.g., Carr, Borkowski, & Maxwell, 1991) has inspired some to attempt to retrain attributional tendencies. Both applied efforts and basic research (e.g., Foersterling, 1985; Stipek & Kowalski, 1989) have documented that attribution retraining can make a substantial difference in the motivation of students who otherwise tend to attribute their poor performances to factors other than effort. Particularly relevant here, John Borkowski and his colleagues (e.g., Borkowski, Carr, Rellinger, & Pressley, 1990; Borkowski, Weyhing, & Carr, 1988; Reid & Borkowski, 1987) have provided the most compelling analyses and data about interventions aimed at shifting the attributions of low achievers in order to promote reading comprehension.

Borkowski has recognized that for low-functioning students, attributing success to effort alone would probably be ineffective. This is consistent with the perspective emphasized throughout this book that strategies, metacognition, and conceptual knowledge also contribute to reading achievement. Thus, Borkowski's group has been teaching students to use strategies to accomplish intellectual tasks at the same time that they persuade students that their successes and failures on academic tasks are due to their efforts using appropriate strategies (Clifford, 1984). Borkowski and his colleagues persuade students that, as they learn strategies, they are acquiring tools that will permit them to improve their academic performances, providing a powerful motivation to use the strategies they are acquiring (Chapman, Skinner, & Baltes, 1990).

For example, in one study (Carr & Borkowski, 1989), underachieving elementary students were assigned to one of three conditions:

1. In the strategies + attribution training condition, children were taught comprehension strategies. They were instructed to self-test while they read, in order to determine whether they understood their reading. The students were also taught summarization, topic sentence, and questioning strategies as a means of understanding text. The attributional part of the training consisted of emphasizing to students that they could

understand text by applying the comprehension strategies, that their comprehension of a text was a function of how they approached it, rather than of any inherent comprehension abilities.

2. Participants in the strategies-only condition were taught the strategies, without the benefit of attributional training.
3. Students in the control condition were provided neither strategies instruction nor attributional training.

What a difference in the strategies + attributional training condition! When tested 3 weeks following the conclusion of the instruction, the strategies + attribution participants were more likely to be using the strategies than other participants in the study, and recall of text was higher in this condition than in the other conditions of the study. In addition, the strategies + attribution subjects were using comprehension strategies in the classroom much more than the students in the other conditions of the study.

Although much more work analyzing the effects of attributional retraining needs to be conducted in order to understand completely its potential for modifying views of self as learner, many who work with learning disabled students in particular are already employing attributional retraining with their students. For example, as learning disabled students are taught comprehension, writing, and memory strategies in a well-known learning disabilities curriculum created by Donald Deshler, Jean Schumaker, and their colleagues at the University of Kansas (e.g., Deshler & Schumaker, 1988), there is consistent emphasis on the role of controllable factors, such as use of strategies, as a determinant of performance. This is because the Kansas group recognizes that the attributions made by learning disabled students often are dysfunctional (e.g., "I am stupid"). Such attributions, if permitted to persist, have high potential for defeating other instruction, since believing that one is stupid is also believing that there is nothing that can be done about it.

Interesting Texts to Read

Throughout the 20th century, going back at least to Dewey (1913), it has been recognized that interest matters with students: high interest increases student engagement and learning from text (e.g., Hidi, 1990; Renninger & Wozniak, 1985; Schiefele, 1992). This insight has prompted many authors and materials developers to attempt to create academic materials that "grab" students.

Richard Anderson and his colleagues (e.g., Anderson, Mason, &

Shirey, 1984) carried out some of the best known work on the role of interest in children's reading of text. Children read sentences that had been rated either as interesting or uninteresting. Interesting sentences were much more certain to be remembered later than were uninteresting sentences, producing a very large effect relative to the size of effects produced by other manipulations (e.g., readability of sentences).

Anderson's group (e.g., 1982) also conducted some extremely detailed analytical studies to determine the mechanisms underlying the interest effect, hypothesizing that more interesting materials were more likely to be attended by students. In fact, that seemed to be the case, with students spending more time reading interesting texts. In addition, interesting texts were so absorbing that readers failed to respond to an external signal (e.g., to press a button in response to a sound heard while they were reading) as quickly as they did when reading uninteresting texts. Even so, greater attention alone did not account for their greater learning of the interesting materials, for when differences in attention and effort were factored out of the learning data (i.e., amount of time spent reading sentences was controlled statistically), there were still large effects of interest (e.g., Shirey & Reynolds, 1988). Thus, interest can affect directly both attention and learning, but only some of the increases in learning are due to its effect on attention to academic content.

Unfortunately, when Anderson, Shirey, Wilson, and Fielding (1987) analyzed social studies and science textbooks presented to children in school, they found them to be dull. They also determined that authors often attempted to make texts interesting by adding stimulating anecdotes. Texts filled with anecdotes, however, often lack coherence (e.g., Armbruster, 1984). In addition, the reader can completely miss the point of the text even while remembering the anecdotes in it. That is, stimulating information and seductive details can be recalled (e.g., John F. Kennedy played football on the White House lawn with his children), although there is no learning of either abstract or general points covered in the text (e.g., Kennedy's administration proposed sweeping social reforms; Garner, 1992; Garner, Alexander, Gillingham, Kulikowich, & Brown, 1991; Garner, Gillingham, & White, 1989; Hidi & Baird, 1988; Wade & Adams, 1990).

While there is not much reason to be sanguine that texts can be made more interesting without also being seductive, we should not dismiss the possibility of making texts interesting altogether. A low-cost way to increase the interest of students in what they read is to permit them to choose for themselves what they will read. This is one of the main motivations of whole language educators to provide students with so much choice.

Whole Language:
Literature and Literature-Based Activities

A consistent claim of whole language theorists and enthusiasts is that literacy-rich environments are motivating to students. In fact, there is considerable support for their assertion.

National Reading Research Center researchers Barbara Palmer, Rose Marie Codling, and Linda Gambrell (1994) asked grade-3 and grade-5 students from 16 classrooms about the factors that motivated them to read. Forty-eight children, varying in reading ability and their motivation to read, were interviewed in depth. In many different ways, the students reported that their motivations to read depended on rich literacy environments.

Thus, *prior experiences* with books were a major motivation for wanting to read, as well as choosing to read particular books. Children reported wanting to read books after seeing them on the television show *Reading Rainbow* or after hearing a book read by a teacher or parent. Similarly, prior experience with books in a series motivated continued reading of the series. For example, the *American Girls* series permits the child to learn more about characters that they have learned to like from reading previous books in the series.

Social interactions revolving around books also matter. The participants in the study reported wanting to read books that their friends, parents, and teachers talked about. Remarks such as the following were common:

> My friend Kristin was reading it and told me about it and I said, "Hmmm, that sounds pretty interesting."

> I got interested in it because the other group . . . [was] reading it, so I checked it out of the library. (Palmer et al., 1994, p. 177)

Book access was also reported as important by the children, who reported high motivation to read books they owned and ones available to them in the classroom. Particularly striking was the importance that the students attributed to the classroom library, consistent with the emphasis in whole language that classrooms filled with books motivate literate interactions with them (Fractor, Woodruff, Martinez, & Teale, 1993; Morrow, 1992).

A hallmark of the whole language philosophy is that literacy instruction should include *freedom of choice*. Consistent with the perspective that choice is important in motivating literacy, the children in the Palmer et al. (1994) study reported they were more excited to read books that they chose to read than ones they were required to read (Spaulding, 1992).

My own predilections are to believe the children, for they are closer to their motivations than anyone else. Many social scientists are skeptical of self-reports, however, especially with respect to motivation. They prefer observations of motivated reading. What would be most believable to the social science community would be observations of greater motivation in literacy-rich environments than in more conventional classroom environments. There is in fact some evidence of this type.

Julianne Turner's (1995) dissertation study at the University of Michigan was a very thorough comparison of motivation in literacy-rich whole language grade-1 classrooms versus grade-1 classrooms which emphasized skills. She studied six grade-1 classrooms in a school district that used whole language and six grade-1 classrooms in a similar district, except that it used a basal instructional program. The whole language classrooms were pretty much consistent with whole language as described in Chapter 1, except that there was quite a bit of teacher explanation about phonics and other skills. This explanation often came in the context of group reading of texts (e.g., big books), however. The basal instructional program included stories and skill work, including ditto worksheets as part of phonics instruction.

One of the most striking outcomes in the study was that the children in the whole-language classrooms used more learning strategies than did the students in the basal classes. That is, they seemed more engaged with the content, rehearsing it more, elaborating on ideas they encountered, planning more, and monitoring whether they were understanding what they read. Thus, whole language seemed to make a difference. Even so, both types of classrooms afforded opportunities for the types of tasks and situations that Palmer et al. (1994) concluded were motivating. Consistent with Palmer et al.'s (1994) conclusions, across both types of classrooms, students persisted most in reading when they were involved in activities like partner reading and reading of trade books, in contrast to when they were doing activities such as worksheets. When children could select texts on their own, they read more. In short, Turner (1995) observed that when the classroom conditions matched those that the children in Palmer et al. (1994) claimed were motivating, students seemed more motivated.

Lesley Morrow (1992; Morrow & Sharkey, 1993) and her colleagues at Rutgers University, in work sponsored in part by the National Reading Research Center, also explored the motivational consequences of instruction consistent with whole-language principles. She introduced a literature-based reading program into grade-2 classrooms. The program included literacy centers that stimulated a variety of literacy activities (e.g., reading, felt-board enactments of stories, listening to taped stories, writing), teacher-guided literature activities (e.g., reading and telling of stories by teachers, student retelling and rewriting of stories, writing of original stories, book sharing), and independent reading and writing periods that permitted student choice of literacy activities (i.e., reading, writing, listening, enacting, etc.). In the whole-language classrooms, there was a great deal of social, cooperative interaction between students as they engaged in literacy activities.

In contrast, students in control classrooms participated in a traditional basal program supported by workbook exercises. Control instruction included small group lessons and seatwork. After completing workbook activities, students read library books. Although teachers occasionally read stories to children in the control classrooms, this was not a focus of instruction.

By the end of the intervention, there were clear advantages for the students in the whole-language classrooms. For example, students in these classrooms were better able to retell and rewrite stories that were read to them than were students in control classrooms. Students in the whole language classrooms outperformed control participants on a listening comprehension test. They also outperformed controls when asked to compose their own stories, using language that was more complex and included more diverse vocabulary than the language of the control participants. Most critical in the context of this chapter on student motivation, the students in the whole-language classrooms read more books and stories outside of school. When the whole-language students talked about their literacy program, they did so with enthusiasm, emphasizing that it was fun.

Collapsing across these studies, there is converging evidence that when classroom life is rich in literature and authentic reading experiences, students are more motivated than when instruction is more consistent with traditional skills and drills. Perhaps the most incontrovertible conclusion with respect to instruction filled with social interactions around reading of real literature is that such experiences enliven classrooms.

Running Start (Reading Is Fundamental)

The main idea of the Running Start program, sponsored by the Reading Is Fundamental organization, is that motivation to read will be encouraged by immersing children in books (Gambrell, 1996). The Reading Is Fundamental group emphasizes that children are motivated to read when they can interact with others with regard to what they are reading, when they are exposed to adults and other children who are enthused about reading, and when the adults in their world have high expectations that they can learn to read. Reading Is Fundamental emphasizes that reading is motivating to the extent that children have choice about what they will read and when they will read.

The Running Start program is a 10-week intervention, with grade-1 children challenged to read 21 books (or have the same number of books read to them) during the 10 weeks. At the outset of the program, Reading Is Fundamental donates a large number (60 to 80) of new books to the library of participating classrooms. The classroom is organized to support student progress toward the goal of interaction with 21 books over the 10-week period, with reading and book sharing common activities in class. Parents and older children visit classrooms to interact with children over books, sometimes reading to them and sometimes listening to the children read.

Motivation to read is encouraged in multiple ways in Running Start classrooms. Children keep track of their progress toward the 21-book goal using a sticker chart. Bookmarks are used to remind children to read, but also serve as rewards for reading. When children meet the 21-book goal, they are given some books to take home and keep.

Linda Gambrell's (1996; Gambrell, Codling, & Palmer, 1996; Gambrell & Morrow, 1995) group at the National Reading Research Center evaluated the motivational effects of the Running Start program. More than 300 classrooms from across the United States were part of the evaluation. The most important finding was that both children and parents were more motivated to read, and to read together, as a function of participating in the program.

In a follow-up, Gambrell and her colleagues (Gambrell et al., 1996; Gambrell & Morrow, 1995) carried out a quasi-experimental evaluation of the Running Start program with economically deprived urban grade-1 students. In general, compared to control participants who did not experience the Running Start program, the program participants read more on their own and with family members. Importantly, 6 months following the conclusion of the Running Start program, the program participants reported more reading and literacy-related activities (e.g., talking about books with parents) than control students.

One of the reasons that the Running Start program had the impact that it had was that it transformed the culture of the participating classrooms. The teachers created more elaborate literacy corners in the rooms, and more time was devoted to silent reading. The students and teachers in intervention classrooms talked to one another more about reading and books.

In summary, Reading Is Fundamental, a well-known charitable organization that has long supplied books to children who did not have them (remember the Ed Asner commercials soliciting support for Reading Is Fundamental?) has now created a grade-1 intervention designed to increase student motivation to read alone and with parents. Gambrell's group at the National Reading Research Center was able to provide evidence of the program's impact on motivation.

A Community-of-Learners Approach: Concept-Oriented Reading Instruction

Ann Brown and her associates pioneered the community-of-learners approach, in which content area instruction is integrated with literacy instruction (Brown, 1992; Brown et al., 1993; Brown & Campione, 1994; Campione, Shapiro, & Brown, 1995). Rather than superficially cover many topics, communities of learners explore a few issues in great depth during an academic year. When students begin to study a new topic, they generate questions that they want to answer. Students are taught strategies for carrying out research. Much of their time is spent doing collaborative research aimed at answering the questions that they have posed. This research will include library research, but can also include making field observations or carrying out experiments or any of a variety of activities that might reveal something about the concept that is being explored. Students also learn comprehension strategies that increase their abilities to find and remember the important parts of texts they read as part of their research. Finally, they do a great deal of writing. The overarching goal is for community-of-learners students to acquire strategic and conceptual knowledge that they can use broadly. The group is generating considerable evidence that students learn skills that transfer as they acquire thorough understanding of the concepts that they research and write about (Campione et al., 1995).

John Guthrie (1996) and his National Reading Research Center associates (Grant, Guthrie, Bennett, Rice, & McGough, 1993/1994; Guthrie et al., 1996) have developed a variation of the community-of-learners approach. They are studying literacy instruction that integrates reading, writing, and teaching of science, emphasizing real-world science observations, student self-direction, strategy instruction, and student collaboration and interaction during learning. Guthrie refers to this approach as concept-oriented reading instruction (CORI).

In a year-long evaluation of the approach, grade-3 and grade-5 students observed concrete objects in their natural world as part of an effort to develop conceptual interests that would motivate their study of the phenomena observed. Thus, to begin their study of birds and the environment, students observed bird nests in the wild. This was followed by other concrete experiences, including attempts to build bird nests, observing and recording behaviors at bird feeding stations, and visiting a collection of stuffed birds. Such concrete experiences provided much learning, illustrated by this report from a student after attempting to build a bird nest:

> We built our nest with leaves, grass sticks, and twigs. Mud too. But first we looked for each of these things at the playground. Clay was to stick our nest together because if we didn't have clay our nest would break. We called the clay mud. I learned that it's hard to make a nest unless you really try to. I learned that birds have a hard time making nests but we read a book that helped us learn and I found out that if you try with a group it might be easy. And you might make a lot of friends. (Guthrie et al., 1996, p. 312)

The concrete observations led to the development of students' questions, and to collaborative brainstorming to come up with questions. These questions would motivate additional observations, reading, writing, and discussions. Questions were displayed on the walls of the classroom as a reminder of what students wanted to discover through their research, reading, and writing. This was science instruction that involved making observations, gathering and recording data, recognition of patterns, and development of explanations for these observations and patterns.

In order to answer the questions that students had posed for themselves, they needed to develop their search skills. As part of CORI, students were taught how to search for books and other materials. They learned how to use tables of contents, indexes in books, headings, and pictures in text in order to narrow their search for relevant information. Students learned to (1) be certain of what they wanted to find out before they searched (i.e., to form a search goal); (2) identify the organization of materials they are searching; (3) extract critical information from sources, constructing summaries and paraphrases of critical material; and (4) abstract across sources, producing syntheses of important ideas and general concepts emerging from the various sources of information. These strategies were taught using teacher and peer modeling followed by teacher scaffolding of these skills as students searched. Of course, because students worked together as they searched, there was also peer scaffolding of skills.

CORI students also learned comprehension strategies, which included identifying the main ideas in texts, looking for critical details, summarizing, comparing between texts, relating illustrations in text to verbal content, evaluating a book, and reflecting on the point of view expressed in a text. These skills were practiced with narratives and expository pieces, with students learning that topics can be addressed and explored in both fictional and factual writing. Students learned how to take notes about main ideas, details, and so on as well.

Virtually all reading was of authentic literature, with a variety of trade books read as part of units. Thus, as students studied birds, they read *Owl Moon* (Yolen, 1987), *White Bird* (Bulla, 1966), and *Wingman* (Pinkwater, 1975). Students also read poems relating to birds. As they read these texts, students were taught about the importance of imagery during reading and how the story grammar elements (i.e., setting, plot, conflict, resolution) combine as part of a story.

By reading materials related to the thematic topic and searching for answers to critical questions, the students became experts about the topic. This expertise was used by students as they wrote reports relating to the concept, developed stories pertaining to focal concepts, and created visual displays (e.g., bulletin boards). As students carried out these activities, they learned how to tailor their messages to particular audiences and how to express meaning in a variety of ways.

Although Guthrie and his associates have yet to produce a controlled comparison of the effects of CORI to alternatives, they have been able to document that CORI students improve in search skills, writing, understanding of focal concepts, comprehension of texts, and interpretation skills. Particularly important here, the majority of students reported greater motivation to read and participate in literacy activities as the program continued. Moreover, the majority of students reported reading more as the year proceeded.

Finally, Guthrie has worked with the group at Benchmark School to determine the feasibility of the approach with middle-school students who had a history of reading problems (Gaskins et al., 1994). Although there certainly were challenges in implementing the approach with such students, there were clear gains in students' search skills and evidence of improved conceptual understanding, with the students viewing science less as the learning of facts and more the acquisition of conceptual understanding.

Summary

Many researchers are studying the nature of instruction that grabs students, motivating them to read and learn. Although there have been frustrations—for example, interesting texts often prove to be more seductive than informative, as they were intended to be—there have been many more successes than failures. Perhaps most encouraging of all, instructional practices that motivate are enjoying dissemination. Despite justifiable reservations about whole language with respect to the development of basic decoding skills, many whole-language practices are motivating, and they certainly are widely disseminated; also Reading Is Fundamental is reaching more classrooms every year. Even if a school does not adopt these efforts, however, much can be gleaned from the motivational research that can be adopted and adapted in any classroom.

CONCLUDING COMMENTS

Americans are barraged with information about how schools are failing. The case typically is made with test scores. Much of the wailing about American students' low and declining test scores is not justified (Berliner & Biddle, 1995). I never lose sleep over test scores. What I do lose sleep over, however, is the documentation of steadily declining academic motivation as students proceed through school. Yes, in part, the declines are artifactual in that kindergarten and grade-1 children are just so darn optimistic and full of enthusiasm, so filled with intrinsic motivation that the only direction they can go is down. Still, there is something wrong when some kids are ready to throw in the towel by the time they are in grade 5 or 6 (or even earlier). I lose sleep over those kids, just as I lose sleep when I realize that even the best readers are less enthused about reading with every additional year they are in school (McKenna et al., 1995). There is plenty of reason for American educators to be doing everything they possibly can to increase student motivation.

One productive way to think about the motivational research summarized in this chapter is to think about the ideas that emerge that can be used in any elementary classroom. Although the case is not airtight, and much research remains to be done before absolutely firm conclusions could be offered, I think there is enough evidence available right now to recommend that every teacher do everything possible to follow these guidelines that relate to student motivation:

• Assure student success. This can be accomplished by making certain that students are attempting tasks that are within their reach. Tasks are motivating when they are appropriately challenging, rather than too easy or too hard.
• Be a teacher who scaffolds student learning. Be a teacher who monitors when students are having difficulties and provide enough support so that students are able to make progress.

- Encourage students to attribute their successes to expending appropriate efforts and their failures to lack of effort or failing to deploy effort appropriately (e.g., using a wrong strategy). This principle is as important for good students as it is for weak ones. The good student who attributes successes to high ability is constructing a personal story that provides no motivation for trying hard. The weaker student who believes that failures reflect low ability, which is unchangeable, has no reason to believe that effort will matter.

- A related point: Encourage students to believe that intelligence is not innate and fixed, but rather everchanging. The smart get smarter by learning more, by learning to use the strategies that smart people use and by acquiring in-depth understanding of important concepts, such as those at the heart of science, social studies, and literacy curricula at their best. People who believe the incremental theory of intelligence have much more reason to try hard than do those who take to heart an entity perspective on intelligence, to use Dweck's terminology.

- Failures occur. Encourage students to interpret failures as a natural part of learning. Discourage students from believing that failures reflect low ability. Students are served well when you foster in them the understanding that failures indicate a need to try harder in the future. Teachers should use student failures to diagnose when and how they can scaffold a student.

- Do not permit failures to persist, believing that failure represents a lack of developmental readiness and that the child will quickly acquire the now-difficult-to-acquire skill when she or he is "ready." For example, the grade-1 student who is having difficulties in learning to decode will be discouraged by continued failure. It is better to explore alternative ways of teaching decoding with the struggling student, doing all that is possible to take advantage of the grade-1 student's great faith in effort. Persistent failure to make progress discourages motivation; every effort should be made to prevent students from continuing to fail.

- Do not encourage student competition. Student competition undermines motivation rather than fostering it. In competitive classrooms, many more students are going to feel like losers than winners. Rather than encouraging competition between students, it is better to reward students for improving on their past performances and to consistently send the message that improvement is what matters.

- Encourage student cooperation and interaction over literacy tasks. When students talk about books, they let each other know what is worth reading and what is exciting to read. Students can scaffold one another, for example, by helping one another with difficult words during pair reading. Students' conceptual knowledge develops more completely when they work together in communities of learners, especially when motivation is high in such classroom communities.

- Play down "grades as rewards" for literacy activities, especially activities that are intrinsically motivating for students. When students begin to be rewarded for doing what they like to do, their intrinsic motivation for the activity can decline. In general, the more a classroom encourages working for grades, the more it discourages intrinsic motivation.
- Make certain that students have access to a wide range of interesting books. Classroom libraries seem to be a critically important source of reading material for students, and hence, it makes sense to do everything possible to assure a rich classroom library.
- As much as possible, permit student choice with respect to what they read and to what topics are the conceptual focus of instruction. Teach children how to find books on the topics that interest them.
- Integrate literacy instruction with content learning. Such integration makes clear to students that the reading and writing skills they are acquiring are useful for learning important ideas, which is especially likely if the conceptual ideas explored as part of science and social studies grab students.
- Favor depth over breadth as much as possible, as is done with communities of learners, choosing a few exceptionally motivating topics as the conceptual focus for the school year.

Not surprisingly, many of these concepts have been encountered in previous chapters. Why? Recall the discussions of excellent teachers presented in Chapters 6 and 7. All of them were very motivating largely because they integrated many of the ideas covered in this chapter into their teaching.

In reviewing what is now known about student motivation, it is clear that there is no evidence whatsoever that any one of these mechanisms is so powerful that it alone is more powerful than the others. Whole-language claims about the power of literature to motivate students must be considered in light of declining motivation for students experiencing frustrations as part of learning to read. Thus, is it reasonable to believe that students in exclusively whole-language environments who are experiencing difficulties learning how to recognize words will remain motivated because of the presence of literature in their classroom worlds? I doubt it. One of the reasons to like balanced curricula is that the motivational gains of whole language have a better chance of occurring if children have the skills to work successfully on the reading and writing tasks that occur in their classrooms. Nothing motivates like successful accomplishment of interesting and appropriately challenging tasks.

SUMMARY

1. In general, academic motivation declines from the onset of schooling through high school. Declines in enthusiasm for and interest in reading parallel the general developmental declines in academic motivation.

2. There are a variety of psychological developments contributing to declining motivation, including developmental changes in how students react to failures: The younger the child, the greater the chance that she or he believes failure reflects lack of effort rather than lack of ability. Older children are more likely than younger children to make comparisons with others, which undermines motivation for the child experiencing difficulties.

3. There are also structural changes in the school setting that contribute to declining motivation with increasing grade level, most prominently increasing competition.

4. There are a variety of mechanisms that are being validated in research as positively affecting student motivation. One is the training of students to make effort attributions rather than ability attributions, to explain both failures and successes. A variety of mechanisms favored in whole language, such as the choice and reading of excellent literature, seem to promote student motivation to read. (This is just one of a number of reasons to favor much of what is offered in whole language, even if the whole-language perspectives on decoding are in error.) The community-of-learners approach promises to increase depth of conceptual understanding as it motivates students to engage academically.

5. There has been a lot of progress in understanding academic motivation in the past two decades. It is essential that such work continue and the results of such work be applied to school reform. If taken seriously, the research findings in this chapter have the potential to turn American schooling inside out and upside down. For example, imagine the ramifications of taking seriously the idea that academic competition and competitive grading be eliminated because such competition undermines intrinsic motivation.

6. Skills teaching as part of balanced instruction increases the likelihood of student success with reading, which goes far in motivating reading. Whole-language proponents have done much to increase the variety of literature that children read in school, consistent with their

approach to motivational enhancement. A balanced approach takes advantage of multiple motivational mechanisms. In the best cases, children feel successful, and thus, are motivated to try. When they do try, they find books that are wonderfully interesting to read and are within their reach because of the skills they have been learning. Balanced instruction is a better bet for motivating students than less complete types of instruction, such as whole-language or skills-emphasis approaches. Recall that a hallmark of excellent instruction as documented in Chapter 6 was that students were highly engaged and motivated, and that this was much more common in balanced classrooms.

REFERENCES

Ames, C. (1984). Competitive, cooperative, and individualistic goal structures: A motivational analysis. In R. Ames & C. Ames (Eds.), *Research on motivation in education* (Vol. 1, pp. 117–207). New York: Academic Press.

Ames, C. (1992). Classrooms: Goals, structures, and student motivation. *Journal of Educational Psychology, 84,* 261–271.

Anderson, R. C. (1982). Allocation of attention during reading. In A. Flammer & W. Kintsch (Eds.), *Discourse processing* (pp. 292–305). New York: North-Holland.

Anderson, R. C., Mason, J. M., & Shirey, L. (1984). The reading group: An experimental investigation of a labyrinth. *Reading Research Quarterly, 20,* 6–38.

Anderson, R. C., Shirey, L. L., Wilson, P. T., & Fielding, L. G. (1987). Interestingness of children's reading material. In R. E. Snow & M. J. Farr (Eds.), *Aptitude, learning, and instruction: Volume 3. Conative and affective process analyses* (pp. 287–299). Hillsdale, NJ: Erlbaum.

Armbruster, B. B. (1984). The problem of "inconsiderate text." In G. G. Duffy, L. R. Roehler, & J. Mason (Eds.), *Comprehension instruction* (pp. 202–217). New York: Longman.

Berliner, D. C., & Biddle, B. J. (1995). *The manufactured crisis: Myths, fraud, and the attack on America's public schools.* Reading, MA: Addison–Wesley.

Blumenfeld, P. C. (1992). Classroom learning and motivation: Clarifying and expanding goal theory. *Journal of Educational Psychology, 84,* 272–281.

Borkowski, J. G., Carr, M., Rellinger, E. A., & Pressley, M. (1990). Self-regulated strategy use: Interdependence of metacognition, attributions, and self-esteem. In B. F. Jones (Ed.), *Dimensions of thinking: Review of research* (pp. 53–92). Hillsdale, NJ: Erlbaum.

Borkowski, J. G., Weyhing, R. S., & Carr, M. (1988). Effects of attributional retraining on strategy-based reading comprehension in learning-disabled students. *Journal of Educational Psychology, 80,* 46–53.

Brown, A. L. (1992). Design experiments: Theoretical and methodological challenges in creating complex interventions in classroom settings. *Journal of the Learning Sciences, 2,* 141–178.

Brown, A. L., Ash, D., Rutherford, M., Nakagawa, K., Gordon, A., & Campione, J. C. (1993). Distributed expertise in the classroom. In G. Salomon (Ed.), *Distributed cognitions: Psychological and educational considerations* (pp. 188–228). New York: Cambridge University Press.

Brown, A. L., & Campione, J. C. (1994). Guided discovery in a community of learners. In K. McGilly (Ed.), *Classroom lessons: Integrating cognitive theory and classroom practice* (pp. 229–270). Cambridge, MA: MIT Press/Bradford Books.

Bulla, C. R. (1966). *White bird.* New York: Philomel.

Campione, J. C., Shapiro, A. M., & Brown, A. L. (1995). Forms of transfer in a community of learners: Flexible learning and understanding. In A. McKeough, J. Lupart, & A. Marini (Eds.), *Teaching for transfer: Fostering generalization in learning* (pp. 35–68). Hillsdale, NJ: Erlbaum.

Carr, M., & Borkowski, J. G. (1989). Attributional training and the generalization of reading strategies with underachieving children. *Learning and Individual Differences, 1,* 327–341.

Carr, M., Borkowski, J. G., & Maxwell, S. E. (1991). Motivational components of underachievement. *Developmental Psychology, 27,* 108–118.

Chapman, J. W., & Tunmer, W. E. (1995). Development of young children's reading self-concept: An examination of emerging subcomponents and their relationship with reading achievement. *Journal of Educational Psychology, 87,* 154–167.

Chapman, M., Skinner, E. A., & Baltes, P. B. (1990). Interpreting correlations between children's perceived control and cognitive performance: Control, agency, or means–ends beliefs? *Developmental Psychology, 26,* 246–253.

Clifford, M. M. (1975). Validity of expectation: A developmental function. *Alberta Journal of Educational Research, 21,* 11–17.

Clifford, M. M. (1978). The effects of quantitative feedback on children's expectations of success. *Journal of Educational Psychology, 48,* 220–226.

Clifford, M. M. (1984). Thoughts on a theory of constructive failure. *Educational Psychologist, 19,* 108–120.

Covington, M. V. (1987). Achievement motivation, self-attributions, and the exceptional learner. In J. D. Day & J. G. Borkowski (Eds.), *Intelligence and exceptionality* (pp. 355–389). Norwood, NJ: Ablex.

Covington, M. V., & Omelich, C. L. (1979a). It's best to be able and virtuous too: Student and teacher evaluative responses to successful effort. *Journal of Educational Psychology, 71,* 688–700.

Covington, M. V., & Omelich, C. L. (1979b). Effort: The double-edged sword in school achievement. *Journal of Educational Psychology, 71,* 169–182.

Covington, M. V., & Omelich, C. L. (1981). As failures mount: Affective and cognitive consequences of ability demotion in the classroom. *Journal of Educational Psychology, 73,* 796–808.

Covington, M. V., & Omelich, C. L. (1984). Task-oriented versus competitive learning structures: Motivational and performance consequences. *Journal of Educational Psychology, 6,* 1038–1050.

Deshler, D. D., & Schumaker, J. B. (1988). An instructional model for teaching students how to learn. In J. L. Graden, J. E. Zins, & M. J. Curtis (Eds.), *Alternative educational delivery systems: Enhancing instructional options for all students* (pp. 391–411). Washington, DC: National Association of School Psychologists.

Dewey, J. (1913). *Interest and effort in education.* Boston: Riverside.

Dweck, C. (1987, April). *Children's theories of intelligence: Implications for motivation and learning.* Paper presented at the annual meeting of the American Educational Research Association, Washington, DC.

Dweck, C. S., & Leggett, E. L. (1988). A social–cognitive approach to motivation and personality. *Psychological Review, 95,* 256–273.

Eccles, J. S. (1993). School and family effects on the ontogeny of children's interests, self-perceptions, and activity choices. In J. E. Jacobs (Ed.), *Nebraska symposium on motivation: Developmental perspectives on motivation* (Vol. 40, pp. 145–208). Lincoln, NE: University of Nebraska Press.

Eccles, J. S., & Midgley, C. (1989). Stage/environment fit: Developmentally appropriate classrooms for early adolescents. In R. E. Ames & C. Ames (Eds.), *Research on motivation in education* (Vol. 3, pp. 139–186). New York: Academic Press.

Eccles, J., Wigfield, A., Flanagan, C., Miller, C., Reuman, D., & Yee, D. (1989). Self-concepts, domain values, and self-esteem: Relationships and changes in early adolescence. *Journal of Personality, 57,* 283–310.

Entwisle, D., & Hayduk, L. (1978). *Too great expectations: The academic outlook of young children.* Baltimore: Johns Hopkins Press.

Foersterling, F. (1985). Attribution retraining: A review. *Psychological Bulletin, 98,* 495–512.

Fractor, J., Woodruff, M. C., Martinez, M. G., & Teale, W. H. (1993). Let's not miss opportunities to promote voluntary reading: Classroom libraries in the elementary school. *Reading Teacher, 46,* 476–485.

Gambrell, L. B. (1996). Creating classroom cultures that foster reading motivation. *Reading Teacher, 50,* 14–25.

Gambrell, L. B., Codling, R. M., & Palmer, B. M. (1996). *Elementary students' motivation to read* (Research Report). College Park, MD, and Athens, GA: National Reading Research Center, Universities of Maryland and Georgia.

Gambrell, L. B., & Morrow, L. M. (1995). Creating motivating contexts for literacy learning. In L. Baker, P. Afflerbach, & D. Reinking (Eds.), *Developing engaged readers in home and school communities* (pp. 115–136). Mahwah, NJ: Erlbaum.

Gambrell, L. B., Palmer, B. M., Codling, R. M., & Mazzoni, S. A. (1996). Assessing motivation to read. *Reading Teacher, 49,* 518–533.

Garner, R. (1992). Learning from school texts. *Educational Psychologist, 27,* 53–63.

Garner, R., Alexander, P. A., Gillingham, M. G., Kulikowich, J. M., & Brown, R. (1991). Interest and learning from text. *American Educational Research Journal, 28,* 643–660.

Garner, R., Gillingham, M. G., & White, C. S. (1989). Effects of "seductive details" on macroprocessing and microprocessing in adult and children. *Cognition and Instruction, 6,* 41–57.

Gaskins, I. W., Guthrie, J. T., Satlow, E., Ostertag, J., Six, L., Byrne, J., & Conner, B. (1994). Integrating instruction of science, reading, and writing: Goals, teacher, development, and assessment. *Journal of Research in Science Teaching, 31,* 1039–1056.

Grant, R., Guthrie, J., Bennett, L., Rice, M. E., & McGough, K. (1993/1994). Developing engaged readers through concept-oriented instruction. *Reading Teacher, 47,* 338–340.

Guthrie, J. T. (1996). Educational contexts for engagement in literacy. *Reading Teacher, 49,* 432–445.

Guthrie, J. T., Van Meter, P., McCann, A. D., Wigfield, A., Bennett, L., Poundstone, C. C., Rice, M. E., Faibisch, F. M., Hunt, B., & Mitchell, A. M. (1996). Growth of literacy engagement: Changes in motivations and strategies during concept-oriented reading instruction. *Reading Research Quarterly, 31,* 306–332.

Harter, S. (1990). Cause, correlates, and the functional role of self-worth: A life-span perspective. In R. J. Sternberg & J. Kolligian (Eds.), *Competence considered* (pp. 67–97). New Haven, CT: Yale University Press.

Harter, S., Whitesell, N. R., & Kowalski, P. (1992). Individual differences in the effects of educational transitions on young adolescents' perceptions of competence and motivational orientation. *American Educational Research Journal, 29,* 777–807.

Henderson, V. L., & Dweck, C. S. (1990). Motivation and achievement. In S. S. Feldman & G. R. Elliott (Eds.), *At the threshold: The developing adolescent* (pp. 308–329). Cambridge, MA: Harvard University Press.

Hidi, S. (1990). Interest and its contribution as a mental resource for learning. *Review of Educational Research, 60,* 549–571.

Hidi, S., & Baird, W. (1988). Strategies for increasing text-based interest and students' recall of expository text. *Reading Research Quarterly, 23,* 465–483.

Jacobsen, B., Lowery, B., & DuCette, J. (1986). Attributions of learning-disabled children. *Journal of Educational Psychology, 78,* 59–64.

Juvonen, J. (1988). Outcome and attributional disagreements between students and their teachers. *Journal of Educational Psychology, 80,* 330–336.

Kistner, J. A., Osborne, M., & LeVerrier, L. (1988). Causal attributions of learning-disabled children: Developmental patterns and relation to academic progress. *Journal of Educational Psychology, 80,* 82–89.

Kloosterman, P. (1988). Self-confidence and motivation in mathematics. *Journal of Educational Psychology, 80,* 345–351.

Lepper, M. R., Keavney, M., & Drake, M. (1996). Intrinsic motivation and extrinsic rewards: A commentary on Cameron and Pierce's meta-analysis. *Review of Educational Research, 66,* 5–32.

Marsh, H. W. (1987). The big-fish-little-pond effect on academic self-concept. *Journal of Educational Psychology, 79,* 280–295.

McKenna, M. C., Ellsworth, R. A., & Kear, D. J. (1995). Children's attitudes toward reading: A national survey. *Reading Research Quarterly, 30,* 934–956.

McLoyd, V. C. (1979). The effects of extrinsic rewards of differential value on high and low intrinsic interest. *Child Development, 50,* 1010–1019.

Morrow, L. M. (1992). The impact of a literature-based program on literacy achievement, use of literature, and attitudes of children from minority backgrounds. *Reading Research Quarterly, 27,* 250–275.

Morrow, L. M., & Sharkey, E. A. (1993). Motivating independent reading and writing in the primary grades through social cooperative literacy experiences. *Reading Teacher, 47,* 162–164.

Nicholls, J. G. (1978). The development of the concepts of effort and ability, perception of academic attainment, and the understanding that difficult tasks require more than ability. *Child Development, 49,* 800–814.

Nicholls, J. G. (1989). *The competitive ethos and democratic education.* Cambridge, MA: Harvard University Press.

Nicholls, J. G. (1990). What is ability and why are we mindful of it? A developmental perspective. In R. Sternberg & J. Kolligian (Eds.), *Competence considered* (pp. 11–40). New Haven, CT: Yale University Press.

Nicholls, J. G., & Thorkildsen, T. A. (1987, October). *Achievement goals and beliefs: Individual and classroom differences.* Paper presented at the meeting of the Society for Experimental Social Psychology, Charlottesville, Virginia.

Nolen, S. B. (1988). Reasons for studying: Motivational orientations and study strategies. *Cognition and Instruction, 5,* 269–287.

O'Flahavan, J., Gambrell, L. B., Guthrie, J., Stahl, S., & Alvermann, D. (1992). Poll results guide activities of research center. *Reading Today, 10,* 12.

Palmer, B. M., Codling, R. M., & Gambrell, L. B. (1994). In their own words: What elementary students have to say about motivation to read. *Reading Teacher, 48,* 176–178.

Parsons, J., & Ruble, D. N. (1977). The development of achievement-related expectancies. *Child Development, 48,* 1075–1079.

Pearl, R. (1982). LD children's attributions for success and failure: A replication with a labeled LD sample. *Learning Disability Quarterly, 5,* 173–176.

Phillips, B. N. (1963). Age changes in accuracy of self-perceptions. *Child Development, 34,* 1041–1046.

Pinkwater, D. (1975). *Wingman.* New York: Bantam–Skylark.

Pressley, M., & Ghatala, E. S. (1989). Metacognitive benefits of taking a test for children and young adolescents. *Journal of Experimental Child Psychology, 47,* 430–450.

Reid, M. K., & Borkowski, J. G. (1987). Causal attributions of hyperactive children: Implications for teaching strategies and self-control. *Journal of Educational Psychology, 79,* 296–307.

Renick, M. J., & Harter, S. (1989). Impact of social comparisons on the developing self-perceptions of learning disabled students. *Journal of Educational Psychology, 81,* 631–638.

Renninger, K. A., & Wozniak, R. H. (1985). Effect of interest on attentional shift, recognition, and recall in young children. *Developmental Psychology, 21,* 624–632.

Ruble, D. N. (1983). The development of social-comaprison processes and their role in achievement-related self-socialization. In E. T. Higgins, D. N. Ruble, & W. Hartup (Eds.), *Social cognition and social development* (pp. 134–157). New York: Cambridge University Press.

Ruble, D. N., Boggiano, A. K., Feldman, N. S., & Loebl, J. H. (1980). Developmental analysis of the role of social comparison in self-evaluation. *Developmental Psychology, 16,* 105–115.

Schiefele, U. (1992). Topic interest and levels of text comprehension. In K. A. Renninger, S. Hidi, & A. Krapp (Eds.), *The role of interest in learning and development* (pp.151–182). Hillsdale, NJ: Erlbaum.

Schmidt, C. R., Ollendick, T. H., & Stanowicz, L. B. (1988). Developmental changes in the influence of assigned goals on cooperative and competition. *Developmental Psychology, 24,* 574–579.

Schunk, D. H. (1991). Self-efficacy and academic motivation. *Educational Psychologist, 26,* 207–232.

Shirey, L. L., & Reynolds, R. E. (1988). Effect of interest on attention and learning. *Journal of Educational Psychology, 80,* 159–166.

Spaulding, C. C. (1992). The motivation to read and write. In J. W. Irwin & M. A. Doyle (Eds.), *Reading/writing connections: Learning from research* (pp. 177–201). Newark, DE: International Reading Association.

Stipek, D. J., & Daniels, D. H. (1988). Declining perceptions of competence: A consequence of changes in the child or in the educational environment? *Journal of Educational Psychology, 80,* 352–356.

Stipek, D. J., & Hoffman, J. M. (1980). Children's achievement-related expectancies as a function of academic performance histories and sex. *Journal of Educational Psychology, 72,* 861–865.

Stipek, D., & Kowalski, P. (1989). Learned helplessness in task-orienting versus performance-orienting test conditions. *Journal of Educational Psychology, 81,* 384–391.

Stipek, D., & Mac Iver, D. (1989). Developmental change in children's assessment of intellectual competence. *Child Development, 60,* 521–538.

Sweet, A. P., & Guthrie, J. T. (1994). *Teacher perceptions of students' motivation to read* (Reading Research Report No. 29). Athens, GA, and College Park, MD: National Reading Research Center.

Sweet, A. P., & Guthrie, J. T. (1996). How children's motivations relate to literacy development and instruction. *Reading Teacher, 49,* 660–662.

Turner, J. C. (1995). The influence of classroom contexts on young children's motivation for literacy. *Reading Research Quarterly, 30,* 410–441.

Wade, S. E., & Adams, R. B. (1990). Effects of importance and interest on recall of biographic text. *Journal of Reading Behavior, 22,* 331–353.

Weiner, B. (1979). A theory of motivation for some classroom experiences. *Journal of Educational Psychology, 71,* 3–25.

White, R. W. (1959). Motivation reconsidered: The concept of competence. *Psychological Review, 66,* 297–333.

Wigfield, A. (1988). Children's attributions for success and failure: Effects of age and attentional focus. *Journal of Educational Psychology, 80,* 76–81.

Wigfield, A. (1994). Expectancy-value theory of achievement motivation: A developmental perspective. *Educational Psychology Review, 6,* 49–78.

Wigfield, A., & Eccles, J. (1992). The development of achievement task values: A theoretical analysis. *Developmental Review, 12,* 265–310.

Wigfield, A., Eccles, J. S., Mac Iver, D., Reuman, D. A., & Midgley, C. (1991). Transitions during early adolescence: Changes in children's domain-specific self-perceptions and general self-esteem across the transition to junior high school. *Developmental Psychology, 27,* 552–565.

Wigfield, A., & Guthrie, J. T. (1995). *Dimensions of children's motivations for reading: An initial study* (Reading Research Report No. 34). Athens, GA, and College Park, MD: National Reading Research Center.

Wigfield, A., Guthrie, J. T., & McGough, K. (1996). *A questionnaire measure of children's motivation for reading* (Instructional Resource No. 22). Athens, GA, and College Park, MD: National Reading Research Center.

Wigfield, A., Wilde, K., Baker, L., Fernandez-Fein, S., & Scher, D. (1996). *The nature of children's motivation for reading, and their relations to reading frequency and reading performance.* Athens, GA, and College Park, MD: National Reading Research Center.

Yolen, J. (1987). *Owl moon.* New York: Philomel.

9

◄O►

CONCLUDING REFLECTIONS... FOR THE TIME BEING

$\mathbf{T}$he overarching conclusion of this book is that balanced elementary instruction—that is, a balancing of whole language and skills components—seems more defensible than instruction that is only immersion in reading and writing, on the one hand, or predominantly skills driven, on the other. A great deal of this book is about how good reading involves the learning and use of word-recognition and comprehension strategies, the effectiveness of strategies use depending, in part, on the reader's prior knowledge about the world, including knowledge built up through reading.

THREE MODELS OF BEGINNING READING AND EARLY READING INSTRUCTION

The great debates regarding reading instruction probably will continue. The main reason for this is that there are competing models of how to teach reading, and the advocates of each are all too ready to make very strong claims about the superiority of their approach relative to other methods. Three instructional models were considered in this book.

Skills-Emphasis Model

According to the skills-emphasis approach, reading depends on the development of a number of particular competencies. Because some competencies are logical prerequisites to others, different competencies are the focus of development and instruction at different grade/age levels.

During the preschool years, or at the latest kindergarten or grade 1, children should to know to differentiate letters from one another as well as be taught the names of letters and letter–sound associations. Children also need to learn that words are blendings of sounds. Such phonemic awareness depends critically on experiences that emphasize the sounds in words and how those sounds can be manipulated. Without phonemic awareness, instruction to sound out words by mapping the letters to their sounds and blending the letters would make little sense (i.e., the purpose of decoding instruction would not be clear).

At first, letter–sound mapping and blending require much effort and need a great deal of support. With practice, associating component letters to their sounds and blending them becomes more automatic. In addition, frequently encountered letter combinations come to be perceived automatically as chunks. When familiar chunks are part of unfamiliar words, they come to be much of the basis for sounding out and blending. As initially unfamiliar words are reencountered, recognition of the word as a whole is increasingly automatic. Such automatic recognition requires little if any effort.

The decreasing effort needed for word recognition frees up cognitive capacity for comprehension of the words being read. That is, decoding and comprehension compete for the limited attentional capacity that is available, the 5 ± 2 slots of short-term memory. One reason that comprehension often is low when students are struggling decoders is that all their capacity is being devoted to identifying the words, with little left over for understanding (LaBerge & Samuels, 1974).

Once words are recognized automatically, their meanings are also accessed automatically. One of the ways that psychologists have demonstrated this is with research on the Stroop effect. My 9½-year-old was so taken with this effect that his grade-4 science project was dedicated to it. Tim presented his friends and some younger children with lists of color words—*blue, red, green, yellow, black, purple, orange,* and *brown.* On one list, each word was printed in the color ink that corresponded to it (i.e., *blue* was printed in blue ink, *red* printed in red ink). On the other list, each word was printed in an ink not corresponding to its color (e.g., *blue* was printed in red ink, *red* was printed in blue ink). His friends' task was not to read the words but simply to name the ink colors in the order of presentation. Consistent with classic Stroop results, Tim found that when his grade-4 and -5 friends attempted this task, it was really difficult for them when the color words were printed in an ink other than the color the word stands for. In contrast, kindergarten and grade-1 students had no difficulty reading off the sequence of colored inks, regardless of the meaning of the word. What was happening? The grade-4 and -5 students' reading of words was so automatic that they accessed the meaning of the words even when they were not trying to read them, and this accessing of meaning produced interference when they attempted to say the name of the different-colored ink the word was printed in. Becoming adept at reading words definitely affects comprehension. With the exception of situations like the Stroop task, automaticity of comprehension typically improves performance.

Word-level processes certainly are not all there is to comprehension, however. For example, scholars from a variety of perspectives are exploring how comprehension beyond the word level occurs and can be facilitated (e.g., Lorch & Van den Broek, 1997; Pressley, 1997). Good readers process the details in text, as specified by word-by-word reading of text, but do not get bogged down in those details as they construct an understanding of the main ideas in a text (e.g., Kintsch & van Dijk, 1978). Good readers are very active in this construction process, selectively attending to informative aspects of text, explicitly attempting to elaborate upon and remember points in text that seem particularly relevant to the reader's reason for reading, and responding affectively to ideas encoded in text.

As previously discussed, skills-development approaches have fared well in scientific evaluations. In particular, instruction aimed at fostering emergent literacy and phonemic awareness skills has proven to affect reading in the long term. Decoding instruction intended to develop sounding out and blending skills has proven potent, as has instruction directed at developing reader knowledge of orthographs and their utility in word recognition. Comprehension instruction that encourages more active strategic processing of text really does make a difference in student understanding (e.g., Pressley, El-Dinary, et al., 1992).

As positive as the evaluations have been of instructional development of particular reading competencies, the skills-emphasis approach often does not appeal to educators. It seems mechanistic and reductionistic, especially to educators who are confronting children who seem ready to try to write, even though they cannot spell; who are enthralled by stories long before they can read many words well; and who use language that seems quite complex. The skills-emphasis approach especially seems mechanistic and unattractive when presented in publisher products that overemphasize the skills, such as published decoding programs that are nothing more than daily worksheets, or when phonics fanatics, as I think of them, literally scream that phonics should be first in grade-1 reading. Such educational hawkers often show little understanding of how literature can be used to develop literacy competencies and enthusiasm for reading, and little knowledge about the important links between writing and development of reading. Moreover, the phonics-first crowd often seems to assume that if the child learns to decode with phonics, everything else will fall into place. According to them, the only bottleneck in learning to read is learning to decode.

The skills-emphasis model does not fail because skills are not critical; it fails because the skills that are the focus of skills-emphasis enthusiasts, especially decoding skills, are not all there is to literacy. The skills-emphasis model is an incomplete model of literacy development, one that does not even acknowledge as important many defensible whole-language practices that are embraced by those who control the American elementary schoolplace—elementary teachers.

Whole-Language Model

An alternative to the skills-emphasis approach is whole language, which takes the position that instruction focusing on the development of specific skills is essentially wrong-headed. Literate people read whole texts and sometimes write them, too. The message from whole language is that if you want children to become readers of texts, have them read texts; if you want them to be writers, have them write. Holistic reading and writing will foster a deep understanding of the nature and purposes of reading; it will make obvious to the child why letter- and word-level processes, developing as a natural consequence of doing real reading and writing, are important.

In recent years especially, whole-language advocates have conceded that skills should be taught, but in context. In other words, the child should be taught the skills that she or he in particular needs for holistic reading and writing. Thus, if a teacher notices that a student is having difficulties with writing plurals (e.g., a Hispanic student who is required to write in English, which uses very different approaches to pluralization than the child's native Spanish), it makes sense to do some explicit teaching of plurals at that point. The reason for such teaching will be obvious to the student in such a context, and the improvements in reading and writing gained from such instruction will also make clear the importance of learning about plurals.

Whole language is premised on a belief that children have powerful language-learning capabilities. The proof of this is that children learn oral language without explicit teaching, simply from immersion in a speaking world. Analogously, children should be able to learn to read and write from immersion in print and print experiences. The flaw in this thinking, however, is that learning to read and write is not much like learning to speak; humans have not evolved to be able to discover how to read and write from immersion in print experiences.

Beyond the conceptual shortcomings of whole language, it has not enjoyed as much validation as alternative approaches, such as the skills-emphasis model. There are several reasons for this: (1) There is a great deal of data that are inconsistent with the fundamental assumptions of the approach, such as demonstrations that only weak readers rely on semantic–contextual cues to decode words. (2) The data that do document positive effects of whole language is not abundant, perhaps because of antagonism in the whole-language community toward scientific study of whole language. (3) Even though there are data documenting positive effects of whole language on some aspects of literacy development, whole language does not seem as certain to result in adequate decoding competency as other approaches. This is a point of emphasis since decoding increasingly seems like a critical literacy competency in the current political context. If the whole-language versus skills-emphasis debate has done nothing else, it has inspired a lot of analyses substantiating how critical being able to decode is for the development of mature literacy.

Whole language has been an attractive teaching model, however. It is extremely child-centered, and educational models that focus on the natural development of children in authentic contexts have a long history of appeal. As appealing as it is, its initial specifications were so vague that many teachers who wanted to could not figure out how to become whole-language teachers . That situation has improved with the publication of many books about educational activities that are consistent with whole-language philosophy. Nonetheless, even a casual reading of these sources makes clear that good whole-language environments demand much of teachers: Excellent whole language teachers must know literature well, understand the writing process, and be committed to monitoring their students intensely in order to identify the competencies that should be developed, the ones students most need to master in order to read and write.

Because of the lack of empirical support for whole language, it is being questioned by policymakers everywhere, so that the teacher who uses it often will do so in the face and wake of substantial administrative resistance. Because students in whole language often do not make rapid progress in word-level decoding, parents are often very concerned about their students: For many parents, reading is being able to recognize the words!

Basically, whole language has the same flaw as the skills-emphasis approach. It is an incomplete model of the literacy development process. It is especially incomplete with respect to its specification of a realistic conception of letter- and word-level learning.

Balanced Teaching Model

There is much that is attractive about whole language, and much that is intuitively sensible. Many teachers have come to the conclusion, however, that children's immersion in literature will be most beneficial if they are armed with the skills necessary to attack the words in books. These teachers also believe that writing is more likely to be rewarding for children if their creative imaginations are assisted by skills (e.g., spelling) that increase their abilities to translate what they can imagine into words on the page. In my own work, the classrooms where reading and writing seem to be going best are ones in which there is a lot of coverage of skills, and a great deal of teacher support as children apply the skills they are learning to the reading of excellent literature and to writing.

The balanced teaching model is eminently testable, and is being tested. I expect more observational and correlational work aimed at establishing the nature of elementary instruction when achievement is high (i.e., similar to work covered in Chapter 6). Comparative studies of the approach also have begun. For example, Barbara Foorman (1996) has provided preliminary reports of a school-year experiment comparing balanced grade-1 instruction to whole-language and skills-emphasis instruction. At the beginning of the school year, the three groups of students experiencing each type of instruction were comparable on standardized measures of reading achievement. By the end of the year, the students in the balanced-instruction classrooms were doing much better than students in either the whole-language or skills-emphasis classrooms.

In relating this outcome I must admit some potential conflict of interest. The balanced classrooms in Foorman (1996) used the 1995-copyrighted version of Open Court. The Open Court team, which included me as a member, was determined that their program would be a strong balance of skills, reading of real literature, and writing, believing that such a mix would maximize literacy achievement. All of us associated with the development of that program were happy with Foorman's results, especially since they came from a well-respected classroom investigator who was not associated with the program.* Even so, I believe that more experimental tests of balance are needed: this would be the case no matter which specific approach to balance had been studied by Foorman. Nonetheless, I also recognize that the expense and technical requirements of school-year-long comparative studies render it unlikely that there will be a large number of such tests. The questions surrounding balance are important enough, however, to justify the expense of such work.

DEVELOPMENT OF LITERACY COMPETENCE

The Appendix at the end of this chapter summarizes much that was covered in this book, laid out along the lines of the ages and stages of development. Much must develop for a person to become a highly skilled reader, which involves efficient processing of individual words during active and selective processing of text.

Literacy development begins long before the child passes through the schoolhouse gate for the first time. Understanding has increased greatly in the past several decades about how literacy development proceeds early in life. With respect to elementary instruction, which is the focus of this book, plenty has been learned about the value of explicit decoding and comprehension-strategies instruction but also about the value of real reading opportunities and daily composition. The most important findings are summarized in the Appendix. The Appendix concludes with a summary of what is known about literacy development beyond the elementary years, as a reminder that literacy development is not a childhood thing but rather a lifespan development.

The complexities reflected in the developmental progression detailed in the Appendix make clear that simplistic notions regarding development and instruction of literacy are not adequate—whether from the whole-language camp or from the skills-first/emphasis enthusiasts. Many simplistic claims about reading instruction continue to be made, however, which are simply wrong. Ten of the most offensive ones are taken up later in this chapter.

*Although a version of Foorman (1996) was accepted for publication in the *Journal of Educational Psychology* as this book went to press, a journal that I edit, the decision making concerning the article's publishability was handled entirely by the associate editor of the journal, Dr. Carole Beal.

THE RESEARCH THAT IS NEEDED

Much, much more research is needed on effective elementary literacy instruction. The great progress to date gives good reason to believe that even greater progress can be made by researchers who are informed by what has been discovered so far.

There are always follow-up studies that are a slight extension of previous work. This section is not about such incrementalism, however. Rather, in this section, I take up some of the big and broad research efforts that are needed with respect to reading education and the development of skilled reading.

More Descriptive Studies of Effective, Balanced Teaching

Much can be learned in laboratory-like experiments about how skills can be developed, and the skills-instruction enthusiasts have provided much such work. Much can be learned about the types of literature and writing experiences that are possible by reading the mostly testimonial writing of whole-language teachers, and the whole-language enthusiasts have provided many testimonials. To understand the complex articulation of skills instruction and whole language that is balance, however, one must begin with observation of excellent, balanced instruction.

Descriptive studies are not so valued in the social sciences as studies that are aimed at evaluating predetermined hypotheses about causes and effects. More positively, however, shifts in educational research toward more qualitative methodologies have led to recent enthusiasm for descriptive work. As one who has done a great deal of descriptive research, I see this as a good sign, especially because this work has produced great insights about what really good elementary literacy instruction looks like. Still, much more is needed if sure conclusions are to be drawn from such work and if the generality of existing conclusions are to be tested. Then, there is a need for comparative studies informed by the observational work—that is, *in situ* evaluations of balanced classrooms compared to other types of instructional environments.

Balanced instruction is more complex than skills approaches or whole language and calls for more complex methodologies to evaluate and elucidate it. That is, scientific work does more than inform scientists: At its best, it also informs practitioners, and to achieve that, thick descriptions are absolutely necessary. People often can learn better from detailed, concrete examples (i.e., cases) than abstract descriptions.

Teacher Education Research

Substantial resources need to be devoted to research on teacher education that helps teachers develop into effective literacy educators, who can deliver effective balanced instruction. Logically, it seems that such teachers must have in-depth understanding of children's literature, a sophisticated understanding of the linguistic structure of American language and vocabulary, and good understanding of the cognitive–instructional models that underlie scaffolded instruction and the most effective approaches to process writing (e.g., Harris & Graham, 1994). Teachers must learn how to mix explanations with students' scaffolded participation in reading and writing. Such teaching requires consistent, detailed monitoring of students as they read and write, as well as detailed understanding of the reading and writing tasks themselves in order to envision how students can be encouraged as they attempt those tasks.

Pamela El-Dinary and I (e.g., Pressley & El-Dinary, 1997) found that it was very challenging for teachers to become balanced comprehension instruction teachers. Complex articulations of components must occur if students are going to learn the decoding and comprehension skills so that they can apply them in real reading and writing. As work on balanced teaching proceeds, it is imperative that the research community be sensitive to the challenging nature of such teaching, making it a priority to conduct research that reveals how teachers can overcome the challenges to becoming maximally effective teachers.

In my view, those education faculty members in colleges and universities who wish to inform young adults about how to be teachers must immerse themselves in elementary schooling. As someone who has done so, I have become very facile at spotting those faculty colleagues who are so grounded and those who are not. There is no need for more books by individuals who have not spent extensive time in the school settings they wish to affect. There now exist powerful observational approaches that can inform scholars about complex settings, such as classrooms: it is the scholars who choose to wrap themselves in those methods and devote their days to on-site classroom analyses who deserve the attention of the educator community. I would have never come to the insights about teaching reflected in this volume without those hundreds of mornings and days in elementary classrooms during the past decade.

My work has made very clear that it is hard to be an effective literacy teacher and difficult to learn how to become one. It is high time to carefully evaluate alternative approaches to teacher development.

Longitudinal Research

As a developmental psychologist by training, it is part of my being to believe in the longitudinal study of development, to believe that much can be learned by following individual children for a number of years. To some extent, there has been longitudinal study of literacy development, but unfortunately, such study has often failed to provide the types of thick descriptions of development and explanations of developmental differences that are needed to make one feel confident that much is really known about the children being studied. Thus, there are now a number of studies examining quantitative indicators of phonemic awareness in 4- and 5-year-olds as predictors of standardized test achievement in the elementary grades. I have never felt that I knew much about these children after reading such studies, however. When thicker descriptions have been provided (e.g., Snow, Barnes, Chandler, Goodman, & Hemphill, 1991), however, important insights have emerged, on such issues as why schooling becomes more important with increasing age as students progress through it. (Homes of at-risk students are more certain to be able to provide support of primary-level skills than skills developed in later grades.) Snow et al.'s (1991) work also made clear in vividly concrete ways the discontinuities in the quality of teaching as children progress through school, as well as the consequences of such discontinuities (Pressley & Palmer, 1992).

Such work is really critical because American students do experience discontinuities in their schooling. The assumption that students receive either whole language *or* skills instruction exclusively fails many times because a student can have a whole-language teacher one year and a skills-oriented teacher the next. Is it possible that if balanced instruction became the majority view, instruction might be more continuous from one grade to the next for many more children? I think this possibility is worth exploring. Moreover, the effects of such year-to-year continuity on literacy development should also be evaluated.

Extending Elementary Reading Principles into the Middle and High School Years

No one could come away from reading this book without appreciating the enormous amount that has been learned in the past two decades about literacy development in the preschool and elementary years. It is striking how much attention has been given to young children's literacy development, however, compared to students in the upper elementary, middle school, and high school years. That really needs to change, because many middle and high school students need reading instruction.

As a researcher who has principally focused on elementary school, I am proud of the many reforms in American elementary education that are linked to research. In contrast, there has been much less reform in the secondary schools, and often the reform that has occurred is not inspired so much by research as by inspiring visions of high school education, such as Theodore Sizer's (e.g., 1996) essential schools. The excitement of change in the local elementary school often is not mirrored by exciting changes in the district's middle or high school.

Amidst the backdrop of little or no research-based change in secondary schools, there is one important exception. Some special educators have made enormous progress in developing, validating, and disseminating effective literacy instruction to students with learning disabilities. The most strikingly effective group on this score operates out of the University of Kansas, with Donald Deshler and Jean Schumaker (e.g., 1988) providing the conceptual and pragmatic leadership. I cannot tell you how many times I have heard secondary literacy educators react to descriptions of the Kansas work with the appraisal, "All high school students need to learn the comprehension and writing strategies that students with learning disabilities are being taught." There is enough research on literacy-strategies instruction at the secondary level for me to respond confidently that such claims are on target (see Wood, Woloshyn, & Willoughby, 1995).

Extending the Dependent Variables Included in Research

Reading researchers have mainly documented reading achievement, measured in a variety of ways. Excellent instruction does more than promote achievement, however. When literacy instruction is going well, life in the classroom seems very pleasant, very peaceful. When literary instruction is going well, classrooms are very motivating places, or at least that is the way it seems to my colleagues and me. I believe that determining whether our observations about the peaceful and motivational characteristics of high-achieving classrooms are valid should be a high priority, for if they are, there is especially great incentive for balanced literacy instruction.

TEN DUMB AND DANGEROUS CLAIMS ABOUT READING INSTRUCTION

There are many strong claims being made about reading instruction, many of which fly in the face of considerable data. In this section I offer what I consider to be the ten dumbest and most dangerous claims about reading instruction that are commonplace in the contemporary conversations about education. Inspired by David Letterman, I present this as a top-10 list, beginning with number 10. Of course, I am aware that others might order these claims differently, or even have alternative claims that they feel should be on the list. Nonetheless, I think by providing such a list—and briefly reminding readers of the evidence that counters each of these claims—I can provide an effective review of some of the most disturbing beliefs about reading instruction that are not in synchrony with scientific evidence.

10. *When otherwise normal students have difficulties learning to read, there is a biological basis for the problem, and thus, instruction will do little good.* In fact, biological dyslexia is rather rare compared to reading failures due to lack of appropriate instruction. Many children who experience difficulties in learning to decode given normal classroom instruction benefit from more intensive instruction, such as provided by tutoring.

9. *Students learn to read in the first three grades, and read to learn after that.* Even learning to decode is far from complete by the end of grade 3. There is also much left to accomplish with respect to comprehension, good reason to continue teaching students to read long after the primary years are completed.

8. *Teachers who use published reading materials or teach skills are being deskilled themselves. Moreover, they are in political conspiracy with right-wing elements determined to maintain the social, economic, and political status quo.* These claims, which are embraced by some whole-language enthusiasts, are not true. In fact, when teachers use published programs, they do not follow the prescriptions in the programs blindly; rather, they pick and choose, using the components and activities of the published programs that make sense in their own reading programs. As for the political conspiracy part, there are many, many very politically liberal people who think that it is a good thing for children to be taught how to read! When I have read the arguments of those who advance the conspiracy theory, I am struck that I can object to almost every claim they make, including the claim that those of us who favor some explicit instruction as part of literacy instruction do not recognize the advantages provided by whole language experiences. That brings up dumb and dangerous claim number 7 . . .

7. *Whole language does not promote literacy.* Immersion in reading and writing experiences increases understanding of the elements of reading and writing, such as the structural characteristics of stories and other types of writing. Hearing and reading stories increases vocabulary and world knowledge. Invented spelling experiences promote under-

standing of the sound structure of words. In short, students in whole-language environments make much progress in literacy. What whole language does not promote sufficiently for many students, however, are letter-level, letter–sound, and word recognition skills, which leads to number 6 . . .

6. *Children will come to phonemic awareness and discover the letter and sound facts (phonics facts) through immersion in reading and writing alone. Teaching these competencies, rather than allowing them to emerge naturally, might do some harm; for example, it could decrease children's motivation to read.* Yes, whole immersion results in some learning of phonemic awareness and phonics, but much more can be accomplished through more explicit teaching of skills than occurs in whole-language environments. The idea that teaching interferes with natural development is an old one with no credible evidence in support of it. Indeed, with respect to motivation, leaving a child to struggle and experience failures and frustrations has very high potential to undermine motivation to read. That brings up the next dumb claim . . .

5. *If a child experiences difficulties in learning to decode, simply wait and the child will learn to read when ready.* Children who are behind in grade 1 stay behind. Rather than waiting and hoping that the child catches on to reading, real progress can be made with tutoring that promotes decoding skills in children experiencing difficulties in early reading.

4. *Short-term tutoring for students experiencing reading difficulties can get them on par with other students, and those students will stay on par once tutoring has concluded.* For students experiencing difficulties in school, sustained, long-term, excellent instruction is more likely to be successful than short-term instruction. A medical analogy for the short-term instruction approach is an inoculation, with benefits expected for a long time following brief intervention. What works in reading development with students who have difficulties, however, is more akin to continued medical care.

3. *Students become good comprehenders if they just read, read, and read.* There is substantial evidence that children become much better comprehenders if they are taught to use the active comprehension processes that skilled readers use. As is true for phonemic awareness and word-recognition skills, students do not seem to discover sophisticated comprehension strategies through immersion in reading alone.

2. *Students should be taught to give priority to meaning (i.e., semantic-context) cues in word recognition.* This is a very dated idea that just has not died because of whole-language theorists' embrace of it, despite analyses making clear that good readers give priority to phonological, letter-, and word-chunk cues in word recognition. In addition, instruc-

tion that emphasizes sounding out and decoding-by-analogy promotes word recognition more than does instruction emphasizing semantic contexts. That does not mean that semantic-context cues play no role. Such cues permit evaluation of whether an attempted decoding based on phonological cues is accurate. Such cues also permit readers to decide which of several meanings of a word makes sense in the context, once the word has been decoded.

1. *Skills instruction and whole language are incompatible. Alternatively, whole language has always included skills instruction, so that there is no need to think about adding skills instruction to it.* Systematic skills instruction has a good track record, and there are plenty of effective balanced-literacy teachers who carry out systematic instruction of skills, scaffolding student use of skills into real reading and writing. Such teachers are proof that systematic skills instruction can occur in the context of extensive reading of literature and student writing. That adding systematic skills instruction to whole language environments has so often improved literacy development is also proof of sorts that whatever skills instruction is in whole language is not enough relative to what students could and should receive.

The case for balanced teaching as detailed in this book is a case for optimism that many children can learn to read better than they would if the 10 ideas just reviewed were to prevail in determining who is taught and how. Of course, one of the points of this book is that ideas as dumb and dangerous as these have prevailed in American schools. More optimistically, I hope that this book permits many more teachers, parents, and policymakers to realize that the thinking reviewed in this top-10 list should not continue to affect educational decision making.

BALANCED LITERACY TEACHING COMPARED TO LITTLE LEAGUE PRACTICE

In December 1995, I participated in a symposium at the National Reading Conference, an organization comprised of literacy researchers of various persuasions. My task that day was to be the discussant for a session on balanced reading instruction. The session took place in a jam-packed room, and the crowd spilled into the hallway. The attendance was so great, given the capacity of the room, that the presenter–audience dynamic was quite unusual: It was impossible as a panelist not to know the audience's reaction because the crowd was sitting against the wall behind the presenters, pushed up to the podium, to the left, to the center, and to the right. It was a little tight in the room.

As is typical in discussions about beginning reading, there were strong reactions to the presentations. After all, the audience included extremists committed both to whole language and to direct instruction of decoding skills as the primary objective of beginning reading instruction. The panelists wanted to emphasize to the audience that it makes sense to forget both the extremes in favor of balance. I could feel the tension between whole-language and skills advocates growing as the meeting progressed, however, and there was potential for a real blow-up during my discussion.

I simply could not say directly what I wanted to say without potentially stimulating a shouting match, but I was determined to get the message out anyway. Several who were in attendance urged me to write up the remarks. I present here the gist of my remarks from that day.

Commentary for a Symposium on Balanced Literacy Instruction

"I come here today not as a literacy researcher, but as a candidate for little league commissioner in my home town. The reason I am running for the position is because I disagree with the two opposing models of minor league, little league baseball. Some of the parents and managers believe that our minor league program should focus more than anything on the development of baseball skills. They are so adamant that some even believe that the minor leagues should not schedule regular games. The other side of the argument is that our 6- to 9-year-olds should be playing baseball as a game most of the time, for such immersion is how a person learns to play the game. At present, our minor league program is much more this second model than the first, and thus, I will talk about my perceptions of that approach first.

"Our 6- to 9-year-olds are playing a lot of baseball games. For some of the kids, this is working just great. Unfortunately, however, many others are not making progress in learning the game. If their understanding of the overall game is developing (i.e., the 6-year-olds know where the bases are and which direction to run should they hit the ball), their understanding of many fundamental details is lacking. How many of you have seen one of our 8-year-olds who did not realize that she or he could overrun first base? How many times have I seen a 9-year-old who does not know how to approach a hard grounder in the outfield? And when it comes to hitting, we have 8- and 9-year-olds who still do not know how to grip a bat, yet alone know that they should be waiting for a pitch in the strike zone.

"I know the argument that by playing the game, the kids will come to like the game. I have to be honest, however, that I see too many youngsters who are bored stiff because they do not understand the game in which they are immersed. I see too many children in tears because they do not even know what they are doing wrong when they make an error or strike out. They know only that they are not playing well. And lastly, I am struck that so many children are dropping out of baseball in the minor leagues and will never play in the regular little league because of what they felt was a bad experience in the minors.

"That is not to say that I favor the other side of this debate. Batting, running, and fielding practice all have their place, but baseball practice after practice without ever playing a game would be a drag. Unless the kids actually use the skills in games, they will never understand why they are learning to overrun first, put their whole body in front of a ground ball, or wait out a pitcher. I remember when I was on a junior high basketball team. The coach ran us through in-and-out weaves of various sorts for practice after practice. Even so, we were totally disorganized in the games. I'll never forget during a halftime screaming session how the light-bulbs went off when the coach yelled, 'Why don't you use those weaves we practiced!!' Suddenly, we realized that those in-and-out patterns could be used in game! Skill drills alone just do not result in kids who can play the game.

"As many of you know, I was a member of a few baseball teams. My memory of successful teams was that there was some practice of skills, typically more early in the season than later, and typically more at the start of practice than at the end of it. After the skills practice, however, came the scrimmage game, with the team divided into two squads that played one another. During the scrimmage, the coaches did a lot of teaching, reminding players especially about how the skills they had been practicing transferred to the scrimmage. Thus, if during the scrimmage a runner did not overrun first, the coach might say, 'Remember how we practiced going past first.' If an outfielder approached to the side of a grounder, the coach might quip, 'Get your body in front of it,' a pointer that would make sense given the earlier drill. What the coach was doing is called scaffolding. The coach knew the kids did not 'get it' completely during the skill instruction and practice. 'Getting it' depends on using the skill in context, and the player is much more likely to 'get it' if given a hint at an appropriate moment than if the moment passes without the coach offering a mini-lesson.

"Now, some of you whole-baseball coaches and parents are going to respond that the skills-practice part of this balance thing will bore the kids to tears. I don't buy it. I need only reflect on how I bounced a tennis ball against a wall for hours and hours and months and months to get good at picking up grounders. How much time did I spend in my youth throwing high poppers to myself to get accustomed to fielding fly balls? I've even heard from some of you that you think the skills practice will interfere with the kids learning how to play real baseball. My response to that is, 'Where's the evidence?' I think you would be hard pressed to identify a single successful athlete who did not do a lot of skills practice. Swimmers and runners practice leaving the blocks, football linesmen practice with the sleds and tackling dummies, basketball players shoot and shoot and shoot, and major league baseball players spend a lot of time in the batting cage and more time in the field shagging grounders and fly balls. If skills practice interferes with learning to play the real game, there are many professional athletes in every sport who do not show the effects of such interference.

"My position is for a balanced approach to our minor league program, one in which practices involve skill instruction and drills plus scrimmages. The practices would be interwoven with some real games, but real games that are structured so that a lot of scaffolding and mini-lessons can take place. Our minor league games should not be about winning and losing but about learning the game in the exciting and motivating environment that is a six-inning baseball game. There should be a score book, but one that is more than a record of the runs scored: a running record of player accomplishments and weaknesses that the coach can review later to reflect on what needs to be emphasized in future practice sessions. The center of attention has to be the improvement of the players, with every kid getting the help she or he needs and getting stroked for making improvements. That's what a balanced minor league little league program should be like in my view."

Balanced Instruction and Student Construction of Knowledge in General

I did not become the little league commissioner. What I am, though, is an accomplished researcher in the area of children's learning, one who has spent a great deal of time reflecting on the conditions that result in the cognitive development of students. As such, I am well aware of the many suggestions made by constructivists that boil down to, "Don't teach, let the child discover." There is a long history of such thinking in education, going back to Dewey (1933) and continuing with the Piagetians (Inhelder, Sinclair, & Bovet, 1974; Kohlberg & Mayer, 1972) to the present generation of so-called radical constructivists, including the whole language theorists. There is also a long history of student discovery that does not result in rapid and certain cognitive development (e.g., Schauble, 1990), certainly not as rapid and certain as can occur through instruction (Brainerd, 1978; Shulman & Keislar, 1966; Wittrock, 1966).

In Chapter 8, I made the case that academic achievement is most likely when instruction is matched to student competence. Whatever instruction the teacher provides should be matched to the level of the students' competence, in the students' zone of proximal development, to use the Vygotskian term (Vygotsky, 1978). There should be no illusion, however, that the student will really understand the lesson from the teacher's presentation. My colleague Karen Harris and I (Harris & Pressley, 1991; Pressley, Harris, & Marks, 1992) have made the case that when a teacher explains a strategy to a student, the student does not really understand it well, but the instruction is a start. If the teacher then places the student in a situation where the strategy can be applied and scaffolds the student's use of the strategy in the situation, more learning will occur. With additional scaffolded practice opportunities, there is more learning still, as the student comes to understand how and when the strategy can be applied and adapted. With increasing experience, there is less need for the teacher to assist the student or even provide a hint that the strategy might be applied. Eventually, the student uses the strategy flexibly and appropriately, coordinating its use with the use of other strategies and knowledge.

If there is anything that can be learned from Vygotsky, it is that cognitive skills and strategies are passed from one generation to the next. Adults guide cognitive development by leading children to think in ways that many children would not discover on their own. (How many parents have taught their children baseball skills that were taught to them by their parents?) There is some explaining in such cross-generational transmissions, but there is much more scaffolding, which is necessary because people do not learn by listening alone but also by doing, which should occur in a realistic context. (How many parents spend much time scaffolding during little league scrimmages?) Adults who are effective in promoting development do not leave development to the child's discovery of skills. (Even the great Babe Ruth owed his development as a baseball player to a member of a previous generation: Ruth cited Brother Mathias, who taught him baseball at St. Mary's

School in Baltimore, to be the greatest person he ever knew.) Discovery learning is the wrong approach to instruction; the case in favor of teaching as scaffolding is much more conceptually compelling, occurring as it does in the evening, when the little leaguer is fortunate enough to have an excellent baseball coach, and during the day, when the little leaguer is lucky enough to be enrolled in a classroom headed by an effective literacy teacher.

FINAL COMMENTS

Much has been learned about what makes sense in elementary reading instruction. The recent version of the great debate has been posed as skills instruction versus whole language, most frequently at the primary level, and most frequently as phonics versus whole language.

Whole language is like little league baseball if players only played games. Their playing of whole games would be substantially impaired by lack of skills. Just as bad, skills emphasis is like little league baseball if it involved mostly infield, outfield, and batting practice. As good as players experiencing such an approach might be at picking up grounders, running down fly balls, and hitting consistently, they would not be baseball players. They would not know how the components articulate as part of an entire game. Baseball, like all sports, involves development of skills and practice in applying those skills in whole games, played at a level appropriate to the developmental level of the players.

Analogously, reading involves development of skills but also practice in their application during reading and writing tasks that are appropriately challenging to students. That is why the balance model of instruction is a better model than either the skills-emphasis approach or whole language. Balanced instruction means much more systematic instruction of skills than does any version of whole language, with its emphasis on teaching only when there is demonstrated need. Balance also means much more involvement with literature and writing than occurs in many skills emphasis classrooms.

When students are skilled in reading and writing and their motivation is maintained through appropriately challenging literacy experiences, they read and write more. Lack of skills, which is a danger of whole language, has high potential to undermine long-term motivation for literacy. Lack of exposure to interesting reading and writing experiences, which can happen in skills-emphasis classrooms, also can undermine motivation for literacy experiences, since children, like everyone else, thrive on interesting experiences and are turned off by boredom. Balanced literacy instruction is the best bet for maintaining and even enhancing student motivation to do literate things, providing students with the skills they need to be successful in reading and writing and having them practice those skills by reading interesting books and writing about topics that are important to them.

The great debate might not only continue, but might do so with new intensity, as the skills-emphasis and whole-language enthusiasts now have a common target for attack (i.e., balanced instruction), albeit for different reasons. This can be nothing more than rancorous bickering, which much of the recent great debate has been. Alternatively, it can be a healthy situation if it leads to additional research on elementary reading instruction. I hope it is the latter, but even if it is not, I am confident that much revealing reading instructional research is yet to come. Thus, the conclusions offered in this book are, for the time being, subject to revision in light of new evidence.

APPENDIX

Landmarks in Development of Literacy Competence (or What Happens When)

0–2 YEARS OF AGE (Infancy)

• Emergent literacy experiences begin; infants who have rich verbal interactions during infancy are advantaged over those who do not.

• A secure parent–child attachment sets the stage for healthier emergent literacy experiences than if attachment is insecure.

• When there is risk of insecure attachment (e.g., because the baby is temperamentally difficult), parents can be taught how to interact with their infants so there is a greater chance for secure attachment.

• Prior knowledge development is schematic from infancy onward, with the children's schematic knowledge reflective of the experiences they have had (e.g., children have schemata for what happens at fast-food restaurants when they pay many visits to McDonald's and Burger King).

2–5 YEARS OF AGE (Preschool Years)

• Many and diverse emergent literacy experiences are possible; readiness for school-based literacy instruction is determined in part by the quality and quantity of emergent literacy experiences.

- Long-term, rich verbal and cognitive interactions with adults result in internalization of verbal and cognitive skills which are critically relevant to reading. Thus, egocentric speech is more prevalent in early preschool years than in later years, when inner speech prevails.

- When parents are not naturally facile at emergent literacy interactions, often they can be taught to be so.

- Learning the names of the alphabetic letters is an important acquisition, as is learning the letter–sound associations. Such learning is acquired in a variety of ways, from interactions with parents to viewing of *Sesame Street*.

- Word recognition skills begin to develop, with preschoolers, for example, able to read logographs (e.g., McDonald's, as long as the name is on the famous golden arches logo). Four-year-olds can use analogies based on word chunks to some extent to read new words (e.g., if child is shown the word *bee*, she or he can recognize that *see* is like *bee* in that both include the *-ee* part).

- There are language difficulties and differences apparent in many children who will later be diagnosed as biologically dyslexic.

- The beginnings of phonemic awareness sometimes are stimulated, through such parent–child activities as reading of rhymes and playing of rhyming games.

5–7 YEARS OF AGE (Last Year of Preschool and Early Primary Grades)

- Academic motivation is at its highest during the primary years. Students tend to believe they can succeed if they try.

- Complete phonemic awareness typically does not develop through emergent literacy experiences alone, but can be activated through instruction during kindergarten, which can have positive impact on later learning. The instruction typically involves a variety of activities aimed at student listening for sounds in words and manipulating the various sounds in words. When such phonemic awareness instruction is added to whole-language preschool and kindergarten experiences, there are positive effects on later literacy development.

- Alphabetic reading begins for many children, including approximations to it at first (e.g., reading a word based on only a few salient letters).

- Formal schooling now includes daily reading and composing from the first days of kindergarten. As students gain proficiency in reading and writing words, the diversity of reading and writing activities expands.

- Children can learn to decode through phonics instruction—through synthetic phonics instruction more certainly than analytic phonics instruction. They can also learn to decode through analogy-based approaches. There is no logical reason that phonics and analogy-based approaches cannot be combined, as children learning via phonics can acquire knowledge of word parts as they experience them and children learning by initial focus on word parts can also learn to blend the sounds produced by word chunks with individual sounds (e.g., blending sound of *s* and *-ee* to pronounce *see*). There is a lot of evidence that effective decoding instruction involves teaching students how to analyze words with respect to component sounds and how to blend those sounds. As students learn to decode, their automatic sight-word skills improve (i.e., words decoded frequently become sight words).

• Although children in classrooms that are exclusively whole language are taught to rely heavily on semantic context cues to decode, such instruction does not produce skilled decoding as reliably as phonics or word chunk analogy-based approaches.

• Excellent classrooms involve a balancing of whole-language experiences (i.e., reading of real texts, composition) and skills instruction. Teachers scaffold student use of skills during realistic reading and writing. There also is integration of literacy and content-area instruction. There is good reason to suspect that classrooms that are either extremely skills-oriented or extremely anti-skills oriented (i.e., skills instruction occurs on an as-needed basis only in the context of reading and writing) are not as effective as more balanced classrooms.

• 20% to 30% of normally intelligent grade-1 students experience difficulties learning to decode. Most of these students can learn to decode with more intensive instruction; a very small percentage are biologically dyslexic, with biologically determined problems in phonological processing and/or perhaps in visual-spatial processing.

7–11 YEARS OF AGE (Later Primary and Upper Elementary Grades)

• Academic motivation tends to decline: this is especially likely the more a student experiences academic failures and frustrations. Students' faith in success with effort declines during the elementary years. Students increasingly view academic frustrations as indications of low ability.

• Classroom competition increases with increasing grade level, with the potential to undermine the motivation of many students, who increasingly notice how they do compared to others and interpret their relative failures as signaling low ability. Good grades given to good readers are not unambiguously beneficial for them either, having the potential to undermine the intrinsic motivation to read that many good readers bring to the task. That is, good readers can come to justify the reading they are doing as motivated by good grades; in situations where there are no grades for reading, there is no longer an incentive to read (i.e., there is an overjustification effect).

• Effective classrooms emphasize that effort matters, sending the message that trying hard fosters achievement and intelligence, failure is a natural part of learning, and school is more about getting better than being best. Rewarding students for improvement rather than performance relative to others promotes academic motivation.

- With increasing grade level, there is greater variability in the core emphases in classrooms. That is, first-grade classes across the country typically are more similar to each other than to fifth-grade classes in the same school. Some core emphases (e.g., encouragement of comprehension strategies use) can make a big, positive difference in the development of literacy competence in second to fifth grade.

- Comprehension strategies can be taught, typically resulting in improved understanding of text, especially if strategies instruction is long-term and thoroughly integrated across the school day. Many times, however, such skills are not taught as explicitly or extensively as they could be taught. Consequently, students are not as active in their reading as they could be.

- Excellent classrooms report a balancing of whole language (i.e., reading of real texts, composition activities) and skills instruction. Teachers scaffold use of skills during realistic reading and writing. There also is integration of literary and content-area instruction.

- Reading of novels becomes an important language-arts activity.

- With greater reading, automatic word recognition increases, as does extent of vocabulary and other knowledge. Those who do a lot of reading become better readers than those who do little reading.

- Writing often emphasizes planning, drafting, and revising processes. Conventions and spelling are emphasized increasingly with advancing grade levels.

- Students begin to experience content area texts, many of which are not interesting. When students have some choice in what they read, motivation is higher.

BEYOND THE ELEMENTARY YEARS

- Skilled reading is both top-down (e.g., predictions about upcoming text based on prior knowledge) and bottom-up (e.g., individual letters and words are processed).

- Skilled readers can read at 200 to 300 words per minute, processing most words, and indeed most letters within words, as they read. Saccadic eye movement is orderly from left to right within each line of text, with fixations on informative words.

- Skilled readers rely more on letter- and word-level graphemic–phonological cues (including recognition of common word parts) for word recognition than do unskilled readers. Unskilled readers attend more to semantic–contextual cues than do skilled readers in attempting to recognize (i.e., decode) a word. Once a word is recognized, however, good readers use semantic–contextual cues to determine the exact meaning of the decoded word in the present context and do so with greater certainty and success than less-skilled readers.

• Skilled readers effortlessly recognize many words (i.e., they have large sight vocabularies). Such effortful recognition of sight words frees up short-term capacity, permitting it to be used for comprehension.

• Good readers remember the gist of what they read, to some extent as an automatic consequence of reading the text. Comprehension and memory of text, however, also are enhanced through the use of a variety of active comprehension strategies, which are enabled, in part, by extensive prior knowledge, permitting construction of bridging inferences.

• Reading skill continues to develop well into adulthood.

• Many adults remain unskilled readers, from those who cannot decode at all to many others who cannot do things attributed to skilled readers in this section of this appendix.

REFERENCES

Brainerd, C. J. (1978). Learning research and Piagetian theory. In L. S. Siegel & C. J. Brainerd (Eds.), *Alternatives to Piaget: Critical essays on the theory* (pp. 69–109). New York: Academic Press.

Deshler, D. D., & Schumaker, J. B. (1988). An instructional model for teaching students how to learn. In J. L. Graden, J. E. Zins, & M. J. Curtis (Eds.), *Alternative educational delivery systems: Enhancing instructional options for all students* (pp. 391–411). Washington, DC: National Association of School Psychologists.

Dewey, J. (1933). *How we think: A restatement of the relation of reflective thinking in the education process.* Boston: Heath.

Foorman, B. (1996, April). Paper presented at the annual meeting of the Society for the Scientific Study of Reading, New York.

Harris, K. R., & Graham, S. (1994). *Helping young writers master the craft: Strategy instruction and self-regulation in the writing process.* Cambridge, MA: Brookline Books.

Harris, K. R., & Pressley, M. (1991). The nature of cognitive strategy instruction: Interactive strategy construction. *Exceptional Children, 57,* 392–404.

Inhelder, B., Sinclair, H., & Bovet, M. (1974). *Learning and the development of cognition.* Cambridge, MA: Harvard University Press.

Kintsch, W., & van Dijk, T. A. (1978). Toward a model of discourse comprehension and production. *Psychological Review, 85,* 363–394.

Kohlberg, L., & Mayer, R. (1972). Development as the aim of education: The Dewey view. *Harvard Educational Review, 42,* 449–496.

LaBerge, D., & Samuels, S. J. (1974). Toward a theory of automatic information processing in reading. *Cognitive Psychology, 6,* 293–323.

Lorch, R., & van den Broek, P. (1997). Understanding reading comprehension: Current and future contributions of cognitive science. *Contemporary Educational Psychology, 22,* 213–246.

Pressley, M. (1997). The cognitive science of reading. *Contemporary Educational Psychology, 22,* 247–259.

Pressley, M., & El-Dinary, P. B. (1997). What we know about translating comprehension strategies instruction research into practice. *Journal of Learning Disabilities, 30,* 486–488.

Pressley, M., El-Dinary, P. B., Gaskins, I., Schuder, T., Bergman, J. L., Almasi, J., & Brown, R. (1992). Beyond direct explanation: Transactional instruction of reading comprehension strategies. *Elementary School Journal, 92,* 511–554.

Pressley, M., Harris, K. R., & Marks, M. B. (1992). But good strategy instructors are constructivists! *Educational Psychology Review, 4,* 1–32.

Pressley, M., & Palmer, B. (1992). Literacy acquisition at home and school. Review of C. E. Snow, W. S. Barnes, J. Chandler, I. F. Goodman, and L. Hemphill, *Unfulfilled expectations: Home and school influences on literacy. Contemporary Psychology, 37,* 18–19.

Rousseau, J-J. (1974). *Émile* (A. Bloom, Trans.). New York: Basic Books.

Schauble, L. (1990). Belief revision in children: The role of prior knowledge and strategies for generating evidence. *Journal of Experimental Child Psychology, 49,* 31–57.

Shulman, L. S., & Keislar, E. R. (Eds.). (1966). *Learning by discovery: A critical appraisal.* Chicago: Rand McNally.

Sizer, T. R. (1996). *Horace's hope: What works for the American high school.* New York: Houghton-Mifflin.

Snow, C. E., Barnes, W. S., Chandler, J., Goodman, I. F., & Hemphill, L. (1991). *Unfulfilled expectations: Home and school influences on literacy.* Cambridge, MA: Harvard University Press.

Vygotsky, L. S. (1978). *Mind in society: The development of higher psychological processes.* Cambridge, MA: Harvard University Press.

Wittrock, M. C. (1966). The learning by discovery hypothesis. In L. S. Shulman & E. R. Keislar (Eds.), *Learning by discovery: A critical appraisal* (pp. 33–75). Chicago: Rand McNally.

Wood, E., Woloshyn, V. E., & Willoughby, T. (Eds.). (1995). *Cognitive strategy instruction for middle and high schools.* Cambridge, MA: Brookline Books.

AUTHOR INDEX

291

SUBJECT INDEX

Subject Index **WITHDRAWN**